BATTLE FOR THE
ELEPHANTS

Also by the same authors

AMONG THE ELEPHANTS

and by Oria Douglas-Hamilton

THE ELEPHANT FAMILY BOOK

BATTLE FOR THE ELEPHANTS

IAIN & ORIA
DOUGLAS-HAMILTON

Edited by Brian Jackman

Doubleday

LONDON · NEW YORK · TORONTO · SYDNEY · AUCKLAND

TRANSWORLD PUBLISHERS LTD
61-63 Uxbridge Road, London W5 5SA

TRANSWORLD PUBLISHERS (AUSTRALIA) PTY LTD
15-23 Helles Avenue, Moorebank, NSW 2170

TRANSWORLD PUBLISHERS (NZ) LTD
Cnr Moselle and Waipareira Aves,
Henderson, Auckland

DOUBLEDAY CANADA LTD
105 Bond Street, Toronto, Ontario, M5B 1Y3

Published in 1992 by Doubleday
a division of Transworld Publishers Ltd

Illustrations as endpapers: *Front* – Namibia – The mysterious far-ranging
rare desert elephant of the Kaokoveld. *Back* – The largest intact
elephant population survives in Botswana, including this herd in the
Okavango Swamps.

A catalogue record for this book is available from the British Library.

ISBN 0385 401922

Typeset in Garamond by
Chippendale Type Ltd, Otley, West Yorkshire.
Printed in Great Britain by
Mackays of Chatham Ltd.
Endpapers and plate section by Cheney & Sons Ltd, Banbury.

To all those who,
in whatever way,
fight for elephants.

Acknowledgements

D ECADES have passed and we are indebted to many. Faces swarm before us of individuals to whom we owe so much, and we are moved by a deep feeling of warmth. Now in the small space allotted, we would like to mention many whom we hope will recognize themselves below.

We remember especially our family, our children and friends, who have laughed with us in good times, supported us in difficult times; and those with whom we have made common cause in far-off elephant ranges, in forests, savannas, deserts and swamps, or in conference halls, lecture theatres, or offices in the battle for the elephants. In particular we give our thanks to: Iain's mother who nurtured her oft-abandoned grandchildren; all those who opened their homes to us in Africa, Europe, America; our hard-working staff at home and in the offices; an array of wonderful assistants; proof readers and patient editors; the photographers who donated pictures; a ranger friend of long standing; conservation organizations large and small who have given money to support us, to buy equipment, cars, aeroplanes, binoculars, and computers, and to keep them all flying, fuelled and serviced; the generous public who responded to elephants in crisis and who kept rangers supplied with mosquito nets and blankets, water-bottles and boots, transport and fuel in difficult times; observers who have endured the 'torture chamber' of aerial counting; lone researchers and hospitable missionaries in far-off places; those who have lived with elephants and understand them; wildlife officials who risk their necks to bring the facts out; research officers who paid for counts out of their own pockets; friendly air controllers; co-operative policemen, reformed poachers, those soldiers at road-blocks who don't harass people; the people of Africa and the politicians who have created refuges for wildlife; scientists who have enriched our knowledge for elephants, imaginative bureaucrats who have rescued forgotten elephant plans from beneath piles of folders; administrators who lobbied in the corridors of power and leaders who have brought the elephant issue before the world; curious journalists, amateur sleuths, undercover agents, wildlife trade monitoring units, financial investigators, economic analysts, biologists and population modellers who probed the ivory trade, delegates who voted for the ivory ban; above all, rangers, game scouts, wardens and policemen, who live at the sharp end of conservation, the unsung heroes who frequently face the bullets and not infrequently lose their lives.

Contents

Acknowledgements   6
List of Illustrations and Maps   11
Authors' Note   13
Prologue   ORIA: Elephant Idyll   15

PART I   *Wings Over Africa*
1   IAIN: *Return to Manyara*   25
2   IAIN: *The Ivory Rush Begins*   33
3   ORIA: *School for Elephants*   44
4   ORIA: *A Final Solution*   54
5   IAIN: *Laagers*   63
6   IAIN: *A Wilderness*   75

PART II   *The Ivory Avalanche*
7   IAIN: *Massacre at Murchison*   89
8   ORIA: *Drought in Manyara*   98
9   IAIN: *The Killing Fields of Kenya*   105
10   IAIN: *Elephant Dilemma*   116
11   IAIN: *The Second Avalanche*   124

PART III   *The Trail West*
12   ORIA: *Footprints in the Sand*   133
13   ORIA: *Elephants of the Sahel*   145
14   ORIA: *Ivory Coasts*   151
15   ORIA: *On the Shores of Gabon*   160
16   IAIN: *The Die is Cast*   168
17   IAIN: *The Turning Point*   179

PART IV   *The War in Uganda*
18   IAIN: *Honorary Warden*   191
19   ORIA: *A Sound of Guns*   200
20   ORIA: *Tembo Two*   210
21   ORIA: *The Cull*   215
22   IAIN: *Hopes and Ashes*   222
23   ORIA: *Clouds of War*   227
24   IAIN: *Kidepo Showdown*   234

PART V   *To Gain or Lose It All*
25   IAIN: *In the Wilderness*   249
26   ORIA: *The Silent Fall*   255
27   IAIN: *Sudan's Bloody Ivory*   263
28   IAIN: *Shadow of Darkness*   273
29   ORIA: *The President's Hoard*   283
30   IAIN: *Ivory Laundering*   293
31   ORIA: *Tsavo Twilight*   309
32   IAIN: *The Turning of the Tide*   315
33   ORIA: *Burn Ivory Burn*   326
34   IAIN: *The Year of the Elephant*   333

Epilogue   ORIA: *The Survivors*   346

Photographic Credits   354
Bibliography   356
Index   360

List of Illustrations and Maps

Photographs

FIRST SECTION   96 – 7
Early Days
Among the Elephants

SECOND SECTION   160 – 61
Westward Bound

THIRD SECTION   224 – 5
War and Utilization

FOURTH SECTION   288 – 9
The End of an Era

The photographic sections have been designed by Barney Wan.

Photographic credits appear at the back of the book.

Maps

Africa   24
East Africa   34
Southern Africa   64
Central Africa   132
West Africa   136
Uganda   190
Central Africa   272
Tsavo   308

Authors' Note

THERE have been many excellent books about the natural history and social behaviour of the African elephant. This book is not a definitive picture of elephant biology. It is a personal tale of events over the last twenty years as they have affected the elephant's struggle for existence, showing how the world reacted to the elephant crisis.

After five years of living with elephants in a small park in Tanzania, and another two writing about them, we became aware of a continental threat to the species caused by a burgeoning ivory trade. We gave up monitoring elephant family life and entered on a criss-cross trail across Africa. Our life moved from the scientific orbit to campaigning for elephants, sometimes in confrontation with fellow conservationists, and to even more violent encounters with poachers in the field. At first we were mostly alone, but later the world recognized the threat to the elephants and finally the trade in ivory was banned in 1989.

There is a spectrum of philosophies on how to deal with the ivory trade and conserve elephants that has become extremely polarized and has led to a bitter clash of ideas. At one end is the belief that the trade should be controlled and promoted so that profits can be used to boost conservation. At the other end is the belief that all trade in ivory is a pact with the devil, which can never be adequately controlled.

We agree with the latter. While there are people we know and respect who adopt the first proposition, we fear that any trade in ivory opens a Pandora's box of vested interests and commercial incentives. At best these exert an insidious pressure towards ever-more interference with Nature, and at worst they give rise to criminal killing of elephants and smuggling of ivory.

As poachers have become better armed, so rangers have become less prepared to take chances. The widely adopted 'Shoot to Kill' policy in the parks is a tragic consequence of the widespread availability of imported military weapons, the aggression of ivory poachers, and a high price of ivory.

Although the arguments expressed have sometimes been bitter, we recognize that men and women of great integrity are found on either side of the ivory divide. The opinions expressed here are our own and cannot be blamed on any of the organizations for which we have worked.

ORIA: *Elephant Idyll*

1969-73, Manyara, Tanzania and Kenya

W HEN you are born in Africa you remember things like the smell of the land when it rains, the flute-like whistle of a boy walking home with his cattle in the dust, the chant of the emerald-spotted wood dove drifting through the trees, or the sound of thunder faraway when all is still and dry.

But some sounds remain in my memory like a haunting love-song, and whenever I hear a distant aeroplane homing in with a red sun sinking at the end of a day, a gentle tingle runs over the skin of my back and my arms and I look up into that empty sky and know all is well. When the elephants call at night, echoing across the valley in a deep rumble all of its own, I hold my breath and cup my hands behind my ears, straining to catch every sound, and the echo carries on and on.

I remember the time many years ago in 1969 when I first came to live in a park in Tanzania. In days gone by when the Maasai walked here with their cattle it was known as *'Amanya-are'* – 'A Meeting Place of Two'. Today this place is called Manyara; a white crusted soda lake edged with flat-topped umbrella trees and fat, leafy baobab trees spread out under the towering cliffs of the Rift Valley.

In this tiny fragment of the earth, four years earlier, a young man with a scientific mission headed along a path towards the foot of these cliffs where a waterfall slid down the rocks. Marking the map with a cross, he dropped his pack and scanned the hillside above the river. Baboons sat atop the white boulders, like markers in a game. The sombre halting call of a ground hornbill sounded, then a big branch was snapped. It would take some time to build a little house. The young man set up his safari tent under the cool roof of a tree and pulled a yellow envelope from the pocket of his back-pack.

He was an animal scientist. His brief was to study the elephant and this was the first time he had met with elephants in the wild. Refuges like Manyara had attracted elephants from far and wide. Finding safety, the animals were now being threatened by their own reduced range and were eating themselves out of house and home. The scientist was to study this problem and set out to recognize each elephant as an individual in order to unravel their social structure.

He was given three years to find a solution. A young Tanzanian park ranger from the Nyamwesi tribe joined him as his bush companion and tracker, and together they wandered far and wide like two young elephant males, collecting samples and clues from the thick web of bushes and vines that grew among the acacia woodlands.

Dressed in shades of green as if a part of the landscape, the two young men became intricately involved with Manyara and its inhabitants. One day like shadows in the undergrowth they looked straight at an oncoming grey mass shattering a thick wall of leaves and branches. A massive figure with outspread ears appeared, followed by a trumpet of *alta voce* – then a camera clicked, no-one moved, and the elephant stopped. A smile cut their faces and their eyes met; it was Manyara's leading matriarch. Cautiously they slid downwind through the bushes, following elephant tracks to collect the next lot of samples: snapshots, leaves, seeds or dung.

It was only by chance that I met this scientist, and our paths would never have crossed, but for the fact that he had learned to fly and came up one day in his ancient aeroplane to Nairobi.

I was dancing wildly, the rhythm of the music swaying my hips, silver chains hung and swung from my waist, and my arms red-brown from the sun were wrapped in silver bracelets moving above my head like the weightless wings of a bird. I was happy.

After eight years of living in the hub of industrial wealth, Milanese materialism and smog, I was back in Africa. My marriage had ended, barren, without bitterness but with some pain. I was over thirty and would have to pick up the loose threads I had left behind and start my life again.

Among the crowd stood a stranger, a stranger in every sense. He did not belong to this rather loud and chest-beating group of revellers – he was shy, with a learned look about him – a man of books, I thought briefly, as I whirled round and caught his glance. His eyes followed me round the room, and I danced towards him, inviting him to join me in my burst of freedom.

'I'm not very good at these dances,' he said. 'I only know how to do reels.' We sat down in the corner of the room. Someone offered me strawberries, and as we picked at the fruit and bit into the cool soft pulp, he told me that he had been living in a far-off place, where he had been studying elephants for three years to get his Ph.D. 'Rather than study the behaviour of mice in Oxford, in relation to the behaviour of humans, I chose elephants,' he explained. From a very young age he had always wanted to live in Africa, and his only port of entry was through science.

'When I first looked at elephants,' he continued, 'I asked myself, is there an elephant society, and if so, how does it work? To find out I first had to learn to recognize elephants as well as I recognize people. I know most of the Manyara elephants, although there are new ones coming in every month.' When he spoke about elephants his voice changed, his eyes lit up, as if he wanted everyone to know.

His name was Iain Douglas-Hamilton, a descendant of an ancient Scottish family. His ancestors, he told me, were feared by all, raiding cattle and killing people, just like the Maasai. I liked that. We had something in common. We admired the Maasai and we sought the unusual in life. 'It's a treat to be at a party in Nairobi. I can never eat strawberries like this in Manyara with a beautiful woman.'

His voice was warm and friendly, his body strong and tanned, clad in an ill-fitting suit. Later, gently catching my arm, he said: 'I was wondering if you would be interested to participate in an immobilization? We shoot tranquillizing darts into elephants. Then we're going to put radio collars on a couple of them – it's never been done before. The idea is to find out where elephants wander and why. I could fly you down there next week.'

The following week I heard the sound of an aeroplane approaching my parents' farm in Naivasha, gradually increasing in volume, until suddenly it swept down over the trees surrounding our home, breaking the silence of the day and landing in one of the back fields where no plane had ever landed before. This man is crazy, I thought. I was riding my motor bike fast. He must have hit one hundred holes. But there he stood, in his green faded shorts and shirt next to a small red-and-white Piper Pacer registered as 5Y-KIX which appeared to be unharmed.

'Are you ready to leave?' he asked, with that same calm voice, but laughing. 'You're crazy,' I said. I threw my arms around him and held on to him. 'Maybe I am, but I'll land anywhere to pick you up.' He sat on the back of my bike, holding his sandals and his binoculars in one hand. 'I shall come here often, so you'd better tell these men to cut some of the trees at the end of the strip.' He stayed for lunch, and we would not let him leave until we had cut the grass and filled in the holes on a strip long enough for *KIX* to take off.

Early next morning we lifted off from our newly made airstrip, skimming the tops of the trees and heading south towards Ol Donyo Lengai, the Mountain of God, standing like a pyramid over Lake Natron. Ahead was another lake – Manyara – where the elephants lived and Iain worked and where our first child, Saba, was born fifteen months later.

On the ground, riding in a battered Land-Rover, was a green clad ranger to meet us. 'This is Mhoja Burengo,' said Iain introducing me in Swahili. 'He is my minder and early warning system for rhinos, apart from being a fine botanist and elephant spotter.'

Below the escarpment we entered a cool forest of tall, smooth trees. Clear streams hurried through beds of ferns and flowering creepers. Hornbills chuckled, baboons barked from somewhere deeper in the woods and a thick, sweet smell of wild jasmine and moss stayed with us as we moved on in a stillness of fragrance and birdsong.

Of all the elephants one was Iain's favourite. He named her Virgo, a young mother aged about twenty-five years old with a single straight tusk and a lively curiosity. Even though she was a wild elephant, and part of a family led by an irreconcilable matriarch who hated mankind in general, Virgo would come close to his car as if trying to establish a bridge of communication. Little did he know that one day he would be able to hold up his first-born child to be greeted by the raised trunk of this elephant at a fingertip's distance.

The forest ends with light and dust, and the distant glitter of the lake; and here under the flat-topped African umbrella trees stood Iain's elephants, grey shadows lazily fanning themselves with huge ragged ears. Like the rhinos that also lived in the forest and rested next to the fallen trees, they were still very wild. Most of them distrusted man and charged on sight and Iain's car had been squashed and impaled several times by these irate tuskers.

The tracking and immobilization operation through Manyara's dense bush was a heart-pounding experience. The elephant went down and Mhoja and Iain wrapped a thick yellow belt around its neck with an araldite-embedded radio on top. They plucked off parasites, thick as raisins, filled glass phials with blood and stretched the tape up and down and around the animal, taking measurements. It was all very new to me.

Bushes and creepers filled the gaps between the acacia canopies, but the elephants had cut wide tunnels which we followed. Mhoja rattled off Latin names of plants which he collected for the herbarium, while Iain checked the faces and ears of the elephants in his 'Who's Who' list. Part of Iain's work was to follow the movements of the elephants but in that thick bush it was extremely difficult. 'Now, with radio-tracking, for the first time I will be able to record every minute of their day,' he explained, and we heard the radio bleeping through the earphones.

It was such a rare treat, walking with Mhoja and Iain. They knew the place and the animals intimately and were the first people I had met who did not shoot or want to shoot elephants. I could spend only a few days then, but I flew back and forth from Naivasha to Manyara many times after that. The cut strip on the farm became the permanent airstrip and we filled the plane with fresh farm produce every time Iain dropped in for a visit. When my parents returned to the farm, I was able to leave and I moved into Manyara. I learnt how to recognize the elephants and monitor the tree damage, how to photograph and sketch elephants, how to identify the plants and, after my baby was born, how to bring up a child in the bush.

Life was simple. We were a small clan of five – Iain and Mhoja, Suleiman the cook, my baby and me. The research camp was in the middle of the park, a nest of small round houses perched on a ledge of the great Rift wall, where a waterfall hissed as it tumbled into a wide sandy river bed that wound down to the lake.

Protected by a circular white wall with an open window overlooking the valley, I could always sleep in peace at night on a mattress on the floor, with everyone I loved most next to me – my man and our four babies: my own, a mongoose and two genet cats. The wind carried the sounds and smells of bushbuck, baboons and buffaloes up to our little hut. Often lions and leopards passed by to drink, but in particular it was the place where elephants strolled soundlessly on the soft sand to dig wells.

Here we spent many hours quietly observing their lives. Out of the five hundred elephants living in Manyara, 103 matriarchs and sub-matriarchs formed the centre of Iain's study group, with all their children. They consisted of twenty-eight closely linked families, each with its own leadership hierarchy; and by the time Iain's study ended, all the resident families seemed to know us and our car as intimately as we knew them. They had learnt to accept us as friendly and harmless animals, as we had them, but we always treated each other with respect.

Our time was running out. Soon we would have to go back to Oxford, to the buildings, books and people, and I was deeply aware of the intensity of each day as it went by. The sun faded behind the hill and long shadows lay across the valley. In front of me was the river I had looked on a thousand times, where family after family of elephants came to drink: Mary, Boadicea, Sara, Leonora and many more. Today, no-one was walking on the sand, but I knew that everything I loved most was here, silently saying goodbye. Beyond were the trees holding their secrets, then the lake and the mountains, and into the empty universe life moved round and took us with it like a speck of dust carried on the wind.

My one hundred yesterdays, my happiness and all that I had learnt there, were a bonus in my life. Not a day had been planned and I hold the memories of those times in the palm of my hand, as precious and as delicate as the pale blue eggshell of the woodland kingfisher that awoke me every morning. One gesture out of place, and it is gone.

When we finished our exile in Oxford and returned to Manyara for a fleeting visit in 1973, new and ominous clouds hung over the future of elephants, with dreadful tales of slaughter as the price of ivory soared. That year we made a film of the Manyara elephants with Survival Anglia, a television company in England specializing in wildlife documentaries. It was an idyllic time. We had returned with our two baby girls. Saba, the eldest, had been joined by Dudu, born in Oxford. One of Anglia's top cameramen had arrived, an energetic and enthusiastic young German, Dieter Plage. With him was his assistant, an attractive, soft-spoken girl called Lee Lyon.

Dieter and Lee were eager to see the elephants, so we drove down into the woodland until we found Boadicea, still presiding over the biggest family in the park. She had risen to this position of leadership and responsibility through her intelligence and courage – keeping the herd out of trouble and meeting any threats to its safety with a display of her own formidable powers. As we approached she kept an eye on us. Then without warning she turned in one swift move, clapped her ears, flung her trunk at us, and let out a piercing scream.

Hurriedly Dieter and Lee set up their tripod. The wind was blowing away, just right for us, but the elephants were uneasy, huddling close against one another. Their almond eyes, set at the side of their heads, are not as sharp as the eyes of primates or cats. But their sense of smell can detect anyone or anything, if the wind is favourable; and their huge tattered ears, one metre long and always in motion, can pick up sounds like radar antennae.

Some of Boadicea's family reached a waterhole. It was a scene we knew well and loved. Skilfully the big rubbery trunks of the mothers drew up the water, emptying the contents with a gurgle down their throats, like thirsty men with their beer, while the babies pushed through the forest of legs, pummelling their feet in the ooze.

Suddenly, as the camera purred, eyes opened, trunks lifted and Boa's head loomed above the others as she moved in our direction, pointing her tusks straight at us. 'Sit still,' Iain whispered.

The heat became stifling. Beads of sweat dotted Dieter's forehead as he held his finger on the button and adjusted his zoom. I heard the click of Lee's camera; there was no other movement as Boa clapped her great ears like the crack of a whip and bore down on the car. A few paces away she skidded to a halt and let out a mighty, ear-splitting scream.

The photograph that Lee took of Boadicea that day is one of the best there has ever been of a charging elephant – ears spread wide, trunk down and curled back, tusks gleaming white, and her great bulk thrust forward through a cloud of dust. It has since appeared all over the world in newspapers, magazines and books that have helped the elephant cause.

Over the years that followed, Manyara remained relatively immune to poaching and arrived in the 1980s with its herds still intact. The park was so small that rangers could easily patrol its length and breadth. Surely this was the one place where the poachers could make no inroads? But every day the price of ivory was rising. For how much longer could Manyara's elephants hold out against the menace now threatening Africa's last wild places?

PART I

Wings Over Africa

'IT is not possible for a free man to catch
a glimpse of the great elephant herds
roaming the vast spaces of Africa
without taking an oath to do whatever
is necessary to preserve for ever this
living splendour'

Romain Gary,
Roots of Heaven,
1958

AFRICA

GAMBIA
GUINEA
BISSAU

SIERRA
LEONE

MAURITANIA

SENEGAL

GUINEA

LIBERIA

IVORY
COAST

GHANA

TOGO

BENIN

EQUATORIAL
GUINEA

MALI

BURKINO
FASO

NIGERIA

CAMEROON

GABON

CONGO

ALGERIA

NIGER

CHAD

CAR

ZAIRE

UGANDA

ANGOLA

ZAMBIA

TANZANIA

NAMBIA

ZIMBABWE

BOTSWANA

MOZAMBIQUE

SOUTH
AFRICA

LESOTHO

SWAZILAND

MALAWI

RWANDA
BURUNDI

KENYA

SOMALIA

ETHIOPIA

SUDAN

EGYPT

LIBYA

TUNISIA

Elephant range

0   500   1000   1500 km

CHAPTER ONE

IAIN: *Return to Manyara*

1987, Manyara, Tanzania

FROM the air, Lake Manyara lay calm and constant, like a silver bubble in a steaming pool, while all around the bare earth was blowing away in the wind. On either side of the white-tipped wings, red dust coiled up into the sky as I came in from the east. It was 1987, twenty-two years since I first arrived in Manyara. Then, I had been sent to look at the destruction of trees by elephants. Now I was returning in my aeroplane to measure the destruction of elephants by man.

I dropped to a couple of hundred feet, bumping in the hot air, and flew low over the Endabash River. The lake was still as I had always remembered it, edged with crystalline salt and waves of pink flamingoes and white pelicans fluttering beneath us. But within minutes something seemed wrong. Instead of herds of elephants one after another, there was nothing but empty bush. Their favourite resting grounds, a swamp at the mouth of the river and the grassy river banks were deserted. By the time I had landed on the crusted mudflats halfway up the park, I was convinced there had been a disaster. Slowly I taxied the plane, turning with a deafening roar which echoed up in the hills, and switched off the engine. I opened the door and fumes from the soda-saturated shore filled the cabin as the wind blew over the speckled sand.

Through the heat-haze a vehicle approached, hired by Nature Watch, the UK-based television programme which had offered to pay the cost of my visit. It was a way I could return to Manyara and see what had been going on in my absence. We unloaded the plane and wound our way to the sandy Ndala river bed, where I had walked barefoot in 1965 and made my home under a tree overlooking a pool where the elephants drank.

In all our travels Oria and I had never shaken off the spell of Manyara. The place was lodged deep under our skins. We yearned to hear the elephants calling to each other across the river, to walk with them in the woodlands and watch as they emerged from the trees to dig wells for clean water in the sand. I wanted to know how each individual had fared.

I knew that some of the matriarchs had disappeared, laid low by disease or presumed killed for ivory. Nevertheless, families were still led by experienced matriarchs. During another brief visit, just a couple of years previously, I had seen several of my old friends, among them many members of Boadicea's kinship group, including Virgo, Diana, Calypso and Bahati.

Over many years, the aerial surveys I had made at Manyara showed an overall increase in numbers. More elephant refugees were coming in from the south and the west to live in the safety of the park. Rumours of increased poaching had reached my office in Nairobi, but when I telephoned the Director of National Parks he dismissed my worries. 'No, I have not heard any reports of poaching,' he said. 'My people have told me everything is OK.'

Knowing how easy the park was to protect due to its small size I should have been reassured; but a certain pessimism continued to nag at me. Nevertheless, I told the Nature Watch film crew that if all went well they could look forward to an introduction to elephants that they would find nowhere else.

When I think of what elephants mean to me I don't just look at them in a scientific way. Elephants are at the top of the league for power and dangerousness, yet this is combined with gentleness, delicacy and something uncannily close to compassion. Here is an animal that can pick you up in her gnarled trunk, hurl you like a cannon-ball, pierce your body with irresistible force or crush the life out of you, and yet who may equally touch you as tenderly as a mother. Among themselves, elephants tend each other's wounds, stand watch over the sick, and bury the dead. There are still great unresolved mysteries about an elephant's life.

Here is an alien intelligence tantalizingly like our own when it comes to family ties, loyalty and love, yet starting from entirely different origins. Here is anger, and when an elephant is angry the earth shakes. Here is love of family. When science does finally cast light on these mysteries, the elephant will probably be an object of greater veneration than before.

The moment when after years, one elephant, Virgo, consented to take food from my hand as I stood in the open with nothing between us was an unforgettable event. When we discontinued the feeding she would still approach, extend her trunk and release a gush of warm air. How much would it take to close the gap? Could one ever be totally accepted? I felt we were on the brink of an understanding, but before I could cross the threshold of that open door events closed in, Virgo's family was swept away and the tenuous bridge collapsed.

The years fell away as I talked again with Mhoja, but when I asked him about the elephants his gaze became sombre. 'Not so good,' he said, and I was instantly silenced. 'A lot of your old friends are gone,' said Mhoja. 'I am finding it difficult even to see elephants.' I could hardly believe it. Elephants at Manyara had been impossible to miss.

Next day was dark and gloomy, with clouds swirling over the Great Rift Valley. I took off with Mhoja for a reconnaissance and immediately felt the exhilaration of flight. I banked in front of the escarpment, a thin plume of cloud trailing from the wing tips like a compass trace. Sitting inside this old machine, it became a part of me and all I felt for this wild place – freedom and harmony drawn in curves over the lovely landscape I knew so well; each valley, river, hill and woodland.

Automatically I began to scan the ground below. For twenty years I had sharpened my eyes to respond to the smallest exposed part of an elephant; a trunk resting against the base of a tree; a grey back vanishing in the foliage; a dark line of dust-red beads on the distant horizon that denoted a large assemblage. My other search-images were of a more ominous kind, bringing sadness and a sense of despair I could never quite overcome, no matter how often I saw them; the rounded sides of fallen animals streaked white by vulture droppings, or a pile of white bones, within a dark circle in the grass where the seeping juices of decay had left their discoloration long after the carcass had rotted away. Using these signs I could interpret what had happened to the elephants.

Now there were dead elephants everywhere. I flew to Endabash at the end of the park where I had been the day before. In the past the elephants which lived here were notoriously fierce. Fugitives from the hunted world outside, they found sanctuary beyond the river and flourished to the point where once, in 1976, we had agonized over culling them to save the habitat. But this time I flew for twenty minutes without seeing a single elephant, until eventually I came across a group of them around my old research camp.

Mhoja, the film crew and I went after them on the ground, but we had not gone more than a hundred yards through the woodlands before we stumbled on the carcass of an old female. I could tell her sex from the small circumference of her tusk sockets in relation to the size of her skull. She was on her sixth and last molar, and must have been a senior cow or matriarch within the family.

A few yards further on we found the skull of a medium-sized bull. Nearby, Mhoja's sharp eyes picked out a small cone-shaped object lodged in a bone. It was a .458 calibre bullet; the type of ammunition used by the Game Department. The implications made me deeply uneasy. At Manyara elephants had always been shot whenever they left the park on crop-raiding sprees, but never to the extent where the population actually decreased.

It was hard to come up with the elephants because the bush had grown so much, mainly in the form of young re-generating acacia trees. The animals were also shy. Eventually we stalked a family from the cover of an ant-hill. Carefully I scrutinized each member as it came into view with my binoculars, but there was not one I knew. They were young animals with small tusks and even younger ones beside them, all very nervous.

Out on the foreshore we found one elephant called Broken Leg. She had been crippled at birth in the early 1960s, and I had never expected she would survive. But here she was all alone in her pain with one long and thin left tusk. She was slashed about with spear wounds, and very thin. It was a miracle that she of all animals was still here.

Next day we made a full aerial count. We started at the south end and worked slowly up the park until every square metre of the elephants' range was thoroughly scanned. There were very few live elephants. When the count was over we added up all those we had seen and they numbered 181 – down from 485 in 1981. At the same time we had been counting dead elephants. The numbers rose quickly, from five to ten, then twenty, fifty until the final toll was ninety-two, and many of them 'Recent', as we say in the carcass-counting business.

On the last day I worked out the movement of the elephants at Ndala and climbed a tree in their line of advance. It was the Boadicea group, that much I could tell, because Virgo was with them, and she was joined by other stragglers and orphans. All the older bulls and matriarchal leaders had been wiped out. Something terrible had happened in the last two years. Boadicea, Leonora, Slender Tusks, Isabelle, and Giselle had died in the 1970s, but now all of a sudden their successors – Diana, Right Hook, Calypso, Hera and Bahati and her surviving twin – were missing.

Virgo and her companions advanced up the hill towards my tree. I wanted to make contact with Virgo once more and see if she would allow me to approach on foot, but when she was still fifty yards from my tree the breeze turned and carried forward my scent to her. At once her head reared and she spun round, tail up, back arched, and fled down the hill, infecting all the others with her terror. This was the elephant who once had allowed me to touch the lip of her extended trunk.

I knew then that Manyara's elephant society had suffered a pogrom. The little paradise we knew had been destroyed and the tameness of its elephants after all their years of peaceful association with man somehow made the crime of their slaughter all the more hideous. What had caused this tragedy was the ivory trade and its growing numbers of consumers. At that time the conventional view of elephant conservation was that it was more important to win the co-operation of the ivory trade rather than try and close it down. Even my own often-times sponsors, the World Wildlife Fund and the International Union for the Conservation of Nature, believed this.

The WWF, with its famous panda symbol, had become the world's leading fund-raising conservation organization, and the IUCN was its scientific partner. Both these bodies worked closely with CITES, the Convention on International Trade in Endangered Species. This was a treaty which had come into force in 1975 to try and regulate the huge world trade in ivory, horn, skins, furs and other animal products taken from the wild. Unfortunately, the treaty had no real teeth and relied on voluntary compliance of the parties. However, all three groups believed the ivory traders should be given the chance to control their trade, and the ivory quota system that I had opposed from the beginning was now in place.

At a critical time for the elephants in the first half of the 1980s, there had been a fashion among these leading conservation bodies to be friendly to the traders, to try to understand them and to see if they had the will or the ability to control themselves. 'What a naïve idea,' I told Julian Pettifer, the Nature Watch anchorman, as the TV cameras recorded our interview for the viewers back in Europe. 'Traders are traders; they do it for money.'

'For the benefit of people who have no idea how poachers operate, how do they kill elephants?' he asked. I knew only too well the wide range of techniques they used. In the Sudan the elephants were ringed with fire so that the soles of their feet became charred and they could only limp along, after which hunters could close in and spear them. In the Central African Republic there were poachers who galloped up to elephants and speared them from horse-back. Pitfall traps were still used, and I had heard stories from different parts of Africa of elephants being poisoned by all kinds of concoctions, such as bananas laced with battery acid. However, by far the most important weapon was still the bullet.

Pettifer raised some of the criticisms that had been made against me; that I had exaggerated the threat to elephants for sensationalism, in order to get more grants. 'I don't have to tell you, Iain,' he said, 'that there are certain individuals who say that the amount of ivory being taken is not excessive and that the elephant is not being overexploited.'

'Well,' I replied, 'firstly, I don't know how reputable they are, and secondly, they don't know the facts. There is no doubt whatsoever that the elephant is being exploited faster than it can reproduce itself and the ivory trade is the cause. If things go on at the same rate there simply won't be any elephants left.'

I went on to explain how Africa had become a dumping ground for weapons, how UNITA rebels had been trading ivory for weapons to carry on their war in Angola, and how big crooks were making money out of elephants at the expense of the countries and the people. The only hope for the elephants was a moratorium on the international trade in ivory. Only if people stopped buying, wearing or selling the stuff would the herds have a chance to recover.

'And what will happen if we don't do something for the elephants now?' asked Pettifer.

'We are going to bear witness to the destruction of the last large herds of the largest land mammal, and we are going to bear responsibility for it, too,' I said.

These were some of the facts and conclusions which I had been struggling to establish for a decade. Now at last the battleground had come to Manyara. I had followed the poachers' trails all over Africa and had witnessed the carnage they had left behind, the tusks hacked out and the corpses left to rot in the sun, but I had never expected to see it here. I wrote a report for the Director of National Parks. At first it was disbelieved, until a second independent count and a full inquiry had been made. Only then did the Parks' authorities accept the destruction of their elephants.

It was not the first time such results and conclusions on elephant population trends in Africa had been doubted. Yet the Manyara massacre was no different from what many scientists had recorded and I had witnessed and reported time and again ever since Oria and I attempted to make the first census of all Africa's elephants in 1976.

So it was that our lives were taken over by the battle for the elephants. It was a battle which would be fought on the field and in the conference rooms. We would join those involved in a never-ending battle for money to pay for run-down national parks and raggle-taggle anti-poaching forces. The battle would be fought from the skies and on the ground, shooting and getting shot at in bloody skirmishes with heavily armed poachers. It was to be a battle against corruption and maladministration at the highest levels; and above all it would prove to be a battle against the co-ordinated forces of a powerful and persuasive lobby orchestrated by the ivory trade.

Even now I am consumed with anger at the sluggish reactions of most of the elephant scientists and the conservation establishment to the unmitigated slaughter of the elephants. And while they argued among themselves, the elephants died and went on dying. Only after the senseless loss of half a million elephants at the hands of the poachers did a majority of the more serious scientists actually concede in 1987 that, as they put it in cold statistical English, the ivory trade offtake was not sustainable.

How had it come to this? To find the roots of the tragedy it is necessary to go back nearly twenty years, to one of the places where the battle for the elephants could be said to have begun.

CHAPTER TWO

IAIN: *The Ivory Rush Begins*

1969–73, Tsavo, Kenya

My plane tossed up and down in the hot African sky like a boat in a stormy sea as I scanned the dusty ground for elephants. Under a vault of deepest blue, the sun blazed relentlessly on an arid landscape of red earth and broken trees that stretched uninterrupted to the horizon.

This was Tsavo in 1969, the greatest of all the Kenyan elephant parks. I was a new pilot with a veteran aeroplane. I had flown in from Manyara, where I was coming to the end of my elephant studies. Wardens and scientists had flown in from far and wide to cover 12,800 square kilometres of inhospitable wilderness and my job was to reconnoitre the ranches adjoining the park boundaries.

As soon as I entered elephant country it began to look as if a tank force had passed through. Many trees had been completely dismembered. Others lay smashed in a scattered wreckage of half-eaten branches, and the deeper I flew into the park the more frequently I encountered whole patches of land with no trees where red Tsavo dust was sparsely covered with grass.

On take-off, David Sheldrick, the park warden, had thrust a five-gallon water container in my hands. 'It's thirsty country,' he said. 'You'd better take this. If you come down you're going to need it.'

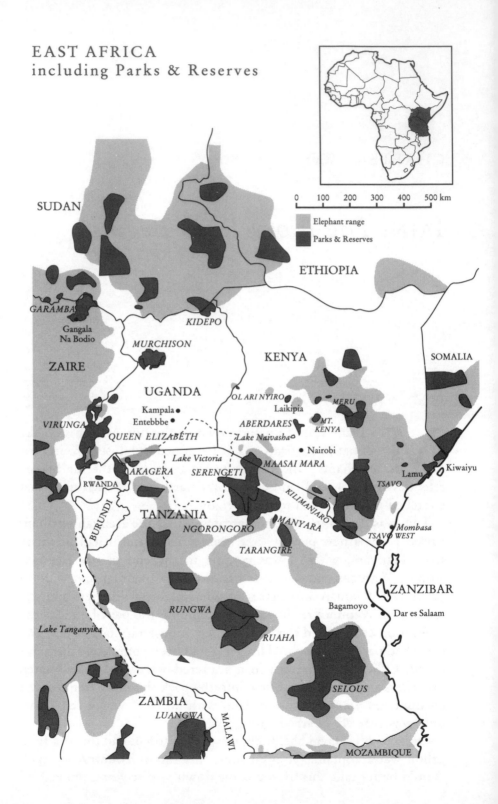

EAST AFRICA
including Parks & Reserves

0 100 200 300 400 500 km

Elephant range

Parks & Reserves

SUDAN

ETHIOPIA

GARAMBA

Gangala
Na Bodio

KIDEPO

MURCHISON

KENYA

SOMALIA

ZAIRE

UGANDA

OL ARI NYIRO

MERU

Kampala

Laikipia

MT.
KENYA

Entebbbe

ABERDARES

VIRUNGA

QUEEN ELIZABETH

Lake Naivasha

Nairobi

Lamu

Kiwaiyu

Lake Victoria

MAASAI MARA

AKAGERA

SERENGETI

TSAVO

RWANDA

KILIMANJARO

BURUNDI

TANZANIA

MANYARA

Mombasa

NGORONGORO

TSAVO WEST

TARANGIRE

ZANZIBAR

RUNGWA

Bagamoyo

Dar es Salaam

Lake Tanganyika

RUAHA

SELOUS

ZAMBIA

LUANGWA

MALAWI

MOZAMBIQUE

The dry wilderness was full of red elephants. We flew for hour after hour and there was no end to them. The next day I flew to the eastern border and found a herd of more than a thousand spread out in the bush, out of sight of each other yet all walking in the same direction, mysteriously aligned like iron filings caught in the field of an unknown magnetic pole. From here elephants could be found right across the Kilifi district almost as far as the Indian Ocean.

During this 1969 operation we counted some twenty thousand elephants inside the park, and there were many others outside. In all, the park and surrounding area was thought to contain at least forty thousand and, given the scientists' tendency to underestimate, there may have been many more. Counting elephants from the air is a tricky business, and it is surprisingly easy to miss not just single elephants, but even whole herds, especially when there is thick vegetation.

At the park headquarters at Voi, rangers in smartly pressed uniforms saluted crisply. Outside stood dusty vehicles of the field force just in from patrol; Toyota Land-cruisers, each flying the pennant of its section, pulling a trailer with water and fuel. This was Tsavo one year before the great drought and three years before the tidal wave of poaching that was to engulf it. I am glad I saw it then, because I know of nowhere yet in East Africa where I could go and find a park as well run as Tsavo in its heyday.

Several of the legendary wardens who had taken part in the campaigns against the poachers in the fifties were there. Bill Woodley, flying his Super Cub, was down from the Aberdare National Park. Bill had been sent out on his first patrol in Tsavo in a clapped-out truck at the age of nineteen, and had located camp after camp of Waliangulu poachers. The Waliangulus had been the master bushmen of this thorny wasteland. They ranged far and wide from the Tana River to the Tanzanian border, taking on the customs and dress of other tribes but always remaining the supreme elephant hunters. With their great bows they could easily drive a poisoned arrow through the thick skin of an elephant, and their hideouts had been common along the Galana River until the Voi ranger force got the better of them.

The fact that there were so many elephants in 1969 was the direct result of the success of those campaigns. Sheldrick, Woodley and some of the other pilots on this count were the men who had made

the parks and defended them. They had seen the rise and were yet
to witness the fall.

As for the elephants, they were quite at home in this country.
After two or three days in the waterless bush they would come
walking out of the distance with a determined, mile-devouring
stride, heading for the river.

Every year in the dry season they dug for water in the sands of
the Tiva River. When they had drunk their fill other animals used
the same holes: rhino, zebra, impala, lion. Some elephants covered
ranges of more than a thousand square kilometres in their endless
search for browse and water. How different were their lives from
those of the Manyara elephants in their park of easy plenty.

When the park was created in 1948 it was still a pristine wilderness,
its only highways the trails followed by generations of elephants –
the oldest roads in Africa. Yet even then, as Bill Woodley found on
his first patrols, ivory poaching was taking place.

Abandoning the practice of placing ranger posts all around the
park, Sheldrick opted for a centralized field-force recruited from
tribes living far to the north. Such men had no local family connections to surrounding villagers. Most of them were nomadic
pastoralists, who were already inured to hardship, excellent trackers
and capable of long forced marches on short rations and little water.
They also had a natural pride and courage, qualities which Sheldrick
used to forge a tough and disciplined force.

Like every good commander, Sheldrick relied heavily on intelligence-
gathering to outwit the elephant hunters. Each captured poacher was
closely questioned and the information received was meticulously
logged in card files. Sheldrick understood these men. He hated what
they did to the elephants but admired their skills in the bush, and
many a veteran poacher, confronted with respect, changed sides
and helped him. Over many years, so thorough did his knowledge
of the poachers become, that despite the tiny size of his field-force
– a mere fifty men to cover a wilderness the size of Wales –
he was able to anticipate raids, unearth hoards of tusks hidden
in surrounding villages and patrol the huge park with unrelenting efficiency.

Finally, after a three-year drive involving the police and the newly
formed game department field-forces, by 1958 no Waliangulus dared
set foot in Tsavo Park. For the next decade poaching was barely
mentioned as a problem.

Sheldrick's methods were taken up further afield by other wardens. Myles Turner in the Serengeti, Peter Jenkins in Meru and Iain Ross in Uganda's Murchison Falls and Kidepo National Parks all built up similar centralized field-forces. These techniques became the well-tested way of coping with poachers, and were so successful that in the late 1960s the poaching menace seemed a thing of the past. No-one could see it then, but it was the abandoning of these standards that gave the ivory avalanche its first decisive nudge downhill.

Meanwhile, protection brought other problems which blinded everyone to the poaching threat. As more and more elephants crossed the boundaries and took up residence in Tsavo, the woodlands continued to disappear. The park's giant baobab trees, standing out like squat concrete columns, were used as a source of food and water by the elephants during the dry months. Now, as the expanding herds opened up the bush, they poked their tusks like swords into the baobab trunks, ripping off the bark to reach the wet pulp within. Many of these magnificent old trees had stood for more than a thousand years. Within a decade many of them were gone.

Sheldrick was the first man to suggest that if there were too many elephants they might have to be reduced by culling. He pressed for research to measure the scope of the problem. But even before the scientists arrived he was becoming reconciled to the changing habitat in which elephants roamed the rolling grasslands like ships in the billowing waves. Although the broken woodlands now looked like an 'elephants' Passchendael', he noticed that as the grasslands flourished so did the grazing species such as zebra and antelopes.

At this time the first scientists arrived, led by Dr Richard Laws, fresh from Uganda where he had studied many hundreds of dead elephants that had been shot in a deliberate attempt to reduce their numbers in the Murchison Falls National Park.

The shooting had been done by a private company directed by a former game warden named Ian Parker. They used military self-loading rifles and had shot two thousand elephants with remorseless efficiency. I had visited both Laws and Parker in Uganda and had been impressed by the force of their arguments. In Murchison there was no scope for extending the park, and culling at that time seemed inevitable.

Laws arranged with David Sheldrick for Ian Parker to come to Tsavo and shoot three hundred elephants so that he could obtain a profile of their ages and examine their reproductive organs as he had done in Murchison before recommending the cull.

By examination of the ovaries he could tell if malnutrition had led to a delay in the onset of puberty. By looking at scars left on the uterus he could see how many calves each female had borne; and from the proportion of pregnant cows he could assess their fertility. Had these signs shown decisively that the rate of reproduction was declining Laws would probably have felt obliged to recommend culling as a way of reducing the excessive numbers of elephants.

But the evidence was not conclusive, and Laws asked the Parks Board if he might shoot another 1,800 elephants before deciding if a major cull was the only way of saving the trees and the park from irreversible destruction.

Alarmed by the speed at which events were unfolding, Sheldrick refused to countenance further shooting. He now held that minimal interference was the proper philosophy for running a park and that 'Nature must take its course' even if the consequence was that a great many elephants might die of starvation. He thought this would be a lesser evil than the precedent of letting gunmen loose in the park, however good their intentions.

The park authorities supported Sheldrick, and Laws resigned in chagrin, with dire warnings of irretrievable habitat changes leading to desertification and a prolonged plunge in the elephant population.

The Tsavo issue was furiously debated. Powerful lobbies grew up for and against culling elephants; but in the end the talking was overtaken by events. A prolonged drought was not long in coming and Tsavo's elephants starved by the thousands. In 1970–71 the plains were full of pathetic, skeletal elephants. Gaunt mothers stood over their dying babies until they, too, became so weak that they crumpled to the ground. Trees and bushes were smashed and splintered beyond recognition. For want of leaves and twigs the elephants ate chips of wood, and Tsavo's woodlands looked as if they had endured intense shell-fire. No one knew exactly how many elephants died. David Sheldrick suggested ten thousand. Others, making reconnaissance flights over the park, estimated far more.

Supporters of the two opposing schools of thought each felt these developments justified their case. The anti-cullers claimed that the drought had produced a natural control of the elephant numbers. The pro-cullers wrote of irreparable ecological damage and desertification. They presented their case as science against amateurism, reason against emotion.

It needed strong nerves to stand by the policy of *laissez-faire*. Peter Beard, the New York photographer who had made Tsavo his special interest, wildly spoke of Sheldrick as 'the murderer of Tsavo's elephants'. But Sheldrick remained firm to his beliefs; and when at last the drought ended thirty-five thousand elephants still survived in and around Tsavo.

In 1973 I went to stay in Tsavo with the wildlife film-maker, Simon Trevor. To my delight the park was green again and Simon showed me where the trees were regenerating. To everyone's surprise another count found the same number of elephants in Tsavo as there had been before the drought. What had happened to the elephants that had died? It was likely that new immigrants from surrounding districts under pressure from poaching had moved into the park.

Despite the deaths of thousands of elephants, nothing had changed and the destruction of Tsavo's woodlands continued. Was there really no way of restoring the balance except by culling? One of the ideas advanced at the time was that elephants and trees have some kind of long-term dynamic cyclical relationship, and that fluctuations of either species should not themselves be a cause for concern.

Another and more ominous theory was that the apparent cycles of elephants could equally well have been produced by periodic exterminations caused by the ivory trade. Tsavo itself had few elephants in 1900 probably due to the historical ivory trade.

Back on the farm in 1973 Oria and I settled down to write about the Lake Manyara elephants. One day a Cessna 185, as black as night, with orange wing tips, swept down on our airstrip. As I approached I could see two tanned and sandaled feet attached to two short spindly legs emerging under the fuselage. Around the plane came a head that looked as if it belonged to a ferocious gnome, until its features relaxed in an engaging smile. It was Ian Parker. This duality seemed characteristic of his personality and persisted throughout his visit.

Parker was, in turn, both stimulating and a little intimidating. Of all the people I met in East Africa he had a unique combination of field experience and a lively and probing mind. He had been a Tsavo warden and more recently had set up his own business which involved culling literally thousands of elephants. After the fierce dispute over Tsavo he was now looking for work.

Never one to remain idle he had begun a study of the ivory trade, pioneering a new line of research by eliciting biological information from the tusks that entered the international market. He believed that by looking at the amount of ivory coming out of Africa he had the best way of finding out how many elephants were left. Conventional aerial surveys could cover only a fraction of the continent and were useless anyway over the vast forests of Central Africa where many, if not most, of the elephants lived. On the other hand, the inspection of tusks could give a good picture of the population from which they were derived. In particular, the yearly breakdown of ivory exported from Kenya could give a broad view of what was happening to Kenya's elephants.

This train of thought led Ian Parker to produce a secret report for Jack Block, Chairman of the World Wildlife Fund in Kenya, on the resurgence of the Kenya ivory trade. In it he related how recently the volume of ivory leaving Kenya had taken off like a rocket, breaking all previous records. The ivory price had started to climb in 1969. Eventually it would rise to become nine times higher than the average value in the sixties. Ivory exports, notably to Hong Kong, followed suit, and Parker thought that the sudden attraction to ivory was a recognition of its value as exportable currency. As such it had become ideal for illegal dealing.

Yet, despite his findings, or perhaps because of them, Parker was convinced that the current high level of the trade meant that the numbers of elephants in Africa must run into millions in order to sustain it.

When he took off from the farm, a copy of my thesis under his arm (very expensive, he said), Parker had left me with much to think about. From now on he became my guru on elephant matters and I consulted him increasingly about my work. His visit might not have done much to clarify my thoughts on Manyara, but it certainly had given me a disturbing perspective on the future.

Shortly afterwards I wrote to the New York Zoological Society, my sponsors at Manyara, telling them I would like to make a general survey of the elephants of East Africa. The controversy over the culling of elephants was still a burning issue, and although most scientists now favoured a 'wait and see' policy, the pendulum could easily swing. I felt it was vital that an impartial survey should be made to predict rates of change in both elephant populations and habitats, over as wide a range of conditions as possible.

Most of all what I wanted to do was to go to the Murchison Falls National Park in Uganda to check whether the elephants were declining to eventual extinction as forecasted by Laws and Parker in 1968. If their predictions were correct then the future of the African elephant would be grim indeed.

Shortly after Ian Parker's visit to Naivasha a seminar was held of all the elephant experts in Kenya, which set the writing on the wall for elephants everywhere in Africa and eventually launched Oria and me on an exploration of their world which continues to this day.

The Nairobi seminar came about because a storm of criticism had blown up around the heads of the Kenya Game Department, principally on the grounds of alleged abuses in the management of elephant hunting. In the end the Director of the Department had been obliged to put a temporary ban on elephant hunting and to order a full-scale inquiry into the allegations.

The row had been brewing at a time when considerable disquiet was already being voiced in conservation circles over a number of poaching incidents which indicated the involvement of people in high places. A cargo of eight hundred tusks intercepted at Nairobi Airport had afterwards mysteriously disappeared. Government cars were reported poaching in the Masai Mara Game Reserve; and when a radio-collared elephant was shot near Tsavo, the dealers and killers were identified but nothing had ever come to court.

The seminar was arranged by Peter Jarman, a research officer in the Game Department. Quiet and unassuming, his excellent organization filled a lecture room in the university with a large gathering of farmers, hunters, wardens and scientists. It produced a rough estimate of 167,000 elephants in Kenya, of which forty-nine thousand enjoyed some form of protected status, and was the first time that a national elephant census had ever been attempted in Africa.

Ian Parker played a key role in the seminar. First he exposed the hunting rackets and the ivory trade. The number of people buying elephant licences each year, he said, bore a direct relationship to the value of ivory and its current high price was obviously responsible for the enormous increase in the issue of licences, authentic or spurious. Then he surprised everyone by claiming that ivory worth $160 million would leave Africa in 1973 – the equivalent of up to 200,000 dead elephants. No one had thought the figures could be so high.

Next, he highlighted the contradiction of locally overcrowded elephants. His view was that historically man and elephant had always been in conflict over space. He argued that as human populations were now rapidly increasing it would be better to shoot the elephants in areas of contention rather than allow them to destroy the ecological balance of the parks as their numbers swelled.

In this paradox of local over-abundance and general decline lay the root cause of the delays that were to put off any decisive action for another sixteen years; but we were not to know it then.

The Nairobi seminar produced an emphatic consensus that poaching was rife in Kenya and that the game laws needed rapid and vigorous enforcement. But, above all, it would be remembered as the first time that people spoke out in public, revealing the extent of the corruption which clung to the ivory trade at the highest levels. Peter Jarman submitted a confidential report to the senior game warden, Jonathan Mutinda, setting out the indictments to which we had all listened. Peter then courageously stepped on to much more delicate ground and mentioned 'Collector's Letters', giving permission to collect tusks from elephants which had died naturally in the bush, which were being notoriously abused as cover for what he called 'illegal or semi-illegal ways of obtaining ivory'. They were issued by the president's office as special favours to certain individuals, often retired Mau Mau guerrillas. The letters were often photocopied and used to develop a widespread trade in poached ivory.

These letters did the game department's reputation much harm, said Jarman. 'Dealers' permits are issued in enormous numbers and their conditions of dealing only from stated premises are widely flouted,' he went on. 'There appears to be a category of people who operate with immunity above the law. Leading personalities, including both assistant ministers in our own ministry, are among those buying from HQ.' He ended his letter, 'All this will be known to you. What I am trying to emphasize is the chaos that surrounds the possession of ivory.'

The Government's response was swift and startling. Within two weeks of delivering his report, Peter Jarman was informed that his contract with the game department would not be renewed, and

Kenya was deprived of an experienced man it could ill-afford to lose. Despite the elephant hunting ban and the fact that the great Tsavo Park was still holding its own under Sheldrick's leadership, the rot within Kenya's wildlife establishment was spreading, and the price of ivory was still rising.

But Kenya held only a fraction of Africa's elephants. There was no telling as yet if the threat to elephants was general. If we could get airborne we could move out to explore their range across the length and breadth of the continent.

CHAPTER THREE

ORIA: *School for Elephants*

1973–4, East Africa and Zaire

ON Christmas Eve, December 1973, in the midst of carols and ribbons and bright paper wrappings, our Survival Anglia film on the elephants of Lake Manyara was shown to millions of viewers. The African première took place on the farm at Naivasha a few weeks later.

Waiting for the sun to set behind the dusty hills, we parked a six-ton truck on the lawn in front of our house and draped a white sheet over the back. Women and children arrived in gaggles and sat together around the lorry while the men gathered on the fringes until the lawn was covered with a multi-coloured throng of all ages. At last the sky darkened and the projector was switched on.

Suddenly an elephant charged out of the screen trumpeting furiously at the audience. Women snatched up their babies, children ran screaming and men raised their sticks ready to throw them at this terrifying apparition. Just at that moment Iain appeared in a Land-Rover, driving helter-skelter in front of the elephant. 'Run, Iain, run,' yelled the crowd. 'Hurry out of the way!'

Encouraged by the success of our opening night, we sent the Manyara elephant film to Tanzania's director of parks, Derek

Bryceson, in the hope that it would help him persuade the authorities to extend the park boundaries which gave protection not only to its elephants but to countless other wild creatures. Perhaps the message of the film would travel even further.

Our gateway to the rest of Africa had always been Wilson Airport, in Nairobi. Its runway was the grey carpet laid out for the arrival and departure of generations of bush pilots ever since the days of Beryl Markham and Denys Finch Hatton, and it was here that I learnt to fly in the little blue-white-and-red Cessna 150, belonging to the Aeroclub school. Day after day I practised my circuits and bumps, and as I banked, lifting up over the Nairobi National Park which borders Wilson, I learnt to recognize some of the animals that lived on the land over which I flew.

Down there an ostrich had laid its eggs. Mornings and afternoons the male guarded the nest jealously, taking his turn to sit on the eggs while the female went out to feed. Then one day as I was flying, the eggs were there no more, and I wondered whether a hyena had stolen them.

The more I flew, the stronger my wings seemed to grow. One day, as I taxied along the runway ready for take-off, my instructor opened the passenger door and jumped out. 'You're on your own now,' he shouted. 'Off you go and good luck.' Slowly the wings lifted off the grey carpet and a smile cut across my face. Alone now with the plane in my hands, I could feel the heat in the small of my back as the earth disappeared beneath me and I started to sing: 'Here I go on my way to join the others in the skies – that is me, that is me – my one and only solo flight – into the wind, across the plains and into the world.'

Below me, on the wide green circle of the park, marched a black ostrich and a brown ostrich followed by a line of little mottled ostriches, each going out into a new world. I waggled my wings; it was a day for celebration. I forgot about earthbound rules in those long five minutes, then turned in for finals. As far as I was concerned, I was now a pilot and felt ten feet tall.

What is more our book, *Among the Elephants*, was finished, and the handsome advance we had received from our publishers would give us the financial independence we needed to pursue a long-held dream. Rather like the old-time elephant hunters, we wanted to satisfy a wanderlust, following the elephant trails into the farthest realms of Africa.

With the cheque in our hands, Iain and I walked up and down Wilson Airport looking for an aeroplane to buy. We examined those parked on the apron and peered into each hangar until eventually we found exactly what we were looking for: a Cessna 185, 1961 model, whose owner was emigrating to Ireland. It was perfect; she had to be ours.

'*Bravo Alfa Delta*', *BAD* for short, was a package of strength. She could take off with four people, full tanks and plenty of cargo without a groan. From the start, *BAD* became an integral part of our life like the elephants, and for the first few years we flew non-stop in pursuit of them.

In the cold early hours when the wind was still and the dawn sky as empty and clean as a crystal glass, we would begin our long flights north, high over mountains, forests and deserts to the shores of Lake Turkana, to the banks of the Nile and on into the tall yellow grasslands of the Sudan. On other days we headed south, flying low over the bush and the seas of dry grass. Below us a pattern of colours on maps suddenly became the Serengeti plains or the snows of Kilimanjaro, or the ocean sands of Kiwaiyu. Beneath the blazing sun, under cumulus clouds or through the arches of double rainbows the small black shadow of our plane marked our long journeys across the immense dusty face of Africa.

On the farm the children grew like the sunflowers in the fields. The sound of their laughter sifted through the thin mud walls of our elephant office. From my desk I could watch them running across the bright green fields, playing and talking with their African nannies as they ambled on their way to the big house to have tea with my parents.

Although Iain and I had our own small cottage, we still considered the big house to be our real home. It is an extraordinary building, a strange sort of castle painted a dark Italian pink with wooden slatted roofs bleached pale by the sun. My parents had built it in the 1930s in Art Deco style, having seen a picture of a West African king's palace in Paris. It stands on a 3,000-acre farm with an avenue of sombre cypress trees framing a distant view of Mount Longonot across Lake Naivasha, which echoed my father's early Neapolitan life in the shadow of Vesuvius.

Sitting on the earth-red sofa in the panelled library, my mother waited with the children for tea to arrive, turning the pages of the tattered story book, *Histoire de Babar*. One of the first pictures showed Babar as a baby riding out on the broad shoulders of his mother. All of a sudden there was a terrible bang, and a wicked hunter who had been hiding in the bushes, stepped out and fired his rifle at Babar's mother.

'Is that Papi shooting the elephant, Granny?' Saba asked. My father sitting at his desk on the other side of the room, grunted.

'Papi, why did you shoot the elephant?'

'That's why we came to Africa. Everyone shot elephants in those days.'

Then tea arrived and all was forgotten as our two little girls scanned the trays of cakes.

If my old papa was responsible for this callous act, my mother should be given credit for the fact that Babar was born in the first place.

Forty-five years had passed since my parents had returned from a year-long elephant hunting safari, where they had walked from Albertville in the Congo, up the western side of Lake Tanganyika and on to Rwanda, eventually returning by steamer across Lake Victoria.

My mother was an artist, a sculptress, and wherever she went she took with her soft crayons, and her sculptor's tools which had been handed to her by Rodin, her teacher and mentor.

Having reached Bukavu six months after leaving Dar es Salaam by train to Ujiji, they sailed across Lake Tanganyika to Albertville, crossed Lake Kivu in dug-out canoes and continued on foot to Nyanza to meet the King of the Tutsis in Rwanda-Burundi. The Tutsi warriors were renowned for their extraordinary height and beauty, and my mother wanted to spend some time painting them.

Approaching the palace grounds, my parents were met by a procession of tall men sent by the King. The hair on their elongated heads was partly shaven and partly woven into moon-shaped combs, called *amasunzu*, an elaborate coiffure worn by noblemen, giving them an even taller look. Next to the King's men, most of them seven feet tall, my parents looked like dwarfs.

The King's palace was a large, round building made of reeds, with a thatched roof and floors covered by leopard skins. Inside sat the *Mwami* himself, so tall, so elegant and with such noble features, together with his favourite wife, who was extremely shy and young and had the cone-shaped head of the Tutsi women, a sign of great beauty and nobility. The *Mwami* welcomed my parents and invited them to stay as long as they wished. My mother, overwhelmed by such beauty and dignity, set up her easel under a tree and began to draw.

My mother was the only member of her family who had ever been exploring in Africa. When eventually she returned to Paris, she told her relatives about her adventures, and in particular about a tiny orphaned elephant that had been looked after by the wife of a Belgian administrator in the Congo. Two of my mother's cousins, Jean and Cecile de Brunhoff, an artist and musician, were captivated by these tales. One day, when their children were ill in bed with measles, Jean began to regale them with stories and to draw pictures of an orphaned elephant which he called Babar.

I had always hoped that one day I would be able to retrace my parents' safari in the Congo. Iain, too, had another compelling reason for going. He was interested in the art of training African elephants which had been known to the ancients in the time of Ptolemy and Hannibal. They had been used in the struggles of empires on the fringe of Africa and all around the Mediterranean, rather in the role of a main battle tank. But knowledge of how to train them had been dead for two thousand years until it had a remarkable revival in the heart of Africa.

In the extreme north-east of Zaire, at a place called Gangala na Bodio, were the remnants of an elephant school. It had been set up at around the turn of the century by Leopold II, King of the Belgians, who dreamt of using African elephants in the same intelligent ways that Asian elephants had served man for millennia.

Three-quarters of a century later there were perhaps ten or twelve elephants still alive at Gangala na Bodio, together with their *cornacs* or trainers. If it was not already too late, Iain wanted us to fly there and learn what we could about training African elephants. Maybe it was the right time to stop shooting elephants and to start using them to earn their keep in the competitive world of the twentieth century?

*

The great central African rain forest spread below us, green and misty, marching a thousand miles to the Atlantic Ocean. The treetops, enveloped in cloud that swept over their heads, resembled a thick green blanket in a steam bath. In places the clouds swelled up into the heights of the sky to form gigantic, unfriendly mountains of cumulus stretching for hundreds of miles, trailing impenetrable curtains of rain.

After many hours of flying we reached the far side of the forest where, to our great relief, we could make out flat ground scattered with clumps of small trees. Elephants holding their trunks above their heads were pushing through tall, rolling green grass towards the brown ribbon of a stream. We had arrived.

Word of our visit had been sent to the warden. Visitors were rare, but the arrival of an aeroplane was an event. The whole village had been summoned to hack out an airstrip, and we landed *BAD* in a narrow canyon of freshly cut elephant grass.

Everyone came out to meet us. On one side stood the nine remaining elephants with their mounted *cornacs*, old men with proud wrinkled faces, still strong and upright. Here were the remnants of King Leopold's dream. Men in uniforms, complete with berets, boots and dark glasses, introduced us to the elephants, of which four of the long-tusked females were instructing *moniteurs*.

From old dusty publications in obscure colonial libraries, and long drawn-out conversations in Lingala, Swahili and French, we pieced together King Leopold's vision of establishing centres in the heart of Africa to train elephants as beasts of burden.

Inspired by the Asian elephants and their *mahouts* (drivers) which he had seen on a visit in Ceylon, Leopold decided to provide the best pilot trainers in Africa and sent out four Asian elephants with thirteen *mahouts* to Bagamoyo. However, this first expedition in 1879 ended in tragedy when three of the elephants died on the one thousand kilometre crossing to Lake Tanganyika, and the rest of the expedition were butchered almost to a man by a fierce ivory baron with his three thousand Rouga Rouga bandits.

Nevertheless Leopold would not accept defeat. What is the loss of a few men, or a few years, compared to the death of a dream, when you are king? Twenty years later in 1899, a report reached Leopold that an elephant had been captured in Gabon and had been successfully trained to work for a mission station. One of Belgium's toughest colonial officers, Commandant Laplume, was dispatched to Uele, an area well known for its forest elephants, with orders to start catching and training African elephants.

Laplume finally succeeded in domesticating three elephants by 1901. By 1910 he had thirty-five under training and the station known as 'La Mission des Elephants' was opened on the edge of the Uele River.

During the following decades, well over five hundred elephants were trained to fell trees, carry logs, and pull ploughs or carts as well as to select and pile bricks. So it went on until 1960, when the fifth Commandant of Gangala na Bodio celebrated sixty years of training elephants in the Congo. By now it had become a station of great importance, and was visited by scientists from all over the world.

Under the Belgian policy of wildlife conservation the wild elephants prospered, too; so much so that crop raiding became a major problem throughout the north of the country. The administration turned to the school as a centre of practical but unsentimental knowledge about elephants, and soon a disciplined squadron of *Chasseurs Cornac* was formed to go out on crop protection. The 'wild animal police', as they came to be known, shot some four thousand elephants a year without apparently making any reduction in the population.

By 1960, however, the African people had become restless under white man's rule, and the continent began to erupt. Despite the anarchy which followed the Belgian withdrawal, Gangala na Bodio continued to function until 1963, when news filtered through that the Simba rebels were approaching and planned to kill all the elephants. Most of the *cornacs* disappeared into the forest, taking fourteen elephants with them.

Two years later, when the rebels were finally defeated by the Congolese army, the *cornacs* emerged like sleepy ghosts from the forest with their elephants. But the ghosts returned to an abandoned and burnt-out station. In vain they waited for someone to breathe new life into the empty shell of Leopold's dream, but no one came back to rebuild it.

One elephant, Wando, who greeted us on our arrival at Gangala na Bodio, was a living witness to the history of this fading vision. She stood by the plane as we stepped out, resting her head on her long, smooth tusks which swept down to the ground like swords, and waited patiently for the ceremony to end.

By talking to the staff and the last of the *cornacs*, after going through the records I worked out that Wando's mother must have been captured by Laplume in 1912, and that her name was Alberte. By 1930 she had been moved to Gangala na Bodio, and in November of that year Wando became only the second baby elephant to be born there. Looking through the old journals I came across photographs of her, only eight days old, walking with her mother and their *cornac*. She became very attached to him, and enjoyed all the scratching and caresses he lavished upon her.

The *cornac* and I mounted Wando's back and sat on a small, thickly woven grass mat to avoid being scratched by her spiky hairs. We ambled through the village, as she had done every day for more than forty years, and followed a path in the tall grass that led down to the river for her bath. The ancient song that accompanied the ritual had probably come with the first *mahouts* from Ceylon. Now the Azande *cornacs* had adapted it to their own tongue and intonation.

An elephant's back seems the most natural place to be when riding through the bush or the jungle. Slowly and silently rocking along between the ground and the treetops I felt tall, stately, and timeless. For days Iain and I talked with the warden and *cornacs* about ways of enabling others to share this experience.

We knew that in Basel Zoo African elephants had been trained to give thousands of people rides every year and to tolerate children running near their feet. In Burma five thousand trained elephants were still being employed; elsewhere in Asia too, elephants were being used for heavy jobs that required powerful muscles and skill, like manoeuvring giant logs from the forest.

What particularly lit a spark in Iain's imagination was the possibility of training African elephants for work on safari. In Nepal at the Tiger Tops Jungle Lodge in the Royal Chitwan National Park, visitors arriving by air are transported by elephant to their hotel and then taken out into the forest to see Indian rhinos and tigers.

'Why shouldn't we bring one of the elephants from Gangala na Bodio with her *cornac*, stage by stage, back to Kenya?' Iain asked me one day. 'We could use her to train a team of young elephants, and start elephant safaris in the Aberdare Forests?'

My own mind ran in another direction. From our own experience on the farm at Naivasha I knew only too well that Africa remains the cemetery of machines, and I sympathized with the warden when he pointed out the rusting tractors which had been brought all the way from Belgium and could not be used for lack of spare parts. In any case with the soaring price of oil, the cost of fuel was prohibitive. Compared with the pathetic life expectancy of a tractor in Africa, the warden estimated that the working span of an elephant might run to thirty, even forty, years. Furthermore the only maintenance an elephant required was the care and affection of its *cornac*, and enough to eat.

Sadly we reflected on the reality of life in Gangala na Bodio. Unless these ideas were received fast, both the elephants and the *cornacs*, who were old, would die at about the same time. The survivors were beautiful in their old age, a rare example of what can be achieved in Africa between man and animals by linking their two lives together. But they had no replacements and no longer had a real purpose. Most of the red-brick houses stood like crumpled packs of cards; the machinery had fallen silent. The horses that had eagerly ridden out to the capture were long since dead. Only the flagpole in the middle of the square revealed the last threads of military style that had established and animated the station for so many years.

Every morning, fanned by the four big palm trees above our heads, we stood beside the warden, his men in fatigues, together with the elephants and a band of ragged children, watching the green-and-black flag slide up into the clear sunshine of another day. Each time it broke at the top of the mast, I wished in my heart that one morning it might rise to the sky and open to a new dream.

But where was the man with the mind like steel, with an arm and hand of iron, who would stop all this waste and once again appreciate for their strength and intelligence these noble creatures of this ancient continent?

All the time we stayed at Gangala na Bodio, Iain longed to cross the Dungu River to have a look at the Garamba National Park into which the *cornacs* had misleadingly told the Simba rebels that they had turned their elephants loose. But access was not easy, for the roads had become almost impassable. We had run short of time and had to be content with viewing the park from the air as we started for home.

Below our plane wild elephants forged through the tall grass like moles pushing along a burrow. As yet little was known about this rich ecological frontier. No one had surveyed the savannah, and an immense canopy spread like a shroud concealing whatever moved in the forest.

Situated at the edge of the interminable Zaire Forest, the Garamba occupies a bowl of long grass savannah between the Zaire River and the trees. Its high rainfall, lush vegetation and low human population were said to provide the most favourable condition for elephants on the continent. Our hunter friends called it the elephant Eldorado, and it was later estimated that twenty-five thousand lived in the Garamba, in a density as high as Manyara. We could not see any damage to the park, but Iain suspected that each year the fringe of the forest withdrew a little further and the rich green savannah of elephant grass advanced.

We had heard disturbing stories of corruption in the park involving illegal trade in fish, meat, skins and ivory. But gazing down from the plane I wrongly thought that with the end of the Simba rebellion, the elephants at least were beyond the worst.

Heading south we looped to our right over the thousands of leagues of dripping forest. Here, where the rainfall is more than sixty inches a year, lay the little-known heart of Africa, always steaming with the rich smell of vegetation. From time to time we spotted small airstrips, narrow rectangles cut out of the trees; closer to the towns they were longer and broader. These had been cleared by prospectors and were frequently used for the smuggling of diamonds and gold. As the prospectors worked their way deeper into elephant country, ivory became their profitable sideline.

If the Tsavo ecosystem had once held forty-two thousand elephants in forty-three thousand square kilometres, how many more browsed through the unfathomed forests of the Congo? Were there one million, two million elephants under the trees? No one could tell us the answer since no one had ever tried to count them.

CHAPTER FOUR

ORIA: *A Final Solution*

1975, Kenya and Rwanda

THE dry season at Naivasha began with hot days of brilliant sun in an empty sky. In the early mornings the cool green lawn spread out under my bare feet. Each step left a thin path of footprints in the dew, leading to where the garden table stood, set with a bright printed cloth, and a dish with slices of moist orange pawpaws forming a circle of new moons.

Breakfast on the farm was always the same. A pot of steaming coffee had its place beside a big jug of fresh milk, with freshly baked scones neatly packed in a basket, dark African honey and home-made marmalade in brown earthenware pots. Above our heads towered the beautiful Naivasha fever trees with their pale green leaves and yellow flowers. Slender grey tails hung down from the branches where vervet monkeys sat sunning themselves, and among the leaves blue-and-gold starlings chattered as they waited for leftovers.

One day news came from Mhoja in Manyara that the great Boadicea had died in mysterious circumstances, possibly killed by poachers. Weeks passed. Iain had flown down at the first opportunity and I had been waiting all day for his return.

Thunder rumbled in the hills and the first rain cooled the winds that raced in waves across the lake as I waited with a knot of anxiety turning in my stomach for the plane to appear. It was getting late and the sun was already sinking fast when I heard the faintest hum of an engine. I knew that sound. The plane dived down to salute me as I stood in the oncoming storm, then spun up into the clouds to catch the last of the light and find a place to land.

The smell of death filled the cabin of the plane, sticking to the khaki cloth of Iain's shirt. On the back seat sat the skull and two bones of an elephant, the remains of Boadicea, the Manyara matriarch, with a letter from Derek Bryceson, the parks director, pushed into one of her bony cavities. The letter gave us permission to keep what was left of Boa.

Anyone meeting Boadicea could not forget her. She was a queen in her own right, with great presence and power, and it was tragic to think she may have fallen to a poacher's bullet. Now, with only her sculpted head to keep her name, she would have a place of honour in a book-filled room, a small tribute we could pay to all elephants cursed with the value of their tusks.

We had wanted to bring back her tusks as well but fate was not on our side. By the time Iain went to collect them, they had gone to Japan. 'For bracelets, trinkets, billiard balls and especially for money,' he was told. The rush for ivory does not wait. What chance had we to stop this race of ivory versus life? The skull now picked as clean as stone was placed beside the door, where it still stands. A memory of all the elephants that once stood tall and roamed the boundless savannah.

In his small thatched office, Iain had finished collecting the many dossiers of information given to him by game departments and scientists all over East Africa. It was the middle of 1975 and we were getting ready to leave for New York, as the American edition of our book was about to be published.

This first book of ours, *Among the Elephants*, had become an international bestseller. Its royalties financially liberated us, but Iain was left as an unemployed elephant scientist. Ideally he would have liked to continue his research in Manyara. But he was overtaken by the whirlwind of poaching which had begun to sweep away elephants all over Africa. Suddenly people were asking him what was happening. We, too, were becoming increasingly worried, and the trip to America was an opportunity to look for funds for our elephant survey. Now, we hoped, was the time to awaken the interest of the American public and alert them to the elephants' plight.

We stopped *en route* in London long enough to settle our two children into the neatly paddocked English countryside with Iain's mother, and then departed for America in the rush and turmoil, leaving behind two bewildered, sad little faces peering through a whirl of legs as the crowd surged past them at Heathrow Airport.

America was like a blast off into space, an upward surge from the bitter-sweet life of Equatorial Africa into the glitter and glamour of the cities where, for a few days, we felt as if the world was at our feet. We were sent from coast to coast, from one studio to another, always explaining how we came to be involved with elephants, and why they were animals worthy of human respect.

In the days before the film of Karen Blixen's classic, *Out of Africa*, very little was really known in America about Kenya. Occasionally we were asked questions about Mau Mau and the macabre rituals of Kikuyu oathing. Otherwise the only tribe anyone had heard of was the Maasai.

An old friend of ours, Jenny Bell Whyte, had organized a dinner party for us, to which she had invited Bill Conway, the general director of the Bronx Zoo. The New York Zoological Society had a worldwide interest in conservation and had supported Iain's field work in Manyara. We had hoped that they would also support the pan-African elephant survey. 'He's a very important man,' Jenny Bell said, 'and very conservative. Don't say anything shocking please, because you're sitting next to him, Oria.'

I was always a bit uneasy when I had to meet Iain's scientific seniors, but promised to be on my very best behaviour, even though I covered myself in Maasai beads and skins. He stared at me from time to time like a cross old parrot, but behind his severe look was a charming and sensitive man who made an inspiring toast in which he expressed the society's interest in Iain's plan, and he promised his full support.

In a studio the next day we heard the news in a friendless room, from a stranger at a radio station, during one of our interviews.

'An American girl has been killed by an elephant in a country called Rwanda. Her name is Lee Lyon. Have you heard of her?'

Lee's shy and sensitive face came back to me in a flash; the two idyllic months she had spent with us at Manyara, sharing our hopes and fears. Now Lee was dead. I was unable to speak and Iain had to finish the interview on his own.

Rwanda is a small, mountainous country of grassy uplands which extend south-eastwards from a chain of volcanoes perched on the great divide of East and Central Africa. Together with its small neighbour, Burundi, it was once ruled over by the Mwamis of the Watutsi, one of whom my mother had met long ago.

In the long contest between man and elephant for space in Africa, it is not surprising that Rwanda presented an extreme scenario in which the expanding human population was encroaching on the home of the country's last one hundred and fifty savannah elephants. An experimental agricultural station growing rare strains of banana was being devastated by their nightly raids; but rather than destroy the elephants the Rwandan government wanted to protect them.

The Akagera National Park, which lay eighty kilometres away, was a possible solution. The park had thousands of buffalo, zebra, topi and roan antelope, but strangely no elephants.

The Rwandans asked for help but their plea came at an unfortunate time. For years every conservationist in East Africa had been worrying about too many elephants and still remembered the scenes of starvation in Tsavo. Elephants were plentiful elsewhere. If they were causing problems in Rwanda, why not just shoot them all?

Bob McIlvaine, a former US Ambassador in Kenya who had become the director of the African Wildlife Leadership Foundation, thought he had found a compromise – an operation to cull the adults and immobilize the young who could later be transported to Akagera. Bob invited Ian Parker, the recognized authority in East Africa on culling, to come to Rwanda. Parker had already personally killed thousands of elephants and his company, Wildlife Services, could organize the shooting. Tony Parkinson, a well-known figure in the animal trapping world, was also invited. When Iain heard about the expedition he asked Bob at the eleventh hour if he might come too and found himself in AWLF's Cessna, flying to Rwanda for a meeting with the Government.

At the research station it looked as if grapeshot had cut swathes through the long lines of banana trees. It was not the first time Iain had seen elephants simulate the effect of shell-fire, but he could sympathize with the distraught Belgian adviser who waved his arms and lamented, '*Les bananes sont terminées*'. No wonder after two

years of seeking solutions in vain the government's patience was
wearing thin.

The first and starkest option was that the Army should wipe out
the elephants and let the local people take the meat. The Government
could keep the ivory, but the valuable hides would be left to rot.

The next set of proposals included the employment of expatriate
experts to prepare and market the hides in the event of the Army
doing the shooting; or alternatively they could take full responsibility for removing the entire elephant population by killing or capture.
These were the options offered by Ian Parker. However, in the
hours he and Parker had spent talking together, Iain was convinced
that Parker was genuinely reluctant to carry out this unemotional
disposal of surplus elephants which he had so often advocated. 'I will
set the price so high that they will not accept it,' Parker told Iain.

The final proposal was Iain's and took everyone by surprise. He
suggested that there was no need to kill any elephants, and since
they had waited this long a few more months would not hurt.

'That would give time,' said Iain, 'to set up large enclosures or
Kheddahs and drive the elephants into them.' It was a system which
had been used in India for millennia. Once they had been tamed in
holding pens over several months, they could be driven in very easy
stages to Akagera.

As Iain unfolded these plans the Belgian advisers whispered
excitedly to themselves. It was obvious they liked the idea. Unfortunately time was the one unavailable commodity. The Rwandans
were unsure, ready to go either way, but scared of the president's
directive that an immediate solution should be found. Iain's biggest
disadvantage was inexperience. The last people in Africa to catch a
complete herd of elephants were the Carthaginians two thousand
years before.

In the end the culling and capture plan carried the day. The
government officials were clearly horrified at the suggestion of a
massacre by the Army and it occurred to Iain that they might prefer
the 'villain' of the piece to be a foreigner. At any rate, Parker's culling
team was hired to shoot all the adults with the help of a military
helicopter to herd the elephants towards the guns.

Tony Parkinson was asked to carry out the immobilizations and
after-care of the small elephants. Any youngsters more than a year
old but under five feet tall would be captured and helicoptered to
a holding pen. Any less than a year old would be shot.

Two films were made of this operation. One was Ian Parker's, who had been given permission to bring his own cameraman to film the killing for his private archives. The second was to be made by Lee Lyon, our friend from Manyara, on behalf of Survival Anglia Television who paid the Government for the right to make it.

Earlier, Lee had been filming in the Virunga National Park, on the shores of Lake Edward. Iain and I went to see her there in a fishing village called Vitshumbi where there were some very remarkable elephants.

Old bulls used to wander between the huts, gleaning corn husks and cabbage leaves put out for them by the villagers. Sometimes, when other food was short, the elephants would eat the catch left out by the fishermen to dry in the sun. It was extraordinary to see them as they moved along the shore like stately ships through a wave of humanity: women washing, fishermen mending their nets.

When her old friend Dieter Plage arrived to see Lee he was charged by one of the old bulls, who was apparently in earnest because he did not stop. Dieter turned to run at the last minute, but was still tied to his camera by his battery cable. Camera and tripod were jerked to the ground, and the bull promptly stamped on them. Dieter passed the whole story off with a laugh, but he was obviously shaken and he warned Lee of the danger.

Iain did not attend the Rwanda culling, but two months later at Wilson we met Ian Parker who had just landed on his return from the operation and was unloading some military rifles from his black Cessna 185. The killing was all over in a few days, he told us. The facts were precisely recorded in a scientific paper entitled 'An Elephant Extermination', written by Parker and his team.

'Elephants were herded in groups by helicopter to the predetermined slaughter-capture site, where the team of four gunmen armed with 7.62mm NATO rifles were waiting for them,' said the report. 'When the elephants were within range – 7 to 30 metres – all adults were felled with shots in the brain.'

The young elephants, once they had been immobilized, were hobbled and tied to a tree or – more commonly – to the nearest dead elephant. After further sedation they were then transported to holding pens where they were kept for a month before being sent to Akagera.

'The project was a technical success,' the consultants concluded; but later in his book, *Ivory Crisis*, Parker said that the African peasants themselves disapproved of the extermination. They could understand the killing of crop-raiders, but to wipe out a whole population – that was playing God, and might provoke divine vengeance.

For the traumatized survivors there would be problems of coping in life without the care and wisdom of the matriarchs and the close ties of their own families. However, the team had taken pains to capture some females as large as they dared, although handling a large elephant without an instructing 'monitor' elephant is not an easy task.

Lee had been with the young caged elephants for three months. She had filmed them as they dangled from a helicopter on their way from one holding pen to another. She had fed and scrubbed them until they recognized her by sound and smell. The young elephants were to be let out one by one into the safety of a peninsula that jutted into Lake Akagera. There, with no mothers or leaders to bring them into maturity, they would have to learn to adjust to their orphaned life as best they could.

As the final day for moving the elephants approached, Lee became silent and pale, and spent many hours in her small home. She wrote her will and letters, leaving a short tidy list of her last wishes; her clothes to be distributed to the people, her photographs and equipment and her love to be left to Adrien de Schryver, the Belgian conservationist she had met while filming mountain gorillas in the cloud forests of Zaire's Kahuzi Biega National Park. She wished to be buried in the forest near her house, where she had lived for a time with Adrien.

From the twin-peaked hill across the lake at Naivasha an aeroplane appeared with a strange registration number visible under the wings. It flew over the farm and then landed, and the pilot stepped out.

It was Adrien. I recognized his lean figure immediately, dressed as usual in faded khaki shorts, a green beret stuck on one side of his head. Lee's parents stood by his side, tall and pale with bent shoulders.

It was easier for us to welcome them on the farm, with the pelicans swirling above us like an ever-turning fan. Here we could stare at the distant outline of Longonot and talk about elephants and what had happened to Lee in Rwanda.

I walked up and down the farm road with Adrien, our heads

bent, looking at our feet. He was talking and I listened to his tale. 'We lived in a small house together. She said one day to me, I am going to die.

'About fifty people were standing in a half-circle, approximately thirty paces from the pen,' said Adrien. 'There were trucks and cars near by. The first elephant had been moved to the freedom gallery. A young male, whom Lee had fed for all these months. She knew him well.'

The gate was pulled up, Lee began filming and the elephant leapt out. His eyes, his mind and his determination went singly in one direction – towards Lee.

Lee, relaxed and unaware, had her eye on the lens, her finger on the button and the camera plugged into the battery belt around her waist, something Dieter had warned her never to do. Without slowing his pace, the elephant smashed into her camera, tripod and all. From the sides of his trunk at the corners of his mouth two little sharp tusks protruded, and he pounded his few inches of ivory into her at least a dozen times, with all his strength and his hatred for man. He must have weighed four hundred kilos.

In vain, someone jumped on to his neck, pulling at his ear. Someone else grabbed his tail; others yelled and beat the elephant, but he would not stop. Lee held on to her short sweet life and tried to pull her dreadfully wounded self under a truck a few feet away, dragging with her the camera and tripod which was still attached to her belt.

A shot was fired, the echoes faded, leaving a profound silence in which life drained away like the arc in the sky of a falling star when even the sound of the settling dust could be heard.

Lee lay dying in a pool of blood like a broken flower. Beside her lay the elephant as if in a dream of daytime sleep, still warm with blood ebbing from his trunk and his blind eyes searching for the sun.

All things end as the day winds down. I lost my friend. I never saw Adrien again though I heard from travellers who had seen him from time to time.

The Rwanda elephant operation was over. The three smallest calves, each about one year old, were adopted by the Belgian warden's wife, and in consequence they became quite tame. Although the other youngsters originated from different family groups, they settled into a stable social unit, and in 1983 three calves were born which formed the nucleus of a new population.

The consultants claimed that the saving of twenty-five elephants obscured the real issue, namely Rwanda's chronic over-population. The 3.6 million people of Rwanda in 1970, they said, were projected to rise to 8.1 million by the end of the century and they gloomily concluded that they did not see how the Akagera Park could be maintained in the face of such human pressures.

Were the elephants of Africa to be overwhelmed by a rising tide of humanity or would they be wiped out by the ivory poachers? Either way seemed a possibility. In Kenya, meanwhile, it seemed that poaching was quite capable of eliminating the elephants on its own, but at last the story was beginning to reach the outside world.

During a visit to England we sought out the advice of Peter Scott, founder of the World Wildlife Fund and the creator of its panda symbol. Peter was also chairman of the Survival Service Commission, a group of specialists who work within the IUCN to protect threatened species of wild plants and animals.

Iain asked him if WWF would launch a campaign for the elephants, but Peter thought this was difficult since the public could not accept the paradox of elephants being endangered over most of Africa and yet being culled in some parks where they were thought to be over-abundant. Nevertheless he agreed that an Elephant Specialist Group should be formed by IUCN, and some months later asked Iain if he would organize it, with Harvey Croze as co-chairman. Harvey was a scientist with whom Iain had counted elephants in the Serengeti, and it was on Harvey's data that the decision had been taken not to cull there, at least for the time being.

We had no funds, and the only place we could find for an office was the hut in our garden at Naivasha. There we pinned a huge map of Africa to the wall – the African Elephant Office was in business!

We decided to try to establish how many elephants survived in Africa. Nobody had ever embarked on such an ambitious project before, but the information was vital if, as we feared, the elephant was threatened throughout much of its range. One of the few regions with healthy elephant populations was Southern Africa, and it was here that Iain intended to begin the great African elephant count.

CHAPTER FIVE

IAIN: *Laagers*

1975, Southern Africa

I had lived in South Africa for six years of my childhood. My mother was widowed during the war and after it was over she married a South African surgeon. My brother, Diarmaid, and I went to live in the Cape under Table Mountain, where the first records on elephants were made by Europeans in the seventeenth century. He was two years older than me and had a scientific bent with a passion for explosives. I was usually the guinea-pig who had to observe his bombs at the moment of detonation from a steel drum which had a hole for a periscope. Curiously, it made for a close bond, which has endured.

We grew up accustomed to freedom and space. We were keen mountaineers and the mountains of the Cape are spectacular, often falling sheer to the sea. Sometimes we threw my brother's bombs hundreds of feet down on to rock ledges where they made satisfying explosions. There was no one to stop us as the coastline was empty. Fishing from exposed cliffs into deep blue waters, surfing from endless white beaches and the crystal clarity of the air were imprinted on us. We were spoiled for ever for life in Europe.

Sometimes we went to see Knysna, a beautiful stretch of forest along the southern coast. Here were signs which read: BEWARE OF

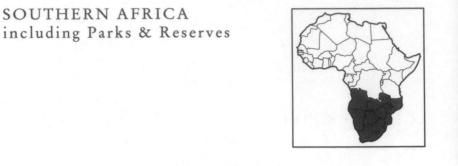

SOUTHERN AFRICA
including Parks & Reserves

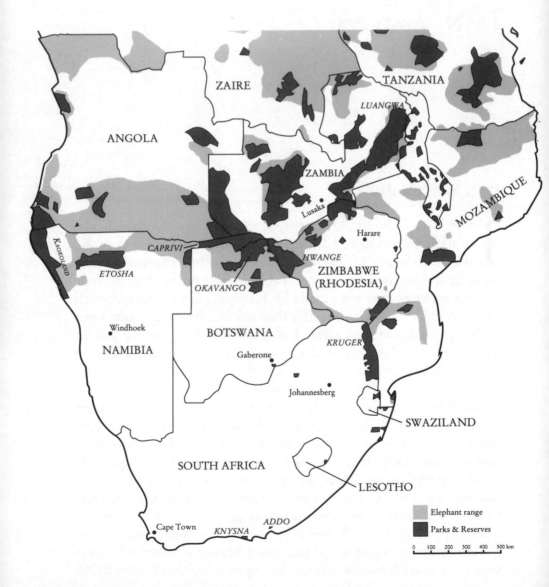

ZAIRE

TANZANIA

ANGOLA

LUANGWA

ZAMBIA

Lusaka

MOZAMBIQUE

Harare

KAOKOLAND

CAPRIVI

HWANGE

ETOSHA

ZIMBABWE
(RHODESIA)

OKAVANGO

Windhoek

BOTSWANA

KRUGER

Gaberone

NAMIBIA

Johannesberg

SWAZILAND

SOUTH AFRICA

LESOTHO

Cape Town *KNYSNA* *ADDO*

Elephant range

Parks & Reserves

0   100 200 300 400 500 km

THE ELEPHANTS and we knew they lurked in the depths of this thick greenery. People were scared of them, but there were said to be only a few left. These, with another nearby pocket in Addo, were the last of the Southern elephants. They had been protected by law since the 1850s. The rest had been shot by the Boer trekkers, along with the bushmen, as they moved east along the coast, and it was not until reaching the Kruger National Park, 1280 kilometres away, that the next elephants were to be seen. I had been there once with my mother and vividly remembered seeing my first wild elephants.

When I left South Africa in 1955 at the age of thirteen to be educated in Scotland I wondered if I would ever go back. Now, twenty years later, I was curious to find out what had happened to the elephants that lived between the Kruger and the Cape. From the few papers that filtered through it appeared that wildlife scientists in South Africa were facing exactly the same elephant problems as we were. Otherwise we knew virtually nothing about the animals in this vast underbelly of the continent.

The chance to discover more came up when Diarmaid, whom I had not seen for years, suggested that he should take a holiday in Africa. His career as a physicist had taken him from Oxford to America where he specialized in building very large lasers for a mysterious company; but his latest passion was flying. Though his mind drove him to live in the midst of cities, he longed to be back in Africa, looking at distant mountains under open skies.

Flying across Africa requires well-planned logistics. In Nairobi I had been told that the Tanzanians were extremely suspicious and would shoot down any aircraft overflying the prohibited zone, which effectively blocked off the whole south of the country. As there was no way we could avoid it, I was immensely relieved when Diarmaid and I were given permission to land there for refuelling only. Nevertheless, it could be a hazardous flight.

Tanzania was supporting the black Rhodesian nationalists in their struggle for power, and a variety of Chinese teams were rumoured to be training guerrillas in the south-west. Over the southern border in Mozambique, FRELIMO, the nationalist movement, had just wrested control from the Portuguese. To the west, Zambia was forbidden territory; so we would have to spend the first night or two in Malawi.

The next lap lay over the prohibited zone. Here I had to change the flying habits of a lifetime and push *BAD* up to 15,000 feet to get

away from trigger-happy Tanzanian soldiers or freedom fighters
in training who might not have heard about our permission. At
last we crossed the mountains marking the Tanzanian frontier and
descended towards Lake Malawi, where we stayed for two nights
with old friends on the Nyika plateau above the shore.

To reach our next stop in Rhodesia we had to cross Marxist
Mozambique, and decided to fly high once again, beyond machine-
gun range, cruising straight over the great Cabora Bassa Dam on
the Zambezi. FRELIMO must have been feeling tolerant or were
totally unaware of our presence and the rest of the flight passed
without incident.

'I speak of Africa and golden joys . . .' Did Shakespeare ever
imagine that one of these could be the joy of flying? Every time
the wheels lift into the air the heart leaps with relief to be free
of an earthbound existence. Tracking over the African wilderness
has made every aviator rejoice, and the exhilaration and sense of
adventure described by Beryl Markham and Karen Blixen are still
as addictive half a century later.

In our new aeroplanes we are enclosed in perspex. The wind
may no longer sing through the rigging above the guttural roar of
a primitive engine; yet much has remained the same. You still pit
yourself against the elements. Thunderstorms can tear your wings
off, and bad weather can get you lost. The wilderness remains
immense and overpoweringly beautiful, and is utterly indifferent to
your fate. Pilots can and sometimes do disappear without trace.

The inclination to fly might be said to be in the blood of the
Douglas-Hamiltons. There were originally four brothers and all of
them flew. The eldest, my uncle and head of our family, was the
first man to fly over Everest in an open cockpit biplane.

My family even flew to Africa. One of my aunts crash-landed in
bad weather below Kilimanjaro, flying a spindly little plane from the
Cape to Cairo in the thirties. She was rescued by the Maasai. Her
husband, the second son, flew a Wellington bomber during the war
from England to Egypt, narrowly escaping a German fighter that
tried to shoot him down. Then he came on up the Nile to Kenya,
where he trained RAF pilots.

After the war another uncle disappeared with his son into the
forests of West Africa when their plane hit the side of Mt Cameroon,
a huge dormant volcano.

My father, the fourth son, flew Spitfires in combat from Malta just over the horizon from Africa. He was later killed returning from a photo-reconnaissance mission over Germany when his bullet-riddled Mosquito crashed on landing.

Flying always carries an element of risk, but I could no more give it up than put out my eyes, and the sheer exuberance of it has sometimes made me forget the hoary axiom: 'There are bold pilots and old pilots, but no old bold pilots.'

To our astonishment Skukuza from the air looked like a small town complete with tarmac roads. Circling above it we gazed down on square houses with gardens, swimming-pools, tennis courts, and a brilliant green rugby field – all this in the heart of the Kruger National Park.

At the beginning of the century there had been nothing at all in this stretch of country just south of the Limpopo River. Ivory hunters and farmers had virtually accomplished the destruction of the entire elephant population in Southern Africa. Realizing the end was near, Paul Kruger, then president of the Transvaal, pushed through a proclamation in 1898 which turned a three-hundred-mile strip into a protected area. Were it not for his determined efforts, this last great stronghold of South Africa's elephants might never have survived.

In 1905 it was estimated that only ten elephants were left; but by 1968 the numbers had swelled close to nine thousand. Paul Kruger, once an ardent hunter himself, did not live to see the realization of his dream, but his descendants are determined that nothing catastrophic will ever happen to their elephants again.

We were met by Dr Piet Van Wyk, a bearded Afrikaaner dressed in a smart black Sunday suit, who drove us into the tourist camp inside an ugly wire fence. We passed a shopping centre full of skins for sale; of zebra, lion, wildebeest, even the furs of small cats like genets, stitched together into a kaross.

Over two thousand black people lived and worked in the park. Three hundred whites formed their own nucleus with a school, a hospital, a church, an abattoir and a clock tower – suburbia maxima. The lodge had one thousand beds inside lines of yellow rondavels and we were shown to one of them. There was no lock on the door. In the Kruger it seemed that nobody bothered about such things.

Piet Van Wyk was the first Afrikaaner I had ever properly met. When he spoke he revealed a deep love of Africa, an almost mystical feeling for the great mother continent. 'We Afrikaaners realize we have had a great deal from Africa and now we want to give something.' He said it with simple but deep sincerity. The paradox was that with external boycotts and isolation the Afrikaaners, who had been settled here for three hundred years, knew little of what was going on outside their country.

Piet told me of a plan, already being implemented, to fence off the entire Kruger National Park. It was no secret, he said, that the fence was primarily for security purposes. Although it would also stop animal migrations, the research team would in future be able to obtain accurate censuses on which they could base their management. Minimal interference was still the basic policy, but animal husbandry was the best training for running parks, he thought, and fortunately many of the technical staff had that background.

To us, fresh from the vastness of the East African bush, it seemed as if the Kruger was managed like a giant game ranch, and I suppose this method is as effective as any; but somehow it seemed as if the wild and true spirit of Africa had been lost in the process. In fact every large mammal population was carefully regulated. They would not risk losing any large species and believed that only by intervening could they prevent extinctions. In former years they had also culled zebra and wildebeest, but now that the bush was thickening up it was no longer considered necessary.

On the other hand, they had felt obliged to start shooting lions again, because they believed that in the dry years the big cats might exterminate the rare and valuable roan and sable antelopes. There were only three hundred roan antelope, immunized each year with shots against anthrax, delivered by dart from a helicopter; and the sable, which had died out in one year had been replaced at vast expense with one thousand fresh animals from Rhodesia.

I now understood why animal husbandry was the sought-after qualification. Compared to the benign neglect of East Africa, more kindly expressed as *laissez-faire*, these policies were interventionist on a grand scale.

One day during our visit a helicopter appeared and manoeuvred to one of the empty helipads. Out stepped three strapping parks men and the pilot. Among them was Tol Pienaar, a tough, leonine researcher with short grizzled hair.

Tol Pienaar was a pioneer in the techniques and practice of immobilizing elephants. I had followed closely his papers about dosage rates and treatment when I was fitting radio-collars to elephants in Lake Manyara. It was said that Pienaar, who had spent fifteen years in the Kruger, knew exactly how many elephants there should be in the park. His helicopters went out to make the tally, and if they were short at the end he would search the map like an anxious cattle herder and send his team back to scour every last hiding-place until all the elephants were found.

In a long interview in his office the next day he explained that the park's neighbours were farmers who could call upon a powerful political lobby in their favour, who had over the years chipped away at the park.

'Dr Hamilton,' said Tol, fixing me with his penetrating blue eyes. 'Our axis runs north-south, but the old migration routes ran east-west. What you must realize is that the Kruger is not a natural unit any more.'

'It breaks my heart to fence the elephants off from the Limpopo,' Pienaar continued, 'but that's what we are going to do; and as there is not enough water we have to give the animals artificial water points.'

The elephants had increased tremendously since the park was formed, Tol reported. At first there were only a handful, but then the bulls came over from Mozambique, followed by cows, working their way south towards Skukuza. Now they were all over the park and a culling programme, taking between five hundred and eight hundred elephants each year from a population of about seven and a half thousand had stabilized them at a level considered to be healthy for the woodlands.

We also heard about Kruger's legendary giant tuskers, whose ivory could rival anything to be seen in East Africa. An elephant's tusks are its upper incisors, and since they continue to grow throughout its life the heaviest ivory tends to belong to the oldest bulls. In the Kruger, poaching was minimal. Furthermore the park staff favoured the big bulls and spared them from culling, allowing them to grow to peaceful old age. Consequently they now had about forty of these old warriors that were known to have tusks of around forty-five kilos and about eight monsters with tusks of over fifty-four kilos. These huge bulls became famous to the wardens and were given African names that mirrored the landscape: Shawu, Shingwedzi, Mafunyane. Already, elsewhere in Africa such tuskers were fast becoming the stuff of legend, sacrificed to man's extraordinary greed. Extraordinary because ivory is essentially no different from any other animal tooth. It is simply a mass of dentine with a hollow at the base containing a pulpy tissue of blood vessels and nerve endings – a digging tool and a weapon.

Our talk moved on to the theory of natural elephant and woodland cycles advocated by my old friend the Tanzanian park ecologist, Desmond Vesey-Fitzgerald, who had always believed so strongly in *laissez-faire*. Even down here the old naturalist had a reputation.

'Dr Hamilton, we don't want any of these Vesey-Fitzgerald cycles in the Kruger Park,' Pienaar told me.

It was sad to think how politics were isolating these ardent conservationists from the rest of Africa. We flew along the Mozambique border and viewed the newly erected security fence that stretched from horizon to horizon. I wondered how it would fare against the elephants, until we dipped down and saw that it was constructed of railway sleepers embedded in concrete, connected with tensioned wire hawsers.

Landing at Letaba on the Olifant's River, we met one of the helicopter pilots. He was an American who had flown in the Vietnam war, and he took us down the river's gorge, skilfully skimming over rock pools and sweeping past cliff faces. Then he demonstrated how he drove elephants for the cull. The first family we found were utterly panic-stricken from the noise of the machine. As the shadow of the helicopter came down they bunched and backed helplessly into each other, making a perfect target. A small baby was almost trampled in the crush and, as they broke and ran, it struggled to keep up. There was no question in my mind that the whisper of the helicopter meant death to them.

The 'cropping' takes place in the afternoon and evening. In the Kruger, instead of using a spotter plane and a team of gunmen on the ground, elephant family units are herded into a tight bunch by helicopter. When they are conveniently near a road, they are shot from the helicopter's window with a dart gun which is accurate to within one hundred yards. As they collapse, rangers and culling scouts on the ground move in and cut the animals' throats to bleed them to death. One of the rangers told us a harrowing story of a drugged, but possibly still conscious, elephant cow who could move only the tip of her trunk which she placed on the hand of a ranger who was about to cut the throat of her calf.

At night, when it is cool and safe from the gaping eyes and clicking cameras of tourists, the huge carcasses are heaved on to a low-loader and taken to the factory. There they are unloaded and winched like whales up into the high-ceilinged processing plant, to be skinned, washed, de-boned, chopped up and put into refrigeration rooms.

From Kruger we flew another eight hundred miles to the Knysna Forest. On the way we passed the towers of the Drakensberg Mountains, wreathed in an eerie, shimmering mist that thickened and threatened to engulf us. At the foot of these mountains lies the Tugela River where the Zulu impis hurled themselves on the guns of the British at the Battle of Rorke's Drift.

The fierce battles between Boer and Bantu – the Zulu warriors flinging themselves against the defensive circle or *laager* of ox-wagons and the Boer settlers fighting back to deadly effect with their muzzle-loaders – are ingrained in the consciousness of every Afrikaaner. It was often said that South Africa's politics are the politics of the *laager*, and their wildlife conservation policies have echoes of the same theme.

The Knysna Forest from the air reminded me of the Marang Forest above Manyara. It was full of steep-sided valleys and I remembered as a child being both fascinated and frightened as we had driven through, hoping to see an elephant but not wanting to be trampled by one.

Years later, I did eventually have a chance to look for the Knysna elephants on foot in their secret fastness. I found their footprints and fresh dung, saw the exotic blue gums which they had stripped of bark, and came close enough to hear and smell them. But they could also sense me and the tracker would go no closer.

The people living in the forest were Afrikaaners who were said to have been left behind by the Great Trek and had formed a small and inbred community. It was impossible to convince them that they should leave the elephants alone, and they would shoot at them with small bore rifles at any opportunity. It was no wonder that the elephants never managed to increase beyond a dozen or so.

Today Diarmaid and I were unlucky again. We looked down on the canopy of trees which spreads to the very edge of this southernmost coast of Africa. Below, waves from the Atlantic and Indian Oceans converged to crash on pink rocks at the foot of the cliffs. Sometimes great whales could be seen undulating through the blue waters, and on rare occasions, it was said, an elephant would emerge from its hiding-place and stand in a clear patch, facing the sea. Round and round we flew, willing the elephants to appear, but in vain. At the time of writing, the most recent information I have on these elephants is already two years old, and they have been reduced to three animals with no chance of survival unless fresh blood is introduced.

From the Knysna we headed north-west for Kaokoveld, behind the Skeleton Coast of Namibia, a moon-like landscape whose deserts were believed to hide beds of diamonds richer than any others in Africa. But more alluring to me was the hope of seeing the last desert-dwelling elephants south of the Equator. Landing at Etoshas Pan we met a co-operative warden and flew with him down to the coast.

What I had not expected as we skimmed a mountain range and caught our first glimpse of the sea was the breath-taking beauty beneath us. Russet, copper and gold gradually dissolved into shades of dun, ivory and finally silver as the mountains sloped down to the rocks in the foothills. From these barren heights, dry river beds of gravel broadened into desert sand and carried the eye to the towering dunes of the Skeleton Coast, dashed by the spray of tremendous Atlantic rollers.

Diarmaid took the little plane down towards this majestic shore-line, and suddenly I felt a chill I had never experienced during all my flying in Africa. On every other flight the temperature had risen the closer I came to the ground; but now it fell dramatically, as we dropped into the current of air which sweeps across the sea from Antarctica and pushes up the coast. This cold wind precipitates any moisture over the Atlantic, producing the notorious fogs that have lured so many ships to their graves on the Skeleton Coast, and starving the Kaokoveld of rain.

The Namib is an ancient desert. Here grows the *Welwitschia mirabilis*, one of the longest-living plants on earth, sending down a thick, tree-like root which can sustain it for two thousand years.

It was the dry season, and not a single river was running. Even so the landscape was as lovely as any I knew in Africa. I kept craning forward to catch sight of an animal brave enough to forage or hunt in the glare of the merciless sun, but few manage to survive here.

Jackals patrol the tideline, and even lions are known to scavenge in the surf for whale and seal carcasses; true sea lions indeed. Further inland I was not surprised to see ostrich and gemsbok, both of which can live without water.

In Kaokoveld – the dry country between the Hoanib and Hoarusib Rivers – black rhinos and elephants have become specialists in colonizing this formidable landscape. Over the generations they have not only come to terms with it, but must have actively sought it as a refuge from persecution.

Unlike other elephants they never damage, destroy or uproot the trees on which their lives depend, even though they chew chips of wood in the driest seasons. In times of drought the elephants may have to travel seventy kilometres to find water – and even then must dig for it in the river beds. Moving by night and drinking only once in three or four days, they preserve precious energy.

Their bodies, too, seem to have adapted to these exacting conditions. Their feet, that travel so far and so often on sand, have spread in circumference; their legs, that have to carry them such long distances, have grown longer. Their average height is 3.5 metres, as tall as any elephants in Africa; and in the last ten years or so, two have been found to be over four metres.

Yet despite nature's miraculous powers of survival I feared that the cause of the Kaokoveld elephants was virtually lost, which was why I so desperately wanted to see them. In 1962 there were said to be as many as three thousand elephants and five hundred rhinos ranging through this and the neighbouring desert. Now I was told there might be only fifty rhinos and two or three hundred elephants left.

The South African government deserves great credit for the populations of game it supports in the Kruger; but its record in Kaokoveld and in the adjoining dry country of Damaraland was cause for shame. The disaster began in 1962 when the Odendaal Commission recommended that the territory should be split up, ostensibly to protect the indigenous population, but arguably for security and political reasons. Rather than protect the wildlife with properly managed scouts, locals were armed with cheap weapons for protection against SWAPO guerrillas. Hunting became a widely known perk of senior government officials, and the illegal slaughter of animals by known individuals went unpunished.

Now, with so few elephants left, I had almost given up hope of coming across them. But suddenly we spotted a family of eight among the copper-coloured rocks on a distant mountainside. Taking care not to disturb them, we circled round to watch them slowly clambering over the broken landscape.

Heading our plane north towards Kenya I felt I now had a fair grasp of the status of the southern elephants. The wholesale destruction in the nineteenth century had been accomplished by relatively few ivory hunters – a fact I found worrying in view of what was now happening in Kenya. Yet the slaughter had led to strict protection in the last corners of their range. Was this to be the pattern for the rest of Africa? Could East Africa still preserve its vast free-ranging herds, or would elephants survive only in *laagers* where numbers were rigorously controlled?

Back home again at Naivasha, Oria showed me a clipping she had just received from *The New York Times* about elephants and ivory. The story had exposed people involved in the illegal trade. I was mentioned as a source of information on the status of the elephant and Diarmaid was worried that I would be linked with the scandalous allegations against highly placed Kenyans which the story contained. It was the first of a number of articles which began to turn a spotlight on the wave of poaching now breaking over Kenya's elephants.

In Kenya, it seemed, no elephant was safe from the poachers' bullets. Yet in neighbouring Tanzania we knew there were huge tracts of empty bush country where elephants still roamed in their tens of thousands. Despite their muddle, the Tanzanians had in Julius Nyerere an idealistic leader, and their system of benign neglect might well be preserving the elephants better than in South Africa.

CHAPTER SIX

IAIN: *A Wilderness*

1976, Selous, Tanzania

ALAN Rodgers was a biologist who lived in Tanzania on the eastern plains of the Selous Game Reserve. Every day he would slog in the heat collecting data, and in the evenings he would drink his bottle of beer. Every few years he would emerge from the wilderness to attend a wildlife conference, his tummy a little rounder from the beer. No sooner had he sat down to dinner than the bread rolls began to fly. It was one of Alan's forms of communication.

Every time I met Alan he rhapsodized about his gigantic reserve, the foot safaris he had made through its trackless bush, the weeks he had been cut off on the wrong side of a flood plain, and the wild country where the elephants seemed to go on for ever. We talked of counting them. Now that day had come.

Selous lay at the complete opposite end of the spectrum from South Africa. It was huge, wild and free, the kind of precious space which East Africa kept intact with no human inhabitants. Until we counted its elephants there was no way we could judge what its future might be in a continent with an ever-expanding human population.

After several years of planning Alan at last persuaded the Danish aid organization, DANIDA, to come up with the money for the first aerial census. The reserve itself at forty-three thousand square kilometres is just larger than Denmark. He asked me to bring my plane and make the census with him. For an elephant counter this was the equivalent of asking a mountaineer to climb Everest.

Alan met me in his car at the airport and drove me into Dar es Salaam. At first the potholes and godowns of the industrial area reminded me of Nairobi. But when we reached the residential suburbs the uncut hedges and smoking piles of rubbish brought home to me the sharp contrasts between Julius Nyerere's socialist Tanzania and Jomo Kenyatta's free-wheeling capitalist Kenya.

Alan drove me down to the harbour front, still lined in many places with nineteenth-century colonial buildings left by the Germans. Across the water lay Zanzibar, the ancient port of the Arab Slavers.

Slaves and ivory had followed the same routes out of Africa for centuries and, as Livingstone and the other early missionaries and explorers came to realize, it is more probable that slavery was a by-product of the ivory trade than vice versa. In the second half of the nineteenth-century the demand for ivory reached a new peak. The Arabs, long-experienced suppliers, therefore had to send their caravans further and further inland when the coastal herds of elephants had been eliminated.

The prevalence of tsetse fly, carrier of sleeping sickness in man and East Coast fever in animals, made it impossible to bring out the tusks by pack train; so slaves were traded or captured as beasts of burden. These macabre processions made their way to the beach at Bagamoyo, just north of Dar, before they were ferried across to Zanzibar. If they survived the journey the slaves could be sold along with the ivory.

With the introduction of firearms, elephant hunting became an altogether easier task. From the coast to the great lakes the whole country disintegrated into a murderous system of chaos and exploitation of man and elephant in which both species became depopulated. This was the miserable state of affairs in Tanganyika when the Germans made their first appearance here in force in about 1880.

The stifling night in Alan's flat, with the smell of drains wafting in through the window on the torpid coastal air, was in marked contrast to the idyll of the sapphire water and palms bent over dazzling white sand that we had left behind that afternoon. But next morning, with a plane full of fruit and vegetables, we sped down the long international runway of Dar and lifted over the new missile sites on the perimeter. There was a civil war going on in Rhodesia, to the south, and the Tanzanians were getting sensitive about strange planes. Alan told me, chuckling through his whiskers, that the game department plane had recently been riddled with bullets by some over-enthusiastic police who had found it parked on a strip in the south-east of the country.

Flying south-west for an hour we reached Alan's base at Kingupira. The Miombo Research Station stood on the edge of the flood plain that marks the eastern boundary of the Selous Game Reserve, which was named after one of the most colourful Europeans in Africa at the turn of the century. Frederick Courteney Selous had started life as a soldier, hunted elephants on horseback, taken Theodore Roosevelt on safari in 1906 and was widely esteemed as a naturalist. When the British and Germans carried the First World War into Africa he was verging on sixty, but the old warrior still took up arms again.

It was immediately clear that the Miombo Research Station was running short of funds. Mapping room, herbarium and workshops lay under dust; the fans on the ceiling were still, the generators silent. Yet, although the game scouts seemed to lack not only buttons and shoes, but discipline too, they were full of good will and charm.

Once away from the eastern plains I realized how the Miombo Research Station had got its name. As far as the eye could see to the retreating horizons spread the broad-leaved miombo trees, lit by the morning sun with the colours of autumn and spring. Herds of elephants browsed in their shade, or peacefully grazed in pockets of pasture, and Alan said these woodlands stretched almost the whole way across Africa to the west coast.

What amazed me as much as the scale of this limitless landscape was the fact that by the end of a whole morning's flying I had not seen a single human being. When the basic ecology and a little history were explained to me I was rather less surprised.

The soil, however well suited to the miombo trees, was too poor for proper cultivation. Furthermore, Miombo provides an ideal home for the tsetse fly, so there was little reward for men to come in and break up the woodlands for crop-raising since cattle and goats could not survive here. The explosion of ivory hunting and slaving in the nineteenth century dispersed what few settlements had taken root; a major slave route ran right through the area to the port of Kilwa. Finally the warlike Ngoni tribe had burst in on the few survivors, further depopulating the woodlands.

On the first morning of the count I settled myself in the pilot's seat with a map of the day's sector on my lap. Alan was in the seat to my right with a camera and notepad, and in the back seat sat our two observers looking to left and right. By flying at two hundred and fifty feet at a hundred miles per hour, and by creating a fixed frame on each side of fishing rods tied to the struts, I could maintain a constant count area for each minute of the flight.

We flew on narrow margins, repeatedly refuelling and taking off again. Towards the end of one day of grind the tanks really did run dry and the engine coughed and stopped. We were five miles from camp and sinking fast. Alan and I had a quick debate about whether the swamp or the wooded grasslands would offer a better crash landing. The right tank was absolutely dry, but I found I could still make the left tank's needle flicker by banking to the right. As we descended in a right-hand spiral, fuel trickled from the tip to the root of the wing and down the fuel lines; the engine picked up and we made it home.

Up the Rufiji River, which runs across the reserve from west to east, the monotonous miombo woodlands were occasionally interrupted where a spring flushed from the hills. Lower down the trees thinned out as they reached the plains, where rings of brilliant green marked a series of waterholes. Always there were elephant families, usually in small groups. These were a good sign, since really large herds more often form as the consequence of unease and harassment rather than from a sense of security.

If all was well with the elephants it seemed so too for other species. I was delighted to see herds of a dozen or more sable. They are perhaps the most beautiful of the antelopes. Tall and black, with streaks of chestnut, their bellies are white and their great curving horns, pointed as rapiers and up to four feet long, sweep back like new moons over their heads.

One of the most striking features we flew over was Stiegler's Gorge. Emerging from this rocky defile, the Rufiji fans out to create an inland delta of shifting sands, lazy oxbows and glassy lakes. Forests of drowned palm trees rise from the water like the columns of a lost civilization, and herds of buffalo graze on the banks. Elephants and buffalo cross with ease, but it has proved an insuperable barrier for giraffe, which are found only on the northern bank.

In 1916 the German rearguard saw to it that the Rufiji also proved an obstinate barrier to the British. On the northern banks is a small tourist camp perched on the side of a low hill, called Beho Beho. Below it a simple slab records the last resting place of Frederick Courteney Selous. The old soldier had returned to his first calling and at the age of sixty he fell here to a sniper's bullet.

The plains to the north of the lower Rufiji are not unlike a miniature Serengeti. Wildebeest, zebra, buffalo, eland and hartebeest abound, and we were continually delighted by the number of elephants we saw, mostly in small family groups, sluicing themselves in the river or contentedly munching the Nile cabbages that floated in green rafts on the water.

As the mornings wore on, the tensions of the observers mounted as they strained to catch a glimpse of any elephant that might reveal itself beneath the mesh of branches. At the same time the concentration of flying the plane, juggling with the height and the turbulence to keep on course, interpreting the map and reading out the transects all at the same time, left bodies and minds exhausted. Before long I learnt that the cabin of my plane had been christened 'the torture chamber'. Often, as soon as the end of the last transect was called, the observers slumped fast asleep in their seats. Then Alan and I would look for somewhere near a river to land and relax. At Lukula we could always swim in the broad, waist-deep, sandy river – keeping an eye open for crocodiles – or follow the whistling calls of a honey guide into the pristine riverine forest.

Sometimes from the air I noticed scars on the ground that had obviously once been sites of towns and villages. Alan's explanation of them further illuminated causes of the extraordinary human vacuum below us.

Soon after the British took over from the Germans at the end of the First World War, they discovered that the demoralized population was suffering from sleeping sickness. Of course it is not just parts of Tanzania that have been afflicted by this particular plague. Historians regard the tsetse, and the infections which it spreads so effectively through tropical Africa, as two of the most significant factors in the continent's history – confining generations of invaders to the coastal fringes, inhibiting the range of the Muslim horseman, the ox-cart and the wheel, and killing off pack animals like the camel and mule which could have saved the lives and dignity of millions of slaves.

In the 1920s and 1930s there was no known cure for sleeping sickness. The only prophylactic was to cut a two-mile cordon through the woods, which effectively kept the tsetse at bay. Since this was obviously impractical for isolated families or hamlets, the Government decided on a simple and drastic solution: the removal of all human inhabitants and the elimination of their rights of occupancy.

In order to prevent people from creeping back into the woodlands, the British began to expand the nucleus of the reserve, which they first named after Selous in 1922. Eleven years later, at about the time of a further outbreak of sleeping sickness, the game department was joined by one of the most ardent advocates of these policies: C.J.P. Ionides, 'Old Iodine', the snake man.

When Ionides arrived in the Selous his first duties were to control the elephant populations in and around the reserve. The elephants here, earlier thought to be in danger of extinction, had begun to recover and to menace the crops of the scattered villages outside. Old villagers told us of an elephant-free existence until 'the Government of the English' arrived.

Alan introduced me to one of his veteran rangers on elephant control, Bwana Madogo. He was a typical product of the old game department: tough and self-reliant with the bluff friendliness of a man at terms with himself. He was left alone with several game scouts under him to get on with elephant control. His work was difficult and dangerous. Many of the scouts were bad shots, but they compensated by creeping up really close. The cost was about five scouts killed every year by elephant and buffalo. With these routine casualties it takes a lot of courage to walk up to elephants in thick maize, when many were probably wounded and angry; but Bwana Madogo did it year after year and had shot hundreds of elephants.

The statistics of control were highly revealing. In the 1920s, about five hundred elephants were shot every year around the Selous. In Ionides' day it was over a thousand, and by the time of our count the figure had risen to just under three thousand on average. Yet this shooting did not appear to have made any impression, and the increasing numbers shot appeared to signify a growing elephant population.

Ionides is buried in the centre of the Selous, on the slopes of the Nandanga Hills. We flew there at sunset and found a huge lone elephant scuffing up the dust as he swung his tusks from side to side, listening to the hum of our machine.

By the time Ionides retired in 1953 the elephants had recovered sufficiently to attract a significant outbreak of poaching. We found very little evidence of it ourselves, but sometimes we broke off to investigate smoke, never knowing if it came from a smouldering tree trunk or the camp-fire of a party of poachers armed with their old muzzle-loaders.

Writing of areas in and around the Selous in the 1960s, Ionides said that they 'were always stinking with elephants and now even more so.' His successor, Brian Nicholson, put a rough figure of thirty thousand on the population, while the chief game warden thought there might be seventy thousand altogether in Tanzania, of which a large proportion was in the Selous. From our observations they had obviously gone on recovering ever since.

At this point we interrupted the survey for a few months so that we could return to monitor it in the dry as well as the wet season. When we came back we spent some days in the small town of Songea, our base, just outside the boundary to the south-west.

Songea was an untidy town with peeling paint and broken side-walks. It obviously had been a tidy station ruled by a British district commissioner once upon a time, but ten years of socialism had run it into the ground.

Posters of Nyerere consorting with the masses were surrounded by books of Mao's thoughts. China's 'great helmsman' had just died and flags flew at half-mast in his honour. Everywhere, radios with African music played at full blast. I tried to ring Oria but could only get a hiss. The operator apologized; his batteries were finished.

In the south of the Selous the country becomes more rugged and the rolling Miombo is broken by lines of terracotta cliffs, sculpted into fantastic patterns by erosion. There are swift streams tumbling down tall mountains to feed the broad rivers of the plains.

In the dry season the miombo trees take on the fiery reds and golds of New England in the autumn. The leaves fall and counting becomes easier. When the trees were bare we began to take aerial photographs of elephant family groups in order to age them from vertical shots.

Sooner or later the tawny plains would rage with the creeping flowers of grass fires, lit by a poacher or wandering honey hunter. Then the land would run charred and grey for as far as the eye could see, the ghosts of fallen trees outlined in pale ash, crisp in every detail down to the last twig, and between them the stark white bones of elephants.

Both we and the plane became very exhausted on this final count. The door of *5Y BAD* would not shut properly; there was a chronic tail-wheel shimmy; and a crack appeared in an elevator. Finally a leak in the fuel tank nearly put a premature end to us and the survey. After Araldite glue had failed to heal it, the day was saved in true African pioneer fashion by the application of soap and a polythene wrapping, held tightly in place with wire.

On one of Oria's visits, we were camping at the foot of the hill where Selous had been killed. Much of his life had been spent shooting elephants, whose sun-bleached bones had long since crumbled to dust, while his own lay anchored under a white slab that bears his name.

'In the immense silence of dawn,' wrote Oria, 'I could gaze through an opening in our tent at the morning beauty of an untouched place. An elephant rumbled near by, and another answered, as if to say, here I am, all is well, and for a moment I dreamt how lucky we were to be with them in this untouched place. Suddenly a gun shot echoed across the hills like some grave, mighty thought, and my senses jumped alert with a pounding heart. A terrible stillness followed. Then three more shots blasted out and I could see an elephant limping away from a line of tents. I fell into my clothes and with Iain ran down the green slope toward the elephant.

'The elephant, a short distance ahead, staggered, carefully selecting his path through the boulders, his right side red with blood. A man ran past, holding an empty gun. He was a game ranger and was going back to his tent to fetch more cartridges while the rest of us followed the elephant.

'The ranger returned with three bullets, but was afraid to approach. He fired from the side, missed, fired again and hit him in the leg, and the blood ran down the crackly skin. Hushed now by an inner sense of death, the elephant began to move away. Iain took the gun from the ranger and sprinted right up to the elephant. There was no choice now. The elephant seemed to know that he was going to be shot, for each time Iain aimed the gun, he turned his head away. Then came a chance and Iain pulled the trigger. The elephant screamed and thrashed the bushes with his trunk, but did not go down, and once again thunder reverberated across the valley. Iain looked at the old and rusty gun and handed it to the scout. "There are no more cartridges," the scout said, "there is only a small gun in the lodge," and he walked away to get it.

'We stood and waited in the thick, wet bush with the elephant moving step by painful step, and in the slanting light even the leaves seemed to be weeping. Caught in this net of horror, I wondered what terrible things the elephant had done to receive such punishment. He was bleeding from one eye. The blood ran down his face, staining his tusks and falling from his mouth. His breath gurgled in his bloody trunk. His foreleg was broken at the knee, and still he stood, his body full of bullets, waiting to die in the dawn. Only the tip of his trunk was moving in the grass.

'A few feet from where he stood a stream trickled by, but the bank was too steep, and falling to his knees he tried with the help of his tusks and his trunk to slide down away from us, and soothe his pain in water, but he failed. And looking at the water he stood, with his trunk hanging over the bank, when the bullets arrived. I felt my eyes filling with tears, and sweat ran down my cheeks as I listened to the sad cooing of a dove and the metal click of a loading gun. Iain walked right up to him, lifted the gun to his heart, and said, "Sorry old chap," and pulled the trigger.

'The scout was standing near by with a confused look. I felt sorry for him, but could find no words of comfort. I lit a cigarette to soothe my soul and quietly asked: "Why did you shoot?" There seemed no reason for my question, for what did it matter now? "Because," he answered, "the elephant was touching the ropes of my tent." '

So wrote Oria in her diary afterwards. Yet however tragic the scene we had just witnessed up by Selous' grave, I recognized the spirit in which the Tanzanian government and game department were looking after this magnificent wilderness. Nor could anything depress my rising elation as I began to collect the findings of our survey, for I knew that the final tally was likely to exceed our most optimistic hopes when we had taken off that first morning at Kingupira.

On my way home I stopped at Dar es Salaam to have a quick look at the ivory store and the records which had been meticulously kept for decades. When I asked to see the books the Tanzanians were immensely helpful and gave me full access, in contrast to the evasions I had met with in Kenya to a similar request. In a warehouse the smaller tusks lay dumped in piles on the ground, while the larger ones were propped against steel girders. The biggest of all weighed ninety kilos and the elephant had been shot by a policeman outside the Ruaha Park eight years before. They had come in from all over the country, for ivory in Tanzania is nationalized. The statistics showed that in the last ten years the average tusk weight had dropped from 8.0 kg to 4.8 kg. In other words most of the big tuskers had been picked off or had retreated to the hearts of the parks and reserves.

It was impossible to tell Oria the results of our count on the telephone, for even in Dar it produced its usual venomous hiss. They would have to keep until I saw her, exciting as they were, and it was with a light heart that I left Tanzania for the cool shores of home, leaving the sweating coastal heat behind.

Thunderstorms pushed me way off course over Lake Magadi until the petrol gauges subsided into inactivity. There were only fifteen minutes left to home. I flew high, past Mount Suswa with a ring of hills before Lake Naivasha. As I came over the lucerne fields on the southern shore the engine cut, and the propeller made ineffectual whirring noises.

'Come on *BAD*, get me home,' I whispered. I knew I still had my wing-tip reserve, so once again I canted the wing up and at about a hundred feet above the ground the engine roared into life and I soared into the sky for another five miles. Oria was there, standing alone and looking up, her red shirt flashing in an emerald field. After sixty days of counting and 220 hours of flying I was home. The counting was over, and so was the fuel.

Then I told her the results: 'We have eighty thousand elephants alive and well in the Selous Game Reserve alone, and one hundred and ten thousand in the whole census zone, give or take fifteen per cent for statistical error.'

The only other elephant populations that could compare were in the Luangwa Valley in Zambia, where Graeme Caughley, a highly respected Australian scientist, had estimated eighty thousand elephants in 1973, and Tsavo, where I believed there were at least fifty thousand, before drought and poaching cut them down by half. Of course there was always the one great unknown – the elephants of Zaire's inaccessible forests; but for the meanwhile in 1976 the Selous carried the largest known population in Africa.

PART II

The Ivory Avalanche

'THIRTY thousand elephants: three hundred tons of ivory, if that. And as the aim of good government is to increase production, I'm sure that this year we shall do better . . . With a little good will, we shall certainly manage, taking Africa as a whole, to kill a hundred thousand elephants a year, and so on till the ceiling is reached, if I may put it that way. It will then be necessary to pass to other species. Ours, I suggest'

Romain Gary,
Roots of Heaven,
1958

CHAPTER SEVEN

IAIN: *Massacre at Murchison*

1976, Uganda

O NE day in 1976, during a break in the elephant count
in the Selous, an invitation came from my friend Eric
Edroma, an enormous, jolly, chain-smoking Ugandan,
who was now senior scientist at the Uganda Institute of Ecology.
To Eric had fallen the task of organizing the third East African
Wildlife Symposium, and Eric, a big man in every sense of the
word, who believed in getting people together, asked me to be there
'without fail'.

The venue for the meeting was the Queen Elizabeth National Park
and although Uganda's relationship with Kenya was going through
a very difficult time, I had strong reasons for wanting to go. The
Uganda elephants had been studied more thoroughly than any others
on the continent by my erstwhile thesis examiner, Dick Laws. Many,
including myself, considered him the leading scientific authority on
elephants, but there was one particular statement of his which had
always worried me: that in the absence of very large-scale culling
the elephants in the Murchison Falls National Park would decline
to virtual extinction.

Here was a chance to see for myself exactly what was happening to
the elephants he had studied with such care, a moderate proportion

of which had been culled on his recommendation, and collect some key data for my pan-African elephant survey at the same time.

The prospect of seeing the Mountains of the Moon and the glorious national parks and their prolific inhabitants was irresistible. Uganda was the exotic heart of Africa, the goal of the explorers, a land of ancient African kingdoms and the source of the Nile, where the first real flow of the river begins its immemorial journey to the Mediterranean.

But while I was very keen to go to Uganda, Oria had considerable misgivings. The country was now under the rule of its self-appointed president, Field Marshal Idi Amin, who had seized power from President Milton Obote. Amin was treated as a joke in the Western press, but this so-called figure of fun was in reality an unpredictable and insatiable killer.

While I was preparing to stick my neck into this dragon's den I met Ian Parker and we made an arrangement to share the costs of the flight. There was no one I would rather have had around in a tight spot. There was also a chance that we would be able to continue up to the parks and visit his old hunting, or rather culling, grounds. We were both intensely curious to find out what had happened to the elephants and the vegetation.

We flew into Entebbe low over Lake Victoria. The day was clear and columns of lake flies rose hundreds of feet above the faded blue waters and green velvet islands. The closer we flew the more I thought about the extraordinary dictator into whose lair we were venturing.

Hundreds of civilians had been arrested by the State Research Bureau. Prominent citizens were not immune. The chief justice was dragged out of the High Court never to be seen again; the university vice-chancellor vanished and scores of innocent citizens were murdered. As talented leaders were killed or fled into exile with stories of atrocities and torture, Amin replaced them with his own military subordinates, some of whom could barely read or write. He appointed himself President for Life, Chancellor of the University, and Conqueror of the British Empire. Orderly government ceased to exist.

Quite apart from human persecution, stories had filtered through of mass killings of elephants within the parks. Two years earlier Bernhard Grzimek, the veteran German conservationist, had told me of an audience with Idi Amin when he confronted the dictator with the rumours. Amin's response was to ban all hunting of large wild animals; but it was merely a cosmetic measure. Sport hunters were an easy scapegoat, and removing the professionals simply left the field wide open to the poachers. Now we wanted to hear what the scientists had to say, and to see the elephants with our own eyes.

Entebbe's brand-new airport building was a black metallic monstrosity, full of steel pillars and sheets of plate glass. MiG jets screamed a crescendo with Russian-sounding voices on the radio as they practised take-offs and landings.

To refuel I taxied over to the old airport where Shell kept Avgas for small planes. A line of MiGs was parked near by, gleaming and immaculate. Imposing as they looked, their days were numbered. A month later they would all be blown to smithereens during the famous Israeli commando raid on Entebbe.

I began to stroll towards the MiGs, but the Shell man became agitated and headed me off. 'Please, sir, it is very dangerous to look,' he said. 'Last week the army boys beat a pilot very badly.'

Hurriedly I returned to the plane while he topped us up, and as soon as he was done we taxied for immediate take-off.

No intimation of violence was evident from the air as I headed west, first over papyrus swamps and then across rolling, sparsely inhabited bush country where chestnut herds of Ankole cattle with enormous gleaming horns grazed the tall grass. In a cloud shadow on the horizon I picked out the snow-capped mountain range of the Rwenzoris, the Mountains of the Moon, the highest source of the Nile, below which lay the Queen Elizabeth National Park.

Meltwater from the snows of the Rwenzoris runs down into Lake George at the north end of the park. These headwaters of the Albert Nile flow on lazily down the wide Kazinga channel, looking from the air almost like a man-made canal, until they reach Lake Edward, where a research institute and a lodge had been built on the small prominence of the Mweya peninsula.

The park has rich volcanic soils and plenty of rain and was famous for its elephants and hippos. To the south lay the Maramagambo Forest, a refuge for chimpanzees and rare, red colobus monkeys; while large herds of buffalo, topi and Uganda kob roamed the Kigezi plains, where prides of lions slept under the scattered clumps of euphorbia trees. At that time it was still one of the finest animal sanctuaries in the world; but to our dismay as we flew in over the park we began to see dead elephants, and automatically we began to count them. Within fifteen minutes we had spotted seventy-eight elephant corpses, against only fifty-eight living animals.

Our host, Eric Edroma, was waiting at the airstrip, and welcomed us warmly; then, through his permanent cloud of cigarette smoke, he nervously informed us that the president was going to open the conference.

At the lodge we met many scientists who had come by road, but not a single Kenyan or Tanzanian; mine was the only plane from a neighbouring country. However, there were many Ugandans in a hospitable mood which I had always associated with the country from previous visits. Some of the scientists were shy and when Eric saw them sitting in isolated groups not knowing each other, he announced, 'This is a cocktail party so that people can mix – so can you all stand up and mix.' This effectively broke the ice and soon all intermingled. Beyond the two huge pairs of arched tusks that framed the entrance to the dining room, black and white participants chatted volubly, in the free and natural way so typical of Uganda; and as the sun went down we stood together gazing at the snowy peaks of the Mountains of the Moon.

Inside the lodge, drummers covered in bells jangled and stamped in unison through a complicated dance. Ancient tattered puttees of some distant colonial origin hung from their ankles. 'You can see the Raj ended some time ago,' muttered Ian Parker.

Next day we waited all morning for the snickering whisper of 'Big Daddy's' helicopter, but it never came. Instead a smartly dressed soldier, Lt.-Col. Onaah, DSO, emerged from a car preceded by a group of terrified civilian officials. Onaah was Minister of Tourism and Wildlife. In the dining room he gave us an effusive welcome. He explained that other state business had detained the president and spoke with a saddened expression of the 'poor animals, whom no one respects', and the Government's determination to protect them. Then his face lit up. 'In future,' he declared to his hushed audience, 'all elephant poachers will face the firing squad.'

At the end of the minister's speech Ian Parker was asked to present a copy of a book he had co-authored with Laws. Inscribed to His Excellency Al Haddji, Field Marshal Idi Amin, VC, CBE, (the exact titles had stretched our knowledge of protocol), the gift was received with a grateful speech acknowledging Parker's role in Uganda's history.

And what was Parker's role in Uganda? In the long and tragic history of the African elephant he could certainly go down as the first man to use automatic rifles on elephant family units. In Uganda, as Laws and he can truly claim: 'large-scale cropping by complete herds was undertaken for the first time anywhere.' Later such concentrated rifle fire would echo all over the continent, sometimes in the name of sound management but more often in pursuit of plundered ivory. Parker has often been accused of acting for profit, and he himself has encouraged this criticism. Culling is an emotive subject, but Parker believed in it and saw no reason to hide the fact that he had shot many elephants, or that he did it for money, and he appeared to enjoy provoking conservationists.

'How did you feel when you did it?' an interviewer once asked him. 'Did you feel any sense of loss?'

'I don't like killing animals,' Parker replied. 'But I would liken my position to a man in the slaughter-house who, as he wields the pole-axe, may have a Bach fugue going through his mind. You can be detached from the grotesqueness and grottiness of life.'

But then sometimes he also appeared to let the mask slip and reveal a less callous side, which, however, he has never allowed to affect the killing.

'The only time that I have ever really paused was during the extensive elephant cropping campaigns that I have undertaken in which all animals are aged,' he told his interviewer. 'One can look back through the animal's life; you slit open the uterus of the female; you can see how many calves she's had; what her reproductive success has been – fantastic – and then you get to look at her teeth and you find, she's older than my mother and I've shot her.'

At last on the third day two Cambridge scientists, Keith Eltringham and Rob Malpas, both of whom had stayed in Uganda through all these difficult years, gave the report we had been waiting for. In 1974 they had found the first evidence that a great elephant killing was underway. Since then, numbers had crashed every year and the evidence of catastrophic slaughter seemed irrefutable.

Ian Parker jumped up at this juncture and said, 'A catastrophic decline is the right description.' He claimed that in 1973 Uganda's minimum ivory export was the equivalent of eleven thousand dead elephants, and the net export was equivalent to twenty thousand elephants. 'One tonne of ivory is equivalent to approximately one hundred elephants,' he told us. Then, in a single chilling sentence he proceeded to spell out the true enormity of what had happened. 'Since forty thousand elephants was the estimated Uganda population for 1969,' he told the hushed audience, 'it means that Uganda lost half its elephants in one year.'

Eric told us that voices within the Amin government had disputed the count and suggested that the elephants had merely moved to the forest. But any denial of the elephant killing was almost certainly a smokescreen designed to cover up high government involvement in ivory poaching; and the matter needed to be handled delicately as there was no telling just who might be the chief beneficiary.

In order to provide irrefutable facts in support of our colleagues, Parker and I offered to fly an independent count in both Queen Elizabeth and Murchison National Parks. We would count not only elephants but also their carcasses. Eric Edroma was delighted, and undertook to provide us with fuel and accommodation.

Every evening Eric laid on entertainments. The band of the Mbarara Simba Battalion was highly popular and the dining-room-cum-conference hall overflowed with local enthusiasts. We formed a flying wedge like a rugger scrum to get into the hall, which was filled with jugglers and fire-eaters, tumblers and troubadours, all going through their paces, to the intricate rhythms of the Simba band.

The noise was deafening. I found myself next to the German ambassador who was yelling in my ear about three hundred tonnes of ivory, that had just gone out on some well-known airlines. Rather reluctantly he admitted that Lufthansa, together with Sabena, had been responsible for many large shipments, which were not illegal at the time. Ian Parker later told me that East African Airways were also taking out large quantities of ivory – often unmanifested.

Flying back and forth over the spectacular landscapes of the Queen Elizabeth Park we criss-crossed a dramatic jumble of volcanic craters holding wooded slopes and still lakes in their depths; worlds within worlds where the elephants came to feed and bathe. Now, all too plain to see, many of the craters were littered with dead elephants.

In the woodlands of the south it was the same, except immediately across the border in Zaire, where some hundreds of elephants had gathered as if seeking safety near a research camp called Lulimbi, not far from Vitshumbi where Lee Lyon had begun her film on the old bull elephants. Next to the fishermen's camps fresh carcasses lay rotting in the sun – grim evidence that the killing had not been for meat. In all we counted 1,230 living elephants and 953 dead.

As soon as we were finished in the Queen Elizabeth Park we flew north past the Mountains of the Moon towards the Murchison Falls National Park. Murchison is the biggest park in Uganda and is bisected by the Victoria Nile as it flows westwards into Lake Albert. The falls themselves are thirty miles to the east, near the lodge at Paraa, just before the Nile leaves the park.

At Paraa Lodge I had a long talk with Agostino Bendabule, a warden who had just been transferred to Murchison. He was a slender man with an aquiline profile and long, delicate hands. One evening after the others had gone to bed, I stayed up discussing his problems and listening to his stories. Once he thought no one could overhear him he was extremely articulate about the effects of Amin's barbarism and whimsical violence.

He told me the Field Marshal's secret police, the State Research Bureau, had visited the park one night and seized another warden, Alfred Labongo, of the Achole tribe. They bundled him into their car and set off for the far end of the park so that they could throw him to the crocodiles; but on the way he had jumped from the car and, using his bushcraft, had managed to escape.

'Life,' said Augustino with a smile, 'is dangerous here for an educated man.' Luckily both he and Labongo survived the rest of Amin's regime and five years later we would all face a different menace together.

When I went out to survey the south bank of the park I found that the emerald plains, mile after mile of undulating grassland, were ideal for spotting elephants; but now they were virtually empty. The first elephants appeared on the horizon as a dark streak which began to move at our approach, sending up a film of dust that hung like mist above the shining grass. They were tightly packed in a mob of about three hundred, surging to and fro in panic as the plane circled.

Ten years earlier Murchison had been a classic example of a park suffering the effects of too many elephants. Long-dead terminalia trees, killed as the hungry animals stripped off their bark, still raised their gaunt branches to the sky. But now everywhere we looked the plain was dotted with white circles of bones. Each circle was a dead elephant. Each corpse went down on the map as a little black cross until the entire sheet was covered with crosses. Here indeed was an elephants' graveyard, but one with not a single tusk. Every scrap of ivory had been assiduously collected.

Neither of us had ever seen such a concentration of dead elephants. Of the eight-thousand-strong herds which had roamed the Murchison plains, we could find only two thousand still alive.

Many dead elephants were concentrated immediately opposite Paraa Park headquarters, and we could not understand how they could have been shot without the knowledge of the park rangers. We were told that it was Amin's soldiers who had done the killing, but I wondered if this was the whole story.

Back at Naivasha I discussed with Oria the implications of what I had seen and heard in Uganda. It was not just that man was competing with the elephant for land; nor that he coveted the elephants' tusks almost as gold. For the first time I had seen what the sudden spread of automatic weapons could do in a country where law and order had broken down.

There was a genuine possibility that the great Ugandan herds were doomed; and if Uganda, a once prosperous and civilized country, could be brought to chaos, might not the rest of Africa follow?

Ian Parker and I analyzed the results of our count and wrote a report for Idi Amin's minister, Lt.-Col. Onaah. In it we demolished the theory that the elephants had moved, and showed they had been killed for their ivory. Parker dug out Uganda's official ivory export figures. They revealed a total of 185 tonnes exported over three years which, he said, represented 18,500 elephants killed. Moreover, we could also show that Hong Kong imports of Uganda ivory over the same three years exceeded the official Ugandan records by five times. It not only indicated large-scale elephant mortality in Uganda since 1971, but also a serious breakdown of law enforcement.

Later in the year as Idi Amin's political situation became ever more insecure following several attempted assassinations, the window to Uganda's elephants was closed for another four years, until he was deposed.

My experience in Uganda brought home to me just how fragile some of Africa's most beautiful parks and most spectacular populations of game had become. They were hostages to fortune, and could be broken just as easily by the turbulence of human affairs as by any natural catastrophe.

Yet, for all that, our travels had also shown us cause for hope. The Selous, with its turbulent past, was now an immense and unspoilt

OPPOSITE – Tanzania, 1973 – Boadicea, Queen of Manyara's matriarchs.

Early days: *CLOCKWISE FROM CENTRE -* Sirocco House on the shores of Lake Naivasha, Kenya, built by Oria's parents after a year of walking and hunting elephants in the Congo in 1930. Iain's Uncle Douglas, then the Marquis of Clydesdale (*left*), with friend, setting off on a tiger hunt in India prior to his flight over the summit of Everest in April 1933 in a single engine bi-plane. Iain walks with Virgo, a wild elephant in Lake Manyara National Park, Tanzania, in 1970. Iain's father, Lord David Douglas-Hamilton (*left*), with friend, stands under a Fairey Battle in 1939 before going on to command a Spitfire squadron in Malta. Oria's mother, Giselle Bunau-Varilla, with the first and only elephant she shot in Rwanda in 1929. Oria's father, Mario Rocco and gun bearer, exhibits a kongoni

he shot in 1930. Forty-five years after their safari, Oria photographs one of the big bulls in Zaire in 1974 that wandered through the fishing village of Vitshumbi.

Attitudes with young: *ABOVE AND BELOW* — Fences are increasingly curtailing Africa's old freedoms. A mother comforts her baby marooned on the wrong side of a fence on a ranch in Laikipia District, Kenya.

ABOVE – Eleanor, as an orphan, spent most of her life with the Sheldricks in Tsavo East National Park. *BELOW* – Here, aged about twenty, after hours with Saba and Dudu playing together, Eleanor, tired of their company, lifted her left leg to scratch (in a displacement gesture) and then very gently swept Dudu off her feet.

Death and Decomposition: *ABOVE* - Elephant skulls were collected in and around Tsavo National Park after a terrible drought in the early 1970s. By studying the teeth it was possible to determine age and sex of the elephants estimated at between 6,000-10,000 dead. *BELOW LEFT* - A skull from a West African elephant shot by a hunter in the early 1950s, was found with seven tusks emerging from the upper skull. *BELOW RIGHT* - Gnawed skulls are often found with teeth marks of porcupines known to eat elephant skulls.

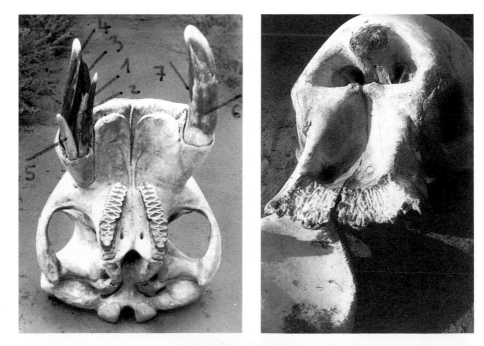

Lions begin to eat a freshly killed bull elephant in Ngorongoro Crater, Tanzania. Six days later, after tusks have been hacked off and hyenas have torn the carcass open, vultures finish off the meat. Three months later only the skull and femurs remain.

ABOVE - Iain in 1970 with *KIX* - his cloth-covered twenty-year-old Piper-Pacer on his bush strip in Manyara, setting up aerial to receive blips from radio-collared elephants. Several times lions had a go at eating the tyres and once a rhino charged *KIX*, stopping feet from the plane.

ABOVE - The faithful *BAD*, a Cessna 185, followed *KIX* and flew for eight years over vast areas of Africa counting elephants. *BELOW* - At the start of his study Iain followed elephants on foot through the thick vegetation. *OVERLEAF* - Iain's house and research camp above the Ndala River at Manyara where elephants came to drink.

Manyara 1973: *OPPOSITE* - Oria with Hadija, a ranger's daughter, Saba and Dudu having a wash in a safari canvas basin in camp.

ABOVE - 1970 - Iain with Saba aged two months in his plane *BELOW* - Virgo and Iain greet each other with a hand-to-trunk touch. *OVERLEAF* - On the shores of Lake Manyara National Park Mhoja and Iain stand with Boadicea's kinship group in April 1978, with Virgo on the extreme right, her son Dudu and daughter Saba next to her.

Nose, Hose and Hand: *TOP* - Bahati with twins Crooked Tail and Straight Tail. *LEFT* - Digging water holes in the Ndala River sand waiting for the clear water to filter through. *ABOVE* - Mary, just before she died, a grand matriarch easily recognized by the big nick in her left ear and long even tusks. *OPPOSITE* - Saba, the elephant, and her mother, Virgo, (*right*) cross trunks and pull son Tumaini out of river.

'Ecole des Elephants': *OPPOSITE* - Zaire, 1974 - Nakofo, aged about fifty, one of the surviving 'moniteur' elephants of the school at Gangala na Bodio, with her *cornac*, Bangonya.

ABOVE - The square at Gangala na Bodio, with Wando, the first elephant born there in 1930, leading the remaining elephants from the school. *BELOW* - The daily line-up, with Wando far left and Nakofo centre. Today, only Kilo *(third right)* and Zombi *(right)* are still alive.

ABOVE - Boadicea's skeleton found by Mhoja below the escarpment. She died in November 1974, presumed killed by poachers. BELOW - Boa's skull in front of the elephant office in Naivasha.

OPPOSITE - 1973 - Boadicea examines the bones of a dead elephant.

Fable and fact: *ABOVE* - Orphaned Babar cries over his dead mother as the bad hunter rushes to catch him. *BELOW* - Small calf grieves on its mother just killed in a cull.

ABOVE - Babar, now King of the Elephants, leaves with Celeste on his honeymoon. *BELOW* - An orphaned survivor of the Rwanda cull leaves its native habitat for a new uncertain life in Akagera National Park.

wilderness. In the tiny park of Manyara, in the great spaces of the Kruger, and the almost limitless expanse of Zaire, the wilderness had survived.

The condition of Uganda's elephants was not unique and it was clear that elephants everywhere were coming under increasing pressure. The rising price of ivory provided a powerful incentive for poachers to pursue them wherever they could be found. Yet still no one could say how many elephants there were. Before we could even begin to protect them, we needed to expand our surveys to a continental level, and to make a study of the ivory trade which appeared to be hastening their decline.

We knew it would cost money. Even as co-chairman of the Elephant Group I could do little without funds, and elephant studies attracted far less interest than they had in Dick Laws' heyday or when our Manyara project was under way. If anything were to be done, we would have to go out to find funds for ourselves in Europe and America.

It would be an uphill struggle to end the slaughter. We would need political support and a lot of money and the elephants would need strong laws and resolute law enforcement. It was very unlikely that we would be able to mobilize any funds in Africa, where economies were struggling or bankrupt in the aftermath of the colonial withdrawal. We would be entirely dependent on arousing support in the West. The publication of the European translations of our book gave us a chance of a free air ticket, and we intended to use the opportunity to lobby for the elephant.

Not long before we set off, Oria's father, Mario, old and fragile, fell and broke his femur. Unable to fit a stretcher in *BAD* and fly him myself to Nairobi, we called in the flying doctor. I lit a fire for the wind direction, and the huge twin-engine plane floated down like a white bird on to our short strip. Having arrived on the farm for the first time by air in 1929, he now left for the last time lying on the floor of the plane, his face drawn in pain, with Giselle by his side. A whirl of dust gathered and blew up into the sky as the plane took off, the rumble reverberating in the hills as if the earth was trembling.

OPPOSITE – A colossus falls, the earth is still: the elephant shot by a game scout in the Selous Game Reserve for innocently touching the rope of a tent.

CHAPTER EIGHT

ORIA: *Drought in Manyara*

1976, Manyara, Tanzania

W E returned from Europe after a successful fund-raising trip. Bill Conway of the New York Zoological Society and officials of the World Wildlife Fund had pledged enough money for us to continue the continental elephant survey. As soon as we returned to East Africa news came that Lake Manyara was in the grip of a drought and the trees were being battered more heavily than ever by the hungry elephants. Derek Bryceson, the Tanzanian parks' director, was worried that it might not be possible to postpone culling any longer and he invited us to fly down in our aeroplane.

The lake was smaller than before, edged with crystalline salt where the waters had receded. Manyara was in the grip of its third rainless year and we knew the elephants would be having difficulty finding enough food.

From the air we could see them, like grey boulders gathered on the shore, casting long shadows in the soft evening light. There must have been at least two hundred elephants out in the open, as if at a meeting, each family a distinct little group, taking turns to drink a cupful at a time at shallow water holes. Others were walking slowly in parallel lines as if directed by some mastermind.

There was the same battered old Land-Rover with Mhoja behind the wheel. His smiling face glowed under his beret and he was still wearing what looked like the same over-sized green jacket of the Tanzania National Parks. Our meetings were always an immense pleasure and it was good to see him again. We shook hands and began to unload the plane, looking around for old bits of wood to wedge under the tyres before winding our way along the lake front towards a mirage of elephants and our old home.

'Have you caught any poachers?' Iain asked as we snaked through the trees on the track to the camp. 'Some,' Mhoja answered, 'but since you were last here we have not lost any more big elephants.'

This was good news. At least the worries caused by the disappearance of so many matriarchs had not deteriorated into an all-out massacre. Derek Bryceson was keen that Iain should include Manyara as part of the pan-African survey and to help get the park extended.

We set ourselves up under canvas among the acacias with our children. From the big boulder where we sat overlooking the lake we could see threads of rain slanting down in the far distance, but in Manyara the drought clung on.

The leaves dropped, the creepers shrivelled, the bushes were all eaten back until there was no foliage left. Then the elephants ate bark and raw wood, but it could not satisfy their hunger. The soil became bare and sandy, and the lush Manyara I had known seemed a dream of the past. The escarpment trees and bushes suffered dreadful damage – of the *Acacia tortilis* only about 40 per cent remained alive out of those present when I first came to Manyara.

Questions whirled through my mind. How would we advise the authorities to deal with the problem? We had recommended extending the park, but it was already three years since Bernard Grzimek, director of the Frankfurt Zoological Society, had offered to buy out the farmers to the south, and nothing had happened.

To leave Manyara alone now was a heavy responsibility for anyone in conservation to bear. Too many doubts and dilemmas had to be resolved, particularly after what had happened in Tsavo. Many felt that active management – a euphemism for culling – had to be the decision of the day; and this caused Iain much agony.

An opportunity to appeal for help came when Aboud Jumbe, the Tanzanian vice-president, visited Manyara with his family. Derek Bryceson arranged for us to meet him and Jumbe needed little convincing. When he next broadcast on the radio, the vice-president announced that the Government was going to extend the park, and warned squatters who had settled on the southern boundary that they had better move out now.

Although we had been unable to establish a firm research project over the past few years, we knew that at least Mhoja had been keeping an eye on births and deaths, arrivals and disappearances within Manyara's elephant community. Now John Scherlis, a young voluntary assistant from Harvard, had joined Mhoja and was making accurate sketches of elephant ears and tusks to bring Iain's identity records up to date. Together they were attempting to solve the puzzle of the unknown 'teenage' elephants, searching through old photos, scanning the ears of tiny babies and looking for every clue with which to compare the older, bigger, jagged ears of today.

Ninety calves were born during Iain's study from 1966–70. Now many were motherless and had found refuge in the safety of other families where secondary matriarchs had taken over some kind of leadership. Most of these juveniles were between six and twelve years old – the eldest would be having their first calves.

Curie, slumbering in the shade of a wide umbrella tree was easily recognizable by her single, straight left tusk, which she used for jabbing any elephant that got in her way. We had always thought she was the sister of Jezebel, a big placid elephant with one straight right tusk which made her look as if she was holding a giant knitting-needle in her mouth – especially when she had her trunk knotted around it as elephants often do. Jezebel had been the matriarch of this family, but had died the previous year, leaving Curie as leader. Now Curie had a chubby little calf, about five months old, whom Mhoja had named Pili, who was huddled up with two smaller babies.

These babies were the twins which Iain had named Straight Tail and Crooked Tail, born to Jezebel's twelve-year-old daughter, Bahati. It was unfortunate that they had to be born at such a harsh time since they were the first elephant twins born in the wild on which regular observations could be made. 'Keep a close watch on them,' Iain had yelled as he jumped into his plane and raced off back to the Selous. Mhoja and John could hardly believe their luck, and word was sent round to all the wardens and rangers that twins had been born in Manyara.

Not much was known about elephant twins but they are probably as frequent among elephants as in humans – that is, about one in a hundred. From the very few observations of elephant twins we feared the chance of both surviving might be low.

A month after the twins were discovered, Mhoja was on an anti-poaching patrol in the acacia woodlands when he heard the loud scream of elephants and noticed hundreds of buffaloes galloping past him in the trees. Moments later he practically collided with Curie who was crashing through the woodland with her family close behind her. For a brief instant the elephants stopped running and Mhoja noticed that Hera, one of the matriarchs, was stained with blood down one side where a deep cut was visible which looked like a spear wound. She seemed unsteady on her feet, and Yusta, standing near by, was allowing her mother to lean against her. The elephants had not noticed Mhoja, who continued to watch as Yusta used the two tips of her trunk-fingers to pinch Hera's wound together and fill it up with mud as if she was trying to stop the bleeding.

Then Curie moved on, heading fast towards the south where the bush was thick and safe, with Bahati and the twins keeping up as best they could. Mhoja cast around for human tracks, picking them up near a tree where there was also a splash of blood. As the footprints moved up the hill he eventually lost them in the undergrowth on the steep slopes of the escarpment; but he thought the poachers must have waited up a tree and speared Hera as she passed underneath.

For a month Curie and her family vanished in the thickets in the south of the park, and Mhoja could find no trace of them. Knowing the area and Curie's restless character, he was apprehensive about the twins. But days before our arrival, Mhoja told us, they had returned to the north of the park and Hera's wound was completely healed. We found Curie up on the escarpment, leaning on one foot as she stretched her trunk as far as it would go to pluck leaves from the upper branches of a tree. All the family was alive, although the twins were much thinner; and with no sign of an end to the drought the elephants were eating shrubs down to the raw wood.

By December there was nothing tender for young elephants to nibble; only a desolation of broken trees and branches. All the elephants were gaunt and thin, with ticks hanging from their skins like black beans. Water was scarce and there were no longer any soothing wallows in which they could plaster themselves with mud and then scrape away the itchy parasites on tree trunks or ant hills.

It was easy to find Bahati. She was now a lonely figure out on the water's edge, with her skeletal twins stumbling behind her. Straight Tail was so weak he could hardly walk any more. His head hung down and he had to rest constantly, standing in the blazing sun while the air seemed to turn molten and run along the lake shore, distorting the distant masses of flamingoes so that they appeared to waver like pink flames in the dancing heat. Somehow, Crooked Tail still managed to keep up with Bahati, walking close behind her tail, where her shadow gave him protection. He was now more aggressive towards his brother when they were together, pushing him away from the nipple and fighting for his own survival.

On 19 December, Straight Tail died during the night. We looked for his body everywhere but found no trace.

Iain, meanwhile, was wrestling with an internal struggle. He was greatly worried by the destruction of the woodlands. The whole escarpment seemed to have changed from where we gazed up at it each day. Gone were the aloes and the paper-barked *commiphoras*. The acacia woodlands appeared to be in ruins and the few surviving trees were going fast. Only the baobabs for some curious reason were left unscarred. 'If people like you don't take some kind of a decision there's going to be nothing left,' was the comment of Alan Root, our wildlife film-maker friend. In a sense it was the same crisis that Sheldrick had faced in Tsavo, where everything had happened on a much bigger scale. But Manyara was so small that it had only a limited capacity to absorb ecological change.

The whole question of extending the park had been handled with the utmost apathy. The vice-president's broadcast announcing the extension was not followed up by legal action. Unfortunately, many of the squatters whom Jumbe wanted to move had already been uprooted from their original homes by the government's Socialist 'Ujamaa' resettlement programme, and it never did prove possible to move them again.

Eventually and with great reluctance, Iain recommended to Derek Bryceson that in the absence of an extension to the park, active culling of elephants in Manyara should be considered. I heard Iain saying: 'Well, if the elephants *have* to be culled, then it should be done in the south, far from the tourist circuits. Shoot the refugees if you have to, but leave our known elephants.'

The days grew overcast, but the weather grew even hotter. Some friends came over from the Serengeti Research Institute to act as observers and we made an aerial count of the elephants. There were still four hundred and thirty elephants alive and very few dead, and in addition we had spotted twenty live rhinos. All was still well. It was a minute scrap of information in the pan-African elephant survey, and yet it was significant; for here at least the elephants were not yet being heavily poached. The rhinos, however, were beginning to take a beating. As the months went by our young researchers came across the bodies of several rhinos, shot or speared deep inside the park.

Iain also counted elsewhere in Tanzania – in the Serengeti, Ruaha and Tarangire National Parks. In the north of the country the high ratio of dead to live elephants showed they were taking a hammering at the hands of the poachers. In Tarangire, which lies on the opposite side of Lake Manyara, he found eight elephants gunned down in a heap; indisputable proof that professional poachers were at work, probably armed with automatic weapons. But Ruaha in the south, and the surrounding reserves and hunting blocks were untouched as yet, like the Selous, and they had even higher densities.

What our counts did show for the first time in Tanzania was that the black rhino was in serious trouble and decreasing even faster than the elephant. The alarm bells were sounded and a rhino specialist group was formed to work in tandem with the elephant group.

We could now start doing our sums. There were 110,000 elephants in the Selous and another 44,000 in Ruaha. The Serengeti supported some 3,000, Tarangire another 3,000, and Manyara 500. When the final totals were complete, Iain estimated 350,000 elephants for the whole of Tanzania. There was also little doubt that the threat to them seemed to be entirely in the north on the Kenya border.

When the counts were finished Iain flew straight to Nairobi. He was lucky. Next day the border was closed unilaterally by the Tanzanians and all Kenyan aircraft were impounded. Exactly what the quarrel was about we never really knew. Our work did not touch on politics although it was affected by it, and Derek Bryceson eventually obtained permission for us to fly over the border and carry on with our Manyara research.

Two weeks after Straight Tail's death, the rains broke with a vengeance, bringing fresh life to the fish and waterbirds in the swiftly rising lake. Soon the park was green again. New leaves sprang from the parched bushes and creepers spread quickly, hiding the dead branches of the drought-stricken trees. Crooked Tail, with that extra portion of milk now vital for his survival, lived on to welcome the cool rain and the tender new grasses which he could just begin to nibble.

With the rains came an amazing and totally unexpected regeneration of acacias which flourished despite the high numbers of elephants. This seemed to fly in the face of several theories about elephants and trees, all of which argued that a high elephant density completely suppressed regeneration. At Manyara it was as if a sudden great pulse of nature had replaced the missing trees regardless of all our preconceptions.

Even stranger, one quarter of the elephants died of disease, probably anthrax. Luckily, Iain's reluctant recommendation on culling had not been carried out. The trees came back on their own, unaided by human interference, leaving us to wonder what would have happened if we had intervened in the natural scheme of things.

CHAPTER NINE

IAIN: *The Killing Fields of Kenya*

1976–7, Kenya

KENYA was now in its twelfth year of independence and the ageing President Mzee Jomo Kenyatta enjoyed great power and prestige. The days when he had been condemned as a Mau Mau leader were long forgotten. In statesmanlike speeches he had reconciled the white settlers and extended a hand of friendship to those who wanted to stay and help to build a new Kenya.

While there was civil war in Sudan, dictatorship in Uganda, and idealistic, but impractical, socialism in Tanzania, Kenya was stable and flourishing.

With an elephant hunting ban, a World Bank loan of $17 million to develop tourism and a government pledge to control all ivory trading, the elephant's chances of survival should have been as good as anywhere in Black Africa; yet Nairobi had become the ivory capital of the continent.

Almost every week the newspapers carried reports of poachers jailed for ivory offences in villages and towns all over Kenya. Magistrates spoke scathingly of the inefficiency of the game department and of a category of people receiving poached ivory who considered themselves above the law.

Revelations in the foreign press the previous year, alleging that the president's family was involved in the ivory trade, had been furiously rejected by Kenyan ministers, who claimed that the sale of government ivory to the Nairobi curio shops was under strict control. Angrily they attacked statistics published in London by the *New Scientist* magazine which claimed there was an elephant population crash.

Our first problem was to get clearance for our elephant project to be on Kenyan soil. We were a bit nervous about this; for although it was to be pan-African in scope, there had been a running battle between the local press and the Ministry of Wildlife and Tourism in which elephants were the key controversy. The hard-hitting articles in the foreign press had been critical of Kenyan corruption and I had been cited as a source of elephant statistics.

The first step was to introduce myself to the ministry, so I went to the office armed with letters of introduction from the WWF and Sir Peter Scott. In the lobby outside I met David Sheldrick, Bill Woodley and Peter Jenkins: three wardens who epitomized to me all the old national park values.

I knew why they were there. A plan was being put through to merge the national parks with the game department, and everything they had built up over the years was in danger. Faced with a surrender of authority to the game department and cuts in their wages, they were on the verge of resigning rather than becoming accomplices to the destruction of the parks. Only a higher sense of duty had kept them at their posts, and the hope that they might be able to alleviate some of the damage caused by the merger.

My interview with the permanent secretary went very smoothly. He approved of the project and gave permission for me to make surveys anywhere in the elephants' range.

In the meanwhile the *Daily Nation* continued the campaign it had been waging against the Minister for Wildlife and Tourism, Matthew Ogutu. They wanted to know why the anti-poaching unit was left short of fuel; why there were 1,300 poachers reported in Tsavo National Park; why morale among the guardians of the parks was low; and why in general the ministry appeared so incompetent. 'Answer or Resign', the paper demanded in banner headlines. It was all heady democratic stuff.

When the minister finally did answer he blustered. 'Whatever was happening in the former Kenya national parks is now defunct,' he declared, 'I am cleaning out those cobwebs.'

I could only presume some of those cobwebs were my friends, the wardens.

The merger was a disaster. The idea was to streamline the two bodies dealing with wildlife. It sounded plausible and apparently logical, but in East Africa the finest wildlife areas had evolved from game reserves into national parks with a whole set of standards and values. They were run by an independent board of trustees and had a tremendous *esprit de corps*. The parks' tradition was one of protection and preservation – while the game department's was one of utilization and control. Add to this the fact that the game department by the early 1970s had the reputation for venality, inefficiency and corruption, and it was obvious why the parks' men were so worried.

Now that I had official blessing I gathered together a small nucleus of people who were interested in helping. My mission in Kenya was to bring out scientific facts about what was happening to its elephants. The precedent of Peter Jarman was not encouraging; but at least I was independent and would soon be free to start collecting data.

As soon as the time was ripe I also wanted to launch an ivory-trade study which would identify the bottlenecks where pressure could be exerted. It would need someone with an ability to probe deeply. Ian Parker, whom I had in mind for this job, had already made a confidential report on the subject naming high-ranking figures involved in corruption. But, I was warned by Richard Leakey, director of the National Museum and a member of the KANU-ruling party, that the 'wounds had not healed' regarding the exposure of the ivory scandals.

Although Kenya was only one country within the elephant's range it was world-famous for its wildlife and its large elephant herds. It was also our home and we decided we would try to survey as much as possible ourselves and to link our results with the work of other scientists and wardens.

There were always problems with counting, and everyone thought they had the best technique. The wardens generally believed in so called 'total counts' in which every square yard of the park was scanned for elephants. At least that was the theory. In practice, as the hours and days wore on, pilots and observers would become fatigued, and the gaps between flight lines grew ever larger, until it was impossible to see all the elephants. It is a curious fact that, despite their size, elephants are peculiarly skilful at making themselves invisible in the smallest amounts of bush. When trees grow thickly they can be missed altogether.

For this reason scientists often prefer 'sample counts' for large areas like Tsavo or Serengeti, using the technique we had employed in the Selous. This was standardized among most scientists counting elephants in East Africa.

But we were now dealing with new conditions in which elephant poaching had become the dominant factor. From our surveys we learnt to tell a disturbed elephant population from one which was unpoached. The large groups we had seen in Uganda and their terrified reaction to the aircraft stood out in stark contrast against the placid calm of elephants in places like Manyara and Amboseli National Park. From now on I looked out for this reaction wherever I went.

Another new idea was to count the many dead elephants there were to be seen and to calculate the ratio of dead elephants as a proportion of all elephants live and dead. This we called the carcass ratio. It became our yardstick for measuring how fast they were being killed and was adopted by many others. So we began to cover the famous parks and reserves of Kenya; Meru, Mara, Amboseli, keeping precise records of corpses like attendants at a morgue.

We aimed to find out how fast an elephant rotted. Then by categorizing the age of each carcass we could calculate how many had died in the previous year.

Our first survey was in Meru National Park, which typified the new problems being faced. Meru is a beautiful, small park of 844 square kilometres, to the east of Mount Kenya, a wild landscape of rocky hills and savannah woodlands, with rushing streams and *commiphora* bush rather like Tsavo. It was administered by Peter Jenkins who ran an extremely tight ship. Peter was a perfectionist. Roads, buildings, vehicles and aeroplanes were all in immaculate condition. Even if it was twenty years old, equipment gleamed and functioned. The local Meru tribe have had a vested interest in the park since its formation. With the wild animals fenced off from their *shambas* (farms, smallholdings), they appreciate the revenue wildlife brings from tourism, of which a proportion comes their way.

After three days of flying we had covered the entire park and had gone further with our sample lines. There were plenty of animals, including rhinos and elephants inside the park, but nothing outside other than carcasses, gaunt white cattle and the camels of Somali herdsmen. The elephants sheltering in the park had voted with their feet.

A freshly killed elephant lies like a fallen colossus. Blood oozes from the wounds. The eyes are glazed, the lashes dusty. In the sun's hot rays the ballooning corpse becomes an obscene parody of an elephant, its legs sticking out like a child's toy. If the belly has been opened the guts come spilling out. Poachers may have taken some meat and opened up the body cavity, giving access to vultures and other scavengers.

Within a day the corpse is covered in vulture excrement. From the air it appears grey with white splashes. If the skin has not been opened it retains its balloon shape until it explodes or until big cats and scavengers have done their work. For several weeks flesh still fills out the contours below undisturbed skin, giving a rounded appearance.

Vultures often give away the presence of dead elephants, and flying over the plains we looked constantly for their rotating spirals. Again and again they led us to fresh slaughters, and each time we felt sick with anger and impotence.

After a month there is just a black stain, with dried-up skin and bones, the corpse shrivelled like a crumpled rag. But this can vary depending on the rain. An elephant killed early in heavy rains may mainly disappear within a month. The softened skin is entirely eaten by insects. The putrescent fluids are washed away. Dung beetles fly in to bury the fibrous stomach contents. In a park like Serengeti with many carnivores the bones are widely scattered. Elephants themselves may pick them up and carry them away, for mysterious unknown reasons. Only the heavy skull remains, a stark white cenotaph surrounded with a faint rot patch where the vegetation has been killed by rotting body fluids.

In drier places the skin may never be penetrated. Without moisture insects are unable to perform their cleaning function. In this case the corpse dries up, leaving bones and dessicated flesh encased in a mummified sheath of skin, surviving sporadic rain for many years.

In Manyara and Amboseli we followed the disappearance of several marked carcasses. The criteria we developed for measuring the age of each carcass gave us a rough guide for our surveys and enabled us to estimate how many elephants had died in the previous year. The rot patch was the key. If it was still present the corpse was almost certainly less than a year old. If it was gone, then the elephant must have died before the most recent rains.

Each survey showed a different aspect of the elephant's status. The immaculately run Meru National Park was a haven full of 'refugee' elephants. The Aberdare and Mount Kenya Forests were fiercely guarded by Bill Woodley and his ex-Mau Mau rangers. In the Lamu district we found the elephants still relatively untouched, living in a beautiful range that swept from the Boni Forest to the offshore coral islands. Elephants still swam out to these islands to sample their varied vegetation. We were puzzled that the Somali poachers had not decimated them since they were so near the border with Somalia. However, their peace would not last for long. Of course, Tsavo was still the most important elephant population, and the news from there was not good.

In June 1976 David Sheldrick told me the results of the latest Tsavo count. He looked tired and dispirited. 'We have lost fifteen thousand elephants in two years,' he said wearily. 'That's forty-four per cent of the population. Not even the drought was able to achieve that kind of drop. I'm afraid that if things go on this way the park will be nothing but an empty shell before the end of the year.'

Sheldrick was a reserved man, not accustomed to showing his emotions, but the pain in his voice was obvious. Arrests of poachers had doubled in the first six months of the year, but although the field-force was still working well it was not containing the situation any more. The five existing sections were being hopelessly over-worked. Under interrogation, the prisoners confessed to Sheldrick and his men that they were working for big shots. Informers spoke about the game department being actively involved in poaching.

The trouble had started in the early seventies when the price of ivory began its fatal climb and Kamba hunters poured into the park. Between one and two hundred were caught in Tsavo each month. Rangers were no longer allowed to cross park boundaries in hot pursuit of poachers, making it much more difficult to operate effectively and to pick up information on the outskirts. Sheldrick had issued a warning back in 1971 that the price of ivory was at a record high and poaching was stronger than ever; but the drought and the starvation of the elephants diverted attention away from the poaching menace for the next four years. It is quite untrue, as has been asserted, that poaching started only after the drought left Tsavo littered with the tusks of dead elephants. The proof was that elephants were poached just as severely in almost all the other East African parks where there had been no die-off due to drought.

Now David Sheldrick had completed a report on the poaching which spelt out in detail the scale of the crisis. It was for internal consumption and he hoped it would galvanize the Ministry of Wildlife and Tourism into action.

He blamed the state of affairs on a combination of factors which included the ready market for trophies, the absence of any arrests of illicit dealers despite their well-known identity, the apparent protection offered to crooked ivory traders by influential people, a general disinterest in any form of elephant protection by those in authority, and a lack of suitably trained officers to carry out anti-poaching duties. He was scathing about some of the products of the Mweka College of Wildlife Management in Tanzania who received a scientific rather than a leader's training.

Today the ex-military men have been entirely replaced as wardens. As Mweka proudly boasts, it has graduated one thousand students since 1963 and virtually every protected area in anglophone Africa is administered by a Mweka graduate, many of them fine men. Yet if elephant trends are a measure of effectiveness then the old military men could be judged a success and the Mweka-trained 'professionals' a failure. That was certainly Sheldrick's view.

Added to this was the effect of drought in Ukambani, the area bordering Tsavo, causing famine among the Wakamba people who desperately needed extra cash to buy food. In the report Sheldrick recommended in the strongest terms that emergency famine relief should be sent to the Wakamba. This was his human interest in the park's neighbours that went beyond anti-poaching. But although food and help of this kind was available, nothing was done about it.

His detailed recommendations were a blue-print for restoring the situation. They included a request that the president's office should order all administrative officers to help curb poaching in their respective districts. But, above all, Sheldrick insisted that the dealers were the weak link in the chain.

This idea became central to my thinking of what should be done in an ivory-trade investigation. If we could penetrate the trade, name the dealers and identify the pressure points in the trade, perhaps we could start to close it down.

November 1976 brought the dire news that David Sheldrick had been transferred from Tsavo. The story spread swiftly across Nairobi, filling wildlife conservationists, both African and European, with quiet despair. He was replaced by a warden who was completely out of his depth trying to cope with the carnage of Tsavo. He resigned after six embarrassing months. His replacement was a man from the game department, after which Tsavo became a killing field for the elephants.

David had arrived in Nairobi, where he had been posted, and had arranged to meet me at the New Stanley Hotel. Over coffee we talked much about ivory, elephants and parks, and before leaving, David handed over a thick register. It contained all his Tsavo ivory data, and he asked me to copy and analyse it for my pan-African report. Otherwise he feared it might be lost to science.

It was the last time I saw him. David's transfer and the destruction of Tsavo's elephants must have been a profound trauma for he died soon afterwards, aged fifty-seven. Simon Trevor's powerful and disturbing film, *Bloody Ivory*, told of Sheldrick's epic struggle, but it left one disturbing question unanswered: 'Why was Sheldrick moved at the height of the poaching?'

With David gone the gates to Tsavo were open. Even more formidable than the Kamba were the Somalis, crack shots and fearless opponents, who now entered the fray armed with modern AK-47 assault rifles. When poaching in Tsavo spread to the nearby Galana Game Ranch, the Somali poachers shot dead the manager, Ken Clark, in a bloody skirmish.

The new junior wardens arrived at their offices several hours after sunrise, dressed in white shirts and platform shoes, and did not go into the field to tangle with the Somalis.

One shock wave followed another, and it was soon discovered that three assistant wardens were involved in the shooting of eighteen elephants near Aruba Lodge. None was convicted; they were merely transferred. Scientists working in the park told us they frequently heard gunshots not far from their homes. Dead elephants were found on the edge of the main roads with their tusks hacked out. The poachers – Kambas, Somalis or park rangers – no longer even bothered to hide the evidence of their crimes from the eyes of the world. With little or no surveillance left in the park, the Somali *shifta* (bandits) poured in with a vengeance.

In the meanwhile there were numerous protests in Nairobi. The wildlife clubs demonstrated in favour of closing down the trophy industry. The government's response was to ban all professional hunting. And so a seventy-year-old tradition was killed off at the stroke of a pen. For all those years it had been properly regulated until the corruption of the game department destroyed it.

When the ban was imposed it was estimated that hunting brought in $2.5 million per year as opposed to $45 million from tourism. But professional hunting was an emotional issue. The system introduced in colonial times at the turn of the century made hunting licences expensive and limited them by setting quotas for each area. Sport hunting in East Africa became a fashionable adventure for wealthy Europeans, but native people unable to afford the licences were not able to hunt at all. In consequence, although the system had worked for sixty years, by Independence there was a strong built-in resentment against the almost entirely white professional hunting industry.

Some African authorities have tried to blame the imbalance of this hunting system, which favoured whites, for the general collapse of the conservation policy in the 1970s; but it is too easy an explanation. Although anti-colonialist sentiment probably did help to end sport hunting in Kenya, the collapse of the park system cannot be blamed on colonial iniquities, nor on the hunters. The country's ivory was stolen by 'big fish', the so-called 'big-shilling Bwanas' who took it with as little concern for morality as bank robbers cleaning out a safe.

In January 1977, under the towering thorn tree of the New Stanley Hotel's café, we met a man, small, tense and intelligent, from the BBC. Peering at us through wire-rimmed glasses, Julian Mounter talked at length about the film he had researched on the slaughter of the elephants, the corruption in Kenya and the money that was being made out of ivory.

Our initial reaction was that he would be an embarrassment. We had pinned our faith on a cool scientific presentation of national elephant trends and did not want to rock the boat until our research was complete. Furthermore, the last thing we wanted to do was to draw attention to the Kenya ivory trade at a time when we wanted to penetrate it. But Julian was a true investigative reporter. Nothing was going to stop him, and in the end we agreed to help.

His film would expose the greed and the ridiculous lies of those in power who protected the dealers. The ivory traders and the 'big fish' seemed to have the killing fields clear to themselves. Indians, Kenyans, Somalis, Europeans, Japanese and Chinese – all had their fingers in the ivory pie, scooping up the tusks big and small. Whoever was involved, one thing was certain: ivory was leaving Africa in massive quantities.

Julian and his team waited for the shops to open. It was a hot day in January and the town centre had more curio shops selling ivory and skins of every description than any ever before. Like any other tourists they slipped across the street from the New Stanley Hotel into a shop proudly calling itself Jewels and Antiques. Inside lay Kenya's lost elephants in every describable shape and size. At once Mounter's men set to work. Spotlights switched on and cameras came to life, tracking the layers upon layers of tusks on the shelves, the tusk-framed mirrors, the fake-tinted antique ivory bracelets, buttons, rings and statues, the thousands of hastily made ivory objects and identical figures carved in the little back room. Together they were worth a fortune. Mr Shah, the owner, attempted to telephone his 'friends in high places' as he called them; but it was too late – the picture was taken.

Under Mounter's guidance the BBC lens followed the ivory trail with the persistence of a hungry aardvark sniffing out termites. Dozens of people unwittingly let out secrets on the 'Who's Who' of the ivory racket and slowly, day by day, the whole sordid story of corruption and slaughter unfolded.

In his interview with the minister, the answers Julian received in response to his carefully prepared questions left no doubt as to who controlled Kenya's ivory trade – in case no one had already been convinced by the flood of stories in the foreign press.

As a parting gift, he left me his personal dossier with the names and notes, the quantities of illegal tusks and the agents involved in the poaching racket. 'I have been told that if you publish these names there is a ninety per cent chance that you will be either deported or run over. I don't know whether it's worth it at this stage in your survey! Anyway thanks for everything and good luck.'

By the end of 1977 we could prove that Kenya had lost at least half her elephants since 1970. We presented this evidence to the

Government and it eventually found its way into the Press. Not long afterwards the first results started to trickle in from another survey carried out by Canadian scientists, and within another year they were complete. Their figures confirmed ours and were devastating. Of all the elephants seen about half were now corpses. With the Kenya results the East African picture was complete. Although Tanzania was still relatively untouched the facts were inescapable. The disease was spreading. Uganda was a black hole, the dense mass of elephants trapped in the parks now spiralling to destruction. In Kenya Peter Jarman's prediction of an elephant catastrophe had come true with a vengeance. It now remained only to see what President Kenyatta's government would do.

CHAPTER TEN

IAIN: *Elephant Dilemma*

1977, Kenya and Rhodesia

ONE day towards the end of 1977, a year and a half into our elephant study, a bombshell arrived in our mail in the form of a draft paper written by Peter Scott. It was headed: 'The Elephant Dilemma.'

Peter, when I had first met him, had been very aware of the paradox that while some elephants were multiplying to the point where they were destroying the very woodlands that sustained them, others were being poached out of existence.

Now he had been criticized by a group of American wildlife professionals as a well-meaning preservationist who had successfully stymied nearly every attempt to reduce game numbers in national parks to manageable levels.

This criticism stemmed from the views of Les Robinette, a retired professor from the Mweka College of Wildlife Management in Tanzania. Robinette had been strongly in favour of culling elephants in the national parks during the controversies of the 1960s. He now reiterated his belief that 'the over-population of elephants in park after park' was the single most important problem requiring attention.

His friends took his views very seriously. They set out to persuade

Peter Scott and other influential figures to join them in a campaign whose objective was to pressurize East African governments into accepting the need to cull their game by threatening to withhold conservation funds.

Peter Scott, while never agreeing to this interventionist approach, was keen to put the record straight and show he was not opposed to culling for the sake of management. His response, written on behalf of WWF, was the paper we had just received.

'As an example of the scale of the problem,' said Peter, 'it is estimated that there are about one hundred thousand elephants in the Luangwa Valley in Zambia, and that for the habitat to recover, that number must be reduced to twenty-five thousand. The idea that seventy-five thousand elephants must be culled will be very difficult for most people to accept. Nevertheless it seems necessary for WWF to begin at once to explain to its constituency this unhappy paradox of world depletion and local over-abundance.'

I was amazed that culling had once more become an issue and wrote back immediately to Peter Scott, saying Robinette was quite wrong in claiming that over-population of elephants was the major problem. It was just this view which seven years ago had blinded us to a much greater threat, that man armed with modern weapons, if he should turn against elephants, could rapidly exterminate them.

Now the rising price of ivory had triggered just such a crisis, even to the extent that elephants living in areas of low human density such as parts of the northern districts of Kenya had been virtually exterminated.

I also pointed out to Peter that 'over-populated elephants' accounted for only about 10 per cent of the continental population. As for the Luangwa Valley, I feared it might already be at risk, given the way ivory poaching had progressed in East Africa, and I could see no case for culling there. In any event the Luangwa elephant population, one of the most important in Africa, had not been surveyed since 1973.

I thought the debate would die away, because whatever the situation might be in Southern Africa, there was no question that culling was now totally inappropriate for East Africa, where poaching was getting worse by the month. However, a year later Peter Scott was still mulling over the idea and in desperation I wrote to him again:

'We feel that the "cull or not to cull" debate is irrelevant to East Africa, with the possible exception of Ruaha National Park. People abroad do not seem to be aware of the suddenness and speed with which poachers can decimate previously "overcrowded" elephant sanctuaries. Elephant populations have fallen like nine-pins in the last five years, in particular those over which the debate raged, such as Murchison Falls, Queen Elizabeth and Tsavo National Parks. We are worried that by the time culling begins in Luangwa the elephant population may already have been decimated by poachers.'

Our view of the elephant's situation was now shaped by further surveys right across East Africa from the Kenya coast down to the great Selous. Since the programme began we had counted elephants in Serengeti, Ruaha, Tarangire, Meru and Tsavo. We had discovered that Serengeti itself was no longer the inviolate 'last wild place', for we had seen far too many carcasses. In the adjacent Masai Mara Reserve in Kenya the situation was even worse, and it looked as if many of the Mara elephants had fled across the border into Tanzania for safety. In Manyara the disease had run its course and the elephants were now secure, but across the lake in Tarangire I had encountered for the first time groups of dead elephants in Tanzania to yield bullets from heavy calibre rifles. The only other elephants to escape heavy punishment in Tanzania were in the south, in the Selous Game Reserve and Ruaha National Park, and I feared that even here it was only a matter of time before the poachers moved in. Already rumours abounded that the Somalis were heading south to look for new hunting grounds.

Further afield, responses had come pouring in from thirty-one African countries in reply to our questionnaire survey, and although counts were few our informants almost to a man reported that poaching had vastly increased. Rhodesia and South Africa were notable exceptions, and in Central African Republic (CAR) and Somalia we were told that the elephants were still leading tranquil lives, although this was soon to change. At this time, according to our sources, in twenty-one of the elephant-range states the species was decreasing.

Nevertheless, the old culling controversy lingered on. In 1978 Les Robinette burst into print with the ideas he had expressed the previous year. His article, entitled 'A Time for Sense not Sentiment on Culling the Game', was an extraordinary piece of work, classing the threat of overcrowded elephants within the national parks as the chief threat to the future of conservation. It was written as if none of the catastrophic poaching events of the past seven years had taken place, and it was backed up by none other than Dick Laws himself.

'For decades,' wrote Laws, 'the political authorities in East Africa have explained away their own very parochial failures by attributing the decline of elephant populations to poaching in the mistaken belief that the problem will evaporate once poaching is controlled. But the problem will not evaporate. The anaesthetic that envelopes it is wearing thin, and soon it will come to the full consciousness of all, that the increasing concentration of any species in arbitrarily restricted areas will result in over-population, habitat destruction, and local – perhaps even wholesale – extinction of that species.

'The question is this,' he continued. 'Should this species be allowed to find its own level in relentless competition with others of the world's limited land and resources, or should this species be brought into balance with the environment and the other species that inhabit it? Today this species is the elephant.'

This, coming from one of the most eminent scientists in the field, was a singularly ill-informed response. Whether he had been right or wrong in the late 1960s, how could Laws have failed to grasp the appalling significance of what had happened since his time in the parks? In Tsavo, the elephants had fallen by more than half. Aerial counts in Kenya now revealed more dead than live elephants. Yet here he was supporting the case for more culling, and dismissing fears about poaching as a parochial East African concern.

It was remarkable how these old Africa hands still had such an influence at the highest level, regardless of how much the true picture in the bush had changed.

Eventually the pressure to cull elephants in the devastated parks of East Africa died away, but those who had taken sides on the issue were furnished with a new cause that revolved around whether or not to ban the trade in ivory. Predictably the pro-cullers now became pro-trade, and the anti-cullers became anti-trade.

In our small IUCN African Elephant Specialist Group, Harvey Croze and I convened meetings in Nairobi from time to time, which were confined mostly to East African participants, unless we had visitors from abroad. We were asked by IUCN to discuss how the African elephant should be listed in the *Red Data Book*, their Domesday catalogue of endangered species, and in view of the preponderance of declining elephant populations, we classified the species as 'vulnerable'.

We also discussed the question of ivory-trade controls, and since the group was far-flung I consulted each member by post. The group had been chosen to represent all shades of opinion on the culling issue, and was now predictably divided. Some wanted a completely open, free market. Others wanted the ivory trade closed down. The issue was quite different from culling in that the policy of one country could affect the trade and the elephants in another. If the culling controversy had been fiercely debated it was nothing to what was to come on the ivory-trade issue.

In the meanwhile, in the aftermath of the Nairobi ivory stampede, Oria and I decided to visit Rhodesia where we were invited to attend the Fiftieth Anniversary of the Hwange National Park. After more than a decade of bush war there was no clear winner, and Ian Smith's minority white government was still trying to cling to power by setting up an 'Uncle Tom' black government under Bishop Abel Muzorewa.

The elephants were reportedly doing very well, and under the circumstances were certainly not adversely affected by Rhodesia's pro-culling philosophy. I was curious to learn more.

Touching down in Bulawayo, our eyes darted from the armoured car running full speed alongside the plane, to a lonely white soldier standing in the open, to more soldiers huddled under another plane and a family saying goodbye to a soldier son.

Inside the airport building young men with cropped hair and combat gear held their guns as they waited to embark. All looked peaceful, but precautions in case of a sudden attack were evident, with more armoured cars surrounding the parking area.

We left for Hwange in a small plane, to be warmly welcomed on arrival by sun-tanned wardens dressed in khaki. Three soldiers with a machine-gun mounted on a Chevy pick-up covered the exit. One warden, our host, a lean and sad-eyed man in his thirties, took us to a zebra-striped combie. He explained that he had just spent two hundred days on call during the past year as a result of the emergency. 'Even my children don't recognize me when I return home,' he said.

We entered the park in convoy, escorted by a strange assortment

of home-made armoured cars. Their bodies were V-shaped underneath to minimize land-mine blasts, with zigzag sides to deflect
rocket hits. Every so often, looking back down the line of vehicles,
I could see soldiers swivelling their machine-guns to face the bush
on either side.

The Hwange anniversary began with a festive air. Tables had
been set outside, laden with a generous spread of roast meats and
hams, vegetable dishes and every kind of pudding. Some guests
wore elegant city clothes but most were dressed in khaki shirts
and shorts. Waiters carrying trays of Rhodesian wines gravitated
among the crowd, while African ministers of Bishop Muzorewa's
government and their wives chatted amiably with white hunters
and farmers. Only a handful of non-Rhodesians including ourselves
were present. Around us, giving the whole occasion a strange sense
of unreality, stood park wardens carrying camouflaged weapons.
Mothers with babies sat on the grass next to Uzi sub-machine-guns.
We had been invited to a party in the middle of a war.

The discussions at this meeting were new to our ears. There was
a lively debate about whether or not professional hunters should be
allowed to shoot elephants in the national parks as an aid to culling.
This idea was vigorously resisted by the parks' people, and I was
struck by their deep commitment. However unsentimental they
might be about culling, which was an accepted way of management
in Rhodesia, they cared deeply about their wildlife.

Culling was, nevertheless, a major part of their programme.
Indeed, their whole conservation philosophy rested on the premise
that wildlife must pay its way or die. Teams operated every year
inside the parks, killing elephants; but, unlike the South Africans,
they preferred to use automatic rifles rather than dart guns.

Oria visited the 'baby pens' not far from where the symposium
was being held. Huddled together in three enclosures were forty
small elephants. Survivors of the cull, they were to be sold to zoos
and circuses in the USA and other countries. Two very tiny ones
were kept apart from the rest in a paddock of their own. One
immediately ran towards Oria, hoping to get some milk; but all
she could do was to give him her thumb which he sucked with his
soft pink tongue.

Oria wondered how much the shooting of their mothers had
affected them. She found it unbearable to think that they would
spend the rest of their lives isolated in concrete stables or in cramped

enclosures, with nothing more to do but to eat what was given to them at regular hours, play with their trunks, and weave back and forth until they died.

Later we were shown the aftermath of a cull – the meat of nearly four hundred elephants drying on low tables in the bush. The park staff did the shooting and wildlife contractors processed and marketed the products.

It was good business. There was no end to the uses which man's ingenuity could devise from the different parts of a dead elephant. Skin from the body, ears and feet was valuable, and could bring in anything up to $200 per elephant. Meat and fat were sold locally. The skin was used for table tops, and the softer belly skins and ears could be used for quality leather goods. Briefcases made of elephant skin fetched $175, and smaller scraps were used for shoes, bags or purses. The elephant feet became foot-stools or umbrella stands, and even the feet of baby elephants were made into pencil holders or cigar containers. The tusks belonged to the National Parks, and were sent to the ivory auctions in Salisbury. Only the bones, trunks and intestines were left in red heaps for the scavengers and flies.

Oria could not accept the arguments used in favour of culling. It was easy, she thought, for armchair ecologists to recommend shooting programmes for management purposes when they had never participated in a cull or studied elephants in the wild.

She opposed the killing of elephants in national parks as abhorrent. Shooting elephants in masses, especially whole families, she found repulsively cold-blooded, reminiscent of Auschwitz and Belsen. She could not erase from her mind the question – was it really necessary?

From my point of view I could see little alternative. However cold the perspective of the Rhodesian wildlife department seemed to Oria, their arguments made sound economic sense. The main point was that the elephants were effectively protected, and the only human predation was precisely controlled. Poaching of elephants for ivory at that time by Africans was virtually unknown, although there had been a few Europeans arrested for this crime. It seemed to me that at worst culling was a lesser evil than the uncontrolled massacres we had witnessed elsewhere and which still posed the greatest threat to the elephant.

Given a well-regulated offtake every year, the system maintained the habitat in a favourable condition for the elephants and other

animals. It protected the woodlands and avoided those large fluctuations in animal and plant numbers which, natural or not, tend
to alarm administrators.

Culling brought economic returns from the animal products, provided material for scientific research and blunted any criticism that
the Government was allowing animals to do what it had forbidden
human beings – namely to destroy habitats by over-exploitation.

Yet still I felt uncomfortable. By playing God, man was pushing these ecosystems and the elephant's way of life ever further
away from any natural state and I was afraid that the temptation
of self-perpetuating economic incentives might prove even more
irreversible than the habitat changes induced by elephants.

CHAPTER ELEVEN

IAIN: *The Second Avalanche*

1977–8, Johannesburg and Nairobi

T OWARDS the end of 1977 Oria and I found ourselves in front of a large audience in Johannesburg attending the First World Wilderness Congress. It was an illuminating occasion. Bill Conway from the New York Zoological Society was there to talk about vanishing tropical forests. Laurens Van Der Post spoke eloquently of the Kalahari bushmen and how they lived in harmony with the wilderness.

Finally the American writer, Robert Ardrey, got up to say his piece. 'I blame it all on God!' he thundered. 'God said to Adam: "Go forth, be fruitful, and multiply." Oh boy, did he ever multiply.' And so human increase was identified as the root of much misery.

Then it was my turn. I had plenty of slides, ending on a grisly succession of elephant carcasses taken on recent surveys. In the case of the African elephant I was not so much concerned with human population pressure as I was with the ivory trade which might finish the elephants even before man had overrun their habitats. 'In 1976,' I told the audience, 'all ivory leaving Africa may have come from anything between 100,000 and 400,000 elephants.'

This statement needs some explanation. I was confident of the lower limit and had reached it in this way. I had a good idea that the minimum level of exports from Africa was of the order of 1,000 tonnes a year. In addition, recent work in Tanzania on a batch of 43,000 tusks gave an average tusk weight of 4.8 kilos. To convert this to numbers of elephants I had to know the average number of tusks per elephant, which is not as obvious as it sounds, given that there are a number of one-tuskers in any population. The answer, furnished by Alan Rodgers, my biologist friend from the Selous, was 1.8 tusks per elephant. If these figures held true for the rest of Africa, then 1,000 tonnes of tusks was equivalent to approximately 115,000 dead elephants.

A figure of this order had been supported by Ian Parker who, as long ago as 1974, had told the American reporter, Karen Lerner, that probably between one hundred thousand and two hundred thousand elephants were exported annually from Africa as ivory. He told her he was quite confident that the minimum going out of Africa every year was equivalent to a hundred thousand dead elephants, and we knew from the trade figures that 1976 had been unprecedently high.

In putting forward an upper limit I knew I was sticking my neck out a long way. To arrive at this number I doubled the higher figure Parker had suggested back in 1974, since some of the key indicators such as the imports of ivory to Hong Kong – the largest single market – had doubled. But despite qualifications I had made, I realized I had a problem when I saw the newspapers. 'SCIENTIST SAYS UP TO 400,000 ELEPHANTS KILLED A YEAR,' screamed the headlines. My speech was widely reported, and several articles implied I had said the African elephant was in imminent danger of extinction, which was not true.

In any case the figures sparked off a furore among the United States conservation lobby. MONITOR, a Washington-based consortium of radical conservation groups, threatened to sue the Department of the Interior for negligence in protecting elephants, and launched a campaign to ban the import of all ivory into the USA. This was formally proposed by Californian Congressman Anthony Beilenson in a bill entitled, 'The African Elephant Bill'.

Congressional hearings were set in December 1977 to determine the status of the African Elephant as a potentially endangered species. Out of the blue, a marvellous opportunity had presented itself. If ever there was a chance of getting an ivory-trade study going, this was it.

The traders themselves were very worried. They knew that my mind was open on the possible self-regulation of the trade and one of them, George Wong, whom I had met in South Africa, offered me a first-class air-ticket to Washington, all expenses paid, so that I could 'present a fair picture', as he put it. In the event I did not avail myself of this intriguing offer as the Congressional Committee themselves paid for my ticket.

It was a great boost on the opening day of proceedings to hear from Oria in Nairobi that President Kenyatta had announced a ban on all trade in ivory to come into effect in the new year.

Kenyatta's decree was a revelation. I could scarcely believe my ears. What made him take that decision? Was it that the price of coffee had soared, providing more lucrative returns than ivory for the moment? Was it the power of the media, the word of the scientists or discreet persuasion through diplomatic channels that finally made some impression? We shall never know. But all those months of flying and counting and endless meetings suddenly seemed worthwhile. If Kenya led the way, maybe others would follow.

On the basis of data which I provided, the elephant was moved on to the threatened list which, the US Fish and Wildlife Service assured me, would give them all the flexibility they needed to tighten controls and even impose a moratorium if necessary.

One of the chief officials, anxious to appease his attackers, asked me what project he could support that would do most to help the elephants. I told him we were still making policy in an abyss of ignorance about the workings of the ivory trade, and he snapped at the idea like a hungry fish taking a fly. 'Get me the evidence, Iain,' he said, 'I don't want to know how you do it; just get it.'

I was interested in the idea that perhaps the traders and carvers might have the ability to regulate themselves. The theory was that they would not wish to destroy the resource on which they depended. I also wanted to discover the particular points within the trade where control would be practical and effective. Most of all I wanted to know how we could combat the illegal traders.

My initial suggestion to WWF that Ian Parker should carry out this part of my study had been blocked somewhere within the system during the IUCN review. He had, however, exposed the Kenya ivory trade and I was convinced he was the right man for the job.

I had already started gathering ivory data. The records which David Sheldrick had given me for Tsavo would give us insights on national park populations, and my assistant, Michael Davitz, a very bright New Yorker, had already spent several weeks in Dar es Salaam, scrutinizing data from over two hundred tonnes of ivory that had passed through the Ivory Room between 1971 and 1977.

In both these sets of data the mean tusk weight had dropped ominously from around ten kilogrammes to less than five kilogrammes. The most likely cause was the selective killing of elephants with big ivory, causing them to become rarer in the population. The Tanzania ivory had also fallen below an average of five kilogrammes. The statistics were yet another indirect warning of the growing seriousness of the elephant situation.

It took just two days to get the proposal back to the US Fish and Wildlife Service, but IUCN insisted that they should manage the contract and it took them a further six months to finalize. I found the delay intensely frustrating. There was a growing urgency to get these studies under way. Parker wrote to me in June 1978 that some ivory had crossed the $120 per kilo mark. He thought this might be a direct response to pressures to get the trade closed. Clearly, he said, traders believed very strongly that an ivory ban would be ineffective and difficulties in supply would drive the value up. He ended with a sinister warning: 'Apparently the second avalanche of hunting is now on its way down the slopes . . . the ivory study should get under way now, when it has a chance of influencing events, rather than many thousands of elephant deaths later, when it will be no more than an historical document to IUCN's immortal fame.'

IUCN accountants fiddled with the details until eventually David Munro, the director-general himself, intervened and pushed it through. The contract was signed and I commissioned Parker to follow the ivory trail. The initial idea had been to keep the study under cover, but it was already open knowledge. In any case, we would soon need to contact the ivory traders. Parker set out armed with data I had collected and introductions to our expanding network of contacts across Africa. He would start in South Africa and Europe, and later go to the Far East. The study had taken a great deal of time and patience to launch, but at last it was on its way.

*

In between the endless round of meetings and reports, Oria and I picked up the threads of our domestic lives as best we could. While I had been giving my testimony to the Congressional Committee in Washington, Oria had driven back to the farm in Naivasha to discover that her mother had suffered a bad fall and broken her leg.

In hospital they did the best they could but it was no use. Finally, weak and disorientated, she was allowed to return once more to the farm, where she died, aged eighty-four. She was buried next to Oria's father.

The death of Oria's mother had come in the middle of Wildlife Awareness Week, a week of events we had organized to celebrate the ivory embargo announced by President Kenyatta and the continued existence of wildlife symbolized by the elephant. The French Cultural Centre put the top floor of their building in Nairobi at our disposal, rent free for a year, and it became the centre for elephant people from all over Africa; a place where ambassadors organized dinners to meet government officials in a friendly atmosphere.

I had returned from Washington in time to witness with amazement and delight the spontaneous demonstrations of young people carrying placards through the streets of Nairobi, protesting at the killing of elephants and calling for the closure of the curio shops.

Margaret Kenyatta, the president's eldest daughter, whom we had both met, had been invited to open the week's celebrations and turned up wearing ivory bangles. I asked her not to wear them, which provoked an extraordinary outburst. 'You conservationists are the ones who say bad things about my father,' she shouted. It was a situation where discretion was the better part of valour and I spent the rest of the afternoon writing a letter of apology and looking for flowers to send her.

Meanwhile, the daunting task of obtaining an inventory of Africa's elephants continued. Earlier in 1978 I had organized a new elephant count in Tsavo which showed there were still twenty thousand left out of the thirty-five thousand animals counted in 1974.

The park was green and the trees were regenerating. Willem Wijngaarden, a Dutch soil scientist working in Tsavo, delivered a seminar to a small group. No one important turned up, but his results, known to only a few scientists, showed that Sheldrick was vindicated in his *laissez-faire* strategy.

By now the president's ivory embargo seemed to be having an effect. Kenya was changing from a frontier country of hunting and adventure to a wiser and more mature nation. Elephants were still being poached but they were dying in fewer numbers.

A few months later, in August, Kenyatta himself died. It was the end of an era, both for the nation and for those who had been implicated in the ivory racket. Now, with Daniel arap Moi, the new President, sworn in, we could only wonder what the future would bring.

By the end of the year (1978) Ian Parker's study was coming along well with good interim reports delivered punctiliously. Step by step he made contact with the traders and acquired knowledge of how the trade worked. This was new ground never covered before, and he came back flushed with enthusiasm about each fresh revelation. Up until then much had been speculation. Now, with the new bridges he was building, I looked forward one day to sitting down with the traders to discuss the idea of self-policing. I thought Parker with his excellent contacts would be my ambassador.

He would give them a sympathetic, but critical, hearing and find out if they had the will or the ability to regulate themselves. The logic seemed convincing. Who would want to destroy their own livelihood by over-exploiting the source of their income?

As insights developed, it became plain that we knew nothing about the ivory trade in Francophone Africa. What was the latest situation in Zaire? Why had ivory exports from the Central African Empire into Hong Kong doubled in recent years and who were the people behind the mysterious stamp of 'La Couronne' found on so many ivory certificates? Although we assumed that the customs records would be likely to be highly inaccurate, what would they reveal? Finally, how did the elephants fare all the way from Zaire to their furthest range in Mauritania. To the world at large this was still Conrad's heart of darkness, the great unknown. There was only one way to find out what was happening there. With Oria as my interpreter and the full support of the US foreign service, we decided to visit Central and West Africa, to fill in the missing gaps.

PART III

The Trail West

'THERE was still in Africa a marvellous,
irresistible freedom. Only it belonged
to the past, not to the future. Soon
it will go. There'll no longer be herds
swirling against the forests and crushing
them in their passage. The elephants were the
last individuals'

Romain Gary,
Roots of Heaven,
1958

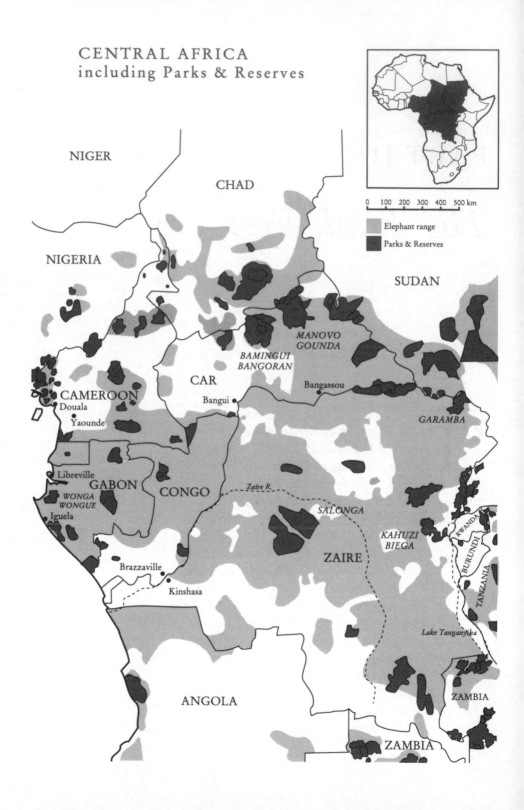

CENTRAL AFRICA
including Parks & Reserves

NIGER

CHAD

NIGERIA

SUDAN

0 100 200 300 400 500 km

Elephant range

Parks & Reserves

MANOVO GOUNDA

BAMINGUI BANGORAN

CAMEROON

CAR

Bangassou

Douala

Bangui

GARAMBA

Yaounde

Libreville

GABON

CONGO

Zaire R.

WONGA WONGUE

SALONGA

KAHUZI BIEGA

RWANDA

Iguela

ZAIRE

BURUNDI

Brazzaville

TANZANIA

Kinshasa

Lake Tanganyika

ANGOLA

ZAMBIA

ZAMBIA

CHAPTER TWELVE

ORIA: *Footprints in the Sand*

1979, Zaire, Senegal, Mauritania

THE sun was already sinking towards the knuckled summits of the Ngong Hills as we left our Nairobi office. All day we had been preparing for an expedition. Now, armed with maps, questionnaires and bundles of files, we were on our way towards that setting sun, 3,800 miles from Nairobi to the other side of Africa. Once more we were on the ivory trail, on a quest that would take us from Zaire to the Sahara where, it was rumoured, a few elephants still lived like fugitives among the dunes of Mauritania.

For centuries ivory had been pouring out of the forests of West and Central Africa. We wondered how many elephants had been killed down the years to keep the rivers of tusks flowing, and wanted to know how strong the trade was today. While Ian Parker was in Hong Kong examining the incoming ivory records, we would be looking at the outgoing ivory from ten francophone countries in the west, including Bokassa's Central African Empire and Mobutu's near-bankrupt Zaire. One of the key people helping our investigation was in Kinshasa, the capital of Zaire, where we would stop briefly *en route* to the threshold of the Sahara.

It was to Timbuktu, to the ancient caravan trading place in the desert, that we were eventually heading in search of the elephants of the dunes. A French teacher, Bruno Lamarche, had written in answer to our questionnaires, claiming knowledge of their whereabouts. This was the first we had heard of elephants still roaming in the desert. A French scientist had informed us that tracks had been seen in Mauritania some ten years ago; but Lamarche, who was living in Mali, had seen the elephants just a short while ago and would be happy to take us there. If they were still alive they would be the northernmost elephants in Africa.

For years Zaire had been the biggest source of ivory in Africa. It was also one of the first signatories of the CITES treaty, and would have to occupy a central role in any attempt to control the international trade. When answers to our first elephant questionnaires had begun to come in they included a report from Zaire by Adrien de Schryver. It was through him that we discovered that an illegal ivory network was operating openly in eastern Zaire as if it were above the law. This was the first evidence we had that the rot had set in beyond East Africa. Little did we imagine the extent to which the Zaire ivory connection would continue to flourish, nor that one day people calling themselves conservationists would suggest that poaching in Zaire was not a threat to the elephants.

Anyone arriving in Zaire for the first time is put to a survival test at Kinshasa Airport. The heat clings like a damp hot towel. On this occasion, no sooner were we inside the building than we were plunged into semi-darkness by one of Kinshasa's regular power cuts. At once a wall of humanity rushed across to the silent conveyor belt and we rushed with it, trying to grab our bags before they disappeared for ever.

At dinner next day in the private house of Bepo Eskanazi, an old-time Swiss businessman, the floodgates of information began to open. Only a week before our arrival a consignment of 175 tusks had been seized in Paris, said one of the guests sitting opposite us at the table. It had been dispatched to a company called 'France Croco', he told us. 'Corruption here is so rife that it could only have been some kind of double-cross which led to its exposure,' Bepo said. Using his knife like an elongated finger to make a point, he explained how Zaire's society was split into two segments. 'On the one side, the poverty-stricken masses; on the other, the suction pumps who take everything. But now,' our host assured us, 'the Army are shooting buffalo and elephants in the north for meat and ivory.'

The US Embassy was our next port of call. They helped us to identify the local hierarchy and to find a working telephone. Then, armed with a folder of introductions, we were ready to tackle the first link in the chain. The director of the Institute for Nature Conservation, the organization responsible for wildlife and national parks, was not around, but we managed to track down his boss, Citoyen Mwangaya Bukuku, the permanent secretary. The interview turned out to be friendly but uninformative. He was sorry that the questionnaires we had sent to him had been lost, he said, but he was anxious to know what we might say about Zaire. He agreed that ivory had always given problems, but the only point he conceded was to confirm that there had been heavy slaughter of elephants in the north – a story which was to be repeated time and again.

His department had provided only certain individuals with permits for the legal export of ivory, he assured us, but none had been issued since last year. We asked him if we could see an example, but he said the certificates were locked in a safe and the responsible person had gone away with the key. Then Citoyen Mwangaya called his driver to take us to our next appointment and promised to show us the ivory permits when we returned.

As we passed the high-rise buildings of Kinshasa, the chic cafés, the dress shops and restaurants indistinguishable from those in Brussels, we wondered how it was that the country was bankrupt. But the driver, a quiet man with a soft voice, told us that he had not eaten meat for so long that he had forgotten the taste.

How different life was for the fortunate few at the top. One of the latest fads among the high-up officials and the select group close to the president was to match their Mercedes cars to the colour of their suits, and drive over the few remaining pot-holed miles of roads along the edge of the huge, sluggish brown river once called the Congo.

Dakar, the capital of Senegal, was the next stop on the trail west. It is an extraordinary city; an exotic blend of French colonial elegance and raw African colour; its markets filled with sacks of indigo and gum arabica; its streets thronged with vendors who swish past in yards of bright cottons, balancing baskets piled with mangoes, paw paws and bananas on their heads.

Dakar was the earliest possession of the French in Africa, and their rule eventually encompassed an area larger than the whole

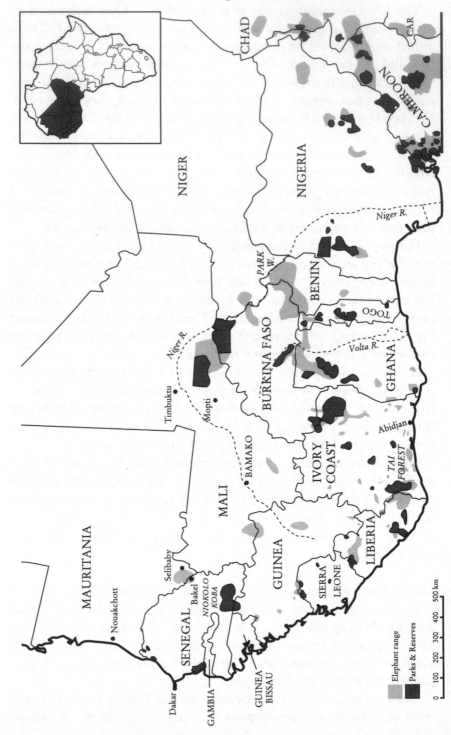

WEST AFRICA including Parks & Reserves

CHAD

CAR

CAMEROON

NIGER

NIGERIA

Niger R.

PARK W.

BENIN

TOGO

Volta R.

BURKINA FASO

GHANA

Niger R.

Timbuktu

Mopti

Abidjan

IVORY COAST

TAI FOREST

BAMAKO

MALI

LIBERIA

Selibaby

GUINEA

SIERRA LEONE

MAURITANIA

Nouakchott

Bakel

NIOKOLO KOBA

SENEGAL

Dakar

GAMBIA

GUINEA BISSAU

500 km

Elephant range

Parks & Reserves

0 100 200 300 400 500

of Europe, containing a vast proportion of the elephants' total continental range. Like so many of Africa's invaders they exported everything that was valuable, including ivory. French African colonial archives are all centralized in Dakar, and we found heaps of ivory records in dusty files, wrapped in yellowed paper and tied with ribbons, kept in the base of 'Le Building Administratif'. Here, in cold statistics and the unemotional language of commerce, the whole tragic tale of over-exploitation in Central Africa was laid bare.

It became clear on studying the figures that the cycle of ivory overexploitation had already happened in the early twentieth century before collapsing between the wars. It was not until the mid-1970s in Central Africa that ivory exports suddenly shot up again, from a few tonnes to over two hundred tonnes per year. This resurgence coincided with the huge increase in price and confirmed our fears that the ivory boom was not just an isolated Kenyan phenomenon.

In Dakar we met some of the traders. El'Hadji Ngore had a shop there and was quite happy to talk about anything. His brother Omar lived in Abidjan, the capital of the Ivory Coast, and traded much ivory from the boot of his Peugeot. The Senegalese merchants and ivory traders are well known across Africa, he told us.

While El'Hadji was talking he pulled tusk after tusk out of a bag and admitted that it was all illegal. 'I can send these anywhere you want,' he said. 'I know the way; it's just a question of some money here and there.' He then offered us a long, smooth and slender cyclotis tusk – typical forest-elephant ivory, weighing 3.5 kilos – which he was willing to sell for as little as $245. The price dropped as quickly as the minutes ticked by. Clearly CITES counted for nothing here; for although Senegal had signed the treaty, neither the trader nor the French customs official whom we had spoken to earlier had ever heard of it.

Senegal still had its four hundred elephants and some other wild animals only because Leopold Senghor, the poet president, had stepped in at the last hour in 1966 and saved them from extinction. Had he not done so, every last animal would have been killed.

In the south a small national park, Niokolo Koba, was to be created in an area where it was unsafe for people to live due to the eye disease, *onchocerciasis*, or river blindness. The making of the park was almost entirely due to the foresight of the President, and he chose a stocky young Frenchman called André Dupuy to carry out his wishes. Coming out of the desert after six years as a commanding officer in the French Foreign Legion, Dupuy was given sixteen men and asked to set up a national parks system for Senegal – a task he carried out with military discipline and organization. With his baggy desert trousers and Foreign Legion crew-cut, Dupuy was tough and talked tough. With Moussa Mane, his Senegalese deputy, he built up an army of three hundred and fifty trained men, making Niokolo Koba one of the best-protected parks in Africa at that time. 'Senegal is not a country for wildlife; it is a country of people, and this is all that is left here,' André had told us when we met him in Dakar. He had been the first person to write and tell us about the last elephants in north-west Africa.

Although his elephants had fewer problems than the harassed remnants elsewhere, Dupuy could never relax his vigilance. Armed men coming from the Polisario war in nearby Mauritania had started shooting elephants in the park. Even though their tusks were not large, the price of ivory had already encouraged an upsurge in killing as poachers and traders looked with increasingly envious eyes towards the haven of Niokolo Koba.

When we told Dupuy what had happened to the elephants in Kenya, Uganda and Tanzania, he could not believe us. But within two years of our visit, after President Senghor had stepped down and handed over to his prime minister, men with automatic weapons entered the park to take the ivory, and not even Dupuy and his well-organized force could save the president's elephants. By 1985 Niokolo's precious herds were reduced to a couple of dozen animals, a heart-broken Dupuy informed us. And yet, miraculously, a relict population of elephants still wandered freely across the Senegalese border with Mauritania. 'They cross the Senegal River regularly,' said Dupuy. But he was worried for their future. Plans for intensive development of the Senegal river banks now threatened even this last precarious refuge.

Elephants had also been spotted a few years back in Mauritania's Assaba Mountains, an American told us. He had heard that they were living at the very top now, away from people, and where food and water were available. All the French hunters we met referred to them as very small elephants, and some scientists speculated that they could belong to a sub-species, *Loxodonta africana pharoensis*. Perhaps these very animals were descended from the elephants described by Pliny nearly two thousand years ago, which earlier still had been used by Hannibal to cross the Alps.

Although the cool months for desert crossings were over it was still possible for us to reach St Louis and take the main road over the Mauritanian border to Nouakchott. From there we could drive eastwards along a good desert road to Kiffa; but then a sudden coup in Nouakchott was announced, and no car hire agency would allow us to go there. Our only chance was to change our route towards Bakel, on the Senegal River, and try to get through from there. Then – with good guides and a little luck – we might be able to find the last tracks of the northernmost elephants in Africa.

Driving out of Dakar was a nightmare. For hour after hour we wove our way between huge, crawling lorries, horse-drawn carts and wandering donkeys, until the city was behind us and the sand began. Away from the sea breeze, dust hung in the air and the sun beat down even more fiercely in the stifling heat.

Villages of mud-brick houses set under huge baobab trees broke the monotony. Pyramids of peanuts and paw paws lined the roadsides, and herdsmen in voluminous robes followed their sheep and cattle through the arid Sahelian bush. Sometimes we passed white horses with red-hennaed tails pulling carts of happy children; but in the distance beyond there was not a wild animal to be seen.

Bakel was motionless when we arrived, its mosques and market drugged with heat, the leaves of its riverside trees hanging limp. There to our dismay we learned that the only ferry had been sunk five years ago. If we wanted to get into Mauritania we would have to cross by canoe and find transport on the other side. In the market-place, men shook their heads, but said we should speak to 'The Libanais'.

The Lebanese trader in his one-roomed store told us he had a cousin in Selibaby, forty kilometres away across the river. He usually came to Bakel once a week to collect provisions. If he agreed to take us to Selibaby we might be able to hire a car there, or find a desert truck that would take us to Kiffa. In any case, even if the ferry had been working, he doubted very much that we would have been able to get there in the Peugeot as the hot sands and the many drifts were practically impassable at this time of the year. In the meantime, since we were *des Anglais*, we should talk to an American couple working for the Peace Corps.

There was nowhere to stay in Bakel, but maybe they could help. Then, while waiting for transport, we could drive to Matam and look for the elephants that crossed the river. It all sounded simple and logical – and quite insane. But go we did. The Americans gave us their water bottles and wished us good luck.

By midday the temperature was over 50°C. At each village we asked if there were any elephants. Very few foreigners, known locally as *toubabs*, had ever passed that way and our presence never failed to attract a crowd. Many of the men had worked in France, and some of them spoke French. They had all heard of the elephants, but none had been seen for a long time.

Every village had its mosque and its square, and the chiefs and elders, always beautifully dressed, came out and sat with us under the biggest, shadiest tree. Away from the shade, the heat rose like an open furnace. By now even the water in our flasks was hot and our energy was draining away as fast as our optimism. But at last one man was brought to us, a Mauritanian, who had seen elephants near Lobali, not too far away. Later that day our hopes rose still higher when we passed a horseman caparisoned like some eighteenth-century brigand, who told us he had seen elephants three times while hunting on the way to Lobali.

When we finally reached Lobali in late afternoon an excited crowd gathered as the *chef du village* emerged from his house to speak to us. We stood in the midst of a great surge of bright-eyed children who stared at us with undisguised curiosity. It was, of course, a man's right to have as many children as God gave him; but how were the elephants going to survive if the human population continued to multiply in every village? Already the trees were going fast, chopped down to make charcoal, the desert cooking fuel.

There exists on the edge of the desert a balance so delicate that the slightest change can have disastrous effects. The people living there are so perfectly tuned to the desert that their limbs practically hum when they walk on the boiling sands in their flowing robes. Like the desert addax antelope or the Dorcas gazelle, their bodies regulate the temperature and provide just the necessary amount of energy. The water they drink, the food they eat, the houses they live in are all tempered for their life in the sands. But now that the pressures of the twentieth-century had invaded their world it would never be the same again. As the people grew more numerous there would come a time when the fragile soils of Africa could no longer support them.

In some countries that breaking point had already been reached.

'The elephants come here every month for a few days, and we chase them off our millet,' the chief of the village told us. One man had counted four elephants; another had seen a group of fourteen with two small ones. 'But to see them,' they all told us, pointing excitedly down the road, 'you must go quickly to Gourel Dra. It's only two kilometres away. There they come every evening.'

We reached Gourel Dra just as the sun was setting. The village head man took us down to the river and pointed to the water's edge. There were tracks but they were old. This was where the elephants crossed over from Mauritania to raid the village crops, he said. There were not many, perhaps only twenty, and they ran away when people shouted at them. They came down from Harr and Testai when it got dry, following the valley to the river.

It would have been too much of a coincidence to have seen them; they had returned to Mauritania and we would have to find them there.

The Lebanese trader's cousin failed to reach Bakel, so early next morning while it was still cool we crossed the river in a small canoe and walked to a huge tree where people sat among the jutting roots, and asked them about a vehicle. A young man with a Land-Rover was willing to take us to Selibaby for $100. The clutch was gone, the gears worked back to front and there were no brakes at all; but at least it was a vehicle.

It was only nine o'clock and already the heat penetrated the skin like hot pins. The scenery was completely different from Senegal, with grass and trees and cattle near the river; but as we left the water and headed towards the dunes the landscape reverted to straggly bush with erosion gullies cut into the pink earth. We drove at high speed through sand as thick and soft as porridge. Twice the car just stopped, but nothing seemed to surprise our driver. He understood the eccentricities of his decrepit vehicle and knew how to fix it.

While he poked his head under the bonnet and stared at the smoking engine, we sought the shade of a dead tree. Half an hour went by. A man with a donkey passed us without a glance, and slowly disappeared over a dune. As the sun rose higher we drank from a goat-skin water bag. Suddenly the engine started and we jumped back into the car, tying up our doors with a piece of rope, and drove on in a cloud of dust across the hot red sands of Mauritania.

It was midday when we saw the village of Selibaby shimmering in the distance. Our driver took us through the main street, with curious crowds on either side as if we were a royal procession. Finally we rolled to a halt outside the Lebanese cousin's shop at one end of the vast village square. The shopkeeper's name was Hassan Chaitou and he seemed disconcerted by our arrival.

'There is no place here where you can stay or eat,' he said as we walked inside. Stunned and silenced, we stood and stared with red, sweating faces. 'You must go to the police this afternoon,' he continued. 'You are in Mauritania now.' But after a few minutes' conversation with our driver his tone changed and he offered us food, iced water and his home to rest in. Chaitou's wife, a good-looking young woman with a mane of black hair, laid the table with plates of delicious Lebanese food. 'There is a house you can stay in,' she told us. 'It belongs to the Peace Corps but no one has been there for a year. You must ask the préfet.'

The Préfet de Police was a pale man, a Moor. 'There has just been a coup in Nouakchott,' he said. 'Four ministers have been imprisoned – all powerful army people.' We already knew about the coup but kept our mouths shut. We presented our letters of introduction and explained our mission. On the wall behind the préfet's head were bloodstains, and we wondered how they had got there.

The préfet stamped our passports and took us to the governor, a tall black man immaculately dressed in black *surwals* and khaki shirt with sandalled feet. 'You will dine with me tonight,' the governor commanded. Then, having left him our letters, we were shown to the simple, but clean, house where we were to stay.

Towards sunset the great square came alive with Tuaregs dressed in blue cloth. Even their skins were blue as the sun fell like a glowing aureole upon the sand and the cooling air caressed the skin like feathers. The wail of evening prayers drifted from the mosque and mingled with plaintive Arab love songs emanating from the transistor radios of the governor's guards.

Later that evening we sat on a carpet spread with cushions outside the governor's residence, sipping cold tea with goat's milk, the cool air blowing from the desert and the glowing moon above us. A bowl was brought by a young man in folded *surwals*, with a pitcher and towel, who poured water over our hands before eating.

Then a big basin of stewed meat and couscous was placed before us.

'You cannot travel to the Assaba Mountains,' the governor told us, delicately scooping up a mouthful of couscous with the tips of his fingers. 'You are not desert people. It is too hot, you will die.' The young man came round and poured hot, bitter green tea, served three times in small cups, as is the custom.

During the *grande sécheresse*, the great drought of the early 1960s which had killed thousands of nomads and their cattle, the governor explained, people had moved into the Assaba Mountains in a desperate search for fodder and had cut down all the trees. 'There might be some elephants left at the very top,' he said, 'but you cannot go there.'

It was no use arguing. There was a pause, and we sat in silence while the moon cast its brilliant silver light across the square. 'We would like to keep elephants in our country,' the governor continued, sitting cross-legged in his long white robe. 'But there are too many people; they are poor and this is a hard country to survive in. You will see. Tomorrow I will give you one of my cars and some guides to take you to the elephants at Harr. It is not far from here.'

The governor was right. We could not reach Assaba now. It was too late in the year, everyone told us. But at least we might find the elephants that had come from Gourel Dra.

Along the windswept track to Harr, in a valley of small acacias, we found what we had travelled so far to see: the prints of a lone elephant bull, preserved in the sun-baked mud. He must have passed through only a couple of months ago, when it had rained. The acacias were being decapitated to feed the goats. Our guide laughed. 'The goats must eat today,' he said. 'Tomorrow, God will provide.'

The arrival of *toubabs* was a great event for the people of Harr. The whole village crowded around us as we talked to the chief, who was dressed in yellow. He was too old to talk by himself, so he called his son, Saumare Youssif, the school teacher, who led us to the conference house of the elders.

There the chief took his place among twenty elders draped like Romans in robes of many colours, some wearing turbans and others with small cotton hats. Both Saumare and his father spoke French. Like thousands of Africans in this part of the world they had been recruited into the French army. Saumare had fought at Dien Bien

Phu, as had Jean Bedel Bokassa, now the self-appointed Emperor of the Central African Empire. Saumare had been wounded by a Soviet napalm bomb and had gone to recuperate in Hanoi, he told us. There, he had ridden an elephant.

The chief spoke and his son interpreted for us, and the crowd pushed closer to listen. He thought we were hunters. He had never met white people who were interested in elephants but did not want to shoot them. 'The elephants come here to eat the millet,' he said. 'They eat everything. They come when it rains and they chase the people. We light fires and we beat tom-toms, and the elephants go away.

'They were here four months ago,' he continued. 'If you want to see them you must come back to Harr next November.'

When the meeting was over the old man invited us to rest in his house until the hot hours had passed. Like all the desert houses its walls were made of packed sand, painted in earthy reds and blues. In the shade stood a huge calabash of water which was kept cold by the evaporation on its smooth clay surface.

'It would be nice to have tame elephants here, if a reserve could be made,' the old man said, holding our hands and wishing us a safe return. It was our turn to speak now, but what could we say to the chief and his son about the future? Conservation was a word which had been heard on the radio, but in reality it meant little to these people of the desert. As for the elephants, it seemed unlikely that they would survive for much longer. Now that their last refuge in the Assaba Mountains had been invaded there was nowhere left for them to run, and so little to eat that in desperation they had become crop raiders. In a land where even the people were struggling to live, it was clear that these last desert elephants had reached the end of the trail.

CHAPTER THIRTEEN

ORIA: *Elephants of the Sahel*

1979, Mali

TIMBUKTU – even the name sounds like a drumbeat from the depths of the African desert, conjuring up visions of veiled Tuaregs, of trembling heat and slow processions of plodding camels strung out across an infinity of dunes. Few people from the West visit Timbuktu; but we had a rendezvous there with Bruno Lamarche.

The only way to get there was via Bamako, the capital of Mali, and continue on one of the local flights. Air Mali off-loaded us in the dusty furnace of Mopti, a busy town astride the great trans-Saharan routes on the edge of the Niger River; but reports of a big sandstorm up-country prevented us continuing to Timbuktu.

'When is the next flight?' we asked.

'When the sandstorm subsides,' the airport official replied.

'And when will that be?'

He shrugged as little flurries of sand swirled across the floor. 'Maybe three days; maybe a week.'

With our bags around us, we sat and sweated in the stifling heat of the shed-like waiting-room, wondering what to do.

In April 1828 a Frenchman, René Caille, became the first European to see the legendary city of Timbuktu and come back alive. In those days, even so far north, elephants were still abundant in the arid Sahel. 'Elephants can be seen everywhere,' he wrote, 'and I can see many good-sized elephant tusks. My host tells me that he can buy plenty in Timbuktu. They are brought in by tribesmen: the Tuaregs, Sourgous, Kissours and the Domans who live on the river's edge. They do not hunt elephants with guns but set out traps; I so regret not having witnessed such an event.'

As early as AD 1100, a seasonal camp for nomads had been established at Timbuktu, where the River Niger pushes through swamps and sand on its way down to the Atlantic. Within this immense wilderness of marshes, dunes and Sahelian vegetation the elephants migrated, adapted and survived. The centuries passed. Empires rose and fell and still the elephants roamed across these vast lands of the Niger, though in ever-decreasing numbers as invasions, hunts and wars took their toll.

By the 1920s most of Mali's elephants had been killed, and by 1930 the big herds of West African elephants were finished. Whatever large herds survived in Mali now huddled together in a vast, shallow depression known as the Gourma, which they shared with the pastoralists. Yet even here they were pursued from time to time by the Bozo people, fishermen of the Niger, who hunted them with harpoons for their meat.

By the time we arrived in Mali the elephants of the Gourma had shrunk to about five hundred, sharing their food and water with 100,000 nomadic Tuaregs and Pheuls and as many as 400,000 head of livestock. During the last two decades the advance of the desert had forced both man and wildlife to adapt to increasingly harsh conditions as lakes and wells dried up. Yet somehow the Gourma elephants continued to co-exist peacefully with the pastoralists. The waterholes were shared, with the cattle drinking by day and the elephants by night.

It was these elephants as much as Bruno Lamarche which had brought us to Mali in the first place. By air the Gourma was not far away; but we were stranded in Mopti and had no idea of how to contact Bruno to inform him of our plight. Two Frenchmen were drinking Perrier at a table near by, with a Malian dressed in the most exquisite saffron embroidered mantle. A small aircraft was parked outside. It turned out that they were pilots, and when we introduced ourselves and explained our mission, one of them happened to be a good friend of Bruno's. He was a big man with a strong southern French accent. His name was Pierre Vernet, an entrepreneur and hunter who had lived in Mali for more than thirty years. 'Don't worry,' he said. 'Lamarche is in Bamako. I saw him this morning, and I will send him a radio message this evening. He will be here tomorrow evening.'

We discovered that Pierre and Bruno had flown many hours together counting elephants. He was eager to help and was very keen that something should be done for these elephants of the Gourma. 'If you like, I can fly you to the Gourma today,' he offered. 'The weather is so bad further north, we will probably stay here now.'

We leapt at the chance and Pierre flew us over the dry, wind-blown expanse of more than twenty thousand square kilometres which the Malian government had set aside in 1959 as *La Reserve des Elephants*. We scanned the shimmering distance, hoping to find a group of elephants he had recently spotted. 'During the dry season,' he shouted over the roar of the engine, 'they join up to form four distinctive groups. The two big groups have approximately two hundred elephants each, with two smaller herds of fifty to one hundred.' We imagined them standing like huge stone monuments on the dry pink earth, but saw only a burning emptiness.

As we flew lower we could see the familiar big round footprints of elephants among the multiple tracks of cattle and camels, criss-crossing the red sand. We landed beside a well-used elephant trail and walked for a mile in the hot wind until we found fresh elephant droppings. Complete silence accompanied us, with only the scrape of our shoes on the sand and the hiss of the wind in the stunted scrub. The ground was like concrete, with not a blade of grass, and the elephants had been surviving by browsing on trees and shrubs and eating the bark. Like Namibian desert elephants they caused little damage to the trees they fed on, as if they knew that this was all they had.

Pierre had hunted here many times. A couple of years back, he and a friend had pursued the elephants in Land-Rovers until they managed to isolate a bull from the herd and finally shot it after a chase of many kilometres. 'Now I don't hunt any more,' he told us. 'Hunting has been closed for two years and my only concern is how to preserve the elephants from extinction.'

In January and February all the elephants massed together in the marshes at Banzena, sometimes five hundred strong. That was when the babies were born, said Pierre. Then they divided up again in their groups and went their separate ways. But although we followed the trail in a wide circle for ten kilometres and afterwards flew for well over an hour and a half, there was not an elephant to be seen.

Flying back with the wind blowing a murky haze of sand far up into the sky, we could just distinguish the olive gleaming coils of the Niger River, the single great artery that kept this land alive.

Lamarche was waiting for us when we landed back at Mopti. He had arrived in a Land-Rover filled with plastic water containers. Packets of powdered soup and dates – his main food – were scattered on the dashboard. A small, thin man with a sensitive, bespectacled face, he wore his hair plaited into one long pigtail. He had spent many years following the Gourma elephants. Travelling by camel with Tuaregs who knew the desert, he had wandered far and wide to understand how animals could live in the barren thirstlands. We talked late into the night, sipping iced mint and Pernod, making plans, taking notes and comparing figures around a table under a fan at a roadside motel.

We knew the Sahel had suffered a terrible drought in 1973 and 1974 and thousands of people and cattle had starved; but we wondered if the elephants' knowledge of the desert and their adaption to extreme conditions had allowed them to survive where others had not. As far as Bruno knew, the only deaths had been caused by European tourists who had chased the elephants for three days to take photographs without allowing them to approach one of the lakes to drink. As a result more than twenty babies died of thirst.

'Even though it is called *La Reserve des Elephants*, there is no government protection in the Gourma area,' Bruno explained. Elephants had been hunted there for hundreds of years and even now about thirty elephants were killed every year by wealthy and influential people from Mopti and Bamako. 'The Lebanese pharmacist in Mopti is one of them,' he told us.

The words of Monsieur Sanogo, Mali's director of *Eaux et Forets*, rang in our ears. 'Mali is a "macho" society where hunting proves your manhood,' he told us in Bamako. 'Hunting is in the mentality of the people and two million people are hunters. In Mali, game belongs to everyone.'

Among the Tuaregs there had been a long tradition of hunting elephants on horseback in the past. Usually they would wait for the elephants to come out into open country and single out an animal from the herd, which they would spear from horseback. Then, with all the speed that a horse could run, they would chase their quarry until it collapsed from exhaustion and loss of blood. Yet then, as now, the nomads never touched the meat. In the old days the Tuaregs took only the tusks and some hide to make tough desert sandals; and even today in the Gourma, elephants are killed only for ivory, although some tribes-people will eat the meat of a carcass left by the ivory hunters.

Most Europeans abided by the hunting ban, said Bruno, but people from Mopti and Bamako still poached for the hell of it. They came in their air-conditioned Range Rovers and sometimes chased the elephants for fifty kilometres. It would have been easy to control the poaching, since there is only one road into the Gourma from Mopti and Bamako; but as Bruno said: 'What can three guards do when there is no gate for control and only a bicycle and two clapped-out mopeds between them?'

With so little protection it was a miracle that there were any elephants at all in the Gourma. Only the remoteness of the terrain and the extraordinary way they had learnt to cope with the harsh conditions had enabled them to cling on for so long. In spite of the bludgeoning heat, the Gourma elephants have evolved what may be the longest migration of any elephants in Africa, walking up to eighty kilometres a day in search of food and water, and often drinking only once every three days. Bruno had mapped their drinking places and their movements covering a distance of approximately eight hundred kilometres. The nomads never complained when the elephants shared their limited waterholes, although they grumbled when their wallowings muddied the water. The elephants to the south of Mali were doomed, said Bruno; but thanks to the remarkable tolerance of the Tuaregs and the inaccessibility of the region, the Gourma elephants might just survive.

Today their fate is inextricably bound up with the survival of the desert people. Following the terrible Sahelian droughts of the early 1970s, aid and famine-relief schemes had created more permanent waterholes, and many nomadic camps had become fixed bases where people were encouraged to grow food on the hot red sands. At the same time, when we arrived in Gourma in 1979, the numbers of livestock were increasing again as veterinary care improved. With the fragile habitat already stretched to breaking point, the spread of domestic animals into the Gourma was leaving even less room for these elephants of the farthest north.

Once many centuries ago, when the Sahara was covered with grass and trees, elephants roamed all the way to the Mediterranean. Now only a few neolithic rock paintings and the name of a well, Ras-el-fil, Head of the Elephant, are all that is left to remind us of that far-off time when the desert bloomed.

When the climate changed the Sahara was reduced from a fertile land to barren sands. But today, over-population and excessive livestock grazing in those countries bordering the desert point to mankind's infinite capacity for destruction as the most likely cause for today's desertification with the loss of trees and declining rainfall hastening the southward march of the dunes.

As for the elephants, the fact that they have all but vanished in the north in less than a century is due almost entirely to man's unrelenting hunger for ivory. The evidence was everywhere, as we had discovered in every country we had visited so far. West Africa was once prime elephant country; but wherever man had penetrated, settled and multiplied, the elephant range lines had disintegrated, and the survivors, both forest and savannah elephants, existed now only as scattered relic populations. For the most part they were no longer of any interest to the ivory trade, having reached such small numbers that it was no longer worth the effort involved in hunting them down.

Now we had reached the northernmost limits of our search. From the ends of Africa, from the Cape to the Sahara, we now had some idea of where the remaining elephants could be found, and in what numbers. We were disappointed that we had been unable to locate the Gourma herds; yet somehow it seemed fitting that all we should see of these last elephants of the dunes were their footprints in the shifting sands, leading away into who knows what future.

CHAPTER FOURTEEN

ORIA: *Ivory Coasts*

1979, Ivory Coast and Cameroon

THE Café Calao in the centre of Abidjan is a typical French brasserie, with chairs and tables on the pavement under a shady awning. The food and the ambience could be anywhere in France. Only the passers-by are different. The people of the Ivory Coast are quite unlike the Senegalese or the Malien; charming, efficient and dressed in a completely different style from the people of the north.

The Café Calao became our favourite haunt in Abidjan. Here we could sit and watch the daily bustle; the men in flowery pink cotton trousers and long painted sandals, and the women in even more colourful dresses with tight bodices and big scarves tied like fluffed cushions on their heads.

But there was a more serious purpose to our leisurely lunchtimes. Across the street, shaded from the sun by grubby cotton sheets, stood a huddle of shoddy stalls offering ivory for sale. This was the Senegalese ivory market, and from our table, while cutting into our *entrecôte, pommes frites et salade verte*, we watched the traders in the same way that we watch elephants, and took notes about their habits.

The sale of raw ivory was forbidden, but it was easy for the traders to get round the law. The least amount of cutting and polishing on a tusk could pass as 'worked ivory', which could be sold legally.

On one stall, about two hundred small tusks, each with identical faces carved on the tips, lay among ivory animals, beads and bangles, sheltered from the sun beneath a big umbrella. We counted another hundred uncarved tusks whose sawn-off tips stood in neat rows on the tables. Altogether at least four hundred elephants must have been killed to supply this one small market. Most of the ivory was small and slim, typical forest-elephant tusks weighing under five kilos each. There was also some rose-coloured ivory, of greater value, said to have come from Cameroon or Gabon.

Slowly but surely, as we made our way around the bulging paunch of tropical West Africa, a picture of the ivory trade was beginning to emerge. Country by country, the jigsaw was falling into place and the story it told – of slaughter, greed and corruption – was to become a depressingly familiar refrain in the months and years that followed.

At the same time we were able to build up a much better idea of how many elephants were left in the various corners of their enormous range from the Knysna Forests of the Cape to the arid scrublands of the Sahel. It was proving to be a long and arduous journey; but wherever the ivory trail led, we would follow. So far in West Africa we had found the elephant range to be broken up into small islands surrounded by seas of humanity. It appeared that human population pressure was just as important an influence as the ivory trade in this area.

Once the Ivory Coast was a densely forested country with masses of elephants. Now the elephants and the great forest trees, the giants of Africa, were both going to their graves.

As in Senegal, most of the elephants were shot out in the early part of the century by French hunters and soldiers. Now, we estimated, no more than one hundred and twenty elephants remained, and the country had actually begun to import raw ivory to supply its carving industry. In 1978 at least twenty-nine tonnes had been imported from Cameroon, Gabon, the CAR and Zaire – enough to have accounted for over three thousand elephants. Even more intriguing was the possibility of looking at any records which might tell us who the importers were.

At the same time the Ivory Coast had lost more than seven million hectares of primary forest in twenty years. This meant that virtually all the forest in the country had been razed, until only the Tai Forest was left unscathed. By protecting the elephants there the Government had spared the forest and all the other species that lived in it.

We went to see this beleaguered forest, driving for hours past a steady stream of heavy trucks heading in the opposite direction, each one laden with huge logs. When we got there, we stood and stared. In there were forest elephants. Here trees and elephants had made a last stand. Yet even here, the centuries-old trees were still being felled, opening the way for squatter families to slash and burn and grow patches of manioc. As we contemplated this last vestige of Ivory Coast's forest, the smoke from the squatters' fires seeped and swirled through the trees like ghosts and the song of the saw mills rang in our ears, reminding us of the power of the logging companies and their political backers whose short-sighted folly threatened these last trees.

Back in Abidjan, buxom Ivoirienne women sat on the ground selling manioc wrapped in banana leaves. Next to them stood huge bowls of steaming rice and fish which they ladled out on to a strip of banana leaf and folded into a neat little parcel in exchange for a few coins.

In the wide covered market, under the hanging kaftans and bales of broderie anglaise, dozens of jewellers were selling ivory, gold and silver. 'You see,' said Birame Diop, 'it's all in the hands of the Senegalese.' What he said was perfectly true. The Senegalese are such successful entrepreneurs that they are even found as far south as Cape Town, trading in ivory.

Birame Diop was himself a Senegalese, a young man we had met a few days earlier. He told us that the stalls belonged to the same families who ran the ivory shops in Treichville, the African quarter. Malians, Senegalese and Guineans, they were all in the ivory business together, with links all over French West Africa; but the Senegalese were the main dealers.

Birame took us into Treichville to see the carvers at work, slicing and chopping up tusks of every size. 'Only a small amount is poached in this country,' he said. 'But we can get as much as we want from elsewhere and sell it all to the tourists.' The Italians were the best customers, followed by the Germans, who bought it to re-sell. The ivory then left the country with the tourists as personal effects and disappeared from the world's ivory trade statistics.

Before we left Abidjan we were given permission to scrutinize all the ivory import and export records. These were well kept in neat files and every consignment was precisely recorded at the airport. Suddenly, another piece of the ivory puzzle clicked into place. Ivory Coast was unique in West Africa in being a major importer, but virtually nothing seemed to be going out. Of the twenty-nine tonnes imported into the country that year, only 1.1 tons of worked and raw ivory had been officially re-exported. The rest was going out in tourists' suitcases without ever showing up in the records.

What was an even greater windfall was to take with us photocopies of the certificates of origin from the traders who had sent ivory to Abidjan, giving dates, places and the quantities of ivory they had handled. There were names and addresses from Zaire, CAR, Cameroon, Gabon and Congo – and Iain and I intended to visit some of them and find out more.

In Yaounde, the capital of Cameroon, the hothouse smell of damp vegetation rose from the steaming earth. It had rained all day, a heavy, drenching rain that drummed on the rooftops and washed down the streets leaving long tide-lines of garbage along the sidewalks.

Cameroon lies on the watershed between West and Central Africa, where the cultures and the climate of the northern desert meet the thick jungle of the south. From here the remaining forests of Africa stretch away down the Atlantic as far as Angola, and inland in a wide sweep through Gabon, Equatorial Guinea, the Congo, Zaire and CAR.

Today, Cameroon's elephants still range in three zones crossing the country from east to west: the northern and central Savannah ranges with their parks and reserves, and the southern forest belt where most of the elephants dwell. Here, the massive tropical downpours and dripping vegetation are the elephants' best protection, turning the earth into a thick red sludge which makes travelling arduous, even on foot.

According to the historian Marion Johnson, ivory from Cameroon was known to be 'very large and of excellent quality' in the 1820s. In one season sixty tonnes were taken out by Portuguese and English vessels; but by the middle of the century the flow of tusks had been intercepted by Hausa traders and diverted across the desert along the ancient caravan routes to be sold in Mediterranean seaports.

This trans-Saharan trade dwindled after the Germans conquered the country, but Cameroon continued to be a valued source of ivory. Searching through the archives of Yaounde we came across export figures for the years between 1899 and 1905, which showed ivory leaving the country at between fifty and ninety tonnes a year. Such a volume clearly placed Cameroon in the forefront of pre-1914 ivory-producing nations.

However, according to official customs statistics, ivory exports in the three years preceding our visit averaged only 1.3 tonnes a year. But these figures were wildly inaccurate. In 1978, customs records showed that only three hundred kilos had been exported to the Ivory Coast; yet we knew from a consignment of documents we had examined in Abidjan that at least 9.4 tonnes had come from Cameroon. Someone, somewhere, was making a killing!

Jean-Marie Zorga was a carpenter by trade but according to Simon Nwara, a young Cameroonian who worked at the US Embassy in Yaounde, he was also a commercial hunter-poacher. It was through Simon that we met Jean-Marie, a man in his thirties, with flared trousers and an immaculate white shirt. Over a typical Cameroonian lunch of giant avocados, chicken stew and white strips of rubbery manioc – the staple food of central Africa – he told us about his hunting forays.

He went out for two months at a time and worked for various rich *patrons*, who gave him a gun and ammunition, and paid him $500 for a big elephant, plus food and transport. Sometimes he also took clients out, but mostly he hunted alone. He had just returned from such a trip, he told us, and had shot two elephants.

He shot every elephant he saw, regardless of the size of its tusks. The deal was that he could keep the meat, which he could give or maybe sell to the local villagers; but the ivory belonged to the patron. For his part, to kill two elephants the *patron* might spend up to $1,250 on licences, cartridges, porters and a hunter, in return for which he might make as much as $4,500 profit, depending on where and how he sold the ivory.

The most-prized tusks, said Jean-Marie, were those of the forest elephant, *le petit*, whose ivory was hard and pink in colour; but finding good tusks was getting harder. To hunt now, he had to take the train as far east as Gayoum. Then he had to travel by *pirogue*, a long canoe, poling upstream for two days, and then walk for at least two more days before he might see an elephant. 'Today,' he complained, 'every elephant with big ivory left in the forest has a hunter behind it.'

Driving south through the forests with Simon and Jean-Marie, we spotted our first talking drum. Cut from the trunk of a special tree, it was slit down the middle and had carved lips at each end. These drums can be heard ten kilometres away and are used to send messages over the hills announcing births, deaths – or the killing of an elephant.

Jean-Marie explained that usually when an elephant was killed, the inhabitants from a score of villages would descend on it to cut up the meat. It was difficult for poachers to conceal their activities. There were so many villages in the forest and the gendarmerie would almost certainly get to hear about it – unless of course you came to some arrangement with the villagers over the disposal of the meat.

Along the forest track to Lomié are a series of Pygmy villages. Even though the missionaries and the Government had pressured them to leave the forest and grow crops, the Pygmies remained hunter-gatherers, living off the forest and what it could provide in the way of game, including elephants. They had always been tremendous elephant killers, said Jean-Marie. He did not hunt there himself, but other hunters had told him that the reason why so few good tuskers were left in the eastern province was because the Pygmies had killed them.

In the forest world of the Pygmy, the killing of an elephant is an important event. Large numbers of people can be fed and neighbouring villages are invited to join in the feast, which is accompanied by much celebration. The fat and grease of the elephant is lacking in other bush meat, and is a special bonus to their diet, and Pygmy myths and legends illustrate quite clearly the high value they place on elephant meat in terms of food, festivity and prestige.

The introduction of guns – first muzzle-loaders and shotguns and then big game rifles – changed the Pygmies' attitudes to elephant hunting and made them aware of the value of ivory. The Pygmies had no guns of their own. It was the Bantu living outside the forest who had the weapons, which they would 'lease' to the Pygmies to hunt elephant. The gun-owners would receive the ivory and the Pygmies kept the meat. It was an arrangement which suited both parties and it remains essentially the same today, except that the

Pygmies now demand gifts of cash, clothing, cigarettes or alcohol as well as the meat.

The Pygmies we spoke to insisted that there were still many elephants in the forest and roared with laughter when asked if there was any danger of them being killed off. 'If only I could buy a gun,' said one, 'I could go out and shoot one whenever I wished.' Yet reports were coming in of more than a hundred elephants being killed in a year, and in many cases ivory was the only motive.

Back in Yaounde, wildlife officials showed us three and a half tonnes of ivory which had been seized from a Frenchman and his Hausa tribesmen accomplices. The only safe place to keep this hoard was in the lavatory. When the guard opened the door for us we saw tusks stuffed to the ceiling, and anyone wanting to use the lavatory had to go outside instead.

As far as we could make out it seemed to be all heavy ivory; typical savannah bull elephant tusks. A court case had been filed, but Victor Sunday Balinga, the soft-spoken Cameroonian director of the *Eaux et Forets*, was not hopeful about the outcome. 'Most likely they will seek political pressure and get their tusks out in the end,' he said. According to Balinga a lot of ivory was being taken out of the country as personal effects, especially by Europeans, much of it smuggled in the diplomatic bag. It was the Ivory Coast story all over again.

Like most of the other *Eaux et Forets* departments we visited in West Africa, those in Yaounde were in a state of crumbling disrepair. There was no money. There were no cars that worked, and no means to stop the poaching. The offices in Yaounde employed about fifty people but we never saw more than a handful at any one time.

The director was dismayed by the speed at which the elephants were disappearing in the south. He had heard of villagers putting away their guns as there was nothing left to shoot, not even small game. (In Cameroon the people eat anything that moves.) 'No one knows how many elephants there are,' he said, 'but enormous amounts of ivory still leave Cameroon each year.'

He went on to explain that although four hundred hunting licences had been issued, not a single hunter had returned to pay his hunting tax or collect his certificate of origin, without which no ivory could be exported. Balinga held up his hands in a gesture of despair. 'Regrettably the customs are very free,' he said.

Just how easy it was to circumvent the system became apparent when we went to see Lambara Aboubakar, a rounded, jovial Hausa in a smart brown-and-gold robe. We met him at the house of his sister, who was married to a journalist and lived in the Hausa district of Briquetrie.

Aboubakar was a businessman, and his business was ivory. He spoke quite openly about it. 'A certificate of origin is essential to pass customs, but I can arrange that.' He grinned broadly and held up a sheaf of examples. 'The only problem is money.'

We asked him how much ivory was available. 'Plenty,' he replied. 'It is like petrol. Some say it is finishing, but the price still goes up.' He laughed and called for his sister to bring more drinks. Then his voice became serious. 'Look,' he confided; 'you supply me with a vehicle and petrol and give me the cash and I can get you any amount of ivory you want. There's plenty in the black quarters where the Hausa live. It comes in every day. All I have to do is go out and get it; a few tusks here, a few tusks there.' He claimed he had recently sold two big tusks weighing over seventy kilos for a price of $65 per kilo. 'Of course one has to pay $15 tax or pay the customs man a bribe,' he added.

In the local ivory markets a Greek dealer offered us a tusk for $3,250 which, he claimed, had just come in from the Central African Empire. It weighed fifty kilos. 'Sure, the price of raw ivory is going up, but there is still money to be made,' he said. It took one of his workers about a day to produce an ivory statue, worth $100, and there was enough business to employ ten carvers in his workshop all year round. 'I have a special order from France; ivory porno in all positions.' He chuckled. 'At least the carvers enjoy their work.'

It seemed as if conservation had come too early or too late to West Africa. 'Cameroon is a very easy-going place,' said the Greek. 'No one works too hard or cares too much. One just lets things go along at their own pace. God and the West will provide the rest.'

Most of the traders were charming individuals and it was easy to talk to them. Yet nowhere did we meet anyone who displayed the slightest sympathy for the elephants or was in the least bit concerned for their preservation. Nor did the traders ever question their own involvement in the slaughter. 'It is the whites who kill all the elephants, all those tourists and hunters who come here the whole time to kill, kill, kill,' said Abdou Moussa, an ivory merchant from Douala, down on the Atlantic coast. Like most of the carvers and ivory merchants, he had never been on a hunt. It was, he confided, too much of an effort and too dangerous.

Inside his ivory store were one and a half tonnes of tusks, some of them quite big. He also traded in diamonds, of which he kept a handful in a knotted handkerchief in his pocket. 'I have all the permits I need,' he said, 'even if I have to pay a lot of people to get them. I can export five tonnes of ivory a year: about five hundred to a thousand tusks. But soon the ivory will be finished here.'

He also bought ivory that came in from the Central African Republic, for a time known as the Central African Empire, under Bokassa's reign, but never ventured across the border. 'Anyone who is caught buying ivory or diamonds over there . . . ' He paused and looked at us with bright black eyes, and put his finger to his temple like a revolver to demonstrate what would happen. When we told him that we were going there soon to investigate the ivory business he shook his head in disbelief. 'You're crazy,' he said. 'It all belongs to Bokassa, the emperor, and is managed by his mistress and her lover, El Dorado.'

He put his arms around our shoulders. 'Why don't you stay here?' he entreated. 'As long as you do your work and mind your own business, you can do anything you want.' That was certainly true, for what little we knew about Cameroon it seemed a stable and welcoming country.

CHAPTER FIFTEEN

ORIA: *On the Shores of Gabon*

1979, Gabon

S o far, in all our travels through West Africa, we had yet to see
a real wild forest elephant. Every day we talked of nothing
but elephants. We moved in a world of traders and carvers.
Through their hands had passed the tusks of thousands of elephants.
We ourselves had seen tonnes of ivory, including the hard, pinkish
ivory of the shy forest elephants. But the animals themselves, wisely
perhaps, had remained hidden.

Not until we reached Petit Bam Bam in the Wonga Wongué
Reserve, President Bongo's private hunting ground in Gabon, did
we see them; and even then they were no more than distant
specks glimpsed through the tall green grass. Helicopter hunting
expeditions and the regular thump of seismic explosions set off by
oil prospectors had made them so nervous that it was impossible
to get any closer. As we rattled down the rutted tracks in an old
Land-Rover, we could see them disappearing, moving fast towards
islands of mist-shrouded forest. 'Don't worry,' our guide remarked,
sensing our disappointment. 'The oil is nearly finished.'

We entered the forest and the trees closed around us, wrapping
us in their ancient silence. Tall branches reached for the sun. Their
green shade hid coiled vines that resembled snakes, moths disguised

BOVE - Mauritanian rangers
utside the governor's office in
elibaby. *RIGHT* - Iain with Pierre
ernet, a French entrepreneur,
nd his men in their desert-
rossing truck in the Gourma,
Iali. *BELOW* - A lone short-
isked northern desert elephant
rosses the Gourma at sunset.

Francophone personalities: *OPPOSITE PAGE, TOP LEFT* - Bruno Lamarche, the French teacher, in Mali. *TOP RIGHT* - Iain with Saumare Youssif and his horse in Mauritania. *MIDDLE* - Counting team in CAR - Jean-Marc Froment, Gustave Doungoubé, Iain, rangers and helpers. *BELOW* - Pierre Guizard poses in a big 'cannibal pot' with his son Rene seated and Makita and Joseph behind him in Gabon. *THIS PAGE, TOP LEFT* - Rene Guizard on the Atlantic shores in Gabon. *TOP RIGHT* - Pierre Vernet squatting with friend on desert elephant shot after a long chase. *MIDDLE* - President Mobutu Sese Seko of Zaire. *ABOVE LEFT* - Lee Lyon with one of the captured orphans from the Rwanda cull before her death. *ABOVE RIGHT* - Mathieu Laboureur with father Jean, behind him, lining up poachers caught in the Manovo-Gounda National Park - CAR.

African Ivory Traders: *ABOVE* - Cameroonian carver exhibiting a pair of carved tusks in Yaounde. *BELOW* - The Senegalese ivory market opposite the Café Calao in Abidjan, Ivory Coast.

ABOVE - A young Senegalese ivory trader at his stall, where Oria counted over 120 small, lightly carved or polished forest elephant tusks, all illegally poached. BELOW - One of Savimbi's UNITA rebels carving an AK-47 out of wood and ivory in Angola. These guns were presented as gifts to high officials who provided arms to Savimbi.

Transport: *ABOVE* - The great trees of the Ivory Coast leaving Africa, by truck, rail and sea for Europe, America and Japan. *BELOW* - one of the Sudanese horses overloaded with poached ivory from CAR. *OPPOSITE* - Elephants from the elephant school in Gangala na Bodio, Zaire, carrying fodder from the bush to the village, where fuel and trucks are unavailable.

Central African Empire: *ABOVE* - Emperor Bokassa at his coronation in Bangui, sits on his gold-plated eagle throne made in France. *BELOW* - Julio Dorado, Bokassa's ivory partner, posing beneath a pair of giant tusks. Together their trade cleared out most of the elephants in the south and east.

Central African Republic: *ABOVE* - Confiscated ivory being unloaded by presidential guards at General Kolingba's army HQ in Bangui. *BELOW* - The President's hoard we saw in the cellar of the barracks in Bangui.

Central African Republic: *ABOVE* - Presidential guards counter-attack armed elephant poachers in Manovo-Gounda National Park. *BELOW* - A small calf waits to die in the shade of a tree next to the faceless corpse of its mother.

ABOVE - A dead elephant in Koumbala, killed by horsemen using razor-sharp spears to cut the sciatic nerve and pierce the intestines. *BELOW -* Hand-made horse bridles, spears and leather-bound pieces of the Koran, used by Sudanese horsemen poaching in the CAR.

Gabon: *ABOVE* - Makita, our tracker and gun bearer at dusk in the lagoon after a long day of looking for elephants. *OPPOSITE AND BELOW* - Feeding on the Atlantic shores, the 'Assala' forest elephants, once believed to be a pygmy species. Recent research shows that Savanna and Forest elephants, and hybrids, live side by side deep in the forest. *OVERLEAF LEFT AND RIGHT* - The Rain Forest provides 1,750,000 km², of elephant habitat. Even here the elephants are not safe from the ivory trade, and even if poaching is solved, man's pollution and habitat encroachment still remain a threat, as invasion by farmers and oil prospectors demonstrate.

as leaves and flowers that looked like brilliant birds. In this hide and-seek world of mimicry, nothing was what it seemed.

The breath of the forest hung thick and moist in the windless air, heavy with the smell of decaying vegetation. Here the elephant was king, the path-maker, moving soundlessly on cushioned feet over an antique auburn carpet of soft, damp leaves. Huge trees arched overhead, filtering the dappled light which fell on his quilted hide. With his outstretched trunk he could pluck nuts from the ozouga tree, and fruit from the douka and mikoumina trees twenty feet above the ground, and draw water from rivers as he ambled on his way.

In evolutionary terms it has been suggested that the forest elephant, *Loxodonta africana cyclotis*, may be even older than its savannah cousin. The smaller body, ears and head are all adapted to life in the forest, and the long, straight, slender tusks are designed for digging down to reach the much-needed mineral salts locked in the forest soil. Their constant tuskings and wallowings open up glades in the forest that let in the light, creating fresh vegetation and attracting other creatures such as forest antelope. Recently, it has been shown that savannah elephants, too, are found in the depths of the forest alongside *cyclotis*. They are both an integral part of this world. Without them, the forest would never be the same.

We came upon an elephant's skull, its braided bones cloaked with a mat of moss. Around us stood the tall trees of the secondary forest, but all the valuable timber had been taken out sixty years ago, our guide told us, and floated away down the rivers.

At Petit Bam Bam there was a lodge on a hillock, where we were to spend the night. Here we met the sinister warden, an obese and charmless man dressed all in black. He had been in Gabon for twenty-seven years, he informed us, and for the past ten years he had been President Bongo's game-keeper at Wonga Wongué.

As we entered the lodge we passed two caged lions and a baby gorilla in a small enclosure. They were looked after by his wife, he said, a peroxide blonde who seemed to run Bam Bam.

The warden invited us into the freezing, air-conditioned living room, where he spent most of the day, with its mustard velvet

---

OPPOSITE – Pygmies for centuries have hunted and lived in balance with Nature. Now guns and cash from traders tempt them to over-kill elephants.

armchairs and stuffed animals on the shelves. It was a strange encounter, coming in from the timeless forest.

As we explained our mission, apéritifs and snacks were passed round by a waiter whom the warden called Mickey Mouse. He crouched like a frog, dressed in a black suit with white gloves. 'Soon you, too, will be hanging on one of those shelves, Mickey Mouse – *n'est ce pas?*' said the warden, his shapeless body shaking with laughter as he thrust his red-veined face towards us. '*Oui, patron,*' came the automatic response, as if a button had been pushed. It was a custom for the waiter to squat in this extraordinary position, we were told. We did not know whether it was because the president was only four feet nine inches tall, or because it was considered impolite to be taller than the seated guests. We departed at dawn with a great sense of relief as the sun rose and the clouds peeled away like veils from the dense green heads of the forest trees.

Flying down the coast we could see black smoke coiling out of the forest over a crimson bed of burning oil. In places, where the land was being laid bare, ponderous machines with gigantic steel jaws opened and closed around the long straight tree trunks, crushing them to the ground.

Grey walls of rain forced us to land at Iguela by the sea. As so often happens in Africa, here we met a man we had heard much about, Pierre Guizard. He had been in Gabon for thirty-four years, having started his life there as a forester; and when the precious okoumé tree had been logged out, he prospected for gold and diamonds.

'The forest has been worked and re-worked,' he said, 'and any tree of value has been removed long ago. What grows now is for the elephants.'

He was a man full of warmth and humour, but with a great feeling for the bush. We were immediately invited to his camp for *déjeuner* – always an important part of the day – where we feasted on roast wild boar, rice, palm hearts and wine. Our book was on the small cane table by the sofa. 'I have also been a poacher and a hunter and have shot many elephants,' he told me with an apologetic smile and a wave of his hand, 'and I have given your book to many people.'

His knowledge of Gabon was immense. He had been all over the country on foot and, like the elephant, had lived in the forest off wild berries and fruit and knew from which trees he could syphon water. 'Now I want a quieter life,' he said. 'I would like to turn this place into a sanctuary.' He fell silent, and in the lull that followed we could hear the shrill voices of West African grey parrots as they clung to the nuts of the oil palms around his camp.

Guizard seemed as pleased to meet us as we were to meet him, and we struck up an instant friendship. 'Ah, if you were not prisoners of time,' he said, 'I would give you a tent, a boat, my son René to look after you and learn from you, and my tracker, Makita. Tomorrow you would see the elephants strolling out of the forest and walking next to the sea, family after family like rocks on the beach. You have come all this way to see elephants. You must stay. I implore you.'

In a straight line across Africa from where we stood was Nairobi. We could be back there in a few hours in a jet, if such a route existed; but we still had to return to Zaire before going home and it would take us many days. Yet when fate had brought us to this place, how could we refuse such an offer? We cancelled all our flights, and stepped into Guizard's *pirogue*, a long, beautifully shaped canoe cut from the trunk of an okoume tree.

René, born of a Gabonese mother, tall with blue eyes and a smile as warm as the morning sun, collected a gun and fishing rod to supply our food. Soon a pile of camping equipment accumulated on the beach, with Joseph, who was to be in charge of *la cuisine*, Pascal to look after the camp, and Makita, the gun-bearer. Together they loaded the big tarpaulin, beds and bedding, pots and pans, water, food and fuel, and made ready the rubber dinghy that would accompany the *pirogue*.

As we were about to set off, Guizard summoned Makita, and in pidgin French made a little sermon. 'Makita, you be with me seventeen years.'

'*Oui, patron*,' came the reply.

'You have shot the elephant with me.'

'*Oui, patron*.'

Then, pointing at us, Guizard said: 'This white man not like white man you know, white man that hunt elephant. This white man look only,' he went on, pointing his finger at his eye.

Makita nodded and answered solemnly again, '*Oui, patron*,' his wizened old face utterly devoid of emotion.

'You take white man to elephant but you not shoot,' Guizard continued. 'This white man look. If elephant charge and flap his ears, you not shoot. If elephant charge and flap his ears and white man run, you not shoot. If elephant charge and white man run and fall, and you see only his sandal between elephant feet, only then you shoot. Otherwise you let white man look. Is that understood, Makita?'

'*Oui, patron*,' mumbled the old man, shaking his head from side to side and up and down, and maybe thinking, How many more things do these crazy whites want to do? But go he would, because hunting and tracking was part of his life.

For the next half an hour we drifted down the creek, and then on over the black water of the lagoon which lay between the forest and the sea, until we came to a grove of trees at the end of a long spit of beach. Here we set up camp and searched for driftwood to build a shelter. We had sweet water from the lagoon to wash in, fallen timber for firewood, and fish and wild game to eat. Gigantic runaway okoumé logs lay half-buried in the sand all along the beach; but there was no sign of life for miles, and no sound but the gasp of the waves upon the shore.

A constant south-east wind blew in from the sea, carrying a sheet of spray over the beach and the trees. Bright green wax-like bushes grow all along the shore, with sweet red fruit like a small peach. Not wanting to leave a trace of human scent on these deserted sands, and with the wind blowing in the right direction, René suggested that, together with Makita and Joseph, we should take the dinghy and explore further up the lagoon, leaving Pascal to look after the camp. But Pascal, terrified of being left on his own, begged to be allowed to come with us. 'But there is no room, Pascal,' René said.

In desperation Pascal turned to us. 'What if a buffalo comes?' he said.

'Then you go up a tree, Pascal.'

'And what if an elephant comes?' he pleaded with a look of utter abandonment.

'Then, Pascal, you climb higher.'

'But, madame, what if the great sleep attacks me?' he moaned.

'Wait for us in the tree until we get back,' I said and walked away.

But Pascal, now shaking with fear, would have none of this. He jumped in the boat and refused to move.

Slowly we glided over the lagoon, the water black and smooth as glass. Pascal squeezed between Joseph and Makita, safe now as a pea in a pod and beaming from ear to ear. Small red forest buffaloes waded in the shallows. White-collared mangabey monkeys dug out shells in the wet sand. Pelicans sailed majestically overhead and crocodiles slid into the water at our approach.

On reaching the next clump of trees we climbed up one to scan the beach and could hardly suppress our excitement. Knee deep in the greenery not fifty metres away stood nine elephants with the open sea and the breaking waves behind them. The unexpectedness of seeing elephants on a beach gave the scene a curious dreamlike quality, like a painting by Douanier-Rousseau. It was something we had always longed to see.

While Pascal remained in the boat, we scuttled like crabs through the undergrowth, with René near by, and peered through the wax-leaved bushes for a better view. Makita and Joseph, meanwhile, stood rooted to the spot with fear, not knowing what to do.

Never before had they been with a white man who did not want to shoot an elephant, or seemed so eager to be killed by one, and the *patron* had said, 'Don't shoot'. The *assala*, the small forest elephant, we had been told by all, was extremely aggressive and liable to attack on sight. We raised our cameras and hoped they would not hear the clicks. A bull with outward-spreading tusks and a great slit in his ear stood facing the sea while cows with calves picked fruit – which was evidently a great delicacy at this time of year – and the youngsters played and splashed in the waves. These elephants were certainly smaller than the ones we knew, with smaller rounded ears waving like fans in the wind, and strange-looking tusks.

Suddenly, there was panic. Our guards were running in all directions as a lone elephant appeared behind us. In seconds we were alone with the notorious man-killing *assala* heading slowly towards us, its slender tusks pointing downwards; but the wind stayed true and we remained motionless in the bushes, hardly daring to breathe, and somehow escaped detection. If we had been poachers – how easy it would have been.

After the lone elephant had joined the others we crept back to the boat on hands and knees, hoping they would not catch our scent. Everyone was exhilarated.

We continued our journey upstream, looking for the elephant crossings among the mangroves whose roots rose out of the water like pallid fingers. In the distance we glimpsed the ghostly shapes of buffaloes and more elephants wading across the lagoon. Altogether that first day we saw twenty-seven elephants standing on the shores of the Atlantic Ocean.

Each day we drifted further up the lagoon. Wherever we had touched the earth, the elephants caught our scent and vanished. Their reaction cast the only shadow on an otherwise idyllic interlude, and brought back the sadness we always felt when animals showed such fear of man.

On the third day, having decided to leave Joseph in camp with Pascal, we came upon a small family of about six elephants quietly eating the leaves which they plucked from some tall bushes. We found a dead tree with good visibility and silently pulled ourselves up it, one step at a time, until we were able to stand on a broken branch some ten feet above the ground. The tree was barely able to support our weight but it was too late to descend. We had hardly straightened up when a big grey head suddenly appeared out of a brilliant green wall of foliage just a few metres in front of us, and lifted a long curling trunk between a gleaming pair of tusks. It was a young cow with a tiny baby almost hidden in the leaves beneath her. Precariously perched on the bough we tried to take pictures, praying that we would not fall off.

For a long time we stayed in our tree, held in a single silence that magnified the sound of the sea and the occasional cry of a forest bird. The elephant stood quietly, folding and unfolding her wrinkled trunk, picking at leaves and twigs, blissfully unaware of our presence, and then disappeared as silently as she had arrived.

As the sun passed down we drifted back to our shelter, fishing for supper as we went, and talking to René and Makita while the sky and the lagoon caught fire. We caught one large fish that was instantly bitten in half by a crocodile, and presented what was left of it to Joseph to cook. The numbers of crocodiles had increased enormously, said René, and were eating up all the swamp-dwelling sitatunga antelope.

Inland, a storm was approaching. Dragging our beds under the shelter we lit a big fire and lay there with peals of thunder exploding over our heads. Soon the first, fat spots of rain began to fall, while Joseph squatted over the coals cooking his fish and manioc and the flames lit up the darkening trees. The rain became a steady downpour of tropical intensity, and Pascal and Makita huddled closer to the fire, chatting endlessly in their strange, sing-song language with its sounds of *bambulu-bambam-bolaba* and its long echoing calls, until night approached and at last they fell silent and we lay for a long time, listening to the rain dripping from the leaves and the pounding of the waves breaking on the beach.

Early next morning we gathered our few possessions and paddled back down the lagoon. We found Guizard fixing his rusty Jeep and offered to pay for our *pirogue* safari, but he would not hear of it. 'There is nothing to pay for,' he insisted. 'We eat a bit of fish and there is meat when we hunt. There is nothing else. In Africa we live like this. If you come here, this is your home; and when we go to you it is the same. In Africa the door is always open.' And so we made our farewells and left the good, great-hearted generous man after a wonderful morning of stories and laughter, while parrots called and the ground steamed warmly after the overnight storm.

At the airport in the VIP lounge we met the Zaire Ambassador entertaining his tall and very handsome finance minister with a delegation of bankers returning from a meeting in Dakar. Champagne was being served in silver goblets. There was more champagne on the Air Zaire flight to Kinshasa, and soon the Ambassador and his minister and most of the bankers were dancing and singing in the aisles of the plane.

CHAPTER SIXTEEN

IAIN: *The Die is Cast*

1979, Zaire, Central African Empire, Washington, Switzerland and Zambia

AFTER Oria left for Kenya I flew back to Zaire to find out who was behind the ivory trade. On the way I studied the telegram we had been given by the US Embassy in Kinshasa. It was dynamite.

It said that with the price of ivory sky rocketing in 1978, Zairians were slaughtering elephants in unprecedented numbers using poison, traps, and even hand-made guns fashioned out of Land-Rover steering rods. The soaring price of ivory had caused entire villages to drop their agricultural activities in order to hunt elephants full-time. Even the diamond and gold smugglers had switched to ivory and the whole shady business of buying, collecting and transporting tusks had become a cut-throat operation. According to government officials around fifteen hundred tonnes of tusks were stockpiled throughout the country – a hoard of colossal proportions.

So blatant had the ivory-trade racket become that the main news-paper in Kinshasa ran a three-part exposé alleging that any Zairian with a permit to buy tusks could commission several other people to find ivory for him. These people in turn would commission others and everybody would operate with a photocopy of the original permit. Clearly I was going to have a busy week!

On arrival in Kinshasa I received a telegram from Ian Parker, who was now in Hong Kong, asking me to find out about the identity of Mwanateba, an ivory trader whose name appeared on Hong Kong certificates.

Back at the Ministry of Environment and Nature Conservation I met a contact who produced the specimen ivory permits he had promised to show me. One of these allowed a company called Sotrequa to collect unlimited ivory; the second permitted another company, Ets Manyi, to export a staggering one hundred tonnes to Vaneco, a Belgian company in Brussels. More information followed.

When I showed these names to my contact at the US Embassy he laughed. 'You realize, Iain, you are picking on all the political heavyweights in Kinshasa?' The military attaché told me he had personally seen soldiers loading ivory into C-130 army aircraft in the north of the country; and a fourth member of the Bureau Politique had a C-130 which he regularly flew down to South Africa with ivory on board. It was also said that ivory was flown from Kinshasa to Gbadolite, the president's home town. There it was loaded on to another plane and flown overseas; nothing needed to go through Customs.

So that was it! Members of the Bureau Politique were immune from prosecution. Even if I could prove illegal dealing it wasn't going to make the least bit of difference. These people were above the law.

Eventually I met the minister, Madame Lessendjina, who went out of her way to assure me of the government's concern for the elephant. She was furious about the consignment of ivory that had been seized in Paris from 'France Croco' and said she was demanding its return. For the future, all they wanted to do, she said, was to clear some stocks. After that ivory would be totally banned. As for the ivory permit I showed her, it was an unfortunate mistake, she said, and in any case its validity had expired.

The director of Zaire's Institute for Nature Conservation was Kakiese Onfine, a tall thin man with tribal scars on his face. I had met him a year earlier at the IUCN general assembly in the Soviet Union. In the name of the president he had made an impassioned speech about Zaire's elephants, explaining the danger of the ivory trade and begging the outside world to help. 'Please do not buy or sell Zaire's ivory,' he implored.

We had worked together and framed an official IUCN resolution appealing to the nations of the world to disallow the import of any Zaire ivory. This request was later circulated by CITES and at the time I was under the illusion that we had won an important battle.[1]

Now I found that the Zairians were very cagey about giving me any information on the status of elephants. According to Kakiese my questionnaires had never arrived; but after the meeting I was approached covertly by an aged French *fonctionnaire*, Gilbert Rollais, who was eager to do his bit for the elephants. 'I have told the department to answer your questionnaire,' he said, 'but they are scared. As a member of the department I will talk to you, but you must keep it confidential.' He then presented me with an insider's view.

Basically the story was that immense slaughters had taken place since 1975 and that elephants had been killed by every technique, from surrounding them with fire in the tall grasslands to mass poisoning at waterholes. These reports corresponded closely with what I had heard from the US Embassy and confirmed my own conclusion that the situation in Zaire was as bad or worse than in East Africa.

A search into the documents led me further down the path of identifying the massive illegality of the trade. I was only able to prove that between one and three tonnes were being exported legally with the correct documents every year. However, Parker's sleuthing in Hong Kong had proved beyond doubt that between two hundred and three hundred tonnes were leaving Zaire each year.

While I was in Zaire I took the opportunity to fly up to Bangui, the capital of the Central African Empire, whose ruler, the notorious self-appointed Emperor Bokassa, enjoyed an unsavoury reputation for avarice, *folie de grandeur* and sadism. He was said to be extremely hostile to inquisitive scientists and I had been told that he had had some beaten and later awarded them with medals! However, his prestige was slipping as he had been accused of hammering nails into the heads of some children who

[1] Shortly afterwards Onfine was arrested and convicted for illegal ivory trading.

had refused to buy school uniforms from the store set up by his wife.

Clive Spinage, an old friend from East Africa with a great knowledge of elephants, was working in Bangui and escorted me around. Clive told me how a company called La Couronne had established a monopoly on all ivory trading and had exported 165 tonnes in the previous year. This made them the largest traders in Africa and explained why I had seen their name stamped on so many certificates of origin in the Ivory Coast.

I decided to take the bull by the horns and visit La Couronne. There I met a charming blonde, Madame van Erpe and her partner, Julio Dorado, a young Spaniard of undeniable good looks, but with cold black eyes. I talked to Madame van Erpe in her swimming-pool while tame parrots flew down and landed on her head. She claimed that La Couronne were Bokassa's associates and that 80 per cent of Africa's ivory trade was controlled by a group of companies to which they belonged, but she would not tell who they were. However, she asked me to sign a copy of our book which she had been sent for Christmas. I opened it up and saw inscribed upon the inside flap the words, '*avec amitié, France Croco*'. Clearly they were on friendly terms with the company that had so enraged Madame Lessendjina with the import of 'illegal' Zaire ivory.

Madame van Erpe claimed that most of their ivory came from Zaire and Sudan and therefore their trade was not harming the Empire's elephants. However, it was general knowledge that La Couronne had acquired their ivory from a network of 'collectors' who issued guns to villagers to bring in the ivory, and had ruthlessly suppressed all competition.

Next day she told me that she had been up to the palace the previous evening and told Bokassa about my arrival. 'What will the doctor say about me?' sighed the Emperor. I thought I had better not give him too long to go on wondering and returned to Kinshasa with all speed.

Just before leaving Kinshasa finally for Nairobi, I took the ferry across the river to Brazzaville, the capital of neighbouring Congo. There I discovered that seventy to eighty tonnes of ivory were exported annually and most of it was illegal, having been smuggled across the river from Zaire in canoes.

At last the picture for the Central African region was complete. It established that in addition to Zaire's own illegal exports, ivory was also leaking out in huge quantities through neighbouring countries: Congo, Central African Empire, Uganda and Zambia. Apart from overexploiting their own elephants these countries were all participants in the haemorrhage of Zaire's once vast elephant population. Only the elephants of Gabon had escaped slaughter and even their small ivory exports were conducted irregularly. The whole Central African ivory trade was massively and irremediably crooked to its core.

No sooner was the West African trip finished than news came that another US Congressional Hearing was to take place in July to discuss a new elephant protection act. The timing was unfortunate. Parker was rushing to finish the Ivory Trade Study, and I would certainly not have time to write a covering report.

The way the study turned out was quite different from what I had expected. Parker's draft made fascinating reading and ranged far beyond his terms of reference, tapping previously neglected or unavailable sources. In massive detail he had assembled statistics from Africa, Hong Kong and Japan which demonstrated how the trade had erupted in the early seventies to levels which had not been seen since before the First World War.

The statistics I had collected from Senegal and Zaire confirmed the same story for Francophone Africa, the home of perhaps more than half the continent's elephants.

The surge in ivory prices was continent wide. Parker believed this was because ivory had been recognized as a new source of wealth like gold or diamonds. It was rare and valuable, both in its raw and worked forms, and was durable and easy to store. Like gold, he thought, its price rise had been triggered by world financial instability, especially in African countries where people were anxious to get their capital out, and could do so by exporting ivory.

His study was pioneering stuff with wonderful sections on the history of the trade and was full of Parker's unique brand of curiosity and black humour. Yet despite the new insights the work appeared to me deeply flawed.

It was evident that Parker had more sympathy for ivory traders than conservationists and his resentment of the conservation movement showed through in passage after passage. The international traders on the other hand, especially the importers, were given a sympathetic hearing. He portrayed them as honourable men who had been slandered by conservationists. By the time the ivory appeared on the international scene it had acquired appropriate documents, by virtue of which it was legal, despite the fact that such documentation was almost invariably acquired through bribery. Traders could not be blamed, he implied, if African middlemen provided them with documents obtained in a crooked way.

At this point it was clear that Parker and I differed fundamentally in our perception of the terms of reference. The objective of the study was to recommend means to regulate the trade and to lessen its adverse impact on the elephants. For me, this was meant to lead to identification of bottlenecks where the trade could readily be attacked.

My aim was to expose illegal traders. Parker, on the other hand, wanted a greater understanding of the traders and an end to their harassment by conservationists. To this end he took the precaution of blanking out all the names of the major importers appearing on the trade documents reproduced in his report.

I was stunned. His ivory study began to read like a whitewash. I could not believe that the stalwart who had led the attack on the overexploitation of the elephants had now utterly changed his tune. Here was a piece of work magnificent in its detail and scope, but marred and twisted in a way that would only harm the elephants.

I went over the report page by page, giving my criticisms and suggesting he softened his venomous jibes against the 'ignorant and emotional' conservationists, by which I understood him to mean the American lobbyists, WWF and IUCN. After all it was they who had sponsored the study.

Far more serious was his discussion of the effect of the ivory trade on Africa's elephants. His major conclusions were that, the ivory trade was not excessive; it had not brought about widespread declines; it had not undermined law enforcement; and other than at a local level, it was not causing the elephants any danger. This was quite unacceptable. I warned him that I would have to oppose him publicly if he persisted with this view, but he would not budge. The die was cast and from that moment on the conservation movement would become increasingly split on the subject of the ivory trade.

In the middle of 1979 I had to go to Switzerland to hold long discussions with IUCN, haggling about the cost of extending my project by an extra six months. There was no feeling of mission in the place, and they had engaged an abrasive Australian accountant who was trying to make it into a quartermaster's paradise. WWF who shared the same buildings were somewhat better than IUCN. At least they were still in touch with humanity, but at dinner with Charles de Haes, the director-general, I got the impression that the organization's image and fund-raising was being given more priority than conservation achievement.

Charles was sympathetic towards launching an 'Elephant and Ecosystems' campaign and said to me, 'We will make you into a Superstar'. I couldn't see it somehow. It all sounded too corny. In the event rhinos became the flavour of 1980 and elephants were relegated to the dustbin of conservation for almost another decade.

After the testimony in Washington there was still six months of writing up to be done, but no money. IUCN eventually agreed to extend my contract by six months at half-pay, and allowed me to take on other commissions in order to top up my earnings.

I was perplexed as to how to deal with Parker's flawed *tour de force*. In the end I sent IUCN a covering letter and advised them to ignore Parker's blunt criticisms. I dismissed the idea of self-regulation in the ivory trade, recommended total bans in selected countries, and warned my American friends to expect a counter-attack from the traders in which they would seize on every fact favourable to themselves. Never in my wildest moments did I expect that Parker would lead this attack, and that I would come to believe he was the leading lobbyist for the ivory trade, and a trader himself.

In September 1979 we had a chance to visit Zambia to count the elephants living in the Luangwa Valley. The flight was five hours non-stop in *5Y BAD*, from Nairobi to Kasama, where we slept in an atrocious hotel infested with noisy whores and persistent mosquitoes. Norman Carr's camp at Chibembe in the Luangwa Valley National Park was a delightful contrast. It was set on the banks of the Luangwa River, shaded by beautiful evergreen *Trichelia* trees, and echoed all day long to the drowsy calls of wood doves. Upstream, crocodiles sunned themselves on sand bars and bushbuck emerged in the evenings to browse along the banks.

Norman was one of those legendary figures in the George Adamson mould. Like Adamson he had even raised two lion cubs and returned them to the wild. As a freelance ivory hunter and then as a wildlife control officer, he had shot hundreds of elephants. It was as a game warden and conservationist in what was then Northern Rhodesia, that he created the huge Kafue National Park in 1957, before retiring in 1961 to pioneer tourism in the Luangwa where he lived still, the grand old man of the valley.

The Luangwa is Zambia's finest national park; a wilderness the size of Devon, filled with baobabs and ebony groves, airy winterthorns and endless aisles of autumn-coloured mopane woodland.

There are plains, too; tall expanses of yellow *kasensi* grass where the Luangwa lions wait to ambush the buffalo as they move down from the Muchinga escarpment at the start of the dry season, and dense thickets in whose shadows lived one of the biggest black rhino populations in the whole of Africa.

But it was for its elephants that the Luangwa was best known. Apart from the Selous in Tanzania it had no rival in Africa. When part of it was counted in the early seventies, scientists had come up with a figure of eighty-six thousand elephants; but the whole valley was thought to hold at least one hundred thousand. But that was before the poachers moved in.

For a week we flew over the woods and floodplains and ox-bow lagoons of the Luangwa, looking for elephants between the meandering brown river and the Muchinga escarpment which rises in the west. The scene was familiar; plenty of live elephants, but also many dead ones.

In the evenings, flying low along the river after the long day's counting, we could see acres of mopane trees which looked as if they had been hit by shell-fire – clear evidence of elephant overcrowding. However, the carcasses told us that poaching was heavy, although not on the scale of Tsavo or Murchison, and this was confirmed by the wardens. It was clear that Luangwa was facing exactly the same sort of pressures from the ivory trade as the East African parks. At this rate Luangwa, the park with too many elephants, would soon become a park with too few.

When our survey was completed I wrote to Peter Scott and reported a 40 per cent drop in elephant numbers since a previous count in 1973, on the strength of which a massive cull had been recommended. It was clear that culling simply was not an option until poaching could be controlled.

By Christmas I was exhausted, but able to look back with some feeling of progress. In the past three years with the help of numerous colleagues we had made aerial surveys of twenty-one elephant populations and confirmed beyond doubt that the ivory crisis had infected all but a few countries in the south of Africa. The elephant's predicament was now firmly on the front pages of major western newspapers. In Kenya our work had undisputedly proved that more than half the elephants had already been lost, a fact which the Government had previously denied but now accepted. Now, with funds from the World Bank, better news was coming from Tsavo. Bill Woodley told me that Jo Kioko, a promising young warden, had driven the poachers out of the park in a series of running battles. We felt that by making elephants an international issue we had contributed to the government's resolve.

All over Africa scientists were now trying to estimate elephant populations. The first overview of the continent's elephants gave us a ball-park figure of 1.3 million. This sounded like an awful lot of elephants. But the evidence, even in famous national parks, gave no doubt that numbers in themselves were no protection.

In addition, our trip to West and Central Africa had revealed the true international extent of the ivory crisis. It had exposed the hub of ivory corruption which existed in Zaire, the ruthless exploitation of elephants by La Couronne in CAR, the ivory free-for-all in Cameroon and the extensive ivory smuggling into Congo. West Africa could almost be written off where large numbers of elephants were concerned, but the Central African countries still possessed the core of Africa's elephants and it was clear from all the reports that if anything they were more at risk than those in East Africa.

What was needed now was an overall conservation strategy. The result was the African Elephant Action Plan, a loose-leaf document based on three years of investigations, and feed-back from the African Elephant Specialist Group, complete with maps, tables and recommendations. It was presented in a readable form and was supposed to cover all the most important factors that would ensure the elephant's survival. But my main concern was to maintain the momentum for some definite action to resolve the immediate ivory crisis.

The Action Plan was therefore based on two principles: that any strategy should reinforce the protected areas, and at the same time tackle the burgeoning illegal ivory trade. I was convinced that the latter was all-important and argued in my reports for selective trophy-trading bans in Africa, including the abolition of all the iniquitous collectors' and buyers' permits, especially in countries like Cameroon, Zaire, Central African Empire and Congo. This I thought would be a major step towards bringing the trade under control. At that time, I had always assumed there could be a moderate, properly regulated trade in Southern Africa and those few countries where poaching was not a problem.

The information contained in the Ivory Trade Studies carried out by Parker and myself provided us with a launching pad for united international action against the illegal trade. IUCN had declared their support for my position on the trade. The US public were ready to move, either by supporting selective ivory import bans or by going the whole hog and calling for a total import ban.

In summing up my views on the ivory trade I did not mince my words:

> *The only way to counter the wider ivory trade is for united international action. CITES provides the framework, but, in addition, there is need for fully co-ordinated police action against the illegal ivory traders. It should mean throwing open all the accounts, documents and trade secrets of the companies dealing in ivory. Searches made through the documents relating to finance of the trade would be very revealing.*

This statement must have been seen as a declaration of war, since ever afterwards I found strange things happening. Mysterious allegations surfaced with my sponsors, from sources that were never identified. I heard second- and third-hand rumours that I had fiddled WWF funds, that I had been paid twice for the same work, that I had been buying ivory up in the Sudan and in Manyara, and in the years to come that I was running guns by air into Uganda. I knew of no one I had worked with who would ever make such statements.

To my consternation I was soon to find that my major critic was none other than my erstwhile consultant, Ian Parker, now representing the European Ivory Trader's Association, and that the struggle to save Africa's elephants would be sabotaged with the active connivance of many within the conservation community on the spurious contention that my presentation was not sufficiently scientific.

At the root of the criticism lay the real uncertainties inherent in counting elephants. Elephant counting was not a precise science. Even aerial counts were not precise, depending to a large extent on the skill of pilot and observers, and were easy to dispute. Many were based on strip samples and ended up with a plus or minus factor, understood by scientists and statisticians, but baffling to wardens, journalists and members of the public. On the other hand, ignoring statistics when speaking to the Press was likely to provoke the wrath of fellow scientists.

Apart from such niceties, reported trends were repeated with such consistency from country to country that there could be no doubt as to the general decline of elephants. In case after case the sudden surge in ivory prices and the reported killing of elephants all occurred in the mid- to late seventies, and where aerial surveys could be made in East and Central Africa, these confirmed negative trends with a mounting ratio of elephant carcasses.

In the event, the saboteurs had a field day with the Action Plan, which was not supposed to be read as a scientific paper, and the concern which we had generated for the elephants was dissipated in the most futile fashion. I did not know it then, but this was the beginning of the ivory conspiracy whose shameful intrigues would hold back the cause of elephant conservation in Africa for another decade.

CHAPTER SEVENTEEN

IAIN: *The Turning Point*

1980, Uganda and Kenya

THE year 1980 began auspiciously. At a meeting with IUCN to my amazement I was given red-carpet treatment, and ushered directly into the presence of David Munro, the director-general. Everyone was keen that I should continue the elephant work. Having ignored all drafts sent to them for the last two years it now turned out they liked the African Elephant Action Plan. I suggested that the Elephant Group, which had been set up by the IUCN Survival Service Commission in 1976, should meet in Nairobi as soon as possible.

However, I was annoyed by a recently published article in *Animal Kingdom*, the magazine of the New York Zoological Society. The author had been provided with a great deal of information from our programme. Although broad in scope and giving all points of view, the tone of the article was decidedly tilted in favour of Parker, and gave credibility to his views on the ivory trade.

It admitted that Parker was biased in favour of the trade, but presented the doubts Parker had thrown on the destruction of elephants in the equatorial forest without counterbalance. The reporter had even gone to meet Vaneco in Belgium, the company whose name I had seen on the Zaire permit for one hundred tonnes, and Jacques

Lewkowicz, the owner of France Croco, both of whom he portrayed in a sympathetic light. It was all sweetness and light where the traders were concerned, and all the more unfortunate for having been endorsed by one of the world's most prestigious conservationist bodies.

In the meantime the doors opened at last to Uganda. Idi Amin's reign of terror had been ended by the Tanzanian army, who were still in occupation, and I was invited by the Board of Trustees of the Uganda National Parks to make a survey of the most important elephant populations. Lifting off from Wilson Airport, I suddenly felt relaxed as we headed for the Africa where few bureaucrats ever set foot. Rick Weyerhaueser, who had worked for me in Manyara, and Patrick Holt who had been with me in the Luangwa Valley, were my companions.

Rob Malpas, the elephant scientist I had last seen at Murchison Falls in 1976, was waiting at Entebbe Airport. Tall and emaciated, he stood there with his skin wrapped around his bones like a Category 2 elephant carcass. Uganda after Amin was *terra incognita* once again and Rob was our guide. He had done courageous work over the years, keeping his head down but bringing out the facts, fighting the battle for the elephants as best he could through research. The park survey represented an opportunity for him to resume his research again on the right lines.

I taxied down to the old airport for fuel, opposite the control tower which had been blasted by the Israelis. Amin's MiGs, close to which I had been warned not to wander, were no longer in neat rows; but their remains were scattered around, riddled with bullet holes.

Rob had seen to all the paperwork, and we were able to go straight on to the Queen Elizabeth National Park without having to spend a single day in the city. The country was said to be in chaos, and the victory of the anti-Amin forces had brought no respite to violence. Faction fighting and armed robbery were now the order of the day.

In Queen Elizabeth National Park we were warmly greeted by my old Ugandan friend Eric Edroma and his staff of Ugandan scientists. On the very first evening we drove to see a group of elephants that had been gunned down by Tanzanian soldiers six months previously. One small skeleton was that of a six year old and was still compact except for the skull which had been hacked to remove its cigar-sized tusks. In another carcass I found three small calibre rounds so close together that they must have been fired in a burst. It was my first sight of AK bullets which later became all too familiar.

At dinner Eric made a charming speech of welcome, as we sat down to a huge meal of *matoke*, rice, beans and bananas in the Mweya Lodge. In Uganda, in spite of the war, friendships were so much easier between the races. Situated on a remote peninsula in Lake Edward, the lodge had somehow escaped the looting and still displayed two magnificent pairs of tusks on its walls – relics of a bygone age of huge bulls that had disappeared from East Africa during the period I had worked on elephants.

We immediately began a count in the Queen Elizabeth National Park. Once more Edroma produced the fuel and paid for it from his own pocket; but my joy of flying and working with a good team was tempered by shock as we discovered the extent of the elephant slaughter. Of the 1,230 elephants I had seen four years earlier we found only 150, most of them tightly clustered around the lodge, where they felt safer. It was desperately sad. The rest had been shot, poached, eaten, finished. I could hardly believe it.

One night not long after my arrival we heard rapid firing of automatics, and at the end of our next count found five dead elephants covered in vultures in thick bush across the water from Mweya. The carcasses were streaked with vulture droppings, and hyenas had chewed the feet, but not a scrap of meat had been touched by the poachers. I had never seen such fresh elephant bodies in a heap and we duly photographed them so that the world could know what was happening. The photographs have been used widely ever since, and whenever I look at them I can still feel the waves of anger that I felt then at this casual killing.

In the south of Queen Elizabeth National Park the vegetation had greatly thickened, and we could only hope that we were missing a large number of elephants under the foliage. However, a ground trip made by Rob Malpas had detected virtually no elephant dung in the Maramagambo Forest, so we could not be optimistic.

We later heard that Tanzanians were on the rampage, shooting wildly in Kampala, and one afternoon our plane came under heavy machine-gun fire at Kasese Airfield near the northern boundary. I could not see the rapid flickers of flame from the guns, but I hurriedly pulled the plane up out of reach. The bullets must have passed very close. They seemed to rip the very fabric of the air, and their sound was quite unmistakable, despite the fact that this was the very first time any of us had been under fire. 'It is in the afternoon they are dangerous,' said Eric, 'because by five o'clock they are all drunk.'

We continued the count curiously elated by this near-miss, and I could not help thinking of something Winston Churchill had once said: 'To be shot at and to get away with it is the most exhilarating experience in the world.' When we found a poachers' camp on the edge of the lake on the way home, with strips of meat hanging in the trees, I swooped above their heads until they fled in all directions or dived off their canoes into the water.

When the counting at Queen Elizabeth National Park was finished we moved on to Murchison Falls National Park, flying past the shrouded Mountains of the Moon and along the great Lake Mobutu (formerly Lac Albert) until we reached Paraa.

There we found Alfred Labongo, the warden who had evaded Amin's State Research Bureau, and who had returned from exile in Tanzania as soon as the Liberation War had ended. He was an impressive figure, a great tall man with a deep voice and a natural dignity and sense of leadership. 'My rangers have not been paid for three months,' he growled. 'It is turning them into poachers.'

The hotel at Paraa was a shell. The roof had a hole blown in it by some explosive projectile, and everything movable had been looted. Amin's troops had retreated through the park, and what they could not take, villagers had removed before order was restored.

It was clear we could not stay at Paraa, but at least the Chobe Lodge was still intact. There we met Mishak Adupa, a young Karamajong warden who spoke with wit and intelligence of how he had organized all the staff to run into the bush with the hotel's valuables when he heard that Amin's troops were approaching. Later, thanks to him, he said, the Tanzanians had given the rangers numerous West German G3 automatic rifles and quantities of ammunition captured from Amin's army. Adupa insisted that despite the conditions the rangers had remained faithful. 'You see, doctor,' he told me, 'it is because I have taught them to love the animals so much.'

We were shown the armouries, stacked with skins, spears and traps, long hippo harpoons, piles of tusks and rhino horns. There was also a curious mixture of weaponry: rocket-propelled grenades,

mortar bombs, home-made guns and long rows of automatic rifles
– all the debris of Uganda's recent ghastly history come to roost in
one of Africa's great national parks.

Chobe made an ideal base for the count, but the flying schedule
was gruelling. We started with a sample count, covering the park
and surrounding game reserves, and including a reconnaissance into
an area optimistically called the Elephant Sanctuary that stretched
right up to the Sudanese border. To our amazement we found that
despite a dearth of buffalo and elephant, one species, the Uganda
kob, had thrived. These handsome antelopes were doing well, both
in Murchison and in Queen Elizabeth Park.

On the North Bank of the Nile we found that the presence of
rangers had deterred the poaching to some extent. Nevertheless, we
soon spotted several freshly killed elephants. Altogether we saw only
2,200 live elephants – a big drop from the four thousand counted
in the 1960s.

South of the Nile our count was traumatic. We flew for hours and
found poachers' camps with meat laid out on low wooden racks and
evidence of much activity, especially the ashes of old camp fires.

Then a sudden excited shout came from Eric in the back seat:
'Elephants, elephants.' Below stood a big herd of 110 animals,
huddled together for self-protection. Behind them lay a swathe in the
tall grass, where they had fled in panic, and when we followed their
path we came upon the sickening spectacle of wounded stragglers
dragging their shattered legs. Further on we found the bodies of the
fallen, gunned down as they had run, scattered like discarded leaves
along the trail, the meat intact but the tusks gone. Afterwards, when
we had completed our sums, the figures showed only one hundred
and fifty elephants left on the South Bank out of the nine thousand
or so present in the late 1960s.

If the bodies had been human, what had happened would have
been called genocide. The situation had never been worse, said
Labongo, even in Amin's time. Automatic rifles were now in the
hands of ordinary villagers. Everywhere, looting was the order of
the day. Amidst extreme poverty, even the smallest elephant was
worth killing for its puny tusks.

The destruction of the elephants had now become an obsession
which seethed inside me. I tried to conceal it as best I could; but
often, exhausted after the long hours of flying and the sickening
spectacle of carcass after carcass, it was the only factor that kept me

going. I could not rest while Uganda's herds were being butchered, its priceless parks ransacked. Long gone were the happy days, the simple life of Manyara when Oria and I had watched peaceful elephants strolling on dappled trails through the quiet forest. It was at such moments that I longed to be with my family. Saba and Dudu were growing up so fast and I was not there to see them.

It was a gruelling time for all of us. Over dinner we could barely keep our eyes open after yet another long day of concentrated flying and counting. We had all been appalled by what we had seen. For me it was partly the contrast between the sheer beauty of the parks and the squalid carnage taking place within them. The fact that this huge tragedy was being played out in some of the greatest natural sanctuaries on earth moved me profoundly, as it moved the people of Uganda; but we were to find it did not move many in the Nairobi conservation community. They were too comfortable, it seemed, and too out of touch to care.

But we were determined to make a record so that we could tell the world. The tragedy of Uganda could not be allowed to go on. One way or another, each of us decided to return as soon as possible, and make a personal effort. Rob already had a plan to resume his elephant research and get a Super Cub to keep the park under aerial surveillance. Rick was all set to accompany him, and Patrick and I volunteered to help the rangers save the remaining elephants from extinction.

A storm swept over the Nile. The wind whistled through the fever trees and the evening sun lit their yellow trunks, causing them to glow warmly against the darkening sky, until curtains of rain hid the park from view, as if God was trying to cover up that dreadful place where man was butchering his most magnificent creation.

For a while I stood and listened to the drumming rain. Tomorrow I would be back in Nairobi, drafting a speech for the Minister of Wildlife and Tourism to open the first full meeting of the IUCN African Elephant Specialist Group in Kenya.

The meeting, in April 1980, turned out to be one of the turning points in my life. Elephant experts from all over Africa assembled to plead their cause. Henry Minga, Sudan's chief game warden, with his heavy build and pugilist's face, had driven across Sudan from Wau. Fred Lwezaula, the head of the Tanzanian game department

was there from Dar es Salaam, and Eric Edroma had come from
Uganda. Bruno Lamarche had flown in from Mali to speak on
behalf of the elephants of the dunes, Clive Spinage was there from
Central Africa, with Anthony Hall-Martin from South Africa and
David Cumming from newly independent Zimbabwe.

An outline of the various elephant projects had been presented
to IUCN and WWF in order that they could approve the spending
of the million dollars collected since the elephant campaign was
launched in 1976. Now the bidding for funds began in earnest,
and a number of moving speeches were made by delegates from
Tanzania, Mali, Sudan, and many others, all of whom were being
assailed by poachers working for the ivory traders. Only Anthony
from South Africa was able to declare that elephant poaching was
unknown in his country.

In a clear voice, Clive Spinage spelt out the gravity of the situation
in the CAR with ivory figures that sounded quite horrific. Since the
overthrow of Bokassa even more ivory was leaving the country than
before. The French had to send in troops to keep order and for
a while the ivory trafficking was controlled. But Spanish hunters,
using all their contacts, had got special permission to send out their
ivory. The Wildlife Department was practically at a standstill. It
had no power, no vehicles, and was in dire need of some kind
of direction. The CAR, home of some of the biggest tuskers still
alive in Africa, had become an ivory mine for anyone with guns,
money and aircraft.

It was clearly time to press on with our twin objectives of tackling
the illegal trade head-on and rebuilding the best of Africa's national
parks. Unfortunately there were powerful interests at work to
undermine our chances of success. Inexplicably I found that one
of the IUCN executives was exceptionally cool towards me, and
what should have been plain sailing became a struggle against the
tide. Although I did not realize it, the tide had already turned
against our view that the ivory trade was the most immediate threat
to the elephants.

After Clive had sat down, Eric Edroma gave a splendid speech,
describing in graphic terms the conditions he was up against. But
Ian Parker and others argued that until Uganda had put its house
in order and was able to guarantee security there was no point
in squandering money on anything. Nevertheless, our Elephant
Specialist Group agreed to make Uganda the top priority.

To my deep dismay, however, IUCN flatly refused to delegate responsibility. Against the express wish of the Elephant Specialist Group, it took all the administrative reins into its own hands, allocating the sums of money which had been raised, and nothing of any consequence came out of it for nearly a year.

I was highly disappointed at the way the meeting turned out. Oria, who was also a member of the Elephant Group, was so upset with the IUCN Survival Service Commission that she sent in her resignation to Peter Scott. Yet we still remained the best of friends with Peter, and when the meeting was over we flew him down to the coast to look at some bat caves on the edge of the Indian Ocean.

When we returned from the caves we found that a madman had smashed the windscreen of our plane while we had left it on the small coastal airstrip. We had to patch it up as best we could, and flew Peter back to Mombasa through huge thunderstorms with the windscreen criss-crossed in camera tape. At the airport he said to me, 'There are going to be problems, but whatever happens, just keep soldiering on.' One way and another it had been a memorable day.

As the months wore on I became conscious of a bad atmosphere. There were problems in getting decisions made, but nothing I could put a finger on. It was like fighting a miasma. The policy of WWF and IUCN at this time veered sharply towards being friendly with the ivory traders. We were not only losing elephants in the field. We were also losing the battle for the minds of those who held the fate of the entire species in their hands. This was a disastrous blow, and its effects would last throughout the 1980s.

By now we were so frustrated that Oria and I decided to turn our backs on IUCN and WWF and devote ourselves, at our own expense, to the battle for Uganda's beleaguered elephants. Looking back, I should have tried to formulate a comprehensive scientific monograph on the results of our survey before leaving, rather than publishing it gradually over the years from the numerous typescript reports I had sent to the IUCN. But I was sick of the intrigues and knew for certain that it was now or never in Uganda.

Even though there was no conservation money available I had at my disposal the Toyota that had served the project, and my aeroplane, the faithful *5Y BAD*. Lifting off from Wilson Airport once more the prospect of Uganda ahead was clean and bright. It would be dangerous, but at least I was free of the chains which had bound me. Eric Edroma had told me he had both good and bad news for me. The bad news was that Kidepo, the wild northern park in the lawless land of the Karamajong, was still closed. The good news was that the Uganda Parks Board had welcomed our offer to help as volunteers. They wanted us to come immediately and to stay for as long as possible. At last I was heading towards real action.

PART IV

The War in Uganda

'I KNOW *there are some really clever
fellows who say my elephants are
symbolic, allegoric, or whatever they
call it. But that's not true at all. My elephants
are a living thing – they breathe, they suffer,
and they die, like you and me. We're doing
a well-defined job here – the protection of a
certain natural splendour, beginning with the
elephants . . . No need to look further'*
                              Romain Gary,
                              Roots of Heaven,
                              1958

UGANDA: Murchison Falls National Park & Kidepo Valley National Park

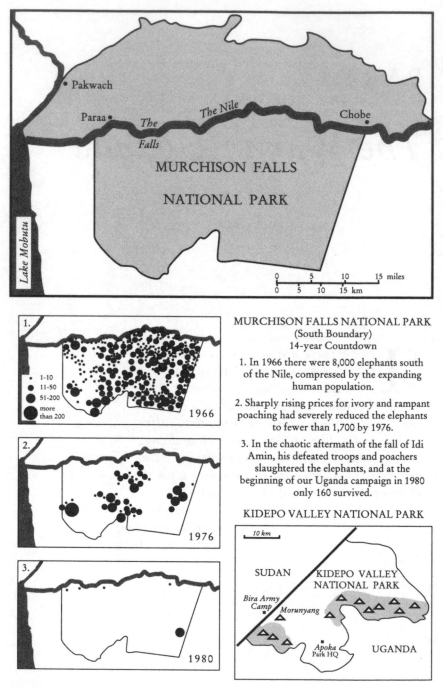

Pakwach

Paraa

The Nile

The

Falls

Chobe

Lake Mobutu

MURCHISON FALLS

NATIONAL PARK

0   5   10   15 miles
0   5   10   15 km

1.

1-10
11-50
51-200
more
than 200

1966

2.

1976

3.

1980

MURCHISON FALLS NATIONAL PARK
(South Boundary)
14-year Countdown

1. In 1966 there were 8,000 elephants south of the Nile, compressed by the expanding human population.

2. Sharply rising prices for ivory and rampant poaching had severely reduced the elephants to fewer than 1,700 by 1976.

3. In the chaotic aftermath of the fall of Idi Amin, his defeated troops and poachers slaughtered the elephants, and at the beginning of our Uganda campaign in 1980 only 160 survived.

KIDEPO VALLEY NATIONAL PARK

10 km

SUDAN

KIDEPO VALLEY
NATIONAL PARK

Bira Army
Camp

Morunyang

Apoka
Park HQ

UGANDA

CHAPTER EIGHTEEN

IAIN: *Honorary Warden*

1980, Uganda, Kampala and Murchison

BACK in Uganda we found the acting head of state, Godfrey Binaisa, had been replaced by a provisional military government. I arrived in Murchison with Patrick Holt to find rangers erecting a couple of Kwik-Pitch two-man tents on the airstrip. Rob and Rick had arrived before us with tents, blankets, uniforms and spare parts. The rangers were clicking their tongues with delight at the load. Such commodities had not been seen in a long time.

Alfred Labongo greeted us with the news that sixty more elephants had been killed in the six weeks we had been away. At this rate they were less than five years from extinction. There had been half a dozen bloody encounters in which some twenty-five poachers had been shot and seven guns recovered. In addition some rangers suspected of trafficking in ivory had been sacked.

More staggering, Mishak Adupa, the charming young warden I had met at Chobe, had been transferred out of the park and was awaiting trial on suspicion of acting as ringleader of the rangers who had killed the elephants we found near the lodge. Alfred said he had become suspicious when Adupa's investigation had become bogged down. When he took over the case himself and put pressure on the rangers the story had come out that Adupa had sent them to shoot elephants and bring him the ivory.

Being short of an anti-poaching warden, Alfred was only too glad of some help which Patrick and I were eager to offer. We were allocated the whole eastern sector of the park and would be based at Chobe with Klau Okong.

Klau was a fellow tribesman of Alfred's, an Acholi from Kitgum. He was a pleasant man and I was able to spend many evenings with him being regaled with stories of scandals within the parks, especially of wardens who in the Amin years had co-operated or connived with the Army in ivory poaching. Klau told me that the rangers in Murchison came from two tribes, the Acholi, who lived around the northern boundary, and the Karamajong, a colourful and martial people from the far north of the country. Poaching by wardens and rangers was the real reason why there were so few elephants on the South Bank, he said. It had been a sanctuary where tourism was not permitted, but this remoteness also meant that it became a poacher's paradise. The South Bank was accessible from Chobe across the Karuma Falls Bridge and we planned operations there to try to save the last remaining herd.

But before we could mount any patrols some food had to be found. There was no money so Alfred instructed the rangers to catch fish from the Nile. These, salted and sun-dried, together with a few beans and some flour scraped up from surrounding small-holders would serve as field rations. In the meanwhile, Patrick and Rob examined the workshops and discovered some vehicles in basically sound condition. They had been mounted on blocks at the time of the army occupation and had somehow escaped looting.

The workshops were near the ferry that crossed the Nile, and as we worked our way through the debris of mechanical bits, looking for valuable items, we saw a patrol come and board the one working launch and set off up the Nile to investigate some gunshots. They were armed to the teeth with G3 automatic rifles and they smiled and waved at us, but looked fierce in their patched denims and ragged trousers.

Chobe was twenty minutes' flight away from Paraa, almost due east along the Nile, and the following day while Alfred was collecting the food we began our air patrols. The park opened like a moving canvas of grass-covered downs, in places dotted with the black shapes of buffalo. To the west palms grew beside a lovely river flowing away to the glittering lake with its backdrop of towering cumulo-nimbus clouds. Elephant trails wound along hilltops drained by tributaries of the Nile and the great river itself attracted us like a magnet. Its dark waters flowed past rocky islands with irresistible force at an ever-increasing pace until they hurtled over the precipice of Murchison Falls.

In this last mile the white water was moving so fast that if you were in a boat there would be no hope of escape. I resisted the river's hypnotic effect and stared resolutely ahead, where a vortex of vultures as small as pinpricks circled to one side of the plume of spray that marked the falls. We closed the distance rapidly, and I caught sight of an empty Land-Rover by the side of the road. It was Rob's. I felt a pang of anxiety until I spotted Rob and Rick walking back to the car. Close behind them were meat racks covered in charred red meat, and the vultures were already gliding down to resume their feast.

Some of the meat looked a bit odd, so I brought *BAD* down low and slow. Then my heart gave a jolt. There was a human being under the meat rack, and another two on either side. All the clichés about crumpled dolls flashed through my mind, but this was the real thing, and in their simple clothes and bare feet, these lifeless figures could evoke nothing but sorrow.

The shock of this gruesome encounter cast a pall on the afternoon and evening, and sharpened a disunity already existing. Rick told me years later that it had been like a horror movie, with the guts of one poacher hanging out, the brains blown out of another, and one of the faces eaten by hyenas, leaving the teeth exposed in a hideous grin.

At supper Rob was silent and moody. Patrick had seen the patrol return bedecked with green boughs, heavy with sweat, exhausted, but jubilant and waving a captured G3 with a bullethole through the stock. Eventually, Rob spoke. 'You realize if you get involved you will be directly responsible for people dying. What we saw today was the work of totally undisciplined men.'

He preferred his own low-key, long-term approach, but admitted this would not save the South Bank elephants. Patrick and I, on the other hand, thought action could not be postponed any longer. The responsibility of what we were about to do and the likelihood of causing deaths gave us great agony of mind. But the rangers' survival often depended on hair-trigger responses. Several rangers had already been killed or wounded. We searched our souls and took a difficult decision, that if poachers carried automatic weapons and were shot, that was an acceptable consequence.

Next morning I went to the armoury to see the captured G3 lying among the spears, hippo harpoons, rockets and mortar bombs that had been recovered in previous skirmishes.

The rangers told me how they had located the gang by day and waited until dark. Then, creeping up by the moonlight, they had caught them around the fire where the hippo and buffalo meat was drying, and opened up on automatic, killing four poachers on the spot.

In the next day both the poachers and the meat disappeared – completely eaten by vultures.

A few more preparations and our anti-poaching patrol would be ready to go. The rangers were keen as mustard, and lined themselves up for a pep-talk from Okong, who told them not to shoot unnecessarily and to bring in prisoners alive. I was introduced to Sergeant Omon, a tall Acholi with a serious face. When he dismissed the parade they turned right, with a snappy salute and a stamp of their feet, the old British army drill.

The days now took on a pattern of patrolling by air and ground. Alfred Labongo joined me for a few days at Chobe and on his first flight we spotted a big meat camp beside the Nile. The rangers closed in, but were spotted too soon. All they saw were about thirty poachers fleeing into the bush; but they recovered much meat and returned in triumph, which boosted their morale no end.

The density of poachers was such that the patrols had at least one contact per day and sometimes several. By day and night the air echoed to the sound of poachers' gunshots booming out on all sides. Patrick, sweltering in the elephant grass with the rangers, expecting a bullet at any moment, sometimes wondered what madness had led him into this green hell, driven by the demands of a demented Scots pilot.

Part of our success was due to the pride we managed to instil into the rangers. They recognized that the outside world was interested in what they were doing. It gave them *heshima*, a Swahili word for pride. Even those who had been guilty of poaching in the past were not incapable of reforming. None was pure but few were totally irredeemable.

It was now that I began to learn the game of anti-poaching. I learnt how the poachers would burn small patches in the grass so that the animals would come to graze as soon as new green shoots sprouted. I discovered how the poachers would smoke their meat beside a river bank to avoid detection, using only smokeless charcoal. I learnt to think like a poacher, and trust no one. Some of them were reputed to be Amin's former soldiers, well armed and dangerous.

I found I could spot the smallest details from the air. One day I noticed a small patch of blood on the ground as I flew over the Wairingo Gate, and later drove down there to question the rangers. At first they tried to lie, but I found more bloodstains on the road, and could see the tracks where an animal had been dragged. The human footprints matched those of one of the rangers, and under questioning from the sergeant the culprits eventually confessed and were dismissed from the service.

One night I joined Patrick in his camp, in order to survey an airstrip in the morning. Sergeant Omon was missing, having gone off in the morning to investigate gunshots inland. That evening the heavens opened and the hyenas wailed as we tried to get some sleep in a camp that stank of rotting meat. Patrick and the rangers lived under extremely primitive conditions with no concession to comfort. Patrick basically didn't care about living normally. He was a compulsive smoker and the deal was that I would pay him in drink and cigarettes, which I did gladly, for I could not have asked for a more loyal partner.

At first light we drove out and intercepted the patrol returning. They had slept out all night in the rain. They were tired and in rags, soaked and bleeding at the knees, but happy. Sergeant Omon brandished a G3, and said in Swahili, 'You see Duglass, we have got what you asked for: a gun and an *adui* not yet dead!' The prisoner was young and his right hand was shattered where a bullet had passed through the palm. Another bullet had hit him in the arm leaving an exit hole the size of a pigeon's egg. When we attended to his wounds the rangers laughed at our concern. '*Adui*,' they cried. 'See how lucky you are, you have *mzungus* (white men) for your friends.'

As the weeks turned into months, Uganda became the centre of my universe, and fighting the elephant poachers an obsession. A crucial moment arrived when Peter Kyeyune, the new director of national parks, confirmed in writing the trustees' plea in ridding the parks of poaching. In doing so he gave me terms of reference which were far more sweeping than anything I would have dared to ask for. I was appointed an honorary chief park warden, and was asked to visit all the parks and take over the rangers and give on-the-spot instruction to the existing wardens. This gave me authority within the organization. From now on I would no longer be a mere adviser, but part of the chain of command.

My plane came under fire on many occasions, although usually I was not even aware of it. Patrick had found some army surplus flak-jackets in Nairobi, which he had bought and intended to sell at a profit in Uganda. However, I purloined the first batch and tested one with a .38 pistol, which only slightly dented it. This was encouraging and I started wearing one in the plane and sitting on another. Not until much later did I discover that General Jack Adams, who headed the US army's helicopter relief of Khe San in the Vietnam War, had told my brother that AK-bullets go through flak jackets like butter. Perhaps it was just as well I didn't know it at the time. General Adams sent me his old combat helmet, with comfortable fitted earphones, which I wore with pride.

I learnt to fly at night, taking off with only the beams of my landing lights to guide me and then patrolling up and down the Nile to look for the tell-tale glimmer of poachers' fires. At times they would fire at the aeroplane and their guns lit up the trees like sheet lightning. Then I would come in to land behind the Land-Rover whose lights dimly glowed at the end of the strip. The biggest danger were the buffalo who loved to graze on the strip at night, but I learnt to drive them off with low-level passes before touching down.

One of the frustrating things we had to endure was listening to the sound of gunshots from across the Nile without being able to do anything about it. In the meantime, I continued my air patrols as best I could. One day I was flying with Klau Okong when he spotted a distant tree festooned with vultures. A quick sweep overhead soon found the familiar trail of flattened grass and the tumbled bodies of fourteen freshly killed elephants.

Next day, Patrick and I set out for a closer look. The rangers moved at a fast pace and it was as much as we could do to keep up. Francis Okello, the corporal who had lately led the attack on the poachers above the falls, was dressed in his green denims. He was with a bunch of lanky Acholi rangers and they were bent on testing us out. When we came up to the dead elephants there were three that had fallen on their briskets, which the Acholis considered was very bad luck for the poachers. 'Those men will all be dead within three months,' they said solemnly. Given Okello's record that was quite likely, for he had proved himself to be a ruthless ranger.

The empty cartridge cases we recovered had an interesting signature. The G3 rounds appeared old and corroded, with distinctive longitudinal grooves and marks where the bullets had ejected. Furthermore the scratches were not all consistent, suggesting that possibly more than one G3 had been used.

The prime suspect in this case was Birigenda, a former park ranger who had moved to Pakwach and now had several members of his gang, all armed with automatic weapons. On the other hand, the AK-cases appeared new, raising the suspicion that perhaps the new Ugandan army was lending ammo to the poachers. I intended to take some of these empty cases to the CID in Nairobi to see if they could tell me their origin.

One of the keys to success was obviously going to be information. We started an informer's fund. Alfred dealt with the intelligence side of operations. Meticulously he began to collect the names of the poachers, porters, their wives, sub-chiefs, buyers and the plans of raids with details of how many animals had been killed. Soon we began to build up a picture of the poachers' routes into the park. We learnt that there was no closed season for poachers. Even when the grass was tall and could cut you like a knife, and the rangers tended to diminish their activities, the poachers kept on coming.

Alfred also discovered the locations of loose guns and the names of their many owners. When poachers were caught the police would interrogate them, and in this way we learnt that some poachers left their weapons hidden inside the park, strapped to the branches of trees. Other stories told of fights that were reminiscent of the Wild West, of shoot-outs, young men in love, of robbery and revenge. The rangers, too, were apt to borrow weapons to settle private scores; and although they knew well how to do their duty, there were few who could be trusted.

The pressure from the poachers was relentless and if anything it was growing in the north. I was afraid that we were already too late to save the South Bank elephants, and that I had underestimated the rate of killing. Reluctantly we abandoned our struggle south of the Nile. There the elephants had all but disappeared and the large group we had seen during the survey had either fled or all been killed. Now the most I ever saw was a nervous group of twenty-five, and after a few months these, too, disappeared.

We now concentrated all our resources in the north of the park. Through George Anderson, our friend from the British High Commission, we became aware that there were a great many embassy people living in Kampala who were longing to get out of the capital and see something of Uganda. George organized some weekend visits, and the diplomats braved the road blocks and drove up to Chobe Lodge, where our anti-poaching operations were based. He also wrote to the quartermaster-general of the British army, asking for old uniforms; and he was particularly insistent that I should meet a young Dutch economist from the EEC, Johann Ter Haar, who was keen on the national parks. I dismissed this idea instantly, wondering how on earth he thought the EEC of all people could help us to save elephants in Africa.

George, however, was undeterred, and not long afterwards a Mercedes station wagon containing two Europeans drew up outside the Chobe Lodge. One was short, dark and muscular; the other lanky with blond hair. Johann, tall and fair, was the Dutchman and the shorter man was his bodyguard, an ex-SAS British soldier hired by the EEC to look after their Uganda delegation. With no one else staying in the hotel it was not long before we had introduced ourselves, and Johann was eager to see for himself what was going on. I flew them both over the massacred elephants and the stench was so bad that we could smell them five hundred feet up in the air. Johann was deeply shocked and I soon realized that he had both the determination and the resources behind him to make good some of our deficiencies. From the ex-SAS man, who was called John, I was to learn a great deal of a more practical nature. This was the first time I had met any of these renowned warriors, who were also destined to play a role in the battle for the elephants.

Away from the front line, the struggle to save Uganda's elephants continued much as before. Our relationship with IUCN and hence with WWF's officials at their Swiss HQ was a constant hot and cold affair, although they did eventually come in with some limited support. The US branch of WWF, however, were staunch supporters of the Uganda effort. So were the African Wildlife Foundation in Nairobi. It was only the people at Gland, in Switzerland, who seemed lukewarm.

I wished they could see Uganda, as a test-case with its lawlessness and loose guns, where if we could win there was still hope for elephants and wildlife in other similarly afflicted African countries. The malaise of the automatic rifle was gaining the upper hand over huge parts of Africa, effecting a Kalashnikov Revolution in the population dynamics of the large mammals. The poachers could be beaten; but only by very well-trained, disciplined units, with efficient communications and quick responses. This was what we were trying to do in Uganda, and although it was a long shot it was the only hope.

I wrote to IUCN after they had rejected my request for funds to cover our basic flying costs, and complained that they seemed totally blind to the need for air support in Uganda, not in six months' or a year's time, but from the moment our survey had identified the appalling magnitude of the crisis back in April. By now I had logged ninety hours flying – all of which was paid for by Oria and me.

By the middle of 1980 I was able to tell Professor Kayanja, the chairman of the Board of Trustees, that with over a thousand elephants alive in Murchison, provided we could institute new tactics and systems of anti-poaching, it should be possible to avert the threat of extinction.

For some months I had felt it was time to bring some heavy publicity guns to bear on the Uganda elephant situation. I also wanted to develop the relationship with the major donors in Kampala. The United Nations Development Programme was led by a charismatic American woman, Melissa Wells, who had been immersed up until now in relieving the famine in the North. The EEC also looked very promising. The West Germans had promised a grader for Murchison, and a chance came to pull these strands together when Oria arrived in Entebbe and I flew down to pick her up.

CHAPTER NINETEEN

ORIA: *A Sound of Guns*

1980, Uganda, Kampala, Murchison, Kidepo

FOR seven years now we had been battling so hard for the elephants that I had barely had time to care for my children, now aged ten and eight. Even the teachers were getting worried and I decided that I would have to spend more time with them.

Living in the pleasant atmosphere of Nairobi's suburbia, I could not fully understand the horror stories coming out of Uganda, whose people were so gentle and hospitable. Then one night Iain called from the apartment of the British High Commission official. 'I'm sitting at the window overlooking Kampala with a whisky in my hand and the gunshots are blaring and pounding across the city.' How could I understand when I did not know how tragically Kampala had changed?

It was difficult to relax in our fight for the elephants. Even the smallest victory was obtained only with the utmost effort; but at least the media had come to our aid. Through them a thin thread of interest was manifesting itself among the general public. The message was spreading far beyond Kenya and the ravaged parks of Uganda: Africa's elephants needed help.

Two months had passed when a truck driver who had come

through Chobe *en route* to Kenya brought word from Iain asking me
to help him establish a base in the parks. 'You have to come here to
see for yourself,' said the message. 'I can pick you up any time.'

Iain was waiting at Entebbe, high-spirited and suntanned, standing
next to *BAD*, which was parked in the shadow of a giant transport
plane unloading food from Holland. Alfred Labongo was with him
and together we walked towards the bullet-riddled airport building.
Inside, broken glass still lay scattered on the floor. Tanzanian
soldiers lazed in the corners of the empty rooms from which
everything that could be moved had been stolen, except for some
stuffed wild animals that stood watching us with their glazed eyes.

With our bags and boxes and camping equipment we piled into
a US Embassy van with some American officials who had been
collecting the diplomatic pouches from Nairobi. There were road
blocks everywhere, but our red CD number plates eased us through
the checkpoints – unlike the ordinary citizens who were thoroughly
searched and frequently robbed.

The evidence of lawlessness was everywhere. Other than government and diplomatic vehicles, most cars had long since had their
head lamps or windscreens removed. The Lake Victoria Hotel and
the red-roofed houses of Entebbe gave an illusion of peace among
the flowering shrubs and trees; but they, too, had been ransacked.

The road to Kampala was lined with burnt-out tanks, and
armoured cars where they had taken up positions among the banana
trees. It had been raining and the heavy smell of humid earth steamed
warmly from the ground. I had not been to Uganda for more than
twenty years. It was still much as I remembered it, but the people
looked frightened and the roads were now cratered with hundreds
of pot-holes.

In Kampala I was impressed by how much Iain had achieved.
Meetings with international aid organizations and simply getting
things to work again had taken up much of his time; but already it
was paying dividends. From office to office and house to house, we
encountered the same warm welcome. The people were so different
from those in Nairobi, where the pursuit of money in whatever
form had overtaken hospitality.

It was *de rigueur* for diplomats to hire their own bodyguards, and
it was here that I met John, the ex-SAS soldier and chief minder to
the EEC delegate whom Iain had met up at Chobe.

'There's not much protocol in Kampala these days,' John said.

'If you are invited for supper, remember to take a toothbrush and change of clothes.' This was to avoid travelling at night, when it was all too easy to get caught up in a cross-fire between *kondos* – a Ugandan name for paid killers.

Early the following morning John escorted us safely back to Entebbe Airport. We were going to Murchison and then on to Kidepo National Park in the north of the country where two rangers' children had died of starvation.

BAD was loaded to the roof and we taxied past a group of Ugandan Catholic pilgrims bound for the Vatican in Rome in a white unmarked Boeing 707. As Iain pushed in the throttle for maximum power I watched the Tanzanian soldiers' guns pointing straight at us as we crossed their line of fire. But within minutes we were off the ground and out above the sparkling waters of Lake Victoria.

From the air Uganda was the way I always remembered it; red earth, rolling green hills thickly planted with banana trees, water and forests everywhere. As we crossed into Murchison we dropped down to the Sacred Nile, with so much history to her name, that beautiful tropical river of crashing cascades and dazzling rainbows, flowing strongly as if eager to be gone from the agony of Uganda.

We did not have long to wait for the horror, for that familiar smell in the air, which by now penetrated Iain's clothes. It came from the scattered half-eaten carcasses, streaked white with vulture droppings and covered with black clusters of carrion birds. Dismembered trunks lay on the ground and broad trails of trampled vegetation left by fleeing elephants radiated from the carnage. Shooting was still going on.

In Paraa the buildings had been emptied by Amin's retreating soldiers. The tourist lodge stood open to the sky, its roof blown off, rooms smashed and gutted. In the midst of the wreckage, overlooking a hippo pool, stood a three-roomed house, built in another era for a royal visit of the Queen Mother. The rangers called it 'Mummy Queen's House'. The bathrooms were still intact, but everything else had been removed, including the electric wire, taps, pipes and door handles. The windows and doors had been smashed and bats had now taken it over.

Iain welcomed me in with a sweep of his arm. 'This is the house I had in mind for us,' he said brightly. I just nodded silently. 'It's very nice, Iain,' I replied doubtfully. 'But I just don't know how we can stay here with the children.'

'It's perfectly all right,' he went on, trying to convince me. 'All we need is to sweep the place out, scrub it down and camp.' He broke off a leafy branch from one of the bushes outside and energetically began to brush the bat droppings off the floor. Compared to the misery of the Ugandans, I suppose I had nothing to complain about.

There were no vehicles at the park headquarters, no fuel or electricity. The rangers were without uniforms and had not been paid for months. Looking into their eyes I could see a faint glimmer of hope; but after talking to them, one could feel that they all had done things they would rather not mention. Iain conferred with Alfred Labongo about the latest poaching where six elephants had been shot five miles from Paraa. Then we left for Kidepo in the heat of the day.

To drive to Kidepo would have required a heavily armed escort to cross the wild and lawless badlands which surrounded the park, and raiders were active all along the road.

We dropped like an eagle from the purple-tinged mountains into a valley of bleached blond grass that ran waving to the horizon. Groups of elephants stood out clearly in the open, feeding unhurriedly in the clear morning light. Iain swung around them again, scarcely daring to believe his eyes. In five months in Uganda, they were the first unmolested elephants he had seen.

BAD was the only plane to have landed on the small strip at Kidepo for over a year, but the grass was cut and the wardens, Agostino Bendabule and Sefa Ndosireho, seemed delighted to meet us. They had been left on their own for many months. At the time we never realized what an enormous relief our visit must have been. Whatever blankets, medicine and food we had been able to spare from our store at Chobe was unloaded into the only working Land-Rover, to the unconcealed joy of the rangers. Wherever we arrived in Uganda the response was always the same. First disbelief, and then delight that they had not been forgotten by the outside world.

From the lodge dining room, shaded from the hot sun by a cascade of orange creepers, we watched waterbuck walk sedately past. Beyond them stood the elephants, encircled by hills. It was quite breath-taking, and the building was not at all like Chobe or Paraa, but clean and cared for, with bright cotton covers on the beds and tumblers filled with fresh flowers on our bedside table.

Agostino and Sefa took us straight to their headquarters, where a surprise had been laid on for us. Two sections of their eighty-two man ranger force were lined up in formation on the parade ground. Their uniforms were tattered and many lacked webbing, but they stood straight and tall, true fighting men of the northern tribes with not an ounce of fat on them, and they held their old .303 rifles with pride.

Only a week ago they had been ambushed and fired upon while on patrol. Sudanese soldiers, camped near the border five miles away, regularly raided the park for meat and ivory. They were well supplied with machine-guns, said Agostino, and had already shot five elephants. Luckily none of the rangers had been killed during the shoot-out, but we counted thirty bullet holes in the Land-Rover.

While Patrick and Iain inspected the men and their arms, I walked to the dispensary as the rangers' booted feet stamped rhythmically on the gravel. Near by, in a straight line, lay the broken vehicles and the workshops.

One truck with Aid food had finally got through to the North, but rations for the rangers were scarce and their families were starving. Thin, saddened mothers held even thinner children with swollen stomachs and sticks for legs. Three of them looked close to death. It was a terrible sight and I could not help thinking of my own children refusing the carefully prepared dishes at home. It was not their fault. It was just the overwhelming difference of our lives which divided those who had an endless choice and those who had none.

I did what I could with my emergency packs to keep them alive. One young woman, still in good condition, had recently given birth to twins. Each one had two little cowrie shells attached to a belt around their waist, and I wondered if they would live. I left rice and milk, sugar and medicine with the emaciated mothers and added rehydrants and vitamins next to the ammunitions, uniforms and radios on our long list of spares.

The Uganda Parks Rehabilitation Programme was massive. Now it was under way we could not stop or even pass on the job to someone else. Being volunteers for such a task sounded glamorous and exciting to our friends in Nairobi. Many talked enthusiastically about coming to join us; but during all the time we were fighting there, not one came out to help.

The battle for Uganda's parks was also draining our financial resources. The heaviest costs were our maintenance bills for *BAD*, who was coming to the end of her life. We added them up and they came to more than $7,000. I rang Iain's mother in London to explain the situation and asked her to take the children for a while. At least she understood and, after a week's holiday together down at Kilifi, they took off for Heathrow Airport.

We were desperate to find funds to get the equipment we so badly needed to the areas where the battles were raging. Priority was ammunition, guns and VHF radios. In Kampala Iain was lobbying with the EEC and United Nations Development Programme to obtain vehicles, fuel, food, uniforms – whatever could be obtained with the minimum of red tape.

In Nairobi, on my way back to the farm, I stopped off at the Norfolk Hotel for a meeting with Colonel John Blashford Snell from Operation Raleigh. He was the only army man I knew and I was hoping that through his contacts he might help me to obtain some arms and ammunition. I told him about the Sudanese raiders in Kidepo, the appalling slaughter of Uganda's elephants, the lack of guns, trained men and communications. Could he help? Before leaving Kampala I had been given import and export permits from Peter Kyeyune, Uganda's director of parks, to find 303 ammunition and send it out to him. Labongo and Iain had seized several G3 and AK-47 automatic weapons from poachers but had hardly any bullets.

'You can buy the ammo in Nairobi,' said Colonel Blashford Snell. 'But what you really need for an assault is to set up a proper communications system with observation points spread around the park.' Whereupon the colonel, known as 'Blashers', sketched out the operation in my diary.

It made absolute sense and introduced me to a whole new world I knew nothing about – military tactics. I dashed out of the Norfolk to order the ammunition from the gunsmith in town, then drove down into the blue Rift Valley towards a small lake where fish eagles sat in the yellow fever trees, calling me back home.

It was another sad day, for I had come up to bury my half-sister, Rosetta, my father's first daughter from his marriage to Irene Ibsen. Rosie, as I called her, was twelve years older than me, and although I had been able to see her from time to time in my life, I had always considered her to belong more to Europe and the Ibsen family than to Africa and us. My father had had a traumatic marriage with Irene, and Rosie had been torn between the two. Before she died, she wrote, 'I want to be buried next to my father.' She was fifty-nine when she died. Now they were bringing her ashes home.

I spent the rest of the day planting vegetables with the women on the farm. Then as the sun set we laid Rosie's ashes next to Pa, and walked back along the jacaranda avenue in the evening light with the purple flowers drifting down on to us like a soft rain as if the trees were weeping.

Iain flew to pick me up together with another EEC bodyguard. His name was Rod, another ex-SAS and looked every inch the part. We loaded the plane with four thousand rounds of ammunition, together with all the boxes, five flak jackets and some sweets for the children in Kidepo.

John, our first ex-SAS friend, was there to meet us and we sped back to his house for tea and talked to Rod about Saudi Arabia, where he had trained the palace guards. John filled us in with the local gossip. It was being said that the elections planned for the following month would not take place and that Milton Obote, the reinstated president, was losing his grip. Only last night, rumour had it, Museveni, an independent military commander, had prevented a coup. Meanwhile, people had been issued with ration cards and the nights still echoed to gunfire.

We were anxious to return to Kidepo with some of the things we had promised, together with an invaluable bonus which the director of parks had welcomed – John and his military expertise.

'Shooting has started up again,' said Labongo when we reached Paraa. This time he thought it was the game department who were involved. We delivered half the .303 ammunition along with medicine and spares and took for Kidepo some automatic rifles and belts of ammunition seized from Amin's retreating army.

Packing *BAD* in the cool air of early morning was a triumph of logistics. Apart from Iain, John and myself, we needed to carry fuel, one AK-47 with twenty rounds, and four G3s with two thousand rounds, plus the rest of the .303 ammunition as well as food, spares, first-aid kit and water containers. The five flak jackets were so bulky that we decided to wear them; but *BAD* lifted off safely between the thorny acacia trees, chasing the warthogs off the end of the strip, and banking slowly with the stall warning screeching in our ears as we flew up into the North towards our fighting warriors.

Ahead in Kidepo, hidden somewhere down there among the trees, the raiders and ivory poachers were waiting. As we approached our goal we could see the Sudanese army camp just across the border.

Landing at Kidepo and unloading the plane was a celebration. No-one could believe the amount of goods we had brought. Happiness for the Kidepo rangers was a new AK-47, and long wailing cries of joy burst out as they held the gun. At last they felt safe.

After a makeshift breakfast of tea and fried spaghetti, we set out for our first lesson in loading and unloading the formidable G3s. Agostino was there to translate for John. He was young and slim, soft spoken, and stylishly dressed in long striped trousers and a spotless shirt, and looked better equipped for a Kampala office than a bush war.

We began with the basics. 'Safety catch on – magazine load – cock – safety catch off – fire,' he called after each smooth movement of the hand.

He handed the gun first to Iain, then one by one to the rangers. It was their first training and the drill was confusing to remember. Then each one was allowed to fire one shot. But what they really wanted to do was to lie down in the grass, put the magazine in the gun and pull the trigger on automatic – brrrm-brrrrrm – at the Sudanese. Some closed their eyes when they fired; others lowered the barrel. They were good people and not afraid to fight, but were out of practice and had little discipline with guns.

The people here were so wild. They loved the noise of automatic fire. It excited them and made them long for war against the *adui* (enemy). Iain's spirits soared. He knew now that they all had a better chance to save Kidepo and its elephants.

Afterwards we went back to the lodge. Below us stretched a sea of waving golden grass, without an animal in sight but filled with an inexpressible sense of peace. Outside the park, terror and famine stalked the land; but here life was simple, sweet and clean. Quick darting sunbirds with iridescent throats hovered around the red poinsettias, and a cloak of orange creepers draped over the porch sheltered us from the sun. How beautiful it seemed; then, in the far distance there began a steady boom, boom, of heavy gunfire as the rangers learnt to use their deadly new weapons.

We stayed out on the verandah as darkness fell, listening to the lions in the distance, and watching the moon sail slowly across the sky. This time and early morning was Africa at its best. Sefa, dreaming of the day when tourists would come to his lodge, pulled up a chair beside me and asked me to teach the waiters how to dress and serve properly at table. When I returned, I promised him, I would bring him things for the lodge. I loved this place. It had all the quality and uniqueness of Africa, and I imagined the hunters roaming over this wild land forty years ago, saying, 'We should make this a national park.' Now Kidepo was a park and we were fighting for its survival.

After a good night's sleep and an early cup of tea, we gathered ourselves into the only Land-Rover, filled it with rangers, guns, ammunition and radios, and set out on our first expedition to the top of Morunyang, the highest hill near the Sudanese border, where we planned to establish the first observation post. John and Iain strode on ahead, working out tactics, while the rest of us wound our way up behind in a single file.

From the top we could look right down into the Sudanese camp and see where they were cultivating their crops inside the park. It was the first time some of the rangers had been up there, and they could not take their eyes off the camp, especially after the previous month's shoot-out.

Having established ourselves and our sentries, we moved off to fire tracers with a G3. Minutes later, our sentries sent a messenger who reported that Sudanese soldiers were running towards their camp and others were jumping into a nearby stream. The whole place was thrown into confusion, with people rushing in all directions, and it caused us great excitement but also some concern as we crept among the rocks to spy on the enemy. 'Lesson number one accomplished,' John announced. 'But what if they come for us in the night?' one ranger asked. 'You are on the top of the world here,' said John. 'No one can come for you if your sentries are awake.'

Driving back through the rain-soaked grasslands, John went over the assault techniques once more. These past two days had totally changed the men's morale, giving them new life and leadership. As for us, it had opened up a new and dangerous chapter in our struggle to save the elephants. This was the sharp end of conservation, where the bullets flew and men died. It was a scary feeling but we were in too deep to pull back.

When we got back from the hill in mid-afternoon, the Italian Fathers from Kaabong, to the south of Kidepo, were waiting for us. They were both surprised and cheered to see us setting up some kind of defensive measures, especially after the months of turmoil. Father Bruno explained how desperate the situation had become. Most of the people were skeletons. The women and children had been deprived of everything they owned and he was badly in need of medicine and food. The mission, too, had been raided but none of the raiders had entered his room.

Evening comes swiftly in Kidepo, and with it, a red sun that turns the hills purple and the grass dark gold. Waterbuck with high curving horns drifted towards the rangers' camp where they felt safer at night while the lions were prowling. Women sang as they ground millet. Life was unreal and full of contrasts – from serene sunsets to skeletal people. Here were the sleek waterbuck walking past my room, protected by men whose families were starving. One moment we were preparing to kill people and the next to keep others alive. The moon and stars appeared and the lions began to roar to each other under the vast African sky while we continued our lessons in the basic tactics of self-defence and guerrilla warfare late into the night.

Uganda in 1981 was a land in torment, so full of hate and emptied of all its wealth. Morals, leadership, and discipline – all had gone, except for islands of integrity such as we found in the parks. Amin had much to answer for. In the continuing chaos we struggled on as best we could.

Our departure from Kidepo was as sad as our arrival had been cheerful; but our visit had been positive and we left with a feeling of achievement in having restored some self-confidence among the rangers. Only Agostino was full of woes. Kidepo was a tough park and he was not made for it. He had been here too long, left alone with too great a responsibility on his shoulders. Sefa was his usual calm self, looking forward to the future and managing his lodge with pride. I did not know it then, but it was the last time I would ever see them again.

CHAPTER TWENTY

ORIA: *Tembo Two*

1981, USA

BACK in Kampala again, I hurried down to the market to buy fruit and vegetables and find some plastic jerrycans for our fuel. I had no desire to linger. There was definitely an uneasy feeling in the city. At night, black cars full of gunmen stalked the side-streets like gangsters in a Chicago movie and there was much more shooting than in the month before. Only two nights ago, nine people had been shot dead not far from where I now stood. I hailed a taxi and piled everything in, and asked the driver to take me straight to the city centre to a rendezvous with Iain.

At last Iain arrived and we rattled back to Entebbe wedged between our jerrycans with just enough hours of daylight to spare to fly back to Nairobi. But this time we had no diplomatic number plates to help us through the roadblocks and were stopped within minutes of leaving town. A soldier sauntered up to us. '*Toka nje*,' he said automatically in Swahili. 'Get out. Where do you come from? Where are you going?' he demanded. 'We are ambassadors,' I yelled from the back seat, 'going to Entebbe.'

'Ambassadors?' His voice rose with incredulity. 'What kind of ambassadors travel like this?' I suppose the soldier had a point, especially with us in our travel-stained khaki clothes from our army training in the North.

'No, we will not get out,' said Iain firmly, flicking open his red diplomatic card, and after much laughter and arguing in Swahili we were finally allowed to proceed.

From Entebbe we flew back to Kenya, to the neat houses and bougainvillaea hedges of Nairobi's expatriate suburbia, a ghetto of affluence in the heart of Black Africa, where ambassadors and ministers met at cocktail parties to arrange development deals over gin and tonics and canapés. It was unreal, coming straight out of a war zone into that comfortable, unruffled world; but we tried to adjust as best we could. We went down to the CID headquarters to identify the empty cartridge cases Iain had picked up in Uganda at the scene of various poaching massacres, and were told that the elephants had been killed with ammunition originating from West Germany, Holland, France, Bulgaria, China and the USSR.

Our children were returning from London and we drove out to the airport to meet them. Two little girls appeared, dressed in blue, radiantly happy with toothy smiles and looking very grown up. How different they were to the children I had just been with in Kidepo. I closed my arms around them relieved we were all alive. We spent some days together on the farm at Naivasha, trying to unwind before Iain had to fly back to Uganda with another load of supplies. For the children, a new school year was beginning. From one day to the next, life took on a full turn with school hockey matches, teas and evening prep.

Before I knew it, three weeks had passed and Iain was back after another exhausting spell in Kidepo. The plane was falling apart and life in Kidepo was hotting up. For once, I prayed that the men were well dug in, that they would remember what John had drilled into them, and that the guns would work.

While in Naivasha for a few days we received an unexpected visit from Hal and Muffy Coolidge, long-time friends from Massachusetts. Hal was perturbed about the rumours he had heard going around in the IUCN. Iain had enemies there, he told us, and he felt there was much character assassination going on. When he pronounced that Iain had been accused of gun-running in Uganda, my chin must have hit the table.

After everything we had been through it was the last straw. 'Gun running?' I blurted out. 'What a bunch of creeps.' Seeing how upset I was, Hal added politely, 'It does look as if these new wildlife people in Switzerland are becoming very pedestrian.' To make matters worse, Iain went down with a bout of malaria; but as soon as it passed he returned once more to Uganda.

I, too, had a journey to undertake; but this time I left our increasingly decrepit old Cessna 185 in Nairobi and took off in Concorde – a little bonus from *National Geographic* with help from Air France – and rushed through Rome, London and Paris to get a change of clothes *en route* to the States. However, this was not a shopping spree. My priorities were to get a new aeroplane and more emergency equipment which was still in short supply.

In Washington my *National Geographic* press conference went off well, and the papers were full of stories about Africa's elephants and their fight for survival. I pleaded with Bill Garrett, *National Geographic*'s editor, to find me someone who could donate us a plane. 'You must know someone, Bill?' I insisted. 'We cannot go on working with what we have.'

Each night at about midnight, as I returned to my various American homes, Iain called me from Kampala. It was morning there and he was just going off to work. One day he put the phone out of the window of the Uganda Commercial Bank building so that I could hear the bullets exploding under his office. 'Listen to the shooting this morning,' he yelled. It seemed extraordinary to hear them so clearly across continents and oceans. Then one evening I returned to find a message from the WWF office in New York, on a note scribbled out by the receptionist. 'Bill Garrett called,' it read. 'He thinks you may have a plane; but you have to depart immediately for Wichita if you want it.' I felt sick with excitement. One mistake, I thought, and I've lost it. Nothing must go wrong. We need that plane. Our whole future and that of Uganda's elephants depend upon it.

Wichita sits in the middle of America surrounded by flat fields of pale yellow grain – like the northern grasslands of Uganda and Sudan but without the raiders. A banker, Bob Langenwalter, was there to meet me at the airport. A dinner had been arranged that evening with the people who were interested in sponsoring the plane. 'Old friends in the oil industry,' he said. 'And hunters who have been to Africa many times.' One of the sponsors who had promised to attend was J. A. Mull; but he was ill with cancer.

I took my place at one end of the table and wondered what to say. How could these kind, comfortable people from middle America understand what we were trying to do?

Just then a tall man with piercing blue eyes and snow-white hair breezed in. He grabbed a chair and sat down beside me. He was frail but his hands had the look of a worker. He looked right into my face and came straight to the point. 'Tell me, Mrs Douglas-Hamilton, how do you intend to save the elephants?' he asked.

It was J. A. Mull, and although he had been advised to stay at home, he had wanted to be there. 'It's a very complicated issue,' I stammered, 'but I will begin by telling you why we need an aeroplane.' I liked this man straightaway. His manner was open and direct, and I had to treat him in the same way.

I tried to explain how we had been counting elephants right across Africa and monitoring their decline. I told him how no one wanted to believe what we were saying until they heard the figures. Uganda was the country most urgently in need of help, I continued. That was why we had moved in to see whether with proper management, discipline and training, it was still possible to stop the poaching. If we could not hold the line in Uganda, I said, I feared the elephants of Africa were doomed.

J. A. Mull had been a keen hunter in his day and I sensed that my story had appealed to the old warrior. 'It seems to me that what you and your husband are doing, counting elephants, is not going to solve the problem. You need proper people and proper guns,' he insisted.

The rest of the evening passed in a daze. It was a wonderful dinner with lobster and enormous steaks; but I could not swallow a mouthful. As the last dishes were cleared away, Bob tapped his glass for silence and rose to thank me for coming to Wichita to tell them about the elephants. Then he said, 'Well, ladies and gentlemen, you have heard what Mrs Douglas-Hamilton said, and I would now welcome your commitments.' Silence followed, and I stared across the table, trying to smile. Then everyone assembled in a small adjoining room for coffee before drifting away.

Afterwards, back in Bob's office, when the last guests had gone, I burst into tears. 'I have failed, I know I have,' I wailed, feeling terrible. 'No, no, you were terrific,' Bob said. 'You'll see; they'll come in with their bids.' He smiled encouragingly. Then the phone rang. 'It's for you,' smiled Bob. 'It's JA.'

'Mrs Douglas-Hamilton,' he growled, 'I think you and your husband are God-damn crazy, but I'm going to support you anyway, and I have called my daughter in California and told her to do the same.' How I loved that man. I wished he could have been there so that I could have hugged him. In the months that followed we wrote to each other often, but I never saw him again.

The following day, Bob and I dropped in at the Cessna factory where our new plane would come from, to see the shells of 185s on the assembly line. 'Build her strong and make her fly,' I said to the workshop manager before leaving, 'because by God she will need it.'

I flew back to New York and waited for my midnight call from Kampala. 'I've got you a plane,' I cried as soon as I picked up the phone, and the message flew out over the Atlantic, across Europe and Africa, to the sixth floor in Kampala where Iain stood looking out of the window.

CHAPTER TWENTY-ONE

ORIA: *The Cull*

1981, Zimbabwe

W E called our new plane *Tembo Two* – *Tembo* being a
Swahili word for elephant – and by July 1981 she was
fully operational. For a couple of weeks we interrupted
our Uganda operations and flew her down to Hwange, where a
meeting of the African Elephant Group was to be held. Much had
changed since our last visit. Rhodesia had now become Zimbabwe.
Bishop Muzorewa and Ian Smith had been pushed aside and Robert
Mugabe was the country's new leader. The war was over. The
armoured cars were gone. So, too, were the young blond soldiers. Many had left the country. Others had returned to civilian life, where they were finding it hard to adapt to a normal
existence.

We were hoping to find an answer to the elephant and rhino
problems; but although it was admitted that a total ban was the only
possible policy for rhino-horn trade, no such idea was entertained
for the elephant. Interesting ideas from Zimbabwe were put forward,
based on its long-term policy of 'cropping' or culling wild animals;
but the meeting proved to be a disaster for the elephant. Iain's
warning from Uganda – that swift fire-brigade action was needed
in order to save the elephants – went largely unheeded. It was not
what the meeting wanted to hear. His voice was ignored as the new

elephant and rhino joint meeting sought to establish that the elephant situation was not as bad as it had been made out to be.

The Zimbabwean delegation, which dominated the discussions, presented their case on long-term culling and the ivory trade as if the situation in Zimbabwe represented that of Africa at large. They were, we were told, a highly trained outfit who were totally in control of their elephants and rhinos.

Zimbabwe's wildlife department was still run largely by white ex-Rhodesians, despite the fact that their one-time enemy now ruled the country. When the African guerrilla armies were in the bush, their political leadership had accused the Smith regime of slaughtering the elephants and appealed to WWF and others to condemn the killing. On accession to power, however, Mugabe recognized the achievements of the department, and at Hwange Iain spoke to one of his ministers who praised their work, acknowledging that it had been inherited virtually lock, stock and barrel from the former regime. The old Rhodesian approach with its devotion to culling and game utilization was continued, and eventually drew the Zimbabweans to support the views of the international ivory traders, with tragic results for the rest of Africa's elephants. But we are running ahead of the story.

In addition, the Zimbabweans were idealistic about sharing the benefits of elephant utilization among the local people. It was curious that these ideas and their practice had originated in a bastion of white supremacy, where they flourished in a more advanced form at that time than in any other part of the continent.

After the Zimbabwean delegation it was the turn of the government representatives of Cameroon, Ghana, Kenya, South Africa, Tanzania and Zambia, who patted themselves on the back and concluded that the elephant situation had improved since the 'abject despondency' expressed a few years ago.

Much credit for this alleged improvement was given to IUCN and WWF, and it now became the accepted elephant doctrine of the conservation establishment. It was said that the dangers of exaggerating the plight of the elephant had been happily avoided. Hwange was widely acclaimed for having been a model meeting, and no one was louder in its praise than Ian Parker.

The end result was that strong measures against the ivory trade never happened, and Hwange led to a damaging complacency which set back the cause of serious elephant conservation for another six years. The formal report did not appear until three years later, and Iain was never sent a draft for comment. The system was by-passing him completely, and he disclaimed responsibility for the conclusions when they were finally published.

A cull had been planned during our stay at Hwange. With a fine sense of irony, at the very time the world's leading wildlife experts were discussing how best to save Africa's elephants, a systematic elephant killing was about to be conducted in Zimbabwe's most prestigious national park, and I was permitted to participate.

The day before the cull I stood on a platform overlooking a pan where the elephants came to drink. All around was a grey landscape of wintry thornbush, pale sand and mopane trees which the elephants loved to eat, heavy with seed-pods. The sun passed down, flattening into a blood-red bubble as it pressed against the horizon. Flights of sand-grouse hurtled overhead, uttering strange, guttural cries and as the air began to cool, elephants, too, began to emerge from the woodlands, drifting soundlessly in a haze of dust that hung and glowed in the fading light.

Three young bulls walking apart from the rest swung down to the water and began to drink, while behind them moved a collection of females and babies and a couple of big males with massive heads carrying heavier tusks. By the time they had all gathered at the water's edge there must have been more than fifty of them. Long after the sun had set, the sky still burnt like the going-down of a great bush fire, the pan aflame and the silhouettes of the elephants, motionless now, stood rooted to their reflections along the shore, at peace with their world as the first stars began to shine. But tomorrow would be different.

Early next morning it was still dark when I awoke. The air cut like a knife and I could feel the cold sand through my shoes; but the kitchen was alive with delicious smells of baking bread and sizzling bacon. The culling team and some of their wives had been in camp for several days. They were used to this way of life and were well organized.

The main culling camp was a hive of activity when we arrived. Already the spotter plane was up. The guns were gathered, the men were dressed for action; yellow overalls for the meat cutters, blue for the scouts in their sinister black truck. The capture cars with their crates were waiting. So were the hunting cars in which the gun-bearers lounged, cartridge pouches strapped around their chests; and the hunters, swashbuckling figures weighted down with ammunition belts and holstered knives, some with radios in khaki backpacks, others holding camouflaged FN rifles, relics from the recent war. Their legs were brown and muscular, crammed into soft leather 'hot pursuit boots', another legacy of the war. A wave of the hand, and slowly the convoy began to move off, testing the wind, and I drove with them.

Clem Coetsee, the rugged-looking chief warden in charge of culling and capturing, had been in parks for sixteen years. He was the eldest of the team, and a highly experienced bushman. He took the lead, wearing an orange blaze on his hat and white shoulder flashes on his sleeveless khaki bush jacket for easy identification from the plane. Moxson, his gunbearer, who had been with him all through the war, stood near by, a wine-red beret pulled down over his forehead to shade his keen eyes as he scanned the bush.

Above us circled the Super Cub. Another young and experienced pilot was at the controls. His voice came crackling down the air-waves: 'I have them in sight – a family of nine – eating – slightly spread out,' and he circled high and slow, guiding us in. Then we stopped and automatically everyone took up their positions.

The sound of the plane drowned out our footfalls, silencing the snap of twigs, the crackle of dry mopane leaves as we crept downwind to where the elephants were feeding. Unaware of our presence, they ambled along, plucking at leaves and branches as they headed slowly in the direction of the pan for their midday drink. It was nearly nine o'clock.

I walked behind Moxson and Clem, sticking to them like their shadows. 'Be ready to run, Oria,' whispered Clem, 'and once we start shooting keep out of the way.'

Above, in his Super Cub, the pilot kept his eyes on the thin brown line of marching men coming in for the kill. Round and round he flew, talking them in. Again his voice came over the radio. 'They're moving quite fast now, heading towards you.' Another wave of the hand, and the killing team fanned out, guns at the ready.

Two senior rangers with many years' service took the left flank, and another, tough as nails – a Selous Scout during the war – took the right. Each man had his personal gunbearer, and trailing further behind came the cutters and the skinners who would move in as soon as the elephants began to fall. And finally there was a quiet technician in charge of research, in green overalls and a green hat.

Suddenly Clem began a fast, crouching run with Moxson at his heels, going straight for the elephants. Then all hell exploded as the bullets burst and hit their prey. Another gunbearer ran with me. The scene was indescribable; dust rising, branches breaking, elephants falling everywhere. One bull screamed in pain. He had been hit in the spine which immobilized his hind legs. On the right flank a cow ran straight into a lethal fusillade and went down as if pole-axed. The herd was surrounded. There was no escape.

The gunmen moved fast now, jumping on to the quivering corpses to deliver rapid brain shots for any that were not quite dead, running over the warm, soft, yielding bodies like ferocious children in an amusement park. The stricken bull instantly collapsed on to his sternum, and from his head a wine-red jet of blood pumped on to the dry ground. His amber-brown eyes were open and seemed to be watching everyone. It was all over in minutes.

The only survivors were two small babies. One was pushing into his mother as if trying to raise her to her feet; but even for him there was no reprieve. Five men pounced on him. A rope was slung around his leg while they held and then tied him to his dead mother's foot. The other youngster, calling frantically, was similarly overpowered.

Hardly had the last shots died away than the men in blue were running in to cut the throats. The researcher, with his chalk, carefully wrote numbers in a white circle on each grey forehead. Then the men in yellow arrived with meat hooks and knives. Each group chose an elephant. A slit down the middle of the back, and with rapid flicks of the knife they pulled off the heavy grey slabs of skin. Then the cutters set to work, hacking and chopping. Ears were peeled off, tusks wrenched out and trunks rolled away until one by one the massive bodies were reduced to nothing but a bloody wreckage of bones.

I looked at one of the discarded trunks and wondered how many millions of years it must have taken to create such a miracle of evolution. Equipped with fifty thousand muscles and controlled by a brain to match such complexity, it can wrench and push with tonnes of force. Yet, at the same time, it is capable of performing the most delicate operations such as plucking a small seed-pod to pop in the mouth. This versatile organ is used as a siphon capable of holding four litres of water to be drunk or sprayed over the body, as an extended finger and as a trumpet or loud speaker.

The trunk has social functions, too; caresses, sexual advances, reassurances, greetings and mutually intertwining hugs; and among males it can become a weapon for beating and grappling like wrestlers when tusks clash and each bull seeks to dominate in play or in earnest. And yet there it lay, amputated like so many elephant trunks I had seen all over Africa.

The men worked hard but there was no singing or whistling. The researcher weighed the ovaries, checked the wombs for pregnancies and measured a foetus, a miniature elephant, perfect in every delicate detail, like a shiny toy with polished toes. All that was needed, I thought, was a key to wind it up and it would start prancing in his hands. In the silence I could hear the sound of the tractors pushing through the bush to collect the meat, and the beating of my heart.

As evening fell and we returned to the camp, I found a young man, a white scarf still tied around his head, hanging up the chunks of meat under the shade of cut branches. In the morning it would be sliced up and laid out to dry on long wire tables. The skins would be salted, the feet scraped into bowls, the fat melted down and the ivory stored for auction. This was Zimbabwe's way of utilizing its elephants, and it was very efficient. The meat would feed the people and the money from the sale of skins and ivory would be ploughed back into conservation. Yet even among the hunters there were many who opposed the culling, and this young man was clearly distressed at having to kill elephants.

Night fell and we sat around the fire. Somewhere out in the darkness a Scops owl began to call, and farther off, the eerie war-whoop of a hyena. The cullers were still in their blood-stained clothes, smoking one cigarette after another to exorcize the aggression which had consumed them. Killing elephants, like many other types of killing, seemed to have a profound effect. Those few moments of highly charged adrenalin, punctuated by the sound of gunfire, when the smell of powder hung in the air, mixed with blood and elephant dung – all this had set off a sort of boisterous cursing reaction which I had witnessed before in Uganda after a shoot-out. One of the wives said, 'They're always like this after a cull. It takes a while to drain away.' Was it just the killing? I wondered. For some it was and had always been a way of life.

For others it was a new life without a war; but none of them liked killing elephants.

I chatted with Clem while he squatted on the bared hip bone of a butchered carcass. Clem was a notch above the rest. Practical and hard-working, he could put his hand to anything. His wife, he told me, could go anywhere in the bush with him. They were used to the life and did not need much entertainment.

By now the symposium had ended and it was time for us to leave. Clem was what we needed, I thought; not those wildlife paper-pushers with their boardroom power games. A few more men like him and we could win the elephant war; but I feared for the future of Clem and his kind. In the new Africa maybe they, too, would become scarce, a vanishing species like the elephant.

Iain had come to Hwange with such high hopes. The group had certainly improved the elephant figures, but neither of us realized the extent to which everything was about to be turned upside down. We said goodbye to Clem, to Moxson and the others, and flew back north to Uganda and an uncertain future.

CHAPTER TWENTY-TWO

IAIN: *Hopes and Ashes*

1981, Uganda, Kidepo

AFTER our first emergency actions in Murchison and Kidepo, the struggle to rebuild Uganda's national parks continued. The parks were led by men who constituted an island of integrity within the body politic, and the parent Ministry of Tourism and Wildlife could not have been more co-operative to outside help, although ministers came and went with regular abandon.

Uganda was still a brutal country. The contrast between the friendliness with which we were greeted and the callous way in which Ugandans treated each other never ceased to amaze me. As time went by and the horrific Amin years receded, Ugandans had to adjust to an even more random violence. Armed robbery, hijackings, looting and rape were the staple diet of Obote's army, and it was doubtful to what extent he was in control. Bodies on the side of the road were a common sight in Kampala after a night of shooting, and as the months went by, the foreign press began to report mass killings.

No one was immune from danger. One evening I was dining in Kampala with John and some friends. It was a real treat and I was just commenting on the excellence of the fish course to our hostess when two soldiers from the nearby barracks burst in through the kitchen and ordered us all to stand with our hands up. One jammed his AK into my ribs and demanded identification. I showed him my IUCN identity card and said I was a diplomat. He was red eyed and looked drugged or drunk.

'We have heard very bad things about this house,' he shouted hoarsely.

'What things?' asked our host.

'Just bad things,' said the soldier, staring with a vacant look.

None of us moved, wondering whether they were about to shoot, and I kept an eye on John in case he went for his gun.

'Are you Christians?' the red-eyed soldier suddenly asked.

There was an ominous silence while we pondered the implications of giving a wrong answer. Then one by one we each attested to our devout Christianity. The soldier beamed.

'Oh, that is very good,' he said. 'I am sorry. We are just doing our duty.' Then they wished us good-night and disappeared into the darkness.

Truly these were extraordinary times; but after months of lobbying, shaking the begging-bowl on behalf of the elephants was beginning to pay off. Oria's fund-raising trip to the States had brought in another $25,000, which was spent mainly on radio equipment. But the best news came when the United Nations Development Project team and the EEC together decided to commit $750,000 for the emergency rehabilitation of the Ugandan parks. This was real money and it made up for the tiny amounts which WWF had been able to put in. Later it would grow to a total of $1.2 million, which was greater than the WWF/IUCN money raised for elephants in the whole of Africa. However, WWF had supported the count which had catalysed everything else.

I was also spending a great deal of time with three senior wardens, Alfred Labongo, Paul Ssale, and Agostino Bendabule, working out a plan for a new anti-poaching force. Paul had been strongly in favour of appointing an expatriate director of parks and three expatriate wardens. What happened instead was that the park service invited me to take up a post as anti-poaching specialist in a new United Nations Development Programme project that was to begin in the New Year. My anti-poaching credentials were still somewhat shaky, apart from twelve months in the field, but I could always turn to the wardens or my ex-SAS friends for practical advice.

My chief adviser was Captain Frank Poppleton, a man in his early sixties who had come fresh from helping to set up a national park system in Nepal. Before that he had been an instructor at the Mweka College of Wildlife Management in Tanzania and I had met him several times at Manyara. His present strength lay in the fact that he had been one of the pioneer wardens in the early days of the Uganda parks, and knew all the ropes.

Having had the whole scene to myself, it was important to adjust to a working relationship with Frank when he arrived. He was a disciplinarian. With piercing blue eyes beneath a shock of curly white hair he could be quite intimidating and I met many Mweka graduates all over East Africa who referred to him as 'that military man'. Most important he had a sense of right and wrong, and enjoyed an enormous respect from the Ugandan staff.

Frank had been in the Seventh Lancers, and the first time he had arrived in Uganda was to help quell riots in the late 1940s. This new job working with me was his last post before retirement. At times he would grow despondent when he thought of how everything had deteriorated since colonial days. 'We're just farting in the wind,' he would say. 'If the Ugandans want to wreck their country that's their business.' But elements of martial ardour in his character could quickly be aroused. When we were in the air with the poachers firing at us from below he was eager to follow them to the bitter end; and every time a message came to Kampala HQ that a poacher had been shot, Frank's invariable comment was, 'Good show'.

Our plans for the training programme took on a new sense of urgency when the Sudanese started heavy poaching in Kidepo and fought the rangers over the carcasses of elephants. Frank and I drove to the scene of the battle. The rangers said they had wounded some of the Sudanese and the elephants they had fought over were still lying in the open with their tusks intact. Around the dead elephants were hundreds of empty bullet cases and Sudanese army mortar canisters, some of which I collected as evidence.

Paul Ssale began recruiting young men in Rwenzori for the ranger course. Tipper trucks arrived in Rwenzori with the would-be recruits, mainly small Bakonjos in their early twenties. We made them run four miles and interviewed the first twenty who came in.

In Kidepo we did the same, but there the recruits were all tough and war-like Karamajong. At least a hundred lined up on the open plains four miles from Karenga. Paul fired a pistol in the air and they were

OPPOSITE – Uganda – Running elephants shot with automatic weapons littered the Murchison Falls National Park in 1980.

ABOVE - Recovering tusks with rangers from a captured poacher, on the banks of the Nile. *BELOW* - Counting empty cartridge cases from a slaughter in Queen Elizabeth National Park.

ABOVE - Rangers in Murchison with new hats and clothes from WWF, take a short break on patrol. *BELOW* - Too late, rangers get to the faceless corpse of an elephant, with tusks already taken out at night. *OVERLEAF* - While flying over the park, we found these poachers, who had been armed, shot by rangers next to their meat racks on the southern bank of Murchison Park.

Uganda: *ABOVE* - John, formerly with the SAS, gives the rangers and us our first lesson in self-defence with automatic weapons in Kidepo, with Agostino Bendabule next to him as his interpreter. *BELOW* - After two months training, rangers armed to the teeth, ready to take on the Sudanese soldiers who invaded Kidepo. Sgt. Peter Lokwe (*bottom left*) with Piramoi (*second right*). *OPPOSITE* - The rangers as we met them on our first visit to Kidepo - thin but proud with ragged uniforms and 303 rifles. *OVERLEAF* - **Northern nomad lands:** *LEFT* - 1956 - Naked Turkanas in northern Kenya cut up hunted bull for a feast of meat. *RIGHT* - 1981 - Armed soldiers feast on poached elephant in Karamoja, northern Uganda.

Zimbabwe: *ABOVE LEFT* – Hwange – First to be cut off the dead elephants are the ears. The animal's skin is carefully dissected into better and lesser sections. *ABOVE MIDDLE* – Live babies are tied to their dead mothers as skinning starts. *ABOVE RIGHT* – As the culler leaps on to freshly killed elephants, a bull receives his *coup de grâce*. *RIGHT* – Chalked numbering starts the day's processing as each elephant is sexed, aged, weighed and valued.

ABOVE LEFT AND RIGHT - Trailers transport skins and meat from the killing place to the processing centres in the bush. *BELOW* - Meat is cut into strips and laid out on long tables to dry in the sun. *OPPOSITE* - Skins are scraped, kept in brine and later packed with salt.

ABOVE AND BELOW - While butchering takes place, the distressed youngsters are pulled and pushed over carcasses into their crates. This one tried to resist with its trunk, as a younger calf from the family, too small to rear in captivity, lay dead near by.

ABOVE AND BELOW - Animal contractors buy the year's supply of baby elephants. Youngsters too big to fit in crates are immobilized with tranquillizing darts, then carried off in small bush vehicles. A hat is placed over the eye to avoid sun-scorching.

off, bounding like gazelles along the road and jostling for position. We drove ahead to wait for them at the finish. But to our amazement no sooner had we settled down than the first arrival came loping in. The fastest man had covered the four miles in sixteen and a half minutes. We were astounded, and I still wonder if the speedometer was reading correctly. The athlete Roger Bannister had trained at international level to break the four-minute mile, and here were these wild, unschooled Karamajong careering into Karenga having averaged his world-beating speed over four miles. We decided they were just what we needed for the arduous profession of national parks rangers, and we planned for the course to start in a few weeks' time.

After the recruiting I was at Paraa for a short spell before the training was about to begin. One day I heard running footsteps and an urgent knocking on the door and knew something bad must have happened. News had come from Kidepo of another engagement with the Sudanese, but worse was to follow. Agostino and Sefa had crashed in their aeroplane. I was stunned. I would have to go up there. I took off at once, taking Miramuibi, the engineer warden, so that we could carry out an investigation.

As I flew into Apoka I could see a blackened wedge of burnt grass, and at its apex, the plane. The cabin was a mound of ash. Only the wing tip and the tail, with its gorilla emblem of the Frankfurt Zoological Society, remained intact. The engine was half-melted and the propeller had wilted and dripped molten aluminium off the tip like a candle. A fragment of the Wildlife Awareness Week T-shirt which Oria had given Agostino, lay among the wreckage and I could just make out the blue casing of a ground-to-air radio which I had lent him when his own aircraft radio had packed up a week or so before.

A young park cadet met us at the strip and described what had happened. The Apoka airstrip was an awkward spot. It was built on a slope and beset by a tearing downhill wind. You could either take off uphill into the strong wind, or downhill with the wind screaming at your back – a choice no pilot relished.

In the event Agostino took off uphill. He became airborne before the end of the runway but there was still rising ground in front of him and the plane was heavily loaded. It had just reached tree-top height when suddenly the starboard wing dropped and clipped the

---

OPPOSITE – Captured baby elephants begin their long lives of captivity, often in solitary confinement, first in crates, then in zoos.

ground, causing the plane to cart-wheel as it crashed and burst into flames.

Agostino and Sefa were both sitting in the front seat and the high wings with their full fuel tanks had collapsed on them as they tried to struggle out. The wind fanned the flames to white heat. Someone had rushed up with a fire extinguisher, but the heat was too intense and the centre of the aircraft became an incandescent fireball.

I went with Miramuibi to see the bodies. It was a hot afternoon and we were ushered into a metal uniport. From inside came a smell of burnt meat and a faint buzz of flies. What was left of the men had been placed in sacks with the charred limbs sticking out, the hands burnt down to the stumps. Miramuibi was stronger than me. I had to go outside and lean against the wall.

There was only one survivor, Mishak Adupa, who was lying concussed in the mission hospital at Karenga. How he got out I will never know. When I went to see him he was still in a bad way. One of his eyes was blocked up, and he could barely talk. He had been transferred to Kidepo while the trustees decided whether or not to pursue charges against him for the Chobe elephant poaching incident; but when I saw him lying on the bed my heart melted and I forgot the killing of those elephants. Maybe I was wrong, but I felt that he embodied the stark contrast of good and evil in Uganda which, though taken to extremes in this country, was also true of all humanity.

The news of the crash brought all the senior staff to the funeral, where for once they dropped their mutual animosity and spoke only with respect for the dead. Paul Ssale made an oration and honoured the men for their devotion to duty. The minister read out the funeral sermon over the grave. The sun went behind the clouds, and as the guard of honour in their new uniforms fired their G3s in salute, the heavens broke and drenching rain beat upon the coffins as they were lowered into the earth.

The tragedy was made all the more poignant because Agostino and Sefa had been so keen to welcome an EEC delegation who were coming to see the work they had put into restoring the park and the lodge. The delegates were due in two days' time and now there would be no one to meet them.

In Nairobi, hundreds of miles away, it was the children's half-term. I flew to Kampala and rang Oria, telling her to prepare for a long journey. Then I flew the remaining five hundred miles to Wilson Airport to collect my family. Together we would honour the wardens' memory by welcoming the EEC delegates to Kidepo ourselves.

CHAPTER TWENTY-THREE

ORIA: *Clouds of War*

1981, Kidepo

THOSE happy days in Manyara when we could fly back and forth in our little plane, drifting over the shimmering lake with the pelicans, seemed far away. Beyond the blue Rift Valley hills would lie the welcoming fields of Naivasha. There was such a sense of excitement when the plane arrived. The farm children hurried to greet us, running as fast as their legs would carry them, shouting, '*Ndege na kuja*' – the bird has come! Then my parents would drive up in their old car, happy to see us alive and well.

Now both my parents were dead and the children had stopped running out to the plane when we returned from our long flights into Uganda, tired and sad at having seen nothing but death. But at least here on the farm we could relax. It was as if the travails of the world could not reach us. Fanned by the cool lake breeze we could unwind in the sun and remember how life had been before the elephant war began. I loved the trees that surrounded the house. They and I were the same age. All my life I had known the smells that rose from the ground, the cries of the fish eagles along the lake shore, and the faces of the people who lived and worked with us.

What had happened to our beautiful Africa? All around us, too much fighting and killing seemed to be going on. Wherever we went the sound of bullets sang in the wind and guns had become as common as bananas.

'We are making real headway,' Iain assured me whenever I got cold feet. 'We have stopped the poaching in Murchison. We've captured dozens of guns and mountains of spears, and we have restored some kind of pride among the men. With the aid money they now have food, uniforms and regular pay, and the EEC vehicles have arrived.' He was so enthusiastic, with his boundless energy and optimistic smile, that I did not have the heart to beg him to stop.

At that time the EEC was involved in all kinds of rehabilitation and development projects in Uganda under a dynamic Dane, Tué Rohrsted, who years later was to play an important role in the battle for Kenya's elephants. The EEC's programme covered everything from repairing the waterworks system in Kampala to supplying hoes to the people in the North, to help them grow more food. Now a group of EEC bureaucrats were flying out from Brussels to assess the aid projects and ensure that the money was being properly spent. While up in the North, the only place that could offer them shelter overnight was the Kidepo Valley Lodge; and it had been agreed that our Dutch friend, Johann Ter Haar, would fly up with the team and Iain would meet them there.

Sefa had been blessed with the same tireless enthusiasm as Iain, always looking ahead at the sunny side of life. When he heard of the forthcoming visit he began his plans. The rooms were scrubbed spotless and the best of the old cotton bed covers changed around, even if the patterns did not match the curtains. He was proud of his lodge and nothing could deter him. Having made his calculations, he took the only working Land-Rover to buy peanuts and chick-peas in the area. He would sell these in Kampala for a good price, and with the money buy fresh fruit and vegetables, tea and coffee and whatever else he could find. This way his guests would be well looked after. Then with Agostino, he loaded the plane. Mishak Adupa was there and wanted a lift, as did the engineer who had come up to repair the cool-room.

In Nairobi it was school half-term. Dudu had fallen and broken her arm and I was about to take her to the hospital to get it set when a call came through from Kampala. It was Iain with the shocking news of the plane crash. 'Oria, you have got to come to Kidepo to receive the EEC delegation,' he pleaded. 'Morale is rock bottom up there and we have to give everyone a boost,' he went on. 'It's essential. Do it for Sefa and Agostino,' he begged.

'I can't this time, Iain,' I replied. 'I'm really sorry, it's the kids' half-term. I can't just leave them here. I'm taking them to the coast,' I answered defiantly.

But he refused to accept any of my reasons. 'I'm coming to pick you all up tomorrow,' he continued. 'I would like you to buy everything that is needed for a week.'

It was a long flight to Kidepo and we did not arrive until late in the afternoon. We landed uphill into the wind. All around us the grass had been burnt by the fatal fire. The plane sat crumpled on a pyre of ash, overlooking the park with its rim of purple mountains. With dry throats the children and I approached on quiet feet as if not to disturb the sleep of the dead. Our silent thoughts tumbled past the wreck as the wind sighed in the grass with a sound of unutterable melancholy.

The EEC delegation had already arrived, and Iain had prepared everything the day before. Luckily they were all out in the park when we reached the lodge. The rangers, immaculate in their new uniforms, had taken them for a game drive in the gleaming new Land-Rovers. Without wasting time, we each set about our duties and I sent the children to check out the rooms and put flowers in the glasses, just as Sefa had done when we first arrived there.

At last, supper was nearly ready. Saba and Dudu, flushed with excitement, had made up the rooms and were setting the tables. The smell of pizzas sizzling on the open-air fire wafted through the dining room. Waterbuck ambled past on their way towards the staff camp, watched by the delegates who had returned from their game drive and were now stretched out on the stoep under its thick hood of golden creepers. Johann was pouring drinks from a cool box filled with iced beer, wine, whisky and sodas. 'We had a fantastic drive in the park,' he declared with a mischievous smile, and I knew that the delegates were pleased.

Then darkness fell, leaving only the mountains rimmed with the sun's dying glow. The new wardens were chatting together, comforted by the presence of other people with whom they could talk about the park and their problems. The waiters arrived with the hot spicy pizzas, and lions roared to one another through the echoing darkness as development was discussed in millions of dollars.

At one end of the table, Iain raised his glass to welcome the EEC support and explained how their involvement had come about. 'You are probably unaware,' he ended, 'that the two Ugandan wardens in charge of this park were killed a few days ago in a plane crash, together with one of our engineers. It has been a terrible blow to us all, and to the programme.' Saddened faces flickered in the candle-light and the table fell quiet, leaving a silence in which the moaning of a distant lion carried clearly across the plain.

After supper, Johann gathered the delegates around him and a long discussion followed. At the end of it, one of the delegates said: 'We have often read about the problems in Africa, the killing of the elephants and rhinos. But when you live so far away in Europe it doesn't leave much of an impression. People just think the countries are badly run and the Governments are corrupt. It is only by coming here today and listening to what you have said, that we have realized what sacrifices it takes to make a national park work, so that we, as visitors, may sit with our drinks and listen to the lions roar.'

Next morning I was awoken by the all-too-familiar rattle of distant gunfire. Nothing else made us leap faster from our beds than the sound of bullets. In a flash Iain was running to the plane. One of the EEC bodyguards had also come running, and together they flew off to the west. Three hours passed. Then a message came through on one of our new radios. It was Iain's voice. 'I am sitting on a gang of fifteen heavily armed Sudanese soldiers. They have killed a giraffe and a kongoni and are carrying the meat. We have been following them all this time but I am running out of fuel. I want two sections from the Army immediately. They are to take the road to Bira. I'm coming back to refuel and collect you. Bring your cameras.'

I sped down to the Army HQ to give Iain's instructions to the lieutenant. Then, leaving the children with our cook, I hurried to the airstrip as Iain landed. As soon as he had refuelled we flew straight back to the scene of the action and followed the tracks that led away from the cut-up carcasses of the giraffe and kongoni. Iain pointed to a game trail that snaked between the scattered thornbushes. 'That's where I left them,' he said, and flew on, low and slow. 'They just kept on walking but did not try to shoot at us.' Only half an hour had gone by, but the meat carriers had vanished.

Round and round we flew over the arid, empty bush, with Sergeant Piramoi, one of Iain's best spotters, sitting in the back.

The river beds were dry and we looked for footprints in the sand and the eagle-eyed Piramoi soon found where they had crossed, and a bit further on we came upon vultures in a tree beside a waterhole. Then we saw the meat hanging on the racks. 'They're here,' Iain yelled, snapping his fingers with satisfaction. 'They're in there – in those trees! I'm going round once more.' Slowly he banked the plane over the tree-tops, pulling up one notch of flaps to gain height, as we peered down through the leaves in search of the enemy.

They were well concealed, waiting for us. Suddenly there was a mighty bang and we were hit. '*Enda juu, enda juu Duglass,*' bellowed Piramoi; go up, go up! And we lifted vertically into the sky. For a moment I thought he had been hit, but he was all right, and we looked for the bullet hole.

'They're in a position of ambush,' yelled Iain. 'I have to stop the men approaching or they'll walk straight into it.' The radio flashed orange lights as he tried to transmit a warning, but it was dead. 'They've hit the bloody radio,' said Iain. Below I could see our men walking up, fanning out with their guns held at the ready. 'Tell them to go back,' Iain shouted, and as he brought the plane down practically to ground level, skimming up and down over the trees, I opened the window and waved my arms and yelled, 'GET BACK, GET BACK,' as loud as my voice would carry.

Again we turned steeply and drove down towards them. I found a scrap of paper and scribbled a note and threw it towards them, watching it as it floated on to a tree. Someone grabbed it, and with relief I saw the lieutenant calling his men back with a wave of his arm.

Only then, as we swung away and headed back towards the lodge did the reaction hit me, and I began to shake. I thought, I must be crazy. How can we be here, sitting in this death trap, with the children on the ground in Kidepo? Not knowing how much damage the bullet had caused, I sat tense and silent as the plane came in to land with the charred grass all around us. Never have I felt so relieved to feel the wheels touch the ground in a perfect landing. Iain jumped out and inspected the plane. A small hole had pierced the back door where the radio was installed; and when the door was opened, that intricate piece of technology was in a hundred fragments.

From now on it was war with the Sudanese poachers as far as Iain was concerned. There was no other way of stopping them, but I was

worried that he would be killed if he kept on taking such risks. My
head spun with a thousand questions. What were we going to do?
We made a plan. Iain flew the children back to Nairobi to resume
their school-days and I went with them, leaving him to go back to
Kidepo to set up the necessary countermeasures to defend the park.
We would be out of contact for at least a week, and in that time I
decided to call some of our influential friends.

One afternoon an American girl who had been working in
Kampala dropped by to see me. With her was a young American
who was training the helicopter pilots of the Kenya Air Cavalry.
He listened intently to the Kidepo story and the battle we were
having with the Sudanese. His face grew serious. 'The United States
supplies arms to Sudan and I'm told they have heat-seeking missiles,'
he said. 'Could they use one on our plane?' I asked. 'Why not?' he
said. 'If they've got 'em, one day they'll use 'em.'

Seeing the dismay on my face, he went on, 'You know, these
days, you can equip a whole army by mail order. You ever hear of
Soldier of Fortune? They can sell you everything you need to keep
your man protected.' As soon as they had left the house I sat down
and wrote a letter to Diarmaid and Meg, his wife.

'It is quite obvious that the Sudanese army are using the park to
feed their men,' I wrote. 'It also appears from our informers that the
tusks go to the commander or the chief in the area. The most likely
thing is that the two of them share the ivory. For the Sudanese to
wander ten miles into Uganda on hunting expeditions is nothing.

'The ridiculous situation is that both sides now are getting aid
from the USA. This is why I am asking you to use whatever influence
you can among your friends, to put pressure on the Sudanese to stop
their soldiers entering Uganda.

'With the race to re-arm the world, and the arms flowing freely
into Africa, what hope is there to protect the wilderness? More and
more men with guns will be running wild, looting and killing. How
many people in Washington actually see where and how their arms
are being used? Those very countries who are supplying the arms
do not always understand that one cannot eat guns, and that food
is the very basic element needed in Africa.

'Please buy me immediately armour-plating to put under the
seat in the plane and around Iain, which can stop a bullet. Also a
bullet-proof helmet, night-vision binoculars and a silencer to reduce
the noise of *Tembo Two*. You can order all this through *Soldier of*

Fortune, whose catalogue you can buy at a bookstall. Otherwise Iain is going to get himself killed, and then, according to African law, you will have to marry me!'

Diarmaid and Meg did as they were asked. *National Geographic* were informed, US senators were lobbied, a visit to the Senate was arranged and Diarmaid went to the bookstall to read *Soldier of Fortune*. He bought the combat gear I had asked for, and sent it to us poste-haste. It was very useful and a great comfort to have in the plane. One week later, Iain was back in Nairobi with two more jagged holes through the plane.

As soon as the plane had been patched up, Iain returned to the front line. When he had gone I wrote in despair to Bill Garrett: 'If we cannot get any support from the USA, no one will be able to get the Sudanese out and there will be nothing left to do but to accept their raiding over the next months. The whole northern part of Kidepo has literally been eaten out by the Sudanese.'

Elsewhere in Uganda the anti-poaching effort we had set in motion had been going from strength to strength. Morale among the rangers was very high, despite the plane crash which had killed Sefa, Agostino and our engineer. When the rangers in Murchison Falls heard that Iain's plane had been hit again they were furious. As one man they came to him with their guns and said: 'Duglass, we are ready to go with you and fight Sudan.' Now Iain was up there with his gang of wild men, waiting to go on the offensive.

The days crept by and I waited for the diplomatic process to take its course and hoped for word to come in time. By the end of the month I had received several anxious calls from our sponsors. 'Whatever happens, tell Iain not to attack,' they begged. 'It's too late,' I answered. 'He's already up there with his men and we are out of contact.'

CHAPTER TWENTY-FOUR

IAIN: *Kidepo Showdown*

1981–2, Kidepo

IN November 1981 I was asked by the park trustees to take command in Kidepo. I had already learnt over the course of half a dozen contacts that the Sudanese were excellent skirmishers. The last time had been with Frank Poppleton on board. From the air I could see them strung out in a line as plain as could be, marching in single file, the porters with great slabs of meat on their shoulders and the men in green, carrying rifles at the port.

There, too, were our own men in the WWF Toyota, closing rapidly. 'Get ahead and cut them off,' I instructed over the radio. It looked as if we had them on toast. But then our vehicle stopped and everyone got out too soon. All of a sudden two green men dropped behind the column and vanished. 'Look out!' I warned Sergeant Logwe. 'They have taken cover.' It was so frustrating to see that our offensive had bogged down. It all looked so easy from the air – toy soldiers walking through the bush. I could not see what was holding up the rangers.

On the ground it looked quite different. The spindly bushes offered an infinite number of ambush sites and the faster you walked the less time you had to scan ahead. Sergeant Logwe was no coward. He had been in dozens of shoot-outs, but this year had been bad, with the loss of one Land-Rover, the wounding of one ranger with a grenade, the accidental wounding of another by the Uganda army, and the deaths of three men who had been killed when I had flown up with Bill Garrett on a visit a little while before.

Now he was cautious. His column advanced and then stopped. The radio crackled again. 'They are shooting. One of our men is hit in the foot. We can go no farther.' So two skirmishers had held up twelve men. The advantage was always with the ambusher. 'Shoot and skoot' was how John had taught us to deal with a superior force. The enemy was employing the same tactic.

Now I had a new plan. I sent patrols to Morunyang, the sentinel mountain, and to other hilltops with instructions to avoid contact and watch and record the activities of the Sudanese. Once we had a detailed picture of their movements I planned to ambush them on their way back. Perhaps that would teach the invaders they could not roam around Kidepo with impunity. We also badly needed to prove that the Sudanese were raiding on our side of the border rather than the other way round, so that we could maintain our diplomatic offensive.

The first section advanced by moonlight to within a mile of the Sudanese border camp and hid themselves in the hills. That night at about ten o'clock they heard shots ring out and watched as a fire was lit on the plains beneath them well inside Uganda. At dawn they watched thirty labourers enter the park, protected by a section of soldiers. Soon afterwards they began shooting, first a giraffe and then a hartebeeste. I took off from Apoka and flew by a devious route over the poachers and then circled over their heads. Our forward observation post saw them dive for cover as soon as they heard my plane approaching. Two of them panicked and ran back across the border to Bira camp; but the rest remained concealed and as soon as the plane had gone they stood up and began cutting wood and grass. Evidently this was principally a foraging party with some poaching on the sidelines, and two of our ranger sections went out to prepare an ambush for them. The poachers, however, failed to show up; but at least morale was improving and the ranger patrols liked being able to talk to each other over the new radios.

On the third day of operations the park was invaded by forty well-armed Sudanese soldiers. The observation post on Morunyang

tracked their every movement and I flew overhead to direct a patrol
to a place of ambush. As I circled above them, the soldiers opened
up with their automatic weapons. One bullet passed through the
wing-tip fuel tank. Another smacked through the side of the fuselage, missing by inches the head of a reporter who had come up
to Kidepo to file a story on our anti-poaching war for the *Sunday
Telegraph*. On the ground our intercepting patrol was also spotted
and came under fire. The rangers fought back bravely until two of
their G3s jammed and they had to take cover. Our attack had
bogged down once again.

I realized the Sudanese soldiers were just too good at bush fighting
for our tactics to work. As soon as they spotted our rangers they
went into a set-piece platoon in attack formation, using their back-up
of two-inch mortars and rifle-propelled grenades. But at least our
rangers were better at field-craft, so I decided to strengthen our
watching-and-waiting tactics and join the rangers on the ground.

I also appealed to Bill Garrett at the *National Geographic* to help
stop arms sales to Sudan until the Kidepo elephant poaching was
brought under control. This message was to cause quite a stir when it
reached the State Department – especially when they realized that we
did not intend to sit back and allow this aggression to continue.

The days and nights which followed now seem so far away.
What I remember best is the comradeship with the Karamajong
rangers, and the shared identity and purpose we had in protecting
Kidepo and the elephants from the *adui*. It always had been a harsh
border up there. On that wild frontier shooting was a normal way
of greeting a stranger, to which a graveyard full of rangers who had
died in action bore eloquent testimony.

I remember sleeping up on Morunyang, nestling in the rough
boulders, bathed in strong moonlight, the cold creeping up on us
as we waited for dawn, taking watch and watch about while the
camp-fires of the poachers burnt beneath us.

At dawn we could focus our binoculars across the border
on to the tiny parade ground where the soldiers formed up
each morning while their officer addressed them. The view was
so clear that we could even see him pointing in the direction
of Uganda. Then the parade dismissed and we could see the
column of men in green uniforms snaking into Uganda with only
their heads showing above the bush until they fanned out across
the open plains.

The best place to force an action was unquestionably Morunyang with its superb command of the ground below. The plan I devised depended on a permanent watch from the mountain top and we hid there for days, counting the numbers of men on parade, noting how many crossed the border and seeing what weapons they carried. In their arrogance, and perhaps remembering the ease with which they had brushed off our attacks, they continued to use the same well-worn track almost every day, while we waited for the right moment. When I was quite sure that the rangers felt confident, I sent thirty men under Sergeant Peter Logwe to sit on a ridge at the foot of the hill and be ready to move into ambush at a given signal. The position I had chosen was on a watercourse that the soldiers crossed every day at the same point. The whole action was rehearsed in detail. We even crept up to the watercourse on foot and selected a place for each individual ranger to take in the ambush.

Back on the ridge, the rangers familiarized themselves with some new Chinese rifles lent to us by the Uganda army platoon, and the captured G3s from Murchison Falls. They tied bunches of grass together and stuck them all over their bodies and through their hair, so that when they froze they became a part of the waving grasslands. We went over the plan for the twentieth time. 'Remember,' I told them. 'Don't fire until they are so close you can almost touch them. And the first man to capture a poacher alive will get a radio!'

Sergeant Logwe was far forward in a nest of grass between the rocks, camouflaged by dense thorn trees. In the evening light I photographed the group against the incomparable Kidepo background. Since the day was over I started leisurely for the main camp, leaving the rangers cooking their *posho* (maize meal porridge) among the boulders like a scene from Romain Gary's immortal novel, *The Roots of Heaven*. On the way back to camp I visited the place where an entire family of nine elephants had been shot by the Sudanese just before the late Agostino and Sefa were incinerated.

As I drove away, the radio crackled into life and the voice of a bright young Karamajong corporal on the top of Morunyang suddenly alerted us that the soldiers we had seen the day before were returning along the ambush track. The airwaves quivered with the news. Was it too late? We had prepared for a full daylight ambush. There would be a moon later, but would they arrive in time? Sergeant Logwe thought it was too late. Then the corporal's voice broke in again. 'They are only two with guns and they are

taking their usual track.' I asked him how long it would take the
adui to get to 'the place of ambush'. 'Sixty minutes,' he replied.
'And how long will it take you to run there?' 'Forty minutes,' said
the corporal.

'So, do you want to go?'

'No, it is too late, they might see us.'

'OK, fine, we'll try again tomorrow.'

'Yes, God will help us, but,' he said, 'the *adui* are taking exactly
that same track.'

Two minutes ticked by in which nobody spoke while each of
us weighed the odds of success. Then Sergeant Logwe broke the
silence.

'*Sasa, nafikiri mzuri kama sisi na jaribu,*' he said. 'Now I think
it is good we try.'

Swiftly his group assembled and ran in the dwindling light from
the ridge to the watercourse. I promised to stay out of sight with the
car so that, as soon as the ambush had taken place, I would drive up
and collect the prisoners and bodies we needed as essential evidence.
Speed was paramount as the ambush would be carried out under the
nose of the Sudanese camp and would need to be completed before
they could send reinforcements.

So Peter ran and I waited while we both listened to progress reports on the enemy movements from our watcher up on Morunyang.

'They are resting now,' came the voice from the mountain.

'How long will they take?'

'Twenty minutes.'

The sun sank below the ridge and the moon rose in the eastern
sky. I sat and waited on the road. Out on the plains the air shivered
to the rumble of lions. Suddenly there was an outburst of automatic
fire. I drove fast towards it, weaving down a rutted track, only to
be brought up with a sickening jolt as the vehicle settled nose first
into a ditch.

'Duglass, Duglass, come quick! We have killed one with a uniform
and have his gun.' This time it was the Sergeant's voice.

'I'm coming,' I told him, 'but I'm stuck in a hole.'

My escort of six rangers heaved, and the Toyota lifted clear and
we raced on through the long grass in the gathering darkness towards
the sound of firing. Behind us came Piramoi in two Land-Rovers
with some Ugandan soldiers in support. A line of dim figures
materialized in front, sparks of light showering from their hips as

they fired their rifles in the air They were quite wild and out of control, and deafening shots echoed from all sides. In the confusion, I could not tell where the shooting was coming from, but already I could feel the fear of the rangers that Sudanese reinforcements were upon them. At the end of the line, Sergeant Logwe and another were dragging a heavy object. I stopped while the rangers hastily hoisted it aboard, then drove quickly on to get ahead and present a less-obvious target. All the rangers from the hit force were moving uphill to get out of the enemy line of fire, although so far the Sudanese had not fired a single shot.

I stopped to let them catch up when a violent explosion rocked the car. At first I thought the Sudanese had opened up with a rocket-propelled grenade, but it turned out later that the Ugandan soldiers had arrived and in their enthusiasm had opened up on us with an anti-tank rifle grenade.

We did not wait but sped on around the foot of Morunyang, and then waited for the men to re-group. The spotters came down from the mountain and told us they thought they had heard voices on the road behind. Were we being followed? The rangers stirred uneasily. The ugly coiling worm of fear gripped them in the moonlight, and I went round each man, talking to them calmly and telling them not to shoot when our last patrols came in. Gradually the whole force assembled. Then we switched on all our headlights and rolled back to camp in convoy, with one lorry, two Land-Rovers and my Toyota. The rangers asked permission to sing – a savage paean of triumph with one man leading in a high, clear voice, and the rest joining in with a wild-eyed, foot-stamping chant.

Still singing we swept into camp and drew to a dusty halt by the armoury. A babble of Karamajong voices rose to a crescendo as they gathered around the slain enemy, and for a moment all discipline was lost. I shouted at them to fall in, and told four men to take the body into the armoury, but was met with a blank refusal.

'To touch the body of the enemy is not good,' said one.

'It burns your eyes out; then next time you cannot see the enemy.'

Nothing I could say would persuade them, and in the end it was I and some few disbelievers who had to drag the corpse away.

Next day the police investigated. The body was where we had left it, within the loop-holed walls of the armoury, and by now the air inside was heavy with the smell of death. The young, clean-limbed soldier was lying on his back, and the police commissioner pointed out the diamond-shaped, tribal tattoo marks on his stomach, awarded for gallantry. He wore a pair of bright blue drawers under his blood-soaked army fatigues. His mouth was open, but his teeth were scuffed with dust from the earth he had been dragged across. A shot had passed through both his legs, but it was hard to see what had killed him. Then we noticed the tiny bloodless hole below his eye. When the policeman turned him over, his body started to hiss angrily with escaping gases, and the gaping crack in the back of his head revealed his brain. Even the hardened Karamajong rangers gagged at the sight, but I felt no remorse. Here was a man who had tried to kill us, and instead we had killed him.

When the investigation was complete the rangers were reluctant to dispose of the body, and refused even to consider burying it. In the end it was tossed out on an ant-hill for the vultures and the hyenas, the same way the Karamajong dispose of their own dead.

Two days later I went back with the rangers to Morunyang and slept up there under the stars, hidden from the enemy among the mottled rocks. It grew very cold and still, and we awakened every so often to reassure ourselves that the sentry was still protecting us from surprise attack. Below I could see the waving fields of grass splashed by the moon, and the dull line of trees along the watercourse down which our rangers had crept two evenings ago. So bright was the moon that even the soldiers' camp a mile away was clearly visible. There, too, lay the poachers' path, running straight as a spear from their camp inside Sudan and deep into the park, littered on either side with the skeletons of giraffe, elephant, zebra and kongoni. The rangers were now waiting in the hills, filled with a new confidence since they realized that the Sudanese were not supermen. By the New Year, I hoped we might be able to stop the elephant slaughter.

It seemed strange to be acting out these minor military tactics that I learnt in the Oxford University Officer Training Corps, but since the Kalashnikov Revolution there was no hope that elephants and their parks would survive without determined and well-trained paramilitary ranger forces. The long legacy of scientific recruitment at the expense of people with military experience had been tried and found wanting. A balance was now needed.

Our diplomatic efforts were also finally beginning to bear fruit. At the same time that we carried out the ambush, President

Gaafar Muhammed Nimeri of Sudan was in Washington trying
to arrange another shipment of arms from America. Oria lobbied
furiously through my brother Diarmaid, begging the National
Geographic Society, the African Wildlife Foundation, WWF and
the New York Zoological Society to contact influential senators.
Edward Kennedy wrote to the State Department, and at last
Nimeri reacted. A senior general was sent down to the Ugandan
border to investigate, and when he arrived no doubt found that
at least one soldier was missing. Exactly what happened I shall
never know; but the raids ceased, and peaceful overtures came
from the other side in messages delivered by the pastoralists who
roamed across the border.

It was August 1982. The sun came up over the Kidepo Valley
with a low bank of mist below the mountain crests, quiet and
mysterious. The days when early morning gunshots disturbed
the tranquillity had long since passed. Dressed in bright civilian
clothes our little group drove in the Land-Rover past Morunyang,
the sentinel mountain, and through the tall grass of no man's land,
where last Christmas the danger of ambush had been ever-present.
We lurched across the flooded watercourse where we had ambushed
the Sudanese in December and drove on towards the border.

From there Frank Poppleton, Alfred Labongo, Peter Logwe and
I continued into Sudan on foot, walking past two old men smearing
themselves with ashes in the shade of a fig tree, and entered Bira
Village, which stood in the midst of sun-scorched plots of maize and
sorghum. Women in western frocks and *kangas* emerged from the
chief's compound and stared at us with undisguised curiosity as we
sat in the shade of a neatly thatched hut with a circle of supporting
wooden columns outside the red-mud walls, and waited while
Sergeant Peter Logwe, looking incongruous in his bright orange
T-shirt, went up to the army camp. In a little while he returned
with a Sudanese lieutenant attired in clean slacks, polished brown
shoes and an Adidas T-shirt. He was a Madi from West Nile on the
Sudan side, and spoke very good English, with which he welcomed
us in the name of peace. We went to his camp beside the dusty
parade ground I had watched so often from Morunyang.

Some of the soldiers had been playing netball. Now they sat in
the shade of a hut, where I could not help noticing the stacks of
well-oiled G3s and a two-inch mortar with a box of high-explosive

mortar bombs. The men stood up as we approached, hard-looking veterans with a firm handshake. Frank said under his breath, 'This is simply unbelievable.'

We sat on polished branches while the lieutenant introduced us in the local tongue. There was a look of amusement in their eyes when he explained that I was the pilot. Alfred Labongo made a speech.

'Greetings, brothers. We come to you in peace and to say that it is wrong for us to fight. Africans should not fight one another. The boundary which you see here was not put there by us, so why should we fight over it? We, on our side, are trying to protect the animals for the benefit of both Uganda and Sudan. We want them to survive so that our grandchildren can see them, too, and can say that their fathers and forebears saved these animals.

'Now that I bring you peaceful greetings from your brothers in Uganda, I want to say that you are welcome to walk through the park or the main roads past Apoka to see your relations in Karenga or to go to the hospital. What we must concentrate on is development, not fighting. What we want is more food, better medical facilities, more education. We do not want to fight.'

It was an extraordinary feeling, to be in the camp of our former enemies while our old adversaries, those hardened veterans in their green battle fatigues, stood in a semi-circle and watched us as Labongo spoke.

As we walked away I chatted to the lieutenant. He told me that when he was in the Anyanya Movement, the Southern Sudanese rebel army, he had met another European. It was the mercenary, Steiner, and the lieutenant had got to know him well. 'Oh yes,' he said with the faintest twinkle of a smile. 'It was he who taught me how to shoot down aeroplanes.'

I loved walking on their territory and shaking the hands of the very men who had tried to kill us on so many occasions. On the way out we met a preacher, a wizened old Sudanese in khaki bush jacket and dark glasses carrying a picture of the Crucifixion, who assured us that hell-fire waited to burn all unbelievers.

By September 1982 our shoe-string campaign in Uganda had developed into a fully fledged aid programme. From the utter disaster of 1980 with the parks in ruins and the staff utterly demoralized, we had turned the situation around completely. In all three parks the rangers were properly fed, clothed and paid. Roads and airstrips were functional and launches cruised on the Nile again as tourists began to filter back.

During those two years I had flown for hundreds of hours and, together with Oria, had helped to raise more than $1,000,000 for Uganda's wildlife. The early volunteer days with Patrick, Rob and Rick had initiated the first serious efforts at anti-poaching and had led to the aid programmes which were now in place.

More important we had reduced elephant poaching virtually to zero. The number of elephants had actually increased in Queen Elizabeth National Park to more than four hundred. In Kidepo we had another four hundred and in Murchison, although elephants had vanished from the South Bank, there were still around a thousand in the North, and not a single fresh carcass to be seen.

At the same time it was extraordinary to see the numbers of young trees springing up along the banks of the Nile. The trees were a symbol of hope, a heartening demonstration of nature's miraculous resilience. With each passing year, they would provide more food and cover for the surviving herds. What a far cry it was from the prediction twenty years earlier that the elephants would eat themselves to extinction.

Uganda had not proved to be the worst-case scenario that we had imagined. Within the parks the situation was better than it had been for years, and I felt that the time had come for me to move on. As chairman of the Elephant Group I was constantly receiving letters reporting further slaughters in other parts of Africa.

From Senegal, Sudan and Somalia came reports which showed that the Kalashnikov Revolution was making great inroads into the elephant populations. I was shocked to hear that even well-run parks like Niokolo-Koba in Senegal, where the protection had been organized by the tough ex-Legionnaire, André Dupuy, were being overrun. The Kaokoveld desert elephants were being shot by South African troops in Namibia, and even in South Africa, Anthony Hall-Martin wrote and told me that one hundred and twenty or so elephants had been poached in the Kruger Park by guerrillas as the war spilled over from Mozambique. If it could happen there, where else on the continent could be considered safe?

Despite these disturbing reports there was a danger that the Hwange meeting might spread the virus of complacency still further over the status of the elephant. In mid-1982 Parker made a scathing attack on WWF and IUCN, in *Africana*, a Nairobi-based wildlife magazine, accusing them of having created a 'Crisis Carnival' over the status of the elephant and the rhino. He also implied, without attacking anyone by name, that the elephant campaigners had not adhered strictly to the truth and had distorted the facts. 'The results published were phoney and ersatz and have not stood up to any analysis,' he said.

Parker claimed that WWF and IUCN had only presented the worst case for the elephants and that it was more likely there were 2.4 million elephants rather than 1.3 million. The Hwange meeting, so he said, had dismantled the carnival. He claimed that the only countries where steep declines in elephants were known to have occurred were Kenya and Uganda, and in any case the situation there had stabilized. On the continent as a whole, causes of pessimism were balanced by grounds for considerable optimism, he asserted, and dismissed all other claims as being unsubstantiated.

These were curious conclusions for one who, only a few years earlier, had warned of the headlong rush to destruction caused by the ivory trade. Everyone who knew Parker did not take him too seriously as he had always been at the centre of controversy ever since he first started cropping elephants. But I have often reproached myself with not answering this article. At the time I was far too preoccupied with life and death struggles in Uganda.

Although I could not yet prove it to the satisfaction of my scientific colleagues, I was convinced that the spread of poaching which had started in Kenya was a rolling wave now sweeping through all these countries with an irresistible momentum, as anybody with their ear to the ground would know.

For all these reasons I decided it was time to leave Uganda. I had great confidence that the highly respected Professor Fred Kayanja, Chairman of the Parks Board, backed up by Frank Poppleton, would continue to steer the parks successfully. Fred was a man who made appointments without regard to race or nationality, which anyway seemed to matter less in Uganda than elsewhere.

Nevertheless, I had some misgivings about the wardens. Some were weary and washed out. With the ludicrous wage structure in existence no one could live on the pittance the Government offered, and almost everyone was fiddling the system in order to survive. One warden uplifted petrol, another looted building materials, and a third stole a rhino horn out of the park armoury.

With these fiddles going on it was hardly surprising that the rangers indulged in their own enterprises. Shooting a few buck for meat and selling it to the local populace was at the mild end of the poaching spectrum. Killing elephants and rhinos for ivory and horn was at the other.

Yet, for all the stories, I still believed that these men did want to see the parks flourish again. It was no good being naïve and shutting one's eyes to the corruption, but with the arrival of international aid, morale had soared. Basically, everyone knew what they were supposed to do, and given a bit of support and leadership from the top started doing just that. I had the feeling that running this enterprise could not be done strictly in black and white, and that shades of grey governed men's behaviour.

Although our parks project continued apace, the country enjoyed no glimmer of light at the end of its dark tunnel and was drifting into chaos. In a raid near Masindi, Museveni's guerrillas ambushed and killed some one hundred and fifty soldiers, and Karamoja had returned to anarchy, with tribesmen even firing on United Nations relief workers. Obote's Uganda had sunk back into its bloodbath and it was all building up to the next round of fighting.

Very sadly, I took my leave of Uganda. Back at Naivasha I had a joyous reunion with Oria and felt all the tension of the past two years draining out of me. It was wonderful to be back in the peace of the farm. No longer did I have to awaken with a jolt to the sound of rifle shots. Instead I enjoyed the bright voices of the children and awoke to the cry of fish eagles, with the prospect of an enormous breakfast on the lawn under the fever trees, and the soothing presence of the lake shimmering in the distance, as if I had never been away.

PART V

To Gain or Lose It All

'A MAN can't spend his life in Africa
without acquiring something pretty
close to a great affection for the
elephants. Those great herds are, after all, the
last symbol of liberty left among us'

Romain Gary,
Roots of Heaven,
1958

CHAPTER TWENTY-FIVE

IAIN: *In the Wilderness*

1982, Kenya

I came away from Uganda believing that if elephants and wild places mattered, no half-measures were going to keep them going. If we wanted the riches of nature to survive our own destructiveness, then people would have to match their beliefs with action. In Africa there was so much more natural wealth than other continents, and no animal symbolized this better than the elephant.

Clearly the long-term threat to the elephants would be an invasion of their habitat by all the polluting behaviour of mankind; but in the short term the far more potent menace of the ivory trade had to be dealt with. Without a much greater emphasis on anti-poaching, law enforcement and draconian control of the ivory trade, it was clear to me that most of Africa's herds would not survive into the next century.

Imagine my disappointment when, having returned from Uganda, I was told rather abruptly that the Elephant Group had been disbanded. It had now been merged with the Rhino Group. Evidently forces had been moving behind the scenes. The new chairman was my friend David Western, commonly known as Jonah, a quiet, intelligent man, boyish in looks, but serious in demeanour. His work was his life, science his hand-maiden, and he had an instinctive feel for the politics of wildlife.

But now he found himself caught between two opposing schools of thought with Ian Parker and me at opposite ends. The people whom he had invited to join the group included some reputable scientists such as Richard Bell, once a contemporary of mine at Oxford, and David Cumming from Zimbabwe. It was good to get some heavyweights involved with the status of elephants, but I wished they would realize what was happening, and throw their full support behind the changes that were needed. From the beginning it was obvious that the Zimbabweans were going to be an increasingly vocal component of this new African Elephant and Rhino Specialist Group, which came to be known by the ugly acronym, AERSG.

Jonah also invited Cynthia Moss, who had assisted me at Manyara in the mid-sixties, to join AERSG. She was studying elephants in Amboseli, and it was a welcome relief to have someone who openly appreciated elephants for their social behaviour rather than as walking ecological disasters or potential mountains of meat and ivory for the masses. In her I had found a doughty champion of elephants as individuals. It remained to be seen if Cynthia would be overawed by the dominant scientists of AERSG.

It soon became clear that the conservation climate had changed while I had been away in Uganda. Support for the ideas I had espoused had been seriously eroded.

In September 1982, I attended the first meeting of the new African Elephant and Rhino Specialist Group and listened aghast to Ian Parker and Esmond Bradley Martin, an expatriate American who had made studies of the trade in ivory and rhino horn. They proposed that the misgivings of former years were no longer justified. There was, they declared blandly, no threat to elephants from the ivory trade.

The essence of their argument was that the numbers of elephants taken by the trade were fewer than I had estimated, that the proportion of ivory supplied by natural mortality, crop protection and culling was higher, and that the increased volume of ivory was due to man's relentless expansion into their range, rather than a response to the rising price of ivory.

Coming from the heat of Uganda, and convinced that the reports I was getting from further afield were true, I found it outrageous to hear the destruction of East Africa's elephants passed off as nothing other than a local event. I spoke out against everything they had said, and put my views on record that we were sitting on the sidelines of a vast catastrophe. In most of East and Central Africa, and in fact everywhere other than a few countries in Southern Africa, the elephant herds were collapsing one after another, and the principal cause of their destruction was the demand for ivory.

However, the new conventional wisdom that would sit with us was that things were not so bad as they had been made out, and a bit of rational tinkering with the ivory trade should set everything to rights. Next day I voiced my dismay to Jonah Western. 'We are sitting on our hands doing nothing,' I told him, 'while the greatest mammalian tragedy of the century is being enacted before our eyes.'

One of the hardest parts of losing the chairmanship of the elephant group was that people no longer automatically wrote to me with snippets of information. 'In this town some people seem to regard information as power,' said Holly Dublin, a later newcomer to the Nairobi wildlife scene. And it was true. I found colleagues at best not bothering to pass on elephant information and at worst concealing it. They knew well that without the oxygen of information one's influence wanes.

I realized with a shock that I was now involved in a struggle of a very different kind. How simple life had been in Uganda, where the enemies of the elephant were instantly recognizable and could be vanquished by positive action. To have any chance of rolling back the hostile forces now ranged against the elephant, I saw that we would have to descend into an arcane numbers game about weights and measures of ivory, about the proportions of 'found' versus 'poached' ivory, and what was the true mean tusk weight. Each false scenario had to be dismantled brick by brick before the belief in the sustainability of the ivory trade could itself be demolished. We were now launched on a battle for ideas, but for the meanwhile it was a desperate rearguard action.

It was also in 1982 that Oria was invited down to South Africa by the animal rights group, Beauty Without Cruelty. The slogan of her visit was '*Ivory Kills – Don't Buy It, Don't Wear It, Don't Sell It*', and she soon discovered a frighteningly high level of activity in the ivory trade. In a letter to Russell Train, head of WWF in America, Oria described some of the glaring anomalies which had aroused her suspicions. She learnt that the Kruger National Park could not produce enough ivory to supply the demand in South Africa. When Oria asked for a certificate of origin for ivory on sale, the reaction of many shop owners was that they did not know where the ivory had come from and that they did not care anyway. Several of the traders admitted that ivory came in from Zaire, Tanzania, Kenya, Angola, Mozambique and Zambia.

Deeply disillusioned with the way things were going I withdrew to Naivasha to reflect on the galling reverses which the elephant was suffering, and on the quality of life in Africa. Like Naivasha itself, Africa has space and peace. But Africa can also be elementally brutal and cruel, as events in Zaire and Uganda had shown. I did not believe there was a universal solution to the ubiquitous problems of the elephants in Africa. But of several things I was certain.

First, the arms race and Africa's chronic political instability were creating a much more dangerous world for elephants – a fact which most scientists and conservationists chose to ignore. Human conflict was unpredictable and could not be fitted into ecological theory. It simply did not appear as a factor to be considered in any of the new World Conservation Strategy documents which were now to be accepted as the conventional wisdom. Yet war, civil strife and political turbulence continued to act as devastating ecological factors throughout the decade. Indeed, in the new wars unleashed in Africa, ivory was a currency of conflict and elephants were slaughtered so that their tusks could be bartered for food and weapons. On top of this the ivory trade was completely out of control and the current policy of appeasing the traders was going to lead nowhere but to further disaster for the elephants.

Finally, I knew that if the wilderness and its inhabitants were going to survive it was going to take a great deal more will-power on the part of the conservationists to persuade politicians to act and donors to give. Elephants were an African heritage, but they were a world concern and would need western aid to see them through a difficult period.

I still had *Tembo Two* and could pick up once again on surveys if I could find them, but that had not been too easy. It had become difficult to get funding now for any elephant monitoring. There was only a limited amount of money available for conservation-orientated research, and the emphasis had shifted towards saving the rhino, which, although justifiable, was not helping the elephant.

In this respect there had been some interesting new developments in Kenya. Some of the private ranchers in the Laikipia District were friendly towards wildlife and their security arrangements, with armed guards to prevent cattle rustling and poaching, were far better than anything the Wildlife Department had provided. Perhaps there were lessons to be learnt here? Anyway, it was to Laikipia, to the wild and broken country beyond the Aberdares, that Oria and I planned to fly with Tembo Two to see our friend Kuki Gallmann, who nurtured forty-five black rhinos and three hundred elephants on a beautiful tract of land called Ol Ari Nyiro.

Kuki's rhinos were doing well, unlike the species as a whole, whose numbers had dropped from sixty thousand in 1960 to no more than four thousand in all Africa. Like the elephants, they, too, had been poached and their horns illegally exported to be carved into Yemeni dagger handles or powdered down for Chinese potions. The world's press had been full of horror stories about Africa's vanishing rhinos; but as far as elephants were concerned, the whole conservation movement seemed to be sleep-walking. How could we awaken the scientists and the public to the elephant holocaust I knew was taking place?

The missing key lay in Central Africa, beneath the rain forest canopy of the Congo River Basin. Nobody knew how many elephants lived in this humid heartland of their range. On the one hand, it was claimed that there was a limitless reservoir of elephants all poised to supply the burgeoning ivory trade. Yet everything I had heard from trusted sources such as Clive Spinage in the CAR suggested a rate of slaughter in the forest at least as terrible as that witnessed on the open plains of Kenya and Uganda. I was convinced the elephants there were going fast; but nothing short of a scientifically conducted survey soon to be started by Richard and Karen Barnes would suffice.

These were the thoughts that ran through my mind like an endless refrain as we flew north to celebrate Kuki's birthday at Ol Ari Nyiro.

CHAPTER TWENTY-SIX

ORIA: *The Silent Fall*

1983, Kenya

THERE was a moment on this 4 June, when the day had no beginning and no end, only a flash as clear as a falling star in a coal-black night, taking with it memories of a lifetime. It was a dry year. The rains had barely touched that barren earth with a little life, when the hot northern wind blew all hope away. In the early hours of dawn we tracked the clover-leaf prints of rhino in the red powdery dust. Walking heads down, our eyes and senses fixed to the ground, we criss-crossed game trails, momentarily stopping to listen, and to smell the wind.

Silently slipping through the *Leleshwa* thickets, we followed the shadow of our tracker, Luka. A small, wiry man, hard as rock and black as ebony, he knew every path and stream, every rhino scrape on this ranch. Suddenly he froze, placing his hand across his lips in a warning gesture of silence. Ahead of him, barely visible behind a wall of sage-coloured leaves, loomed a great grey mass, smooth as a boulder, its big head lowered as if bowed down by the weight of the horn on its nose. An ear flicked. A tick bird fluttered. Marking the position on a map we crept stealthily away.

The walk had been a short one, only three hours, softly lit by the rising sun and with the sweet smell of the Carissa flower,

Africa's bush jasmine, all around us. This was one of the few places where black rhinos still abounded and it was only because of the determination of the owners, our friends Paolo and Kuki Gallmann, their hard-working manager Colin Francombe and the bushcraft of their security patrols, that they had been kept alive.

Ever since he bought Ol Ari Nyiro, Paolo had wanted to keep Laikipia wild. He hunted buffaloes and lions when they threatened herders or killed his cattle and sheep, but protected the rhinos and elephants. At times Kuki, his wife, a slim and elegant woman, whose eyes were as soft as the pale breath of dawn, and Emanuele, her young son, walked with him. Paolo and Luka had taught them how to walk and then freeze without breathing, how to read spoor and follow the call of the honey-guide bird to bees' nests in the trees. Here they could collect and eat the fresh honey and throw a piece of the comb to the bird in recognition for guiding them to this place.

But now Paolo and Emanuele were both dead. Luka had lost his leader. 'Shauri ya Mungu,' he said. 'It's all God's will,' wiping his eyes with a tattered handkerchief when we scraped the red earth and stones on to Paolo's grave. And now the boy was dead – killed by the bite of a puff-adder. Barely a month and a half had passed since we had buried the boy next to Paolo. The snake was lowered with him. We slept out that night around the new mound of earth, with five big fires blazing and the wind blowing through our hair. Elephants were all around. The planets passed by and then the hyenas called. Luka squatted next to the graves, shaking his head. Later that night he came back looking for the hole, for he was certain the snake would find its way out to get its revenge.

But today Luka spoke only occasionally, his mind concentrated on the stalk. 'I will stay here and look after Kuki,' he murmured. 'Ever since her son died, she walks like a warrior now and has no fear.' Kuki was learning to live alone on her ranch with her three-year-old daughter. She had become the guardian of Ol Ari Nyiro and every living thing within its boundaries, and Iain and I had promised to help her, so whenever we could we would fly over the great ridge-back mountain to be with her, discuss new plans and hold her hand. Today was her birthday.

By taking the shortest route home from Ol Ari Nyiro, we would be on our farm within forty minutes. I had taken over the management there at the beginning of the year. After my parents had died my brother and sister wanted to sell up. The farm was in debt and land-grabbers with the help of greedy politicians had been scheming to take it over. Hearing this news as the New Year dawned in Nairobi I sped to the farm. There, alone at night and unable to sleep, I patrolled the place like a lioness in its territory. The atmosphere was tense and I realized that the farm and the people were in need of much attention. Assisted by old employees, I sifted out those behind the 'coup', and helped others with their problems, until life at Naivasha had returned to normal.

Fondly we embraced Kuki and made our farewells; then Iain, Saba and I flew off into the blue. She stood below, a lone figure in the wide umber valley as we swooped down in salute, passing in front of her a few feet from the ground to the far shoulder of the ranch. Running westwards with the wind towards the Rift, we peered into the deep, dark Mukutan gorge, thick with African cedar trees the colour of moss, sombre as a tomb. Beyond sparkled Lake Baringo, ringed with bleached ochre sands that sifted down long ago from the unforgiving crags of the Rift. Then climbing through the freedom of space with the hum of our beautiful *Tembo Two* ringing in our ears, we headed home towards Naivasha.

Perhaps I had been dozing. It took me a few seconds to recognize that something was wrong. Then the adrenalin jolted my body forwards, but the safety belt bound me to the seat of the plane. I heard the words which I dared not utter, 'Engine Failure', and the wind sifted over us with a sinister whistle as the wings glided in the silence of the air currents.

Instantly my eyes scanned the broken land for an open space. All pilots are trained for that moment they pray will never happen. As if in a dream I felt a hand check the fuel valve, then the magnetos, and reach for the fuel booster pump. The engine sputtered into life again, and I felt the fear drain from my body like an outgoing wave at the edge of the sea.

But then once more that terrible silence filled the cabin, and I heard Iain's voice, terse and clear.

'Mayday, Mayday, Mayday, this is November 61494, I have engine failure, ten miles east of Baringo, three on board, does anyone read . . . ?'

'November 61494,' a crisp voice crackled above my head. 'This is Ethiopian Airlines, what is your heading and height?'

'We are heading west towards the lake, altitude one thousand feet, unable restart engine. Am making a forced landing. Cannot talk any more – out.'

All these years, flying with Iain for thousands of hours across Africa, looking for elephants, searching the bush for carcasses, for poachers carrying meat and tusks, being shot at, landing with punctured tyres, racing the sun, and never once had we suffered engine failure. Somehow we always got to where we were heading. But today when we were going home on an ordinary flight, in a clear African sky, it seemed that our luck had run out.

'We're going in there.' Iain pointed at a small opening, dotted with trees. I saw the ground rising steadily, deep gulleys of dry river beds with bush and trees everywhere, and knew that impact was minutes away. All life crystallized into a single thought – were we going to live or die?

This was it. There was no escape from this cabin now. What a way to end our lives. All I wanted was a last look at my family – my husband, Iain, and then my daughter, Saba. Iain, his face framed by his earphones and glasses, was stern, tanned, his cheeks still finely layered with dust from the morning walk; his brow furrowed with concentration. He was dressed in khaki, as I had known him all our life together. He and *Tembo Two* had only just returned after being tested to the limits in Uganda. How cruel, I thought. How ironic, having come through the flames of war to die on a routine journey home. Saba sat on the seat close behind me. Her brown, almond-shaped eyes met mine, slightly confused and apprehensive, her blond mane falling around her sensitive face. Her hands clasped a box containing a long thin snake, an egg-eater, which had belonged to her friend and hero, Emanuele, whom she had seen lifeless only weeks before.

'Put the box on the floor and hold tight,' were my last words. I looked at her face one more time, and thought of our other daughter, Dudu, who had been sent off to cope with books and figures in a school far away in London. I did not believe death could be so easily accepted. A great calm hung over me in that silent fall as a million memories, my whole life, my hopes and all my dreams flashed by in seconds.

In front of me for a thousand miles stretched the great Rift Valley where I was born. I knew it so well. I had walked, ridden, hunted and flown over it all my life. My father, a First World War pilot, had also landed his Gypsy Moth with engine failure fifty years ago on a farm on the edge of another lake, Naivasha. He had come to Africa as a hunter, with his pith helmet, khaki clothes and guns, looking to the elephant to make his fortune. He bought the farm and turned his energy to shape the land. Together with my mother he built our home on the side of a hill, where I grew up with my brother and sister.

It was on this farm fourteen years ago that Iain had set down his tiny, cloth-covered Piper Pacer in the cattle boma on his first visit. He still looked much the same, though his face was lined now with the markings of life. Then came the day when he flew me in a race against time to a hospital, as I wrestled with stomach cramps. Would Saba be born in the plane? I had wondered at the time. And now, was she going to die in one?

For a decade we had been on the move, tracing the plight of elephants all over Africa in a battered old Cessna 185. Now with our new plane life would be easier, safer, I had thought. How could this happen in *Tembo Two*, after surviving her fighting days? She had tasted a fair share of Africa but she was still only two years old. I remembered my parting words to the Manager of Cessna as I left the factory: 'Build her strong and make her fly like an eagle; she will need it.' The picture of J.A. Mull and his hunting companion Harald Mayer was in the pocket of my seat. Today she would show her real strength. I watched the dust devils whirl in the distance and the great clouds form a rim above us as the mottled land lifted up its great body to hit us, and felt pins of fear prick my skin.

Flying in Africa was a part of our life. It was like the rain, unpredictable and magical. One waits for the rain, constantly watching the clouds, feeling the moisture in the air, listening for distant thunder, checking every sign which may bring the rain closer to one's land. In Africa our lives are determined by the rains. The long and the short rains and the times between – these are our seasons. When the flies increase it is a sign of rain. When the safari ants cross the paths in thick brown ribbons it is a sign of rain. When the coucal sings – its liquid notes like the sound of water falling from a bottle – it is a sign of rain. When the elephants suddenly migrate to far-off places – it has rained.

But when the rains fail, and the wind turns into dust devils twirling the parched earth into the skies, and people and animals grow thin and hide from the sun, and the leaves crackle and dry, and your eyes swim in emptiness when you look at the sky and you pray for the rain – then the days have no beginning and no end and it seems as if it will never rain again. Each rainless sky-blue morning I would awake thinking the same thoughts. Now here was just such a day as I had known before and I wondered, how strange that it should end like this.

'Open the doors,' Iain said. Automatically I obeyed. Suddenly the tops of the trees seemed to be erupting from the earth. I looked across at Iain. 'I'm sorry, Oria, we're going into the trees,' were his last words and I remember thinking, how typically British to remember your manners and apologize seconds before death.

Sun streamed upon us as we plunged like a melting Icarus. Branches brushed against the metal floor and still we tumbled deeper down into a rushing sea of leaves. Then standing bold and upright at the remotest gate of hell, two trees held out their solid arms to deliver their final blow. We were breaking up. With a sound like thunder, the metal cracking and buckling around us, we hurtled to destruction. Then came one last shuddering jolt, and all movement ceased. No one stirred and we were enveloped in a silence of drifting dust.

'Get out!' Iain yelled. My door had caved in against me and the cabin reeked of spilled fuel. One wing had smashed through the rear window like an axe, halting inches from Saba's head; but the wing on Iain's side lay limp against the ground and his door was open.

In a flash of frantic energy we scrambled clear. Saba was soaked in fuel from head to foot. 'I can't see,' she yelled as I dragged her towards a broken tree and waited for the plane to explode. Only the distant clanking of a cow bell could be heard. No birds sang. Even the insects had been stilled as the sound of the crash rumbled and echoed in the hostile hills. Then frantically licking Saba's eyes I wiped her face on my shirt and examined her body for wounds until her sight came back. 'My snake, Daddy, please get me my snake.'

Each one of us had our own priorities. Like frightened animals we approached the wreck, cautiously picking out pieces from its crumpled body. *Tembo Two* was dead. But we were alive.

Someone arrived from nowhere. An old man draped in a red blanket, carrying his stick and stool. He held out his hand and touched us. 'Has anyone been hurt?' He spoke to us in Swahili, looking us up and down as if he could not believe that we could have stepped out of such a crash without a blemish. 'Come and sit here,' he said, and led us to the shade of an umbrella acacia tree. 'It will soon get hot.'

More men arrived, some carrying long, leaf-bladed spears. The old man ordered someone to cut branches and make a shelter under the dome of leaves. As we retrieved our belongings from the plane, Iain tried contacting the Ethiopian Airlines captain. 'We are on the ground, no one is injured,' he radio-ed. Then Iain switched to the local security network. The aerial had snapped and had to be tied to the tip of one of the men's spears which he held high above his head so that we could transmit. A rancher's wife answered and word was sent out to rescue us.

Tall red men settled around us, like birds on a branch. Not knowing how long we would have to remain under this tree, I began to prepare for a long wait. 'Is there water? Can someone fetch it – and firewood – and some pots?' I asked the old man. Instantly he gave his orders in Maasai. Standing on one leg, leaning on his stick, he pointed his long black arm towards the plane. 'It is luck. We have a dam here built by an old District Commissioner many years ago, but no one has used it for many years. My wives will bring you their pots.'

Soon beaded women arrived with big bowls of brown muddy water. A fire was lit and water began boiling for drinking. I washed Saba's eyes. From the plane we found some of the *Ein Man Packung* boxes, which had been given to Iain in Uganda by the German relief food emergency agent. It was a strange mixture of provisions to have in the bush, but we had coffee, tea and sugar which would mask the taste of the cow dung and mud in the water.

'We need runners,' I said, and soon volunteers came up to take some of our SOS letters through the bush to the nearest road. 'Sometimes a car goes by the main Mukutan road,' the old man explained, 'then it can pick you up.' Six young clay-headed warriors draped in short pink cotton *shukas* pulled their spears from the ground and strode off with their elongated bouncing strides into the thick bush, carrying our letters.

The old man sat next to us on his small stool cut from the root of a tree, and sniffed his snuff. Dark clouds swept over us and it began to rain, sending up puffs of dust as the drops hit the dry land. 'You have brought us rain.' He sneezed and spat, feeling the fire and the rain. An old man's blessings. We drank tea together and waited under the roof of our hide for the sky to clear.

A plane circled the area, running up and down the valleys, but it was still too far away, and we explored the hills searching for ways out of the bush. 'If no one comes today, I will leave at dawn to look for help,' said Iain. Then darkness folded around us and the fire was stacked with heavy logs to see us safely through the night. *Tembo Two* lay crippled and white as a ghost beside us. The first planets blinked and the sorrowful wail of hyenas came drifting out of the trees.

We had been offered a slaughtered lamb by Kuki to take back to the farm, and though it had been covered with fuel, we placed the meat on the burning embers to roast and sat with the red men watching it cook. It sizzled and smoked, and when it was ready the men cut pieces for all to eat, slicing through skin and flesh with their sharp *simis*. Eyes sparkling, faces shiny with grease, they ate with the sounds of gnawing and munching, spitting and belching. All the meat was eaten and one by one they left us. The old man beat the ground with his stick and straightened up. 'Thank you,' he cried. 'God is with us.'

We huddled together on a piece of the broken wing, trying to sleep. Jackals scurried by to pick up the discarded bones, crunching them in rapid bites. Night noises surrounded us, and in the far distance a faint drone broke the lull. Then lights were upon us and voices coming closer. Our runners had returned with the one car that had passed by. It was a friend from Lake Baringo with the police, looking for the place where the bird fell.

We were taken away late that night. Rumours floated around Kenya that we had crashed. Some said we were loaded with ivory, others that we had no fuel. Kuki sent us a bottle of champagne and her lorry and we returned a week later to pick up the wreck, cutting our way through the overgrown thorn-bush on the old District Commissioner's road to the place where our own road had so nearly ended.

CHAPTER TWENTY-SEVEN

IAIN: *Sudan's Bloody Ivory*

1983–4, Kenya, Sudan

THE loss of *Tembo Two*, written off without a chance of claiming on the insurance, was a great blow to our survey plans. In time we bought another Cessna 185, but for the meanwhile I was grounded and out of work, and becoming increasingly frustrated over my inability to shake my fellow scientists and conservationists out of their complacency towards the ivory trade.

So far the pro-trade lobby had carried the day. They had managed to present a united front to the world with their theories of sustainability; but as the year of 1983 wore on, like an old tusk that has lain for a long time in the sun, the first cracks began to appear in the façade of their arguments.

One of the first things Jonah Western had done on taking over the Chairmanship of the new African Elephant and Rhino Specialist Group was to establish a newsletter which came to be called *Pachyderm*. It was a quick way of publishing the essence of any scientific paper on elephants or rhinos, and it became an insiders' forum for the continuing battle of ideas on elephant policy.

I availed myself of the columns of *Pachyderm* and published an article headed: 'Africa's Arms Race Hits Elephants', which clearly identified the rising price of ivory and the breakdown of law and order as prime factors of elephant destruction rather than the human population increase.

Soon afterwards I met Murray Watson, an ecologist, at Wilson Airport who told me that the elephants of Somalia had been virtually finished in the previous five years. Despite many cries to international donors, the Somali wildlife authorities had received nothing, and as a result their elephant population had collapsed. Sadly I conveyed this news to Peter Jackson at WWF, who was still writing elephant stories for the Press, telling him that the same was true for Sudan, and much of Chad, the CAR and westwards through the Sahel.

It now came to light that Sudan had been exporting 200 to 300 tonnes of ivory every year for the last four years. I had known that elephants were being butchered in southern Sudan by Arabs from the north with the tacit connivance of the Army and had reported it to AERSG at the very time that the apologists of the ivory trade were making their pitch to spread complacency. Henry Minga, the Sudanese Director of Wildlife, had reported these slaughters to us in 1980, and Robin Hurt, a highly experienced professional hunter, told me the same story when I was in Uganda. At the time I had passed this on to the group at Hwange, and published it in WWF annual reports, but to no avail. Now the epic proportions of the tragedy being played out in Sudan were at last recognized and the fact accepted by the conservation establishment.

In October 1983 *The Sunday Times* of London carried a major story by Brian Jackman under the banner headline: SUDAN'S BLOODY IVORY TRADE KILLS 100,000 ELEPHANTS. It referred to massive shipments of illegal ivory being 'laundered' by influential and unscrupulous dealers in Sudan in order to facilitate legitimate sales overseas.

The story described how ivory from all over southern Sudan was finding its way to Khartoum by lorry and camel train, on the backs of donkeys and sometimes quite openly by air. Eye witness accounts told of piles of tusks at Juba Airport and the Sudan Airways office in town, waiting for a flight to the North.

In 1975 Sudan's total export of tusks amounted to just one tonne; but since 1979 it had exported at least nine hundred tonnes of ivory – the equivalent of more than 100,000 dead elephants. Four years of uncontrolled slaughter in southern Sudan and its adjoining territories had turned the region into one vast elephant graveyard. In that time

Sudan had risen from nowhere to become the biggest single source of raw ivory in Africa, and the ivory traders of Khartoum had grown rich on the profits.

Indeed, it was said that one Sudanese firm in Khartoum had become the largest single private exporter of ivory in Africa. Its head was Mohamed Awadalla el Awad, who ran his business from Khartoum but also had an office in Hong Kong. At that time, something like one quarter of all the world's ivory was passing through his hands. In 1982, according to the Hong Kong traders, he sold 220 tonnes of ivory worth at least seven million dollars. In 1983, import documents revealed that he had exported a further 164 tonnes in six months to Hong Kong. 'And that,' said Esmond Bradley Martin, who was then vice-chairman of the African Elephant and Rhino Specialist Group, 'makes him the biggest ivory trader of all time.'

Every consignment sold by Awadalla was perfectly legal and was always accompanied by a valid permit from Sudan. But in Hong Kong he was disliked by the other traders because Sudanese ivory was acknowledged to be the poorest in Africa. The tusks dried out too quickly when they were brought from the humid south into the fierce dry heat of Khartoum, and tended to crack badly after they had been cut.

But where had Khartoum's ivory mountain come from? In 1975, when Sudan's elephant population was last counted by Murray Watson, the total stood at 134,000; and not even the large and highly organized poaching gangs which were then operating in the south could have wiped out 100,000 elephants in four years. All the evidence suggested an annual toll of about ten thousand elephants. In other words, these figures confirmed that much so-called 'Sudanese' ivory had been entering the country illegally, and that Khartoum had joined Bujumbura in Burundi as a major clearing-house for ivory poached all over Africa from Zambia to Zaire.

There was also the mystery of the 315 tonnes of ivory sent to Saudi Arabia in 1977. This colossal consignment had not appeared in Sudan's own export records, which indicated that only twenty tonnes had left the country that year. Looked at simply, the ivory had been shipped to Saudi Arabia illicitly, pending arrangements for its sale elsewhere.

Thus did Sudan become the latest tragic example of a country overtaken by the Kalashnikov Revolution. In 1982, Arabs from northern Sudan armed with automatic weapons, spilled down into the south of the country, riding on horses in gangs fifty strong, and cleaned out the last of the country's big tuskers. At the same time, ivory had become the currency of personal monetary advancement in Sudan, particularly among the armed forces, police, prisons and wildlife departments.

The Sudanese were very upset by *The Sunday Times* story and the publicity it engendered. They demanded an apology but the paper stuck to its guns; and two months later, after much behind-the-scenes activity by the CITES Secretariat, Sudan banned the export of all unworked ivory.

What made *The Sunday Times* story particularly interesting to me was its sources. In December 1983, *BBC WILDLIFE* Magazine carried a news item which revealed that they were none other than Esmond Bradley Martin, Jonah Western and Ian Parker.

In the BBC magazine story, Bradley Martin was strongly critical of the role played by the CITES parties, arguing that an opportunity to halt the trade had been missed when the Convention had met in Botswana in April 1983. 'Everyone knew what was happening in Sudan, but no decisions were taken to tackle the problem,' he said.

In response to Bradley Martin's allegations of too little, too late, Chris Huxley of the CITES Secretariat responded by saying: 'For two years we have been negotiating with Sudan, and this has now borne fruit. This may seem a long time, but the Kenyan ivory crises took five or six years to resolve.'

It was strange that Huxley was trying to pass off the slaughter of 100,000 elephants as a success for CITES, and saying that the Kenya ivory crisis had been solved.

That same year Ian Parker's book, *The Ivory Crisis*, was published with a dedication 'to truth'. Coming out after the Sudanese revelations, it looked curiously dated, harking back as it did to his position of the year before, which denied any ivory crisis. 'I hope to show that there is no ivory crisis,' he declared in his introduction, 'but a very real crisis in conservation philosophy.'

Once again I marvelled at his mercurial brilliance and his depth of knowledge, in particular of the Wata bowmen who had hunted the Tsavo elephants in Sheldrick's day. But then, almost in the same breath, he could describe the current anti-poaching measures as a 'witch-hunt'. He repeated the arguments about the diminishing trade, and claimed that the off-take of elephants for ivory was largely sustainable. 'Could it be that elephants are not disappearing after all?' he asked. 'That whatever the fact may have been in the past, there is no crisis today? That it is, in short, contrived?' Here lay the central theme of his attack on conservationists at large and IUCN and WWF in particular, whom, he said, had led the world to believe there was a crisis over the African elephant, knowing that the public would dig deep into their purses to support such a cause. It was ironic that WWF and IUCN were being attacked from both sides, by Parker for exaggerating the threat to elephants, and by me for being complacent about it. Such is the life of great organizations!

Parker's views caused a great deal of confusion and even gained a wide credence among those who were not familiar with the facts. The whole policy of support for anti-poaching and tougher measures to curb the ivory trade was thrown further into doubt. The book also stooped to a seamy level of personal innuendo directed against the ivory trade's fiercest critics. I reasoned at the time that this was a calculated red-herring. The real issue was whether or not the elephants were being killed excessively for ivory. If the author could not sustain his thesis then the rest of his case simply fell apart.

Late in 1983 some evidence came to light which confirmed my suspicions. It came in the form of a telegram addressed to the African Wildlife Foundation in Washington and apparently approved by Sandy Price, the AWF director in Nairobi, Jonah Western and Ian Parker. The telegram had been sent in 1981. What it said was that AWF's programme to make the ivory trade the focus of their programme in 1982 was totally inappropriate.

It suggested that CITES was working successfully where ivory was concerned, that ivory moved openly in international trade and was easy to monitor through published import statistics. It stated that tackling the illegal trade could be done only by confrontation with governments, and that in any case the trade was declining, and did not pose any immediate crisis for elephants. It asserted that loss of range, due entirely to human population increase, was at the root of current ivory production, that the western public had been misled over the African elephant situation, and that AWF's desire to concentrate on the ivory trade emerged from this.

Coming to light so soon after the Sudanese publicity blitz, the position was of course completely untenable, and I was not surprised when Jonah denied having read the telegram and informed me that it had been sent without his approval. Sandy Price, who was not a scientist, had sought the advice of elephant experts and was in no way to blame for the views expressed. She confirmed that Parker had drafted the contents of the telegram following a discussion between the three of them, and that she had sent it assuming that it had been duly approved.

I wrote to the head of AWF in Washington and informed him that his foundation had been used as a vehicle for propaganda inimical to the survival of elephants. In fact the incident of the telegram cleared the air somewhat between Jonah and me, and from then on he listened more carefully to my views. I was inclined, however, to think that this episode in which AWF had been used was not isolated, but was part of a pattern of incidents which propagated views favourable to the ivory trade. These had been occurring ever since I first took a strong stand against the ivory trade in 1979.

Sandy Price felt badly about the telegram and offered me space in the AWF newsletter to present my views. I was therefore able to challenge the assumptions made by Parker, which in my view gravely underestimated the numbers of elephants represented by ivory-trade exports, and to rebut his view that concern about elephants being killed for ivory was essentially misplaced.

Another small crack in the pro-trade façade emerged when Jonah and Tom Pilgram, a mathematical modeller, analysed thousands of tusk weights and measurements. They proved that most of the older elephants had gone, indicating heavy over-exploitation. They also showed how the trade might cause a population crash, ending with the masterly understatement: 'If it would be premature to view our results with alarm, it would nevertheless be unreasonable not to view them with concern.'

Early in 1984 the European Community quite spontaneously came up with a resolution tabled by a British MP, Mr Stanley Johnson, to ban the ivory trade. This provoked such a furore of outrage from the conservation establishment that the legislators who had proposed it were quite taken aback. They agreed to re-draft their proposals so that they would strengthen controls, but not make any outright ban or inhibit the legitimate trade in ivory so beloved by the CITES secretariat. Even so, the secretariat, led by Chris Huxley, were against any legislation, saying that their proposed quota system should first be established.

In March I was passing through Europe and was given a chance to put the opposite view to IUCN and WWF with CITES in attendance. I expressed my surprise that IUCN and WWF appeared to be so close to the ivory trade that the public was confused as to whose camp they were in. I said they were throwing away a golden opportunity to help the elephants.

My talk clearly made some impression. One of the most difficult of the IUCN officers now had the grace to concede that I had been right about the danger to the elephants all along. The CITES contingent remained implacably uncommunicative and left without saying anything; but Charles De Haes, the director-general of WWF, immediately instructed all WWF national organizations to support the European Parliament's call for tighter controls on ivory imports.

In Kenya and Tanzania the business of counting elephants in the field had ground completely to a halt. There had been no proper survey for many years and an attempt to make a census in the Serengeti was frustrated by a cover-up.

I had been invited by Holly Dublin, an American field scientist, to fly for her in the Masai Mara and count the elephants and buffalo. It seemed a marvellous opportunity to co-operate with the Serengeti scientists to cover the whole of this magnificent ecosystem – something which had not been done since a previous count of mine in 1977. But, having obtained the go-ahead from the Tanzanian authorities, the proposal fell into a hornets' nest of rivalries and professional jealousies. In the end we covered only part of the Serengeti where we found hardly any elephants and plenty of carcasses.

Even some of my closest friends and colleagues put pressure on me to keep quiet about the Serengeti situation and to let WWF and IUCN exert diplomatic influence. I was highly sceptical that this would achieve anything given their supine behaviour so far regarding elephants, but since this was what my friends thought, what could I do? Yet again the truth was going to be muzzled for political reasons. Another elephant population had hit the deck and no one was going to say anything about it. Looking back over my life there is nothing that grieves me more than the times when I have quelled my anger and remained silent on these issues.

Nevertheless, I collaborated with Holly Dublin to write a paper reviewing twenty years of data on the Serengeti and Mara elephants. Her recent counts and rangers' reports suggested that heavy poaching was reducing the Serengeti herds and driving more elephants across the Kenya border into the Mara, where the animals were more vigorously protected. Sadly, like all scientific papers, it was published long after the events it described. And it could not bring back the Serengeti elephants.

These past two years had also been wasted for the elephants at a continental level. Not only had action against illegal traders failed to materialize, but a new and potentially disastrous system, originating from a suggestion made by Ian Parker at Hwange, had been supported by AERSG at meetings I could not attend for lack of funds, and endorsed by the international community through the CITES treaty. The idea was that each elephant range state should set a quota for ivory exports. From the start I was deeply suspicious of these ideas, but little did I know just how destructive they would turn out to be.

In late 1984 CITES commissioned Rowan Martin, a senior biologist in the Zimbabwe Wildlife Department, to draw up procedures for this ivory quota export system and to make a new continental estimate of Africa's elephants. I was keen that Rowan should get his population figures as accurate as possible, and with some difficulty managed to secure three hours of his time when he visited Nairobi, where I showed him the updates to the African elephant data I had been working on.

Amid all these confusions it was easy to lose sight of the meaning of our life. I even argued with Oria about the very essence of my beliefs of what was right and wrong in the cause to which I had devoted myself. She thought the idea of national parks was a white man's creation for the white man, and one of the most alien of all the concepts we had forced upon Africa.

Where was our star we used to follow? We lived in a faraway park in a faraway time. We wrote our book and made our film and we struggled for an international endeavour. We had some success, took some spills and could now only watch impotently as others made mistakes and the elephants continued their rush to destruction. Was it time to turn and fight again, or to cut our losses and quit? If it was only a losing battle, why persist?

One of the hardest things to bear was to find myself so out of sympathy with the co-workers in my field. Five years ago I had looked on these people as friends or allies in the battle for the elephants. Were they the ones at fault or was there something wrong with me? I put it all down to accumulated depression and being without an aeroplane for too long.

It was not until April 1985 that my cloud lifted. A big elephant count was offered to me in the Central African Republic by WWF and United Nations Food and Agricultural Organization (FAO), which I could carry out in my new Cessna, *5Y-AOT*. I decided to accept it, but not without some trepidation, for it involved a journey across the wildest part of Africa with no ground support. It would be like the Selous count all over again; except that this time I was nearly ten years older. However, once I hit the road I knew the excitement would build up, and with it the all-consuming motivation that leaves nothing to chance and drives one on to the very end. Above all, it was the most important part of Africa in which the elephant's population trend had never before been scientifically measured.

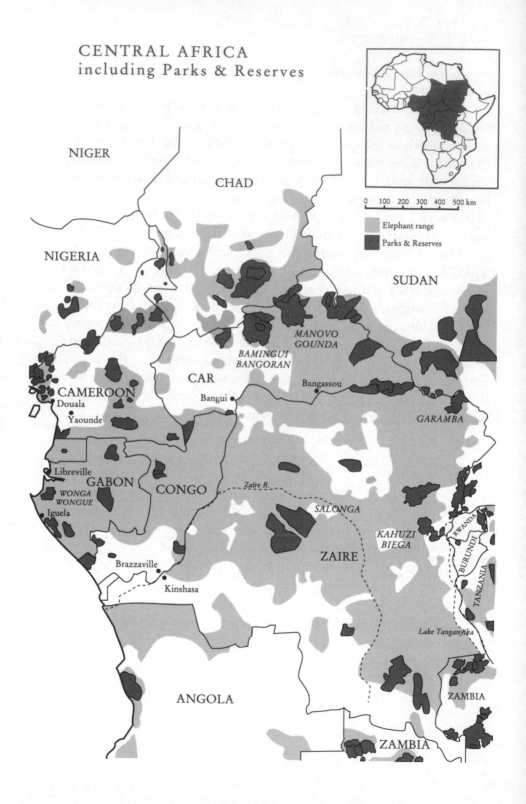

CENTRAL AFRICA
including Parks & Reserves

NIGER

CHAD

NIGERIA

SUDAN

0   100 200 300 400 500 km

Elephant range

Parks & Reserves

MANOVO GOUNDA

BAMINGUI BANGORAN

CAR

Bangassou

CAMEROON

GARAMBA

Douala

Bangui •

Yaounde

Libreville •

GABON   CONGO   *Zaïre R.*   *SALONGA*

WONGA WONGUE   *KAHUZI BIEGA*

Iguela   RWANDA

ZAIRE   BURUNDI

Brazzaville •   TANZANIA

Kinshasa •   *Lake Tanganyika*

ANGOLA   ZAMBIA

ZAMBIA

CHAPTER TWENTY-EIGHT

IAIN: *Shadow of Darkness*

1984, Central African Republic

THE Central African Republic is one of those forgotten, impoverished land-locked countries in mid-most Africa, surrounded by vast unfriendly neighbours. In the early 1960s when African countries sought independence from their colonial overlords, David Dacko, a schoolteacher with a background of French education, became the first president. Although France retained true power, it offered the fledgling republic its protection, aid, advisers and a stable currency. All this Dacko gladly accepted in exchange for his country's freedom.

A few years later, Dacko was forced out by Colonel Jean Bedel Bokassa, who had served in the French army with distinction, collecting a decoration from De Gaulle in person.

Bokassa felt that corruption in Dacko's government had reached such levels that only he could save the Republic. But he was no better than his predecessor when it came to empire-building. Each day brought new ideas of greatness. Like his friend Idi Amin, he soon promoted himself to general and was later elevated to field marshal, with costumes from Paris dripping with medals.

In true Napoleonic style, Bokassa declared himself 'Emperor', and his country an empire. It was a great moment for a simple man from a small village, and he was determined that the world should know it. He ordered an infinite selection of the best that France could offer: gilded coaches with mottled horses; an elaborate gold-leafed throne for himself and minor ones for his favourite son and his wife Katherine, soon to be Empress. There were costumes and clothes galore and ermine-rimmed cloaks encrusted with diamonds and embossed with Bonaparte's 'B' for Bokassa. Food, wine and flowers were flown in from Paris and miles of red carpet laid on streets abounding in puddles. In all, Bokassa's imperial junket amounted to well over $20 million. He did not care. Somehow, someone would pay.

Until 1976 elephants were plentiful in CAR. The best estimate was that there were at least 100,000, and the country was a favourite hunting retreat for the French President, Giscard d'Estaing. But, as I had discovered during my last visit in 1979, the killing of elephants had begun in earnest when a company called La Couronne took over the country's ivory trade.

When La Couronne and Bokassa became business partners it was open season on the elephant. Under Bokassa, poaching was controlled by the emperor himself and La Couronne became the conduit through which the tusks were sent to France. Between them they had effectively seized the ivory-trade monopoly. All the country's elephants and ivory were his, said Bokassa, and anyone caught disobeying his orders was to be flogged to death.

Illegal hunting was well organized. In 1978 alone it claimed at least four thousand elephants, and that was probably only half the number; while more ivory came in by canoes from Zaire. At the same time, Chadian and Sudanese horsemen were competing with Bokassa for ivory by increasing their killings in the North.

By now Bokassa, deep in debt and steeped in alcohol, was helpless to prevent his empire crumbling as his ever-increasing follies required more and more money from ivory. Eventually, following close on the heels of Idi Amin, who had been ejected from Uganda in April 1979, his empire finally came to an inglorious end. While he was on a visit to Libya seeking aid from Qaddafi, the French stepped in from Chad and put David Dacko back in place. The people went wild as the country was released from oppression, but reports especially from the east of the country indicated the elephants had been decimated.

In that brief period of frenzy following the emperor's fall from power the elephants took an even greater tumble as hunters and traders arrived from all sides to join in the free-for-all; but by March 1980, elephant hunting was closed. CAR agreed to join CITES and all ivory trading was banned.

This was the situation Clive Spinage had reported to our elephant group in 1980 – yet the massive evidence of elephant slaughter had been largely ignored.

Then came another blow. Following the Hwange meeting the CAR's ivory trade was re-opened in December 1981. Whether or not there was a connection I cannot tell, but traders and business opportunists poured in once again to make a killing, while the conservation world quietly sat by. After three more years of waiting and empty talking, I had been asked by an unknown young Belgian, Jean-Marc Froment, to survey what was left. At last WWF was thoroughly alarmed and generously paid the flying costs.

The flight across Africa to Bangui and the northern CAR would be a venture into the unknown for me. This vast region was a wilderness the size of western Europe, described by hunters as richer in elephants than anywhere else. The only person I knew who had been there recently was Robin Hurt, who warned me that Arabs from the Sudan were invading the country in search of ivory.

At the Missionary Aviation Fellowship in Nairobi I sought out some pilots who knew Zaire and could advise on how to make the flight to Bangui, the CAR capital. I learnt that radio aids were either inoperative or non-existent. But the main hazard was the weather, with huge tropical thunderstorms one hundred miles across. 'Don't even think of trying to fly through them,' one pilot warned me. 'They can break an aeroplane in pieces.'

What I needed most was an experienced observer to help me count the elephants. Luckily Joan Root, an old friend of ours and a superb aerial spotter, was free to come. We had already worked together in the Mara and Serengeti, and Joan was eager to see a new part of Africa.

Eventually we were ready to go. The head of the United Nations Development Project in Nairobi was an old Zaire hand who had been there in the 1960s and who regaled me with stories of uprisings and atrocities. Missionaries' hands and feet had been cut off, Italian pilots chopped into little pieces, and a couple of French pilots had been caught by Pygmies and strung up from a tree in a small bamboo cage for five years. 'I don't know if it will do much good,' he sighed, 'but here is a UN identity card, and some letters of recommendation.' I tucked these away securely with the rest of the equipment and a sheaf of permits in the aeroplane. Thus does the modern traveller go equipped into the heart of Africa.

Our first stop was Entebbe, after which there was a fuel gap of nearly a thousand miles before Bangui, far beyond the limits of my range. I planned to land in the Garamba National Park in Zaire and refuel from jerry-cans. Jean-Marc Froment had said he would try to get a drum of fuel to Bangassou. Fly twice around the town, he telexed, and a drum would be delivered to the strip.

From Entebbe we flew high over the Murchison Falls and spoke on the air-to-ground radio with the warden, telling him we would be back for another chat in a month's time. All was well with the elephants, he said. The rangers were still holding the line against the poachers.

Then we flew over Idi Amin's West Nile homeland and headed into the unknown, sticking to a compass course and navigating carefully with the map until we found the Dungu River on the edge of the Garamba. Our friends were there to meet us, including Tatala Tatika, the warden, whom I had not seen since 1974. Tatala confirmed Robin Hurt's story of the invading Arabs who were now coming in great bands to raid Northern Zaire for ivory. There had been several clashes with the Army and a large number of Arabs had been shot; but he feared they would be back again, more heavily armed and as determined as ever. 'It is a question of the price of ivory, dear Doctor,' he said. 'When the price went up is when our problems started.'

Next morning as soon as we were airborne again we started to look for elephants. For the first ten minutes within the protected confines of Garamba we sighted one family after another. It was obviously a high-density area and there were no carcasses. This southern end of the park was full of elephants, who, as so often is the case, had recognized the sanctuary they could expect near the park headquarters. But the elephants ended abruptly at the park boundary and for the next five hundred miles we saw only two groups of six and two couples, all running scared in the area where Robin Hurt had been.

The airport at Bangui was full of French fighter planes. Jean-Marc met us and ushered us through Customs. He was a soft-spoken, bearded young man of medium build, fit and wiry looking. We drove down dusty streets lined with red flamboyant trees, past Napoleonic arches and ultra-modern French architecture, until we reached his home on the edge of the brown Oubangui River. His wife, Ingrid, an attractive blond woman in her late twenties, kept us well supplied with coffee and food as we plunged into preparations for the survey.

'There are two areas to be surveyed,' said Jean-Marc, 'each one stretching for some thirty thousand square kilometres.' One was centred on the Bamingui-Bangoran National Park and the other on the Manovo-Gounda-Saint Floris Park. They took these curious names from the rivers which formed part of their boundaries. While Ingrid and Joan marked out boundaries and transect lines, we hovered over the maps Jean-Marc had assembled, and Mozart lifted our spirits with the soaring notes from *Amadeus* as if we were already airborne.

The survey was going to be the first step of Jean-Marc's battle-plan to unlock many political doors that had so far remained shut. He wanted me to make a political statement at the end of the count and ask the president to forbid the killing of elephants and end the iniquitous system of licensed ivory collection known as *la Collecte*. This system authorized certain individuals to collect ivory from animals which had died of natural causes; but they went further and gave out guns and ammunition to the villagers to shoot elephants. One of the key people to meet, said Jean-Marc, was the French military adviser, Colonel Mansion, who controlled the presidential guard.

Jean-Marc and Joan went ahead by car, with supplies for one month, while I flew with Ingrid, skirting some enormous storms on the way. They quite dwarfed anything I had seen in East Africa, but eventually the way was clear to the north and we managed to pick out the airstrip deep in the bush which Jean-Marc had marked on the map.

I knew that the most unaccountable feature in every aerial survey was the capability of the observers, and now was the time for Joan to transfer her knowledge to Gustave Doungoubé, our local counterpart. For several days we flew over the various species, checking minutely the accuracy and note-taking of each of the observers until I was confident that we would get consistent results.

And then began our days of counting. We started by flying long transects of about one hundred and fifty kilometres each, which took us from the steamy Guinean Forest in the south, out across wide plains in which grey granite kopjes lay marooned like islands in dry seas of grass. On over Sudanian woodlands and thorn scrub we flew, to the drought-stricken Sahel in the north, finding thousands of cattle from neighbouring Chad which had been driven south for lack of grazing.

In the heart of Bamingui-Bangoran was the Vassoko-Bolo Reserve, an ecological holy of holies, where nature was supposed to be so strictly guarded that even scientists should not venture there. Instead we found four thousand cattle belonging to the Mbororo nomads of neighbouring Chad. As I flew low over the rust-coloured beasts with their huge horns we could see women and children riding on the backs of the cows, and the men with their pointed hats running alongside or riding small ponies. These fascinating people ranged across a huge swathe of CAR, Chad and Niger, and like all the nomads were suffering from the terrible Sahelian drought.

Compared with East Africa it was vast, reminding me of parts of the Selous. The languid rivers that broke the monotony were thoroughfares for poachers and we saw some of their camps. The densities of wildlife were very poor. A few years earlier it was said to have been full of elephants. Now we saw only bones, day after day, and I realized that we were just clerks of death recording yet another holocaust.

Clive Spinage, working for the Government as a UN consultant, had put forward a blueprint for running the parks; but nothing had been done except the creation of a school for game guards, who were supplied with sporting rifles and who, from 1979 to 1983, formed the core of the anti-poaching force. Jean-Marc had served as an instructor, but unfortunately, political support for conservation was lacking and, as is often the case, the equipment provided was finally used for precisely opposite purposes. One day the game guards returned home from patrol and were met by United Nations officials who collected their guns one by one, and handed them over to a senior politician. It is thought that these guns were later distributed to the ivory collectors. The politician who authorized the seizure of these guns had already made a fortune by issuing collectors' licences at a handsome price, and kept a water bottle made of rhino horn on his desk which he sipped at intervals in the misguided belief that it would improve his sexual prowess. In any event, word soon spread that the park was defenceless and the poachers swarmed in for the kill.

One day, after hours of flying, the frequency of dead elephants thickened and we came to the presidential park at Avakaba, formerly Bokassa's *Imperial Domaine*. We wanted to land to break the monotony of flying and to see what the presidential palace looked like. A vast tarmac runway big enough for jet airliners opened before us, and we taxied to a huge apron, overlooked by flood-lights and watch towers. Armed guards escorted us to a car in which I was alarmed to see bloodstains on the back seat, and drove us to the president's palace. Here we were offered tinned sardines in a room with blue-green walls and plush velvet chairs. It was here that Bokassa had held lavish parties with long-legged hostesses imported from Europe. And it was here, too, that a general had sent out orders for one of the last endangered rhinos to be shot to provide the medicine necessary to make his new reign strong and vigorous. Jean-Marc spoke animatedly with our hosts, explaining the purpose of our count.

Afterwards I asked Jean-Marc about the bloodstains in the car. 'Oh, it's just hunting for the pot,' he said, 'a way of life in Central Africa.'

After seven days the Bamingui-Bangoran count was finished. Altogether, we had covered thirty-two thousand square kilometres but seen elephants on only eight occasions. We still had the Manovo-Gounda-Saint Floris complex to complete, but first Jean-Marc and I would return to Bangui to service the plane.

No sooner were we back in Bangui than a call came through for Jean-Marc from Security. It was Colonel Mansion and he wanted to see us immediately. We were going to meet him sooner than we had expected.

The colonel was brisk and businesslike. 'So you have seen cattle in the park?' he said. 'Where exactly did you find them?' We looked at the wall map full of military symbols and found Vassoko-Bolo for him, where we had flown over four thousand cattle and their herders. '*Bon!*' he exclaimed. 'Now I will send a Jaguar to look,' and then giving us a sidelong, wolfish grin, 'and maybe another to shoot!'

'So you're going back up north?' he went on. 'I want you to tell me immediately whenever you see illegal activities in the park: poachers' camps, nomads, fishermen, wounded elephants, fresh carcasses – and especially horsemen.'

We now learnt the reason for his sudden interest. While we had been counting in Bamingui, the president had flown by helicopter to Manovo, with Colonel Mansion escorting him in a second helicopter. They had found some fresh elephant carcasses, and when they decided to investigate, the president's helicopter had come under fire from poachers. Colonel Mansion immediately led a counterattack with some of his French and CAR paratroops. They arrested twenty-four poachers, shot their camels and horses and confiscated two hundred and twenty tusks found hidden in the camp. This extraordinary encounter had happened on the Niao River near a place called the Grande Saline, where the elephants come out of the forest to eat the salt, and was in the very area we were going to next.

In Bangui I also met Jean Laboureur, an old French hunter who had persuaded the president to allow him to take over the best park in the country at Manovo, and to carry out all anti-poaching operations there. At some stage he had fallen out with the resident warden and the question of who would run this park had then developed into a gigantic struggle involving senior French politicians, the president of CAR, Peace Corp volunteers, white hunters and the Ministry of Waters and Forests, all of whom had lined up on one side or the other. At one stage Laboureur had been thrown out, but now he was back and it was the park warden who had been ousted.

Jean-Marc had avoided being drawn into this conflict, but I was aware of deep and dark passions that fuelled this feud, and found it curiously reminiscent of conservation politics in East Africa, with a unique French cowboy element thrown in. Laboureur was now very much in the ascendant. He chased poachers and hunted in the park on an entirely unofficial basis, but with presidential backing, and he seemed wary about Jean-Marc's plans to elicit massive EEC aid to help save the elephants.

'I am the only one doing anti-poaching in the north,' he boasted. 'Our methods are brutal; brutal, but necessary.' These apparently included shooting suspected poachers on sight, a policy now becoming widely adopted in Africa as the ivory conflict escalated.

The aeroplane had been consuming too much oil, which worried me a little. The engineer, however, gave the plane a thorough compression check and pronounced the engine *'Parfait'*. Jean-Marc and I took off for the north country, but met a huge thunderstorm and were forced off-course. Below a small hill at Sibut I found a missionary airstrip, one of the very few possible diversions, and at the same instant the plane was hit by the first surging gusts of the storm. I made a trial run to see if we could land, but the ferocity of the cross-wind made it impossible, and a down-draught forced me to rev the engine to maximum. I told Jean-Marc I would try once more and if we could not land we would return to Bangui. Then the choice was taken out of my hands.

Engine failure! It was just two years since my last one. For a moment it looked as if we would land in a swamp short of the runway; but then a gust picked us up and the cross-wind died just long enough to drop us on to the extreme end of the strip. The storm now broke and in lashing rain we were collected by a group of Baptist missionaries in a huge, brand-new American pick-up truck. They referred to themselves as the 'Burning Wicks', and gave me a book which was long on allusions about lone candles in a dark place. Our forced landing was no coincidence, they said. 'Make no mistake; God is in the driving seat, and it is not too late for you to turn to the Lord and be saved.'

Next day I found that the throttle axle had broken, and all the cables were dangling uselessly. Given the extreme improbability that it should have broken at the one moment we were over an airstrip I had no counter-arguments for our kind friends. The broken axle did not delay us for more than a day. We hitch-hiked back to Bangui, where our flight engineer fashioned a replacement, and soon we were able to meet up with Joan and Ingrid in Manovo.

Another six days of dodging thunderstorms and the count was virtually completed. It was spectacular country with great cliffs dissected by tumbling waterfalls and lazy, winding brown rivers. Ancient elephant trails were deeply etched into the escarpment walls and so easily visible that the French had put them on their maps. But the invasion of nomads with tens of thousands of cattle was severe, and although Manovo had more elephants than Bamingui, there were also more fresh carcasses. In places we flew over piles of scattered white bones where masses of elephants had been killed together – probably by automatic weapons. Elsewhere we saw fresh dead elephants spread over a square kilometre, with savage gashes in their hind quarters, the work of the elusive horsemen and their long spears. Evidently, Laboureur's 'brutal methods' had not stopped the poaching.

Once again the dead outnumbered the living, and everything was more intense than in Bamingui. In the north of the elephants' range we found only their tracks in the mud, left over from a former season. Eventually, only one count remained to be done. We took a break and flew down to Bangui. A message had come over the radio that Clive Spinage would join us for the tail end of the count; and even more welcome was the news that Oria was also on her way.

CHAPTER TWENTY-NINE

ORIA: *The President's Hoard*

1984, Central African Republic

EVERY afternoon in Bangui, torrential rains preceded by howling winds descend on the city; yet life goes on at its own pace with the rain and the forests and the isolation. Elephant grass sprouts from the pavements and the roads are lined with heaps of garbage, each with its group of rooting pigs.

Grey uniformed police patrol the streets. 'They're always looking for *ginza* bribes,' Iain laughed, 'but here, when they whistle and wave you down, the French just zoom past at full speed and so do I.'

We arrived at a small restaurant tucked under some trees. Inside, fans whirled and French music played. The *patron* led us to the table where Jean-Marc Froment and Clive Spinage were sitting. I had not seen Clive for five years. He was still the same, though perhaps a little rounder at the waist with the good French food. We opened a bottle of wine to salute the day and the tempest hit us as if a dam had exploded on top of the roof.

I could well understand why Iain and Jean-Marc had struck up a close friendship. Shut up in the tiny cabin of our plane for the past month, they had been through some heart-stopping moments and had developed a mutual esteem, clocking up numbers of skeletons and elephants for hour after hour.

The restaurant was filled with hunters and French soldiers – officers in smart khaki uniforms and tough-looking troopers in their desert, sleeveless, open battle dress. It felt as if we had put back the clock of life many decades, to the days of Beau Geste. Le Docteur Dooglass was already well known here in Bangui, and encouraging greetings were hailed across the room – '*alors, les elephants, ça va*' – as he passed by. 'Iain is a sort of a mystery,' Jean-Marc told me. 'No one really understands what we are doing, not even the French; and as you may have noticed, they run this place.'

Beyond Bangui, the manioc fields end and the forest begins, broken only by sporadic villages bordering the main road to N'délé, a small northern town in between the two national parks, where powerful Senoussi sultans reign. All trade in ivory and diamonds passes through their hands. They are Muslims of Arab descent and have always had enormous power in this area.

For over a century various Muslim despots – descendants from Sudanese and Chadian sultans – had fought for power here. In time the Senoussi sultans triumphed. They took over this whole northern area of CAR and established N'Délé as their slave-trade capital; and when the French in CAR and the British in the Sudan eventually put an end to slaving, the raiders continued to hunt elephants. The hunting was carried out by horsemen carrying spears, as firearms were prohibited, and it was from them that the spear-hunting technique had derived and been perfected ever since. Their usual technique was to single out a running elephant, for one rider to gallop ahead and distract it while a second would come in from behind and thrust his spear deep into its hindquarters to sever the sciatic nerve. This would paralyse the elephant, allowing the hunters to finish it off at leisure.

Even now in this part of Africa raiding is still a way of life and the horsemen's ruthless reputation usually ensures that they can obtain anything they want from the villagers.

The remaining area to be counted was part of the Manovo-Gounda-Saint Floris National Park on the border with Chad – the horsemen's favourite hunting ground. Although Iain's plane was never shot at, the poaching here was even worse than in Uganda, with raiders coming in from all sides.

As we circled in search of carcasses or poachers' tracks, I noticed how the rivers opened out into finger-like streams, known as *brêtelles*, where graceful trees with smooth pale trunks massed together, forming the airy gallery forests. It was among these trees with their beautiful names, the Terminalia and the Khaya, the pale Isoberlinea, the grey-blue Daniellia, that the last of the elephants were hiding.

It had taken us nearly three hours of flying to reach the Koumbala River, where Iain and his team were comfortably camped in a safari hunting lodge. The census so far had revealed catastrophic results. Up here in the North the elephants were practically finished. A first analysis of the two parks indicated 7,900 dead, and only 4,300 alive. The horsemen were after anything now – even young females and babies with very small tusks. Jean-Marc was determined to stop the slaughter and put an end to the collection of ivory once and for all. He was young and he had hope, backed by a great sense of dedication; but he would need all the support he could get from the president and the international wildlife conservation movement.

In a local strong-room we were shown accoutrements captured from the horsemen during a series of counter-raids launched by the police and by Laboureur's own anti-poaching team. Tusks, skins, saddles and spears had been seized as well as two thousand litres of honey. The saddles and bridles were hand-made, with cruel bits fashioned out of beaten twisted metal, and the men carried extra spear heads tied to their saddles and rode with elaborate necklaces of leather amulets draped across their chests, containing fetishes or verses from the Koran for protection against the evil moment.

Back in Bangui driving down the Avenue de l'Independance when the census had finally been completed, we passed the giant mirror-fronted office block belonging to La Couronne. 'Dorado!' muttered Iain. With little ivory left in CAR, La Couronne was putting all its energies into diamonds. Between them the Dorado brothers had established a powerful business empire linked to Antwerp and Madrid; but one of them still operated from Bangui, I had been told, and I was determined to confront him if I could.

I had spent only one week in the CAR, yet already it felt as if I had been away for months. Evening settled upon us in a blaze of tropical crimson as the sun went on its way. Sipping our iced pernods, we stared at the maps, and rolls of film accumulated on our elephant counts. Every figure would be analysed and annotated.

We pored over aerial photographs which showed thousands of tiny dots – the russet-coloured Mbororo cattle with their sweeping lyrate horns. Each one would have to be pin-pricked and counted; and when all that was done, and the number of elephant carcasses had been totted up in neat columns, another forecast of elephant declines could be disclosed, ready for dissemination around the world as if a great new theory had just been unearthed.

It was an exacting task but we ploughed on almost mechanically, overwhelmed by the enormity of the tragedy our survey had revealed. Thought piled on thought as the timeless river rippled by. Frogs gurgled in the mud and mosquitoes whined in thick layers around our feet. The rain poured down ceaselessly in impenetrable curtains half-lit by the yellow light from the windows. Through this gloaming world we tossed as in a waking nightmare in which grotesque images of carcasses floated up towards us and faceless people chopped and stabbed elephants in a frenzy of senseless savagery. Ten years to count Africa's giants, and still we were counting, while the nations of the earth covered up their ears as if to shut out the unbearable sound of the elephants rushing to their doom.

Since our return to Bangui, it had proved impossible to arrange an appointment with Monsieur Pablo Dorado, so I drove to the glass monument in the oncoming storm. A guard let me in through the front gate and I hurried up the steps. The hall was empty, hushed by the fanning of air-conditioners. A receptionist prowled past me and disappeared. Half an hour later she reappeared to inform me that Monsieur Dorado was not available.

The following day I returned and said I would wait. There was nothing to read so I stared at the door, waiting for a Dorado who had arrived in this country as a humble salesman, peddling shirts around Bangui. Like so many others we knew, Africa's elephants had served him well.

At last a voice ushered me in. A slim, dark-haired man with an angular Mediterranean face was speaking intensely on the phone in Spanish. He waved me to a chair and continued speaking, pacing up and down in his polished moccasins.

After what seemed like an eternity he put down the phone and I introduced myself. We spoke in French. 'I know who you are and I know everything *le Docteur* Hamilton is doing,' he said.

For a moment I was taken by surprise. 'So you met my husband?'

'*Non*,' he answered abruptly.

'Then he must have met your brother when he was here in 1979,' I replied. 'Does he still trade in ivory?'

'*Non*,' said Dorado. 'We stopped trading years ago after the *Collecte* was first closed.'

Nevertheless, La Couronne had resumed trading on a massive scale in 1982. We had it on good authority from one of the Portuguese hunters who had been working for Dorado.

'I only deal in diamonds now,' Dorado continued. He stared at me coldly. There was no sympathy between us. He had made his position quite clear, but I ignored the hostility in his voice.

'As a matter of fact,' I continued, searching for the right words, 'I wanted to ask you – as one of the world's former leading ivory traders – what would you do about the elephants if our roles were reversed?'

A flicker of a smile played across his face as he considered my question. Then he leant forward across the table and I felt his gaze fully upon me. 'Madame Hamilton,' he said, 'what your husband is doing is a waste of time. He is well known and respected but he will get nowhere. To save the elephants you must close the ivory trade – world-wide.'

He paused and leant back in his chair as if to study the effect of what he had said. 'Nothing but Draconian measures work here,' he went on. 'They will try everything to get around the rules. Close the trade. It's the only chance for the elephants.'

Dorado was right, of course. But it was galling to hear our views vindicated by Dorado himself – once the biggest ivory baron in Central Africa.

One morning as we were having our *café au lait* and croissants in our house in Bangui, there was a telephone call for Jean-Marc. The conversation was short and explicit. '*Oui Colonel. Non, Colonel. Tout de suite, Colonel.*' He put down the phone and gave us a conspiratorial grin. 'That was Mansion,' he said. 'He wants the results of the count and carcass pictures. He wants to show them to the President and he wants them today!'

It had not been easy to meet Colonel Jean-Claud Mansion. 'As the French commander of Kolingba's presidential guard, he was arguably the first or second most powerful man in the country. Mansion had arrived in CAR before the overthrow of Emperor Jean Bedel Bokassa by French troops in 1979 and has survived attempts by civilian officials in the French government to recall him to France. Unlike Bob Denard, who ran the Comores for so many years, Mansion is not a vulgar mercenary but is subject to official co-operation agreements between Paris and Bangui and is believed to be paid directly by the French Defence Ministry. Among Mansion's tasks is securing the Central African government against external subversion by Libyan or Middle Eastern interests. The administration of the presidential guard is carried out by Madame Mansion.

'He's the most powerful man here, you'll never see him,' I was told by some of the French expatriates I had recently met. But here I was, on my way to his headquarters on Basa Bayen, the only hill in Bangui, overlooking the Oubangui River on its lazy journey through the forest to the sea.

A formation of the president's special guards stood outside under the trees, tough troops dressed in camouflage clothing with a black panther on their rolled-up sleeves, AK-47s strapped across their chests, and dark red berets.

I was shown into Mansion's office to be greeted by a tall, slim French soldier. Dressed in the same combat clothes as his élite force of security men, he carried himself proudly as if conscious of the long history of French wars behind him in far-away countries. Colonel Mansion was something of a legend in Bangui. Had he found life in France too tame after Indochina? I wondered. Here he could be someone, with his Vietnamese wife who lived and worked with him in the president's compound.

'Some people say you run the country; others, that you are a mercenary. Who exactly are you?' I asked, as soon as we had been seated. He leant forwards, arms folded across his papers, and an amused expression flickered across his handsome face. 'I don't really know myself,' he chuckled.

Mansion explained that he was paid by the CAR government, and had several French officers under his command, as well as two hundred tough presidential guards.

OPPOSITE – Hundreds of red elephants dot the landscape near the Voi River in Tsavo East National Park, Kenya, as they seek safety from poachers.

ABOVE – Flying over Africa's wild and beautiful parks bring moments of great joy as when flocks of pelicans and elephants join on the lakes edge. *LEFT* – The end of *Tembo Two*, our third plane, was one of our saddest days. *RIGHT* – Coming in to land on the shores of Lake Manyara at the end of a day's counting.

Anglophone personalities: *THIS PAGE, LEF*
- Zimbabwe, Rowan Martin, radio tracking
MIDDLE, LEFT TO RIGHT - Joe Kioko, now
deputy director, of KWS. Erastus sets off i
1990 on rebuilt Michigan bulldozer paid fo
by donors. Joyce Poole relaxes with he
special equipment for recording an
emitting infra sounds. *BELOW LEFT* - Davi
Sheldrick, chief park warden of Tsavo Eas
from 1948 - 76, interrogates poacher. *BELO*
RIGHT - Tué Rorsted, EEC delegate, wit
Bill Woodley and ranger in Tsavo Wes
OPPOSITE PAGE ABOVE - President Danie
arap Moi with Wildlife Minister, Katan
Ngala and Richard Leakey, after appealin
to the world to stop the ivory trade. *MIDDL*
LEFT TO RIGHT - Joan Root logging live an
dead elephants. Ian Parker. Patric
Hamilton, with his Super Cub. *BELOW LEF*
- Chief warden, Peter Jenkins and Sara
stand with the counting team. *BELOW RIGH*
- Stanley refuels a plane in Tsavo East.

ABOVE - Musth bulls, over thirty years of age, fight for dominance during mating. BELOW LEFT - Chief Park warden, Stephen Gichangi from Tsavo East, inspects a confiscated tusk. BELOW RIGHT - Newly equipped by Kenya Wildlife Services, Corporal Mohamed on anti-poaching patrol. OPPOSITE - 1990 - Flames rise over the five tonne pyre of poached and captured tusks making 18 July 'Elephant Day'. Kenya's poached ivory will be burnt every year on this day in an attempt to reduce the commercial value and enable elephants to survive.

Wars of Africa play havoc on people and elephants alike. *ABOVE* - Uganda: victims of the civil war ended in 1986. *BELOW* - Karamajong rangers clean basin of bullets donated by the Tanzanian army in 1981. *OPPOSITE* - Windhoek, Namibia: caught in the act - a confiscated haul of illegal ivory from war-torn Angola, with Portuguese traders and associates.

ABOVE TOP - Manyara 1973 - Mhoja with Dudu and Saba. *ABOVE* -
Manyara, 1990 - Mhoja with Saba and Dudu.
OPPOSITE - Drama at Manyara: Maridadi tries to rescue Bottlebrush's
baby stuck irretrievably in the mud.

'What are you going to do about the poachers in the North?'
I asked him.

'Everything is decided by the Head of State,' he said, looking me
straight in the eye with his soldier's stare. 'I have no power to take
decisions. I only present him with plans for discussions.'

'But you have seen the results of our surveys,' I pleaded. 'Unless
you can take action within the next few months we are afraid it will
be too late to save the elephants in the North.'

'Madame 'amilton,' said the colonel, 'we already confiscated half
a million dollars from a certain person in this country. We searched
his premises and found twenty-six big tusks. The judges will have
the final say.

'Ninety-five per cent of the traffickers here are foreigners,' he
went on. 'I have my eye on everyone's bank account here and I
know what they are up to. One Senegalese was found with 496
tusks. He was taken to court and found guilty, but he had big shots
behind him and the judge let him off.' He shrugged his shoulders,
narrowing his eyes at the thought. 'Of course we want to stop the
elephant slaughter, but the Government has no money to mount a
major operation.'

'So what do you need?' I asked.

He stood up and paced back and forth in his room, looking out
into the square as if he was suddenly planning a military onslaught.
'Give me $500,000 and I will do it,' he said abruptly. 'That is what
we need to mount a proper operation in the North.' He spun around,
smiling. 'So, Madame 'amilton, find me the money and we'll clean
up everything.'

He sat down and stared at me with challenging eyes. 'I'll do my
best,' I promised, 'but if you wait for a year the elephants will
be finished.'

There remained one other favour I wanted to ask him. 'Colonel,
we would like to weigh and measure the tusks which you captured
the other day when the president's helicopter was fired on,' I told
him. 'It is very important as it will demonstrate what size elephants
are being killed.'

He pursed his lips. 'The ivory is kept in the president's residence,'
he said, 'and I do not know what he will say.' But then he smiled

---

OPPOSITE – Eleanor lifts a trunk full of flowers as Tsavo blooms. Her future
and that of Tsavo's elephants looks better now than for many years.

and held out his hand. 'Don't worry,' he said. 'We will try to help *le Docteur.*'

Following that first encounter, Iain and I met up with the colonel a couple more times, and gradually he took us into his confidence, showing us how he wanted to clean up the poaching. Then one day we received a telephone call from him. The president had finally agreed that we could weigh the ivory.

'The ivory is kept in the security cellars underneath the president's home,' Mansion explained when we arrived at his office. 'Three of my men will accompany you.'

We followed them across the parade ground to the entrance of the cellar and then down a steep flight of steps to find ourselves in a dimly lit gallery with water streaming down its sides.

A heavy door was unlocked and we entered a large room filled with the familiar gleam of ivory. This was it – the president's treasure-house – piled high with tonnes of tusks of all sizes. There was a colossal fortune here, some of it collected from the rotting corpses which Iain and Jean-Marc had been counting in the North, or from poachers. Boxes of ammunition covered one entire wall, together with piles of confiscated weapons – spears, muzzle-loaders, machine-guns and ceremonial swords from Bokassa days.

Quickly we set to work with our scale, tape and basket. To weigh the tusks we suspended the scales from a spear laid across two piles of boxes. The air was humid. Sweat dripped off our bodies like the water dribbling down the walls as each tusk in turn was lifted into the basket to be weighed, measured and returned to the pile. When it was over, we found that the average tusk weighed no more than 3.4 kilos, and most had come from females.

Before leaving we called on Mansion again to show him the ivory measurements. 'They're killing all the young elephants, colonel,' I told him. 'Most have not even reached the age of reproduction.' He nodded in sympathy and confirmed that the president had agreed to meet Iain before our departure.

Knowing that the president was a keen photographer, we had carefully prepared a set of big colour prints and pasted them into a book to present to him at the meeting. Then Iain and Jean-Marc dashed around Bangui, trying to borrow some respectable clothes. In their travel-stained shirts and khaki bush shorts, neither of them was in a fit state to be presented to the Head of State. But eventually, looking like Wall Street executives complete with brief-cases, they were ushered into a reception room where the president sat dressed in a smart uniform.

Iain, having memorized his speech in French, was able to address him without an interpreter. 'Your Excellency,' he began, 'the Central African Republic was famed in Africa for its big tuskers, but there are serious problems.' Then he opened the book of photographs.

Beautiful landscapes of elephant country filled the first pages, showing the Falls of Matakil overlooking the seemingly endless parklands of the northern CAR. As the pages turned, elephants appeared, ambling undisturbed between the grey Daniellia trees with their pale yellow leaves. Then suddenly there were no more live elephants; only corpse after corpse, each with its ghastly wounds delivered by the spears of the horsemen.

The president's initial expression of delight turned to horror as one rotting body followed after another. He threw up his hands. 'What shall I do?' he sighed.

'The only answer, *Monsieur le President*, is to ban *La Collecte*, close the trade and mount a major assault on the poachers,' said Iain.

The president nodded. He understood. For it was only a few weeks since he had witnessed the killing at first hand when he had suffered the indignity of being shot at by poachers, and knew what these photos represented.

Before leaving, Jean-Marc and Iain promised the president their full support, conscious of the heavy responsibility they now carried on their backs. As for the book, it would remain in the president's office, a pictorial witness to the curse of ivory and the menace of the horsemen as they pranced through the forests on their dance of death.

After our survey, when we had flown back to Nairobi, we heard that President Kolingba did ban *La Collecte*. Colonel Mansion swept the northern parklands with his presidential guard, his helicopters and ground support. Yet despite all the activity his troops never saw a single mounted poacher. It was as if they had vanished into the bowels of the earth, and they stayed clear of the park for about a year; but it was impossible to sustain helicopters and vehicles in the field for long.

Yet our efforts in the CAR were not wasted. In the long term, they helped to establish one of the most ambitious and expensive

wildlife projects ever launched in Africa. Jean-Marc worked on it.
Roads were built and the country was opened up. An old French
soldier trained the anti-poaching force, who were recruited from
the Sara and Banda tribes, and everything was paid for by the EEC.
Jean-Marc headed out on long patrols with the men and slowly their
morale and discipline grew, until eventually they were capable of
taking on the horsemen in a series of fierce skirmishes. The threat
to the elephants of northern CAR had not been lifted; but at least
we had won them a vital reprieve.

CHAPTER THIRTY

IAIN: *Ivory Laundering*

1985–7, Zimbabwe, Kenya, Somalia, Burundi, Singapore and Canada

THE elephant count in the Central African Republic was my first lucky break in a long time, and I owed it mainly to Jean-Marc Froment who had asked for me by name to come and carry it out. It had enabled me to re-enter the battle for the elephants, but in real life, rather than sitting at a desk and drumming my heels in frustration.

It had been a joy to be back in the field working once more with a dedicated and idealistic colleague. Above all it allowed me to make the most of the fact that as we had known all along, the great elephant populations of Central Africa were collapsing and the propaganda put out by the pro-ivory lobby had merely kept this fact at bay through the specious argument that there was no scientific proof. Now we had proof in plenty of a massive collapse due to overexploitation of ivory. What we had uncovered was the end game of a major disaster being played out not only in CAR, but also in Sudan, Chad and Zaire, and outwards in each direction from Senegal to Somalia.

Immediately following the CAR count another meeting of the African Elephant and Rhino Specialist Group was held at Victoria

Falls in Zimbabwe, in September 1985, and I flew down full of anger at the elephant slaughter we had seen. This time, I was not going to let the meeting go by with the customary blend of complacency.

By now David Cumming, the Zimbabwe Wildlife Department's senior scientist, had taken over the running of the AERSG from Jonah Western. Cumming was respected and well liked, but he was also a man deeply imbued with the Zimbabwean policy of making its elephants pay their way through the sale of meat, skins and ivory, and I knew my views would find little sympathy with him.

The main subject for discussion was the new ivory quota system which, it was said, would bring the trade under control by governing the number of tusks that could be legally exported each year. The concept was that each country with elephants would declare an annual quota of ivory to be exported, which would be kept within sustainable limits. Every tusk leaving Africa would require an export permit, and the issue of such permits would be controlled by the African states with elephants, in collaboration with the CITES Secretariat.

Rowan Martin's report on his recent pan-African tour provided the intellectual underpinning of the new system. Rowan Martin was a strong character who passionately believed he was on the right course for the elephants. If I thought his policies were wrong I still respected the integrity of the man. An immensely skilled debater, a highly able radio-technician and computer wizard, he was also one of the finest bagpipers that ever set foot in Africa. I will never forget sitting in Rowan's house in the middle of the bush, the evening sunlight fading as he strode up and down playing the *piobaireachd*, the plaintive notes of my tribal kinsmen in faraway Scotland. The music stirred a sweet-sad feeling of rebellions, lost causes and battles against the English. It also proved irresistible to a tribe of bats, who one by one plummeted out of the darkening sky and fastened upon Rowan's tweed jacket until his silhouette bristled with their black shapes against the sunset.

Rowan's pan-African report was justified by the good that would come to conservation from the commercialization of the species through ivory sales, and was very much in line with the World Conservation Strategy, which saw man and his needs as the centre-point of all conservation endeavour. Needless to say, the pro-ivory trade CITES Secretariat were strongly in favour.

The battle for the elephants was now one of debate, of arguing, cajoling, persuading; and the Zimbabweans were strong debaters. But support came from an unexpected quarter in the form of a memo from Chuck Carr, the officer in charge of the New York Zoological Society's influential Wildlife Conservation International division. Chuck pointed out how he had changed his mind since the Hwange meeting. He was now convinced that there was indeed a crisis for elephants and was not prepared to be misled into complacency again.

This was a good moment for me to point out that four years of trying to appease the ivory trade had got us nowhere, and that even as the Hwange meeting had been dismissing the threat to elephants they were being wiped out of southern Sudan, northern Zaire and the CAR. Chad had already passed through a holocaust in 1979 when civil war had engulfed the country and its elephants. Yet populations depressed to 10–20 per cent of their normal level had not been sufficient cause for AERSG to trumpet its alarm to the world.

I criticized Rowan Martin for being too cautious and going out of his way to avoid any sense of crisis. The overall continental rate of decline of 1.8 per cent per annum which he proposed seemed to fly in the face of the overwhelming evidence we now had from East and Central Africa.

Then Jonah weighed in, attacking the optimistic predictions of how many elephants lived in the tropical rain forest. While recognizing that local extinctions were proceeding apace, Rowan appeared to believe in some mythical hinterland where there were five hundred thousand elephants alive and well in the forests of Zaire – hence his belief that Africa's elephants were declining overall at such a slow rate. Since the corner-stone of the utilization policies embraced by CITES was set on the assumption of high numbers in the rain forest, getting this wrong warped the whole essence of his report – which nevertheless was published by the CITES Secretariat essentially unchanged.

However, the quota system was there to stay. The only positive thing I could see in its favour was the possibility for tougher international controls on the trade and a crackdown on illegal dealers. Yet Chris Huxley, the CITES officer, had said that CITES itself was not allowed to have any connection with police enforcement, and I could see no reason why illicit traders should not go on acquiring quota certificates in the same way that they did before, by straightforward bribery and corruption.

However, I was assured that data-sheets would accompany these documents marking each individual tusk. The importing authority was supposed to check off each individual tusk and return the corrected document to the exporting authority, with a copy to the CITES Secretariat. It would all be computerized and any fraudulent transactions would be instantly reported and intercepted.

Shortly after this meeting I wrote to David Cumming expressing my opposition to the quota system. I could not understand how AERSG could give its blessing to ivory trading in African countries where the elephant had been drastically reduced or was in danger of extinction.

I respected Zimbabwe's wildlife management, but while selling ivory might be a good thing for Zimbabwe elephants, it was a bad thing for the elephants in the rest of Africa. With few exceptions, other African countries did not have the machinery in place to regulate a trade which was quite out of control.

What the Zimbabweans did not want to understand was that their system was not immediately exportable to the rest of Africa. Nor had it yet stood the test of time in Zimbabwe itself. Meanwhile, for more than 90 per cent of Africa's elephants, the best recommendation over what to do about ivory was: don't buy it, don't sell it, don't wear it.

The ivory quota system, having been steamrollered through at the 1985 CITES conference in Buenos Aires, was now in full swing. All my worst fears were confirmed and 1986 became the year of ivory laundering. Right or wrong, the conservation establishment had nailed their colours to the mast and would go down with the wreck when it sank, as it surely would.

Had the quota system led to a major drive against the illegal traders who flourished within it, the whole thing might have been worthwhile. This could have happened if the CITES Secretariat had used its leadership to draw all interested parties together; but instead they developed a siege mentality, hiding the wealth of information about the ivory traders from the eyes of those who wished to control their worst excesses. The organizations committed to the operation of the ivory quota system, that is CITES and TRAFFIC – wildlife trade monitoring organization backed by IUCN and WWF – became a closed circle. Protection of the traders became the actuality, and all my attempts to persuade them to set up a log of trader activities or even a list of ivory traders were frustrated.

When it emerged that some 60 per cent of the CITES Secretariat's 'ivory unit' operations were financed by the ivory trade it was easier to understand why they had behaved with such secrecy and protectiveness, although it is only fair to record that the CITES parties had agreed that the ivory unit should be allowed to raise finance from external sources.

The rules of the ivory quota system allowed any new country joining CITES to wipe the slate clean so that all tusks held in its possession would be registered for sale. The idea was to gain adherence to the treaty of these new parties. But the result was that ivory stocks previously considered suspect because they were un-documented could now be legally traded with CITES' blessing – and doubled or even quadrupled in value overnight. Whatever CITES' true intentions, registering these enormous hoards amounted to an ivory amnesty which allowed hundreds of tonnes of contraband tusks to enter the market. It was a massive loophole and the traders were quick to exploit it to the full.

On 16 March 1986 the *Sunday Standard* of Nairobi carried a story headline: THE IVORY SALE TO BEAT 'EM ALL. It described the extraordinary sale to be held in Somalia, of seventeen thousand tusks that could fetch up to $3.72 million – exceeding the legal sales of any other African country in that year. The tusks themselves represented the slaughter by poachers of some twenty-three thousand Somali elephants – not to mention what had been smuggled in from Kenya – in the early 1980s.

This was the first of the three great ivory sales orchestrated under the CITES ivory quota systems in 1986, and the story contained several justifications of the trade by Chris Huxley, the CITES official who was the driving force behind them. 'Until recently,' he confessed, 'the Convention's attempts to bring the ivory trade under control were more or less a total failure.' He claimed that dealers now had been forced to move from 'laundering' to pure smuggling.

'In a sense, smuggling is preferable as the case is clear-cut, the Government concerned can immediately confiscate the ivory and prosecute,' said Huxley. 'With laundering, this was not often the case as some kind of documents would usually arrive later.'

   He expressed confidence that the system was beginning to bite and claimed that the illegal trade – worth $50 million and representing 80 per cent of all ivory leaving Africa – had already been cut to 50 per cent.

   But while the Somali government sat on its ivory stocks in Mogadishu, other tusks said to have originated in Somalia had been sold fraudulently on forged documents. In addition, larger, more valuable tusks were disappearing from the government containers, to be replaced by smaller tusks of unknown origin.

   'We're very anxious that the sale's done openly and gets cleared up as soon as possible,' said Huxley mysteriously. 'There are people who are exploiting the situation.'

   Behind this intriguing newspaper quotation lay an extraordinary story that remained concealed for many years within the files of the CITES Secretariat. It appeared that Dr Murray Watson, the consultant originally hired by the Somalis to handle the ivory, had clashed with Huxley over its sale. The consultant CITES favoured was Ian Parker, who, for 3 per cent of the gross, was prepared to sell all the seventeen thousand tusks on behalf of the Shirre company, the owners according to the Somali government.

   A few years later I saw a letter on the headed notepaper of Somalia's National Range Agency, addressed to the CITES Secretariat complaining bitterly at the way they had handled the whole transaction. In particular the letter queried their reasons for introducing Ian Parker as a consultant and adviser on the sale when, so it alleged, he had a vested interest in at least one of the companies bidding for the ivory. At the time this relationship between CITES and Parker was not generally known.

   Huxley on his mission to Mogadishu claimed that Murray Watson had miscounted the number of containers in which the ivory was held. He also insisted that most of the tusks had not been produced in the last two or three years, but had been held by the Government since at least March 1982. In fact this did not contradict Watson, who said that the ivory was derived from slaughters that took place mainly between 1979 and 1982.

   Eventually the differences were resolved one way or another and Somalia requested an ivory export quota of 17,002 tusks, the whole of which was to be sold and exported before the end of 1986. In the end it all went out illegally, plus other consignments of equal or greater volume, and was reported as an infringement to the CITES conference in 1987.

A similar operation now took place in Burundi, where eighty-nine tonnes of ill-gotten ivory also received the blessing of CITES. The importance of Burundi was its strategic position in the heart of Africa. It was only a tiny republic but it had become a key player in the ivory stakes and a major staging post on the long trail leading to the ivory godfathers in Hong Kong, exporting mountains of tusks from the neighbouring countries of Tanzania, Zaire, Kenya and Zambia.

The legalization of the Burundi stockpile would never have been possible without the help once more of Ian Parker, the consultant recommended to the Burundi government by the CITES Secretariat to clinch the deal. Parker became involved in the Burundi scandal early in 1986 after two CITES officials, Chris Huxley and Joe Yovino, were approached by Zulfikar 'Zully' Rahemtullah, a wealthy Kenyan businessman considered to be the major mover in Burundi and one of the biggest illegal ivory traffickers in Africa at that time. In Tanzania, where he controlled a lucrative poaching and smuggling network, Rahemtullah went by the name of Zaidi Baraka until the Tanzanian CID discovered his true identity.

In 1986, Rahemtullah was the owner, through his local agents, of some sixty tonnes of ivory held up in Burundi. He offered the two CITES officials a 'donation' of $50,000 to help him obtain the certificates needed to sell his tusks. Huxley and Yovino refused and reported back to the secretariat in Switzerland, where everyone was taken aback at the size of the ivory stock.

According to Eugene Lapointe, secretary general of the CITES secretariat, what happened next is unclear. But in September 1986 Parker flew to Burundi as the official Burundi government consultant with the task of legalizing the eighteen thousand tusks he found there. In his capacity as middleman, Parker met Rahemtullah and struck a deal whereby he would be paid 3 per cent of the gross profits. Rahemtullah agreed, and Parker personally marked and registered each poached tusk as legal, and signed the vital export permits alongside the Burundi presidential seal.

This single, sorry episode was one of the most ironic events in the entire history of the African elephant. Here was a country with no elephants sending out ivory equivalent to a herd of ten thousand animals.

But the most scandalous deal of all was the immense legalization which took place in Singapore, where 270 tonnes of poached raw ivory had been stockpiled. Once the tusks had been registered under the CITES quota systems and provided with permits, the owners were free to put their contraband on the open market. Overnight, a handful of traders made a fortune, because the now 'legal' ivory had doubled in value. Among them was K. T. Wang, one of the biggest ivory overlords in Hong Kong. Thanks to CITES he received an enormous windfall, after which the grateful trafficker donated about $20,000 to the CITES Secretariat, according to the London *Observer*.

Many conservationists were appalled. As Craig van Note, vice-president of the US-based conservation consortium, Monitor, observed: 'The fact that ivory gets legitimized by governments doesn't make it any less poached.' But the only response from the CITES Secretariat was a press conference in which they claimed that the quota system had already slowed down the rate of poaching.

In all these dealings the importance of Hong Kong as the world market-place for illegal ivory could not be underestimated. Over the years this British Crown Colony had become the driving force for elephant poaching in Africa, and Britain bore a heavy responsibility for the carnage it caused.

The Hong Kong traders were always several steps ahead of the CITES system, moving with ease from one country to another to get round the laws and regulations. When one exporting centre was in danger of being closed down, they simply moved elsewhere.

When Hong Kong stopped raw ivory imports in 1984 the traders set up factories in Macau to be 'laundered' by the simple expedient of carving the tusks. As carved ivory was considered too difficult to control, it could then be moved on quite legitimately to Hong Kong.

When this became more difficult there was an exodus of traders to Singapore, where they were rewarded in 1986 by the CITES amnesty. And when Singapore itself joined CITES in 1986, the Hong Kong traders set up carving factories in the United Arab Emirates and Taiwan.

By the mid-1980s the real power behind the Hong Kong ivory trade had fallen into the hands of a few influential and very wealthy families. Over the years they had developed syndicates which now controlled most of the ivory supplied to Hong Kong's ivory manufacturers. Their influence permeated every part of the trade, from Africa to Europe, the Middle East and the Far East. These were the men whose families grew fat on the huge trade in poached tusks.

Some of the illegal traders were well known to the CITES Secretariat which made attempts to thwart them, yet still they flourished. According to *Asia Week* magazine which published a damning exposé of the trade in 1988, the Poon family were the controllers of the biggest ivory empire. They were headed by two brothers, Poon Tat Wah (George) and Poon Tat Hong. When CITES legalized the poached ivory stockpile in Singapore in 1986, the Poons are reported to have made US $7.5 million, overnight.

The Lai family, exposed by TRAFFIC, were also powerful. They were headed by Michael Lai, a Hong Kong resident. The family owned ivory factories in Hong Kong and Singapore, including the Kee Cheong Ivory Factory. Consignments of poached ivory they had stockpiled in Singapore before it joined CITES were later exported back to Hong Kong, and in 1988 Kee Cheong donated $10,000 to the CITES Secretariat.

But perhaps the most successful trader of them all was K. T. Wang, a suave Hong Kong businessman involved in shipping hundreds of tonnes of poached ivory out of Africa. He had strong connections with French-speaking African countries, developed while working for twenty-five years with French diplomats and for the French Consulate in Hong Kong. Like the Poons and the Lai family, he, too, had benefited hugely from the CITES ivory amnesties. His ivory often passed through Europe, where he had close business links with Jacques Lewkowicz, the owner of *Société Nouvelle France Croco*, an ivory and reptile skin trade company with a web of contacts throughout Africa. In the 1970s Wang and Lewkowicz were the most influential traders in Europe, handling hundreds of tonnes of poached ivory from the Congo, Zaire and CAR.

Using their fortunes, the ivory barons were able to set up an almost foolproof network of supply routes to keep an endless river of tusks pouring into Hong Kong. It was they who, through their syndicates and men on the spot in Africa, provided arms and cash for the poaching gangs and ensured protection by bribery at every level, from police and bent customs officials to game rangers, army officers, diplomats and government ministers.

All along it was clear to me that the battle for ideas still remained to be won, and this was going to be done only with clear documentation of the elephant disaster, rammed down the throats of the establishment in a quantified format. We also realized that public opinion was a vital issue if we were to get anywhere at all.

In early 1987 Oria and I were invited by an American benefactor, Singer Rankin, to give a talk in Pittsburgh. We called it 'The Unknown Crisis' and spoke of the quiet disappearance of the elephants which was being ignored by the world. Among the audience were Paul Schindler and Diana McMeekin from the African Wildlife Foundation, an organization respected by the powerful hunting lobby and by senior conservationists. Within a year they had launched a major campaign to save the elephant.

Another stroke of good fortune came when the United Nations Environment Programme installed a new geographical computer in their Nairobi headquarters.

It belonged to UNEP's Global Environmental Monitoring System, which looked at issues that ranged from the greenhouse effect to polluted seas, and threatened species. Two old friends of mine from Oxford were in charge: Michael Gwynne, an eminent ecologist and Harvey Croze, a former elephant ecologist from the Serengeti. We had enough data about the elephant to make it worth putting on their giant mapping computer. It was a wonderful opportunity to assemble and analyse all the figures on the African elephant which we had collected over the last decade.

A young graduate from Dartmouth University volunteered for the work. Anne Burrill had a figure like Jane Fonda, piercing blue eyes and a mind like a computer chip. She could scan and transcribe thousands of figures and never make a mistake. Together we logged every single piece of information on the African elephant across an entire range of more than five million square kilometres, to find out which factors were the most important in determining elephant density. Her work was of the highest quality and had great political implications for the elephants.

In May 1987, all the members of the African Elephant and Rhino Specialist Group met at Nyeri, in Kenya below the Aberdare Mountains. Anne had produced dramatic computer maps of the elephant's range throughout Africa, and all the factors affecting it. There were my flight lines across the wilds of northern Zaire, together with the most up-to-date details from Zimbabwe and all the continental information summarized and analysed geographically. Anne dazzled us with her demonstration of modern computer technology.

The meeting proved to be a crucial one in the battle of ideas, where the scientists were no longer able to resist the impact of new facts. Richard Barnes, a Cambridge scientist, had been working for five years in the forests of Gabon, often in the most appalling conditions, perfecting an ingenious method of estimating elephant densities by counting their droppings. He now reviewed all the forest data with other Central African representatives and concluded that poaching had been devastating and the elephant numbers were much lower than Rowan Martin's extrapolations.

Even the most conservative die-hards now had to admit that the ivory-trade levels could no longer be justified on scientific grounds and I was delighted when the chairman, David Cumming, agreed to inform CITES of this fact in no uncertain terms.

Down in Kenya's Amboseli National Park, in the dry country that lies below the snows of Kilimanjaro, Cynthia Moss had been studying elephants since 1973. She knew all the Amboseli elephant families intimately, and she spoke up now to defend their freedom. Her work had brought in a host of keen young newcomers, one of whom, Joyce Poole, had been invited to Nyeri to speak on her elephant behaviour studies. A petite figure with soft green eyes, and a quiet voice, that hid a steely will, she stood up shyly before the self-assured and dominant males of the AERSG. She then told us not about population dynamics nor the ivory trade, but about how elephants behaved in this one population which the ivory trade had somehow passed by.

She spoke of how the Amboseli elephants communicated to one another, explaining the complexity and subtlety of elephant social life. She had identified more than twenty-five distinct calls the elephants used, during the thousands of hours that she and Cynthia Moss had spent carefully observing them. She explained the significance of the big males whose very age was a proof of their success, identifying them as carrying the best genetic stock for survival. She felt that above all they should be preserved, yet they had been the first to go elsewhere. Their huge tusks, which stood them in such good stead against their rivals, were also their greatest liability, given man's extraordinary ability to distort all things natural. She ended with a plea that the ethical implications of 'harvesting' such animals should be considered.

There was an uneasy shifting in the seats of the self-confident Zimbabwe alpha males, where old bull elephants had just been referred to as 'dead wood' that needed culling. They were impressed, and one admitted that her talk had made him wonder if they were doing the right thing. Unfortunately his doubts did not last for long, and any idea of an ivory ban was rejected. But the paradox was there. Just as we were beginning to understand these mysterious and intelligent creatures, our species was threatening them with near extinction.

The most exciting discovery was only just beginning to emerge. Katharine Payne was an American scientist best known for her work on whale communication. By concentrating on the songs of the Humpback Whale, she had begun to unlock the secrets of how these huge creatures were able to contact each other across miles of ocean by means of infra-sound. Now Katy wanted to switch to elephants. She came to Amboseli and struck up a fruitful working relationship with Joyce Poole where they combined their expertise to confirm that elephants, too, were able to communicate with each other over a distance of several miles by emitting low-frequency calls inaudible to the human ear.

After the meeting Cynthia, Joyce, Oria and I met in a rebellious mood to make a private battleplan, and decided that we would stick together for a campaign to end the ivory trade. I was in favour of knocking America, Europe and Japan right out of the market, along with any African States that would go for a unilateral ban. Cynthia laughed at the idea that AERSG might muzzle us. She was writing her book *Elephant Memories*, and she vowed that she would use it to appeal directly to the world. Oria was also invited to lecture in America on behalf of the Smithsonian Institution, and Joyce's detailed papers on elephant behaviour were all in the process of coming out. Here were three amazonian warriors who would be hard to ignore in the battle for the elephants.

In the light of the AERSG meeting Anne Burrill and I refined the elephant database. Anne worked like a slave, night and day, actually camping on the floor of UNEP in order to get the report ready for the next CITES conference which was due to be held in Canada in June. I wrote to WWF to suggest that they should act now and take a public position on actively discouraging ivory buying. WWF's response was to withdraw an air ticket they had promised me. But I went anyway, thanks to the National Geographic Society who funded my attendance.

At the conference I found that Christine Stevens, an energetic campaigner for a more humane attitude to animals, had taken up our cause and made it the centre of an elephant exhibit calling for strong action against the ivory trade, telling people not to buy ivory. At last the facts were out for all the delegates to see, and Dave Cumming, as he had promised to AERSG, spelt out in stark terms the conservation disaster that had struck the elephant.

What was beyond my understanding was that, despite the obvious need to lower the demand, the conservation establishment, epitomized by WWF and IUCN, could not bring themselves even to recommend that people should not buy, sell or wear ivory, let alone support a trade ban.

To ban the trade completely we would have to persuade CITES to place the African elephant on its 'Appendix One' list of endangered species which could become extinct if commercial trade was not controlled. Animals which already enjoyed such total protection included gorillas, rhinos, and what was left of the great whales after years of commercial slaughter – a terrible echo of what was happening to the elephant. At present elephants received only the minimum protection offered by 'Appendix Two'.[1] This listed threatened species which could become endangered if uncontrolled trade continued. Animals traded in this category – elephants included – required special permits from CITES.

At the conference I met a couple of Greenpeace men who had badges with Environmental Investigation Agency written on them. They were Allan Thornton, tall, dark-haired and intense with a deceptive air of being friendly to all the world, and Dave Currey, well built and fair-haired, with a humorous twinkle in his eyes. I asked them what the badge meant, and they explained that they were investigating the trade in marine mammals, particularly the exploitation of seals, whales and dolphins. I told them it was time for someone to make a similar study of the ivory trade. They were interested, but seemed too busy to be able to spare

---

[1] During the fourteen years they were on 'Appendix Two' well over half the elephants of Africa disappeared.

time for elephants. Yet somehow I had the strong feeling our paths would cross again.

Our report looked good in its orange covers, and for the first time under the banner of the United Nations Environmental Programme (UNEP) the elephant declines were indisputably documented. In a later glossy UNEP pamphlet about the African elephant, based mainly on our work, the CITES Secretariat were asked for their comments. They tried to present a sanitized version of elephant exploitation according to their liking, which put the blame for elephant decline on human population increase rather than the ivory trade. I managed to get this distortion deleted, but they still managed to insert a piece at the end which said that any ivory-trade ban was sure to fail.

By now I had become convinced that the establishment was unable or unwilling to tackle the illegal ivory trade. WWF, IUCN and TRAFFIC all seemed paralysed by the uncompromising pro-trade stance of the CITES Secretariat. Clearly the time had come to investigate the ivory traders, as had been recommended by AERSG, but which had not been followed up. I felt it would be better if such operations were taken right outside the auspices of CITES lest they compromise any operation. When in London I took the opportunity to meet some specialists in the field of investigation, and was convinced this was the only way to expose the rottenness that seemed to reach every level of the ivory trade.

At the end of the year I found myself one notch further allied to Jonah Western. Although he would not yet go for an ivory ban, wanting instead further dialogue with traders, he threw his full weight into confirming that the trade was the principal cause of elephant decline, and coined a splendid phrase referring to elephants as 'flagships for conservation'.

There now followed one other significant event. I returned to Manyara to make a census and discovered a disaster had befallen this supposedly safe elephant population. My Manyara report was given a somewhat grudging acceptance by the park authorities, who had denied there was any problem, and for a while it was embarrassing to return there. But that was the price for revealing the truth.

Reports were now also coming out of Tsavo that the situation there was once again rapidly deteriorating. It was in Kenya that the whole ivory crisis had started, and it was in Kenya that the first solutions had been tried. A hunting ban and a massive injection of World Bank money for anti-poaching had some limited success in the late 1970s; but ten years of under-funding, bad management and corruption had taken their toll. The ivory racketeering which had been quietly festering under the surface had now come out into the open again, and this time the poaching was in the hands of real killers.

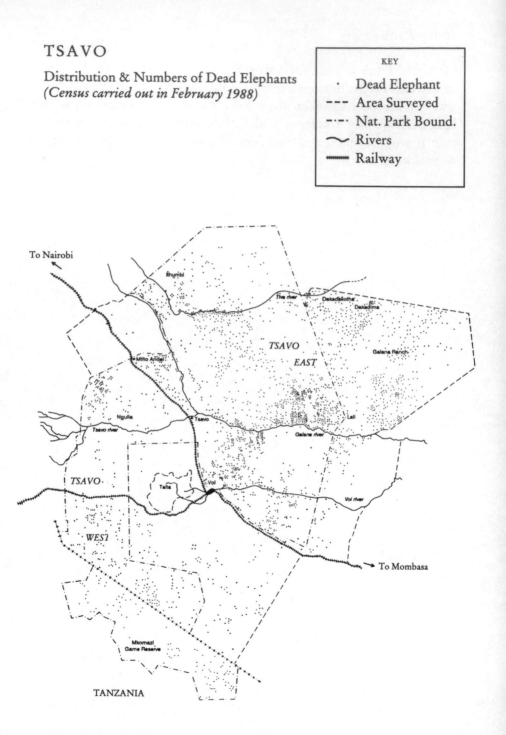

TSAVO

Distribution & Numbers of Dead Elephants
(Census carried out in February 1988)

KEY

· Dead Elephant
--- Area Surveyed
-·-· Nat. Park Bound.
～ Rivers
+++++++ Railway

To Nairobi

Ithumbi

Tiva river

Dakadhkotha

Dakadima

TSAVO

EAST

Galana Ranch

Mtito Andei

Ngulia

Tsavo river

Tsavo

Lali

Galana river

TSAVO

Taita

Vol

Vol river

WEST

To Mombasa

Mkomazi
Game Reserve

TANZANIA

CHAPTER THIRTY-ONE

ORIA: *Tsavo Twilight*

1988, Kenya

TSAVO, that giant wilderness of red earth, thorn-bush and blue faraway hills was still a wildlife paradise. True, the black rhino no longer came boiling out of the commiphora scrub as you passed by; but the national park which David Sheldrick had guarded as fiercely as if it had been his own private kingdom still offered the visitor a sight of eland, oryx and giraffe. Cavalcades of zebra and buffalo cantered away in the morning light and at night, lions roared across the starlit plains. Even the leopards, so cruelly persecuted for their fur in the 1970s, were increasing again. Only the elephants, Tsavo's greatest glory, were hard to find. In 1969 there had been over forty thousand. Now you could drive all day and not find even fresh spoor.

The Wakamba of Sheldrick's day had given way to the notorious *shifta* – heavily armed gangs of Somali bandits – sometimes also aided and abetted by corrupt wardens and park rangers. There had been a respite in 1978 when Joe Kioko, a young African warden of Tsavo East, aided by Bill Woodley from Tsavo West, had driven the poachers out of both parks. Joe Kioko was replaced by Patrick Hamilton and the elephants continued to live in peace until Patrick, too, was transferred out of the park in

1983 when the poaching started up again. The Tsavo story had come full circle.

The situation became so bad that eventually in 1987 special pleading to President Moi was needed to shake up the Wildlife Department. The Director was sacked and our old friend and one-time park director, Dr Perez Olindo, was put back in the chair, exactly eleven years after the National Parks were forced into a merger with the game department, when everything went to pieces. The president gave him a free hand to hire and fire as he saw fit, but no sooner had he reached his office than the intricate threads of power and tribal politics began to bind his hands.

Perez had resigned from the newly formed Wildlife Department in 1976. 'I did not want to witness the decline,' he said.

Back in office he had found the department totally bankrupt.

After Central Africa and the Selous, we knew that Tsavo had to be one of the most critical elephant strongholds left in Africa, where the trend would have profound political implications. All kinds of horror stories were circulating in Kenya about the mass killings of Tsavo's elephants by the *shifta* gangs, but no-one had carried out a total count since 1980. Now, with Perez Olindo at the helm again, Iain suggested that a census of rhinos and elephants should be made in Tsavo, and that he would be prepared to give a hand in organizing it.

Perez agreed and asked Iain to find the money and organize the count. With the scientific facts at his fingertips Perez could start cleaning up the mess. However, despite the financial problems, he brought with him his innate cheerfulness and a new wave of optimism which was a great change. For the first time in years, the director's door was open to visitors, and also to the Press. But inside that office, Perez struggled to keep up with a mountain of problems.

Nairobi was well informed about the plight of Kenya's elephant populations, and when we picked up the phone to raise the funds for the survey, the East African Wildlife Society, other NGOs, the business community, friends, tour operators and safari lodges all gave generously. Others offered food, accommodation and drinks, and the pilots volunteered their time. We intended to pull all the international and local wildlife organizations together on this count, and for the first time in ten years a proper aerial survey in Tsavo was launched, with members of the Wildlife Department keen to participate. Teams poured in from all parts of Kenya and we went on ahead to set up the logistics and accommodation at Voi, in Tsavo East, while others put up camps or stayed in lodges near their counting blocks.

The house where our friend Simon Trevor, the wildlife film-maker lived, was only a stone's throw from our tent and he offered us the use of it, which was a great help. There we met Chupa, the honey badger, a delightful young creature with long claws and sinuous powerful arms. She ran around manipulating things with her paws with a fluid sort of precision which I never anticipated. Her strong jaws could have chopped off our fingers, but she treated us with extraordinary gentleness.

After twelve years scant traces of David Sheldrick's reign remained. Sturdy buildings like the hangar, and Stanley, the aircraft's attendant, were an exception. Stanley had been trained by David for maximum reliability and minimum time loss. Aeroplanes were instantly re-fuelled as soon as they landed, oil checked and screens washed. Everything was neatly inventoried in the store's books. He knew exactly how much fuel had been used and how much was still available. Amid the chaos of the past ten years, it was marvellous to see that a man of his calibre had remained as straight as an arrow and always ready.

Eight planes had arrived for the count. Now, in the golden light of an African morning, they were being prepared. 'One of the problems here is not enough proper control over the issue and expenditure of ammunition,' Simon told us as we fuelled up. 'Even tourists are complaining of gunshots at night and all the dead elephants they see by the side of the road.' Like many of the wardens who had attended the Mweka Wildlife College, the training of those at Tsavo had been theoretical, oriented towards offices, and of little practical value. 'No senior officer goes out on patrol with his men any more,' Simon added gloomily.[1]

One by one, the rangers approached us with lowered voices, explaining how thankful they were to see something happening at last in Tsavo. 'Things are very bad here,' one muttered, but did not dare to venture on with his comments. We knew that some rangers and parks' staff were involved in the ivory racket, shooting

[1] Despite this general tendency, some of the Mweka graduates became superb wardens.

elephants, guiding poachers and making deals with traders; but the question 'who?' was answered with a look of silent fear. As Patrick Hamilton, Perez Olindo's special observer, flew around the park he found many carcasses within a kilometre or less of the road. There were so many they became known as 'roadsiders' and the recovery of the .303 calibre bullets which had killed them was proof enough to him that it was not the *shifta* but motorized poachers, almost certainly Tsavo's own field-force in their national park Toyotas.

Bringing in the results from a count always arouses much excitement, a blend of scientific investigation and treasure-hunt. A large map of Tsavo lay spread out on the table, with the transcriber marking in live and dead elephants – fresh, recent and old – as everyone stood around. Already, by the end of the first day, more skeletons than live elephants had been counted. Bandits – and maybe rangers too – were covering up many more carcasses with cut branches to hide them from vultures, which in turn would have helped the pilots locate them.

The total count in 1988 of the Tsavo ecosystem including the Galana Ranch and Mkomazi National Park across the border in Tanzania produced a minimum of 5,363 elephants – a 79 per cent decline since 1972. Given the undercount factors there were probably around six thousand elephants in all. We also counted 2,421 dead elephants. But since carcasses and skeletons are even harder to see than elephants and many are missed in these counts, the real numbers were expected to be much higher. We calculated that between five thousand and seven thousand had probably died or been shot within the previous eight years, which meant that for the last three thousand days, an average of two elephants had been killed every day. Few male elephants over the age of thirty-five now existed in Kenya, and groups of orphans were a common sight on these intensive counts.

The report made radical recommendations, including the cleaning up of corrupt elements within the Wildlife Department, but the corridors of silence prevailed in the Wildlife Ministry after it had been delivered. We were told that a copy had also gone up to the president, but this was never confirmed. However, the cat was out of the bag. The report was widely circulated. It created a stir of interest within the EEC, UNEP, WWF and IUCN and was warmly acknowledged in a letter to us by Richard Leakey, chairman of the East African Wildlife Society. Leakey had not until then been actively involved in the politics of elephant conservation, but suggested that a delegation of six thousand children from the Wildlife clubs should protest to the president, demanding protection for Kenya's last herds.

Meanwhile, poaching in Tsavo and other parts of the country worsened. Somali bandits now turned on tourists and local people as well as elephants, holding up vehicles and demanding food at gunpoint in the villages. The General Service Unit were sent in to help the police to crack down on the bandits, but always the Somalis seemed to outwit or outgun them. The government forces were no match for any bush-wise *shifta* coming to a waterhole, who needed only to see one pair of bootmarks to set up an ambush or melt away into the endless thorn scrub. The police inspector in Voi told us one day that the Somali poaching in Tsavo was the worst he had seen in seventeen years.

Patrick Hamilton visited us frequently. Always neatly turned out in his khaki uniform and green beret, he was known to his friends as *Chui* – the Swahili word for leopard – having once made a detailed study of these beautiful cats. We talked one night on the verandah under a brilliant moon with all the night noises around us and the stars shining above, a sad story of his frustrated efforts in the Wildlife Department. The place was full of rotten people, undermining Olindo all the time, he told us. 'I used to love flying over Tsavo,' Patrick went on. 'Now I'm beginning to hate it because every time I go out I see fresh carcasses, and there is nothing I can do about it.' He clenched his fists as he spoke, his anger boiling inside him. It was difficult to find any words of comfort for Patrick. We had seen it all before, and could only agree with his hopeless conclusion.

One evening we were informed that a massive operation was going on in Tsavo. One poacher had turned himself in to save his old father who had been arrested. We can call him Abdi and he was a Somali. He told the police at Voi he was ready to co-operate, and later handed in an AK-47 with one hundred and fifty rounds. The first person he informed on was the warden of that time, as well as several other influential people in that area. Among some of the accusations hurled at the warden was that he had been sending rangers out to shoot elephants on the very days that we were conducting the count.

We met Abdi one day soon after Christmas 1988 who told us an extraordinary story. One day he had decided to turn himself in when he saw an orphaned elephant walk into a mosque in the area where he had been poaching. A devoted Muslim, Abdi felt that if the elephant had come to the mosque he was bringing a message for peace. However, Abdi still needed some money, and shot a few more elephants for their ivory, including a cow which collapsed on top of its small calf and squashed it. Abdi was so upset he could not eat. Two days later news came that his wife with one of his children had capsized in a canoe as they were crossing the fast-running Tana River and both were drowned. He knew then he had been punished by God. 'I will never kill another elephant,' he said, spitting on his hand and holding it up to heaven. The tusks he would hide in a pig hole, then cut special marks on the trees surrounding it and take a bearing. Later, when he found a buyer, he would take him straight to the spot where he had buried his hoard. 'There are still eight gangs working in Tsavo,' he told us. 'As for those rangers and that warden,' he said with contempt, 'they are *gasiya* (garbage); worth nothing.

'Once we sold the ivory, we would go to town – Mombasa or Malindi – stop off at the barber, buy some new clothes, a watch and a pair of sunglasses and walk about the streets. After a good meal and some women, the money was finished.' He whistled across his finger in a gesture of finality. 'Very little money ever got back to our families.'

By the end of the year Abdi had disappeared. No one knew where he went to. Maybe, like the elephants, he, too, had been killed and become another sad statistic in Tsavo's long and bloody history.

CHAPTER THIRTY-TWO

IAIN: *The Turning of the Tide*

1988–9, America, Zambia, Kenya

T HE world woke up to the desperate peril of the African elephant in 1988. At last our long campaign was getting through. Oria and I joined forces with Cynthia Moss, Joyce Poole and Katy Payne, and we each publicized the elephants' plight around the world. As the year went on many other voices were added. Daphne Sheldrick highlighted the tragedy of individual elephant orphans. Christine Stevens, in Washington, was at the heart of what WWF personnel referred to as the 'Humaniacs', the humane societies that campaigned for animal rights who now called for a complete ban on all US ivory imports.

The stream of elephant consciousness had broadened into a river. Across the Atlantic Brigitte Bardot supported the 'Elephant Amnesty', launched by the French scientist, Pierre Pfeffer; and in London the *New Scientist* carried another story in which I was quoted as saying: 'If a Government cannot or will not control poaching, there is no reason to assume that it will operate a functioning ivory registration scheme.'

It was now accepted that world consumption of ivory had to be reduced; but how? With a real commitment on the part of the East African governments and donor agencies, there was no doubt in my mind that the poaching tide could be halted. But without this commitment I feared the elephants would nose-dive to the low hundreds in most countries.

When Katy Payne spoke in favour of a ban to the full WWF/USA board she had a terrible time and was told to stick to research. Cynthia's book, *Elephant Memories*, was an instant hit, but when she and Joyce went to Washington, they were condescendingly told by WWF that they did not understand the big picture. Africa's elephants were a more complex resource than could be understood from Amboseli, said the WWF officials. However, WWF embraced many shades of feeling and one of its trustees, Prince Sadruddin Aga Khan, started pushing for a complete re-think on WWF's elephant policy.

The prince's concern led to more agonizing among the WWF leadership as they tried to decide how to respond. It was a hopeless situation. Caught between polarized advisers, they were unable to slip off the dilemma which impaled them.

Meeting followed meeting. At one held by WWF in Lusaka, chaired by Prince Bernhard, and Prince Sadruddin, in April 1988, I pleaded that it was not enough just to condemn the illegal trade. Civilized people had got to realize that buying, wearing or selling ivory killed elephants and that only a reduction in consumption could save them. But the Zimbabweans were resistant against all logic to lower the demand for ivory by discouraging its sale. 'This is a patronizing colonialist attitude,' was Rowan Martin's rejoinder. 'Make no mistake,' he said. 'At CITES Africa will vote as a bloc in favour of the trade.'

Then, to my surprise and dismay, Perez Olindo, of all people, director of Kenya's National Parks, spoke out against a trade ban. 'Why have bans not worked where they have been tried?' he asked. 'Maybe they are not a solution. Kenya recognizes that ivory has a value, and so do elephants. What do we do with the ivory arising from natural mortality? Even in our African communities ivory always had a value. Do we now say it has no value? It will not be taken seriously. For us the ban on ivory has not worked.'

I felt Perez was wrong in believing that a value always had to be attached to tusks. He was not willing to make a break with the thinking of the past which insisted that the ivory trade could never be stopped. A better policy on tusks was to devalue them. All our experience of twenty years told us that any value attached to tusks would result in them being over-exploited.

Of course, Perez was only talking about the banning of the trade in Kenya; but he was supported by other wildlife directors at the meeting and their influential views won the day. For the timebeing WWF would neither recommend a world-wide ban nor a campaign against buying ivory. However, many of their executives were deeply anxious about the public support they were losing and all the time the elephant body count continued to mount inexorably. My last three surveys could not be ignored. In Central Africa the elephants were down by 80 per cent. Selous was down by half and Tsavo had lost at least three-quarters. The science was now good enough to demand a change and it was obvious to us that it was only a matter of time before WWF and the rest would have to swing round behind us and go for a total ban.

Yet sceptical voices persisted. 'The key to conserving elephants is adequate finance for Africa's National Parks,' said Ian Parker, who now argued that chronic under-funding lay at the root of the failure to stop the poaching; while even Jonah Western was reported as saying a blanket ban would be ineffective and would only drive the ivory trade completely underground.

A final testimony before a US Congressional Committee in July 1988 represented WWF's last stand in favour of the trade. A debate on Congressman Anthony Beilenson's Elephant Act was in progress and an embarrassed Bill Reilly from WWF/USA had to defend the thoroughly discredited ivory quota system and put forward WWF's ivory tax proposal. The idea was that ivory imports would be taxed so highly that demand would be reduced and the proceeds would be used for elephant conservation.

I hammered the total failure of the system, and the success of the ivory dealers in exploiting loop-holes. The 'Humaniacs' stole the high moral ground from WWF as defenders of the elephant. From now on, Christine Stevens and her twenty-five strong consortium of wildlife groups at the heart of the campaign were not going to stop until there was a total world-wide ban on the ivory trade. The African Wildlife Foundation persuaded by Cynthia and Joyce came out with a powerful advertising campaign against ivory fashion. 'Accessories to Murder' was how they described women wearing ivory.

In the months that followed, WWF/USA played a vital role in pushing the reworked 'Elephant Conservation Act' through Congress. The act gave the quota system a limited time to prove itself, after which a total US ban would become mandatory. It banned ivory from nations like Somalia with a record of illegal ivory trading, and also threatened to ban ivory from all intermediaries. This threw Hong Kong traders into a panic and forced them to freeze all trade with the States to avoid jeopardizing their industry.

While this saga was being played out I undertook a study for the EEC in the Masai Mara Game Reserve. Tué Rohrsted, my EEC friend from Uganda days, was now based in Kenya and was keen to improve the management of the Mara which was being swamped with tourists. The Mara is where the northern Serengeti plains spills over the Tanzanian border, forming the richest wildlife area in Kenya. Large prides of lions roam the reserve, and every year in July and August its red-oat grasslands are host to the spectacular migration of wildebeest and zebra which trek north from the Serengeti National Park in search of fresh grazing. Since the border between the two countries is only a line on the map the animals are free to come and go as they please. Our task was to come up with a plan for a $1.5 million budget to enhance the entire ecosystem.

Holly Dublin joined our team. Diminutive and sparrow-like, with a mind like a razor, she had impressed me when we had worked together on the Serengeti elephants in 1984, and her latest counts confirmed that the Mara's elephants had continued to increase since then.

The Serengeti and the Mara elephants lived in two different worlds. The Mara elephants had been persecuted during the great poaching wave in the mid-1970s, but were now well protected under the eyes of rangers and legions of tourists in their mini-buses. These resident elephants had now been joined by refugees from the Serengeti, where poaching still raged unchecked. Finding peace north of the border, they attacked the Mara's riverine woodlands with gusto; yet the dreaded word 'culling' was not heard.

In the Serengeti it was another story. There, across the invisible boundary, elephants ran at the slightest sense of man. Survivors congregated on the open plains near Seronera Lodge in pathetic, shell-shocked groups; and in the north of the park, with the elephants gone, the grasslands were being invaded by small spiky acacias.

Our team recommended regional co-operation. With political goodwill the two countries could successfully manage this vast and priceless wilderness as a model of conservation *sans-frontières*. Open the border and Mara's excess tourists would flood into the northern Serengeti bringing in money, roads and better surveillance. With protection, refugee elephants would drift back to control the spread of acacias, leaving the Mara's woodlands to recover. At one positive stroke, ecology, poaching and economics would be tackled; but sadly not even Tué Rohrsted's red-tape cutting capability was able to move the officials involved.

However, the EEC once more looked as if it might step in to help the elephants on a pan-African scale. In Brussels I went to see Vanni Puccioni, an ardent conservationist who had already rescued our Uganda park's proposal when it had disappeared under a mound of files. Now we made a plan to harness the huge resources of the twelve European States to save and survey the elephant throughout its range.

I recommended that the project should be routed through WWF. Whatever our past disagreements, they now had John Hanks an elephant authority in his own right to run their Africa programme. He understood the deadly peril and massive illegality of the ivory trade. Our objective was to diminish the flow of ivory out of Africa and provide direct protection for elephants in selected national parks.

At the end of October 1988 a special CITES committee gathered in the UNEP building in Nairobi to consider how to deal with Burundi and the illegal ivory trade. It was a chance for all the forces for and against the trade to meet and lobby their cause. Jonah Western – still a neutral in this battle – wanted to launch an Ivory Trade Review Group that would look at the elephant situation from every angle. CITES were sponsoring a rival ivory trade study by Ian Parker. It was an extraordinary occasion, with ivory traders and conservationists rubbing shoulders or glaring at each other across the table.

Parker had brought in Graeme Caughley, the Australian scientist renowned for his work on Zambia's Luangwa Valley elephants. When Caughley fitted a logistic curve to the ivory data and predicted an imminent collapse of elephants due to overkill, everyone listened, and I could not help smiling at the thought that it was Parker, of all people, who had catalysed this crucial contribution.

I had considerable misgivings about the Ivory Trade Review Group to begin with, as I thought it might be just another attempt to build a conservation empire. But it truly was a response to the horror of the elephant slaughter. In any case I decided to throw in my lot with Jonah's vision. Steve Cobb, an Oxford zoologist, brought together and co-ordinated a diverse and talented team of economists, ecologists, population modellers and journalists with self-effacing charm. WWF contributed two thirds of the funding. My role was to collate the information on elephant numbers and trends, the bedrock of any decision to be taken. The only real dissent came from the CITES Secretariat, who had now become totally identified with the Zimbabwean point of view and remained as uncooperative as ever.

At an unofficial level several amateur enthusiasts also began to nose around the trade. The most effective of these was the Environmental Investigation Agency (EIA), the London-based conservation sleuths I had first met in Ottawa, CITES 1987. Allan Thornton came to see me one day in London and said, 'Iain, we have launched an investigation and we want you to be the first to know.' By then they had already carried out a daring undercover operation in Dubai to expose the notorious Poon empire, in the United Arab Emirates. They even managed to photograph one of Poon's secret carving factories in the Persian Gulf region, proving that a huge illicit trade was going on in so-called 'worked' ivory, consisting of lightly polished tusks that were then sent on to Hong Kong. It was just another example of how easily the ivory trade was able to flout the system.

Contacts such as Allan Thornton and his team were unearthing all kinds of useful information, and alongside Steve Cobb's official Ivory Trade Review Group we developed an extremely effective informal network to probe the darkest corners of the traders' world.

Then there was Ambrose Carey whom I met by chance in London. The last time I had seen him he was only nineteen and had just driven my Toyota from Nairobi to Uganda. It had been a turbulent period and he had spent ten days with the rangers on anti-poaching patrols.

Now he was twenty-five years old, tall, good-looking and self-assured. When he heard of my interest in the ivory trade he said he might be able to help, as he was now a junior member of a company called KROLL Associates, who specialized in tracking down crooked commercial operations. Known as the CIA of Wall Street, they employed accountants, former intelligence men and SAS officers, private detectives, one-time FBI agents, prosecutors, academics, terrorism experts, investigative reporters and computer specialists – in fact men and women with the very skills we needed to crack the ivory trade.

KROLL prided themselves on their far-flung contacts at the intersection of finance, law enforcement and intelligence, and they were particularly good in Hong Kong and South Africa. In London they were run by Patrick Grayson, a former Guards officer who agreed to let Ambrose donate his spare time to the elephant cause, and allowed free use of all their computer-search facilities. This was to be one of the most fruitful arms of the network now developing to penetrate the inner workings of the ivory trade. Ambrose immediately began scanning all newspapers for the words 'elephant' and 'ivory', and very soon we had a network of interested journalists digging into the subject.

Prime investigators eventually proved to be a major help to the South African police in investigating and exposing the illegal ivory and rhino-horn trade in South Africa. Increasingly we heard that South Africa had now taken over from Burundi as one of the chief conduits for illegal ivory from all over Africa. In July 1988, Craig van Note, an American conservationist, increased the polemic against South Africa – 'that CITES-member nation which projects the image of a conservation-minded model for Africa but which is in reality one of the largest wildlife outlaws in the world.'

In his testimony given before a Congressional committee, van Note accused the South African military of having encouraged Jonas Savimbi, the flamboyant UNITA rebel leader, of destroying perhaps one hundred thousand elephants to pay for his war in Angola. Although van Note was short of facts and there has been no evidence to back his figures, other sources have confirmed that many tusks had been carried back to South Africa by army planes or trucks, and it is rumoured that the South African military still holds a stock-pile of Angolan ivory. Savimbi even gave an exact replica of an AK-47 carved in ivory as a personal gift to President P.W. Botha.

Amid growing criticism in South Africa, Defence Minister Magnus Malan flatly denied that his forces had ever been involved in such dealings. But Savimbi himself, in an interview with *Paris Match*, said that all the help his UNITA movement received from the South African Defence Force (SADF) had to be paid for with Angolan ivory or teak.

More salt was rubbed in the wound, when Colonel Breytenbach, a member of the SADF, came forward to speak out against what had been happening in Angola. 'Elephants were mown down indiscriminately by the tearing rattle of automatic fire from AK-47 rifles and machine-guns,' he said. 'They shot everything; bulls, cows and calves.'

Not all the ivory passing through South Africa came from Angola. Many tusks came from elephants poached in the Luangwa Valley which were said to be finding their way south from Zambia in sealed railway boxcars, suggesting collusion at a high level on both sides of the border. The railroad was run by the South African government and all enquiries into allegations of ivory smuggling ran into a wall of silence.

Another shadowy source of illicit ivory was Mozambique, where the South African-backed *Renamo* guerrillas were locked in a bloody civil war with the left-wing government. It was alleged that *Renamo* rebel forces, helped by ex-Rhodesian special forces, had killed tens of thousands of elephants in recent years to help finance their insurrection.

South Africa's embarrassment was complete when De Wet Potgieter, a journalist on the Johannesburg *Sunday Times*, exposed a whole illegal ivory network centred on Pretoria. For a long time the traffickers had been exploiting the wide-open frontiers of South Africa, Botswana, Namibia, Swaziland and Lesotho, which together form a single customs union. This meant that once a container had entered the customs union at any point it could travel freely with no risk of being opened.

But in September the smugglers' luck ran out when a truck *en route* from Zaire to the Pretoria premises of South Africa's biggest ivory dealer, Chong Pong, was stopped by customs officers on the Botswana border. Inside they found more than four hundred tusks, ninety-four rhino horns and a stack of copper ingots. All together the haul was worth at least one million dollars.

No doubt most of this ivory and the rhino horn would have found its way to Hong Kong or Taiwan. For years I had wondered how it was that South Africa had been exporting more ivory than could possibly be accounted for by the elephants culled in the Kruger

National Park, their only major legitimate source. Now we knew and waited to see if the South African government would move against the renegades in their midst.

Layer by layer, we were peeling away the secrets of the ivory trade to reveal its rotten core. All through 1989 tales of the criminal abuses of the ivory quota system continued to come in. Big consignments were stopped at Heathrow Airport, and the Burundians were still scheming to export their latest stock of illegal ivory. We were now working with our friends at TRAFFIC who at last began to reveal the traders' identities. TRAFFIC is the world's largest wildlife trade monitoring network with its headquarters in Cambridge, England. Had they been willing to target individual traders earlier, the story might have come out much sooner and saved the lives of many elephants. But now great credit was due to them for unravelling the Far Eastern ivory market. There Tom Milliken, their man in Japan, made an outstanding contribution which included the identification of all the main ivory-trading families and their *modus operandi*, as did Tom Meulenaar, their operative in Belgium. In Britain the names of some of these families became almost household words after the *Cook Report*, the ITV's hard-hitting investigative TV programme, homed in on the Poons in Hong Kong, uncovering every branch of their ivory dynasty. Kevin Dowling, the terrier-like reporter who had done most of the leg-work for the programme, later gave me all his findings. He said it was known that Poon had already held talks with the Governments of Zaire, Congo, and CAR to set up carving factories there. I passed all this on to TRAFFIC, where Tom Milliken had meanwhile identified the Lai family as the latest up-and-coming ivory agents to keep an eye on.

With his wispy blond hair and knowing eyes, Kevin had an easy familiarity with devious and dishonest behaviour which it was his *métier* to uncover. He called me quite unexpectedly one day from Birmingham when I was visiting London, and by the evening he was on the doorstep of my mother's house where I was staying. His probing questions showed that within weeks he had grasped the ivory story and already acquired a profound insight.

I took a snap decision to trust him with my secrets and told him everything I knew about the trade, short of my sources. He reciprocated and over the months that followed regularly updated me on his uncoverings of the Poon empire.

Kevin was generous with his information and allowed me to share it with our network. In the meantime, Steve Cobb had roped in a number of heavy-duty journalists including Martin Meredith, an experienced commentator on Africa. In Zaire, Martin was able to confirm that nothing had changed. The ivory free-for-all continued, with Mobutu's close advisers, high-ranking government officials, military commanders and leading businessmen all helping themselves. How could anyone have ever believed that ivory-trade controls could work in countries like this?

The firing up of the Press meant that much of our intelligence-gathering about the ivory trade was done for free. Suddenly it was a good story. The gloves were off, and an almost united conservation movement was telling the media that the African elephant was in serious trouble. When I flew to London at the end of May 1989 for an elephant action meeting, the bubble had already broken. On either side of me in the Tube from Heathrow, people were reading newspapers with banner headlines on the plight of the elephant.

Britain had just announced an instant ban on all ivory imports and was pressing ahead for a European decision at the Council of Ministers. The public and the politicians had moved ahead of the scientists. However, we sat solemnly enough later in the day when the Ivory Trade Review Group met in the London Zoological Society boardroom to consider its verdict. Steve Cobb called the meeting to order and told us the world was hanging on our decision. Jonah had now come round and advocated a ban, and his force of personality persuaded many to this view. One by one each person opted for the ban. Even Professor David Pearce, the environmental economist, who did not really believe in bans, gave his assent. It was an interesting example of group psychology. No one wanted to rock the boat at a time of crisis.

The report which Steve Cobb and his team finally produced was a *tour de force*. For the first time we had elephant estimates based on solid field work from the great unknown forests of Central Africa. Richard Barnes' teams had finally penetrated these forests and proved that there was no untouched reserve of elephants present. The forest elephant survey revealed in far greater detail than ever before the chaotic failure of the ivory quota system in Central Africa.

For the rest of Africa the last great intact elephant population was now to be found in Northern Botswana, ranging north across the Caprivi Strip into Angola and east across the Zimbabwe border into the Hwange National Park. So far it had escaped the depredations of the ivory trade, but we were not sure it would continue to do so. By contrast a recent count showed that the Selous population had continued to plummet at an even faster rate than before, which unfortunately was more typical of the continental situation.

Perhaps the saddest chapter in the Ivory Trade Review Group report was written by Joyce Poole who had visited the main East African elephant populations to reveal that many elephant families had been shattered. Not only were the bulls gone, but matriarchs had been decimated, families left leaderless, and mature bulls were so sparse that in places she doubted that enough survived to fertilize females in oestrous.

It was now blindingly clear throughout the continent that all but a fraction of the trade had swept past the puny monitoring efforts of CITES and the conservationists. Five countries had dominated the export of ivory over the 1980s: Sudan, Burundi, Central African Republic, Congo and Zaire. In the ten years, between seventy-one and seventy-nine thousand tonnes of ivory, representing something of the order of seven hundred thousand elephants, had been sent out of Africa. This figure tied up well with the losses indicated by the census figures and successive continental estimates which I had collated for over a decade.

The shipments in the early days which failed to alarm people were very much larger than the trade in its later days. Most of the vast volumes of ivory exports revealed by TRAFFIC were never nailed down to individual traders.

The main economic force behind the ivory rush was revealed to be the increased prosperity of ordinary citizens of Japan, who could now afford to buy the ivory Hanko seals, prized status symbols with which they signed their letters. The dominant position of the Japanese in the trade gave them the power to make or break any attempts at an international ban, and it was widely believed by conservationists that the Japanese were unreceptive to global ecological concerns.

However, in this the conservationists were wrong. A delegation from the Ivory Trade Review Group went to Japan to argue the elephant's case. The Japanese politely listened to the arguments, weighed the evidence and came to the conclusion that they should join the Western nations in the immediate ban pending the next CITES meeting in October, when the whole vexed question of elephants and the ivory trade was due to be debated.

CHAPTER THIRTY-THREE

ORIA: *Burn Ivory Burn*

1988–9, Kenya

I N 1988 the poaching in Kenya had escalated out of control to the point where parts of the country became unsafe for visitors. A group of German tourists had been held up and shot by Somali *shifta* on the southern side of the Ngulia Hills, not far from the entrance to the Tsavo Park.

Lurking behind bushes, the bandits had pulled out their AKs and fired at the first car. They shot out the tyres and wounded a passenger and one of the drivers. 'Money, dollars and cameras,' they yelled, eyes blazing in their thin, wild faces as they poked a gun through the window. Then, taking the loot, they had fired again and faded away into the rocks, leaving the terrified survivors of the ambush to look after the wounded as best they could.

We had just landed in Tsavo West, when the news of the shooting came. It had happened at least an hour before, but we immediately took off in our plane and scanned the area for any sign of life, flying up and down over the carbon swirl of rolling lava. Nothing moved. The *shifta* could have hidden in a thousand holes and crevices, waiting for darkness. Accustomed to a harsh life of banditry, all they needed was tea, an AK-47 and a handful of food. With this and some sprigs of *miraa*, the bitter

leaves which many Somalis chew as a stimulant, they could keep
going for days.

With its curved magazine and stubby barrel, the AK-47 was the
most deadly weapon of destruction ever used in the long history
of the African elephant. Its inventor was Mikhail Kalashnikov, a
twenty-eight-year-old Red Army sergeant who dreamed up this
formidable but easy-to-manage assault rifle while lying badly
wounded in a hospital bed in 1941. The Second World War had
ended by the time the first *Avtomat Kalashnikova* began to roll
off the production line in 1949; but soon, spread by Russia and
China in the name of world revolution, they poured into Africa
in their millions. And here, inevitably, they fell into the hands of
the poachers, who used them on the elephants with devastating
effect. Instead of picking off single animals, as was the case in
the old days, a Somali bandit with an AK-47 could gun down a
whole family.

Over the past year, increasing numbers of tusks had been finding
their way north to Somalia, and many Kenyans had begun to wonder
if the slaughter of their elephants was a deliberate attempt by the
Somalis to destabilize the country.

The Somalis have never renounced their claims to large tracts of
northern Kenya. Even so, such theories still sounded far-fetched –
until the London-based *New African* magazine published a letter
apparently signed by Somalia's President, Mohamed Siad Barre.
Dated 19 March 1987, it authorized 'Comrades Omer Hassan
Khayare and Hussein Barre Hassan to bring elephant tusks from
Kenya to Somalia.' The Somali Embassy in Nairobi quickly issued
a denial, but the magazine's editor insisted that he was right in
believing that the letter was genuine and that it had come from a
'leak' in the office of President Barre himself.

Kenya's thriving, wildlife-based tourist industry is the country's
main source of revenue. Kill the elephants, scare away the visitors
and the country's economy would soon lie in ruins. So it was with
some dismay that we heard George Muhoho, the Wildlife Minister,
claim improved efficiency in protecting the game. He was speaking
at a press conference in Nairobi on 29 August 1988, just two days
after Somali poachers had shot dead three rangers in the Kora
National Park where George Adamson lived with his lions. Muhoho
also admitted that poachers had shot ninety-two elephants since May
(but we believed many more were killed) and expressed 'regrets'

over the killings, but assured his audience that the affected areas were safe for visitors.

This was too much for Richard Leakey, the distinguished palaeontologist who was chairman of the East African Wildlife Society and director of the National Museum. Two days later he unleashed a pointed attack on Muhoho's failure to contain the poaching, accused his ministry of paying 'lip-service' to conservation, and challenged him to tell the truth about the killing of the elephants.

Next day Muhoho struck back. Why, he asked, should the society doubt the figures he had issued, which showed that Kenya still had twenty-two thousand elephants? And he challenged Leakey to name any 'high- or low-ranking person' involved in poaching.

Leakey was not to be silenced. The figure of twenty-two thousand, he said, was 'misleading'. There were no more than twenty thousand elephants in Kenya and possibly a great deal fewer. Then he dropped his bombshell. The minister, he said, had already received a confidential list naming people inside his own ministry who were involved in poaching. The document had been presented to Muhoho more than a month earlier and had been gathering dust ever since.

For Muhoho, it was a disastrous performance. But at least the acrimonious exchange with Leakey had put the crisis on centre stage, sparking off a national debate over the fate of the elephants and the inability of the Wildlife and Tourism Ministry to bring the poachers to justice.

Only a week before the Kora shooting incident, our daughter Dudu had been visiting George and his lions and had come across two freshly killed elephants in the bush. Daily we received reports on such activities. During the previous fortnight, fifty-eight fresh elephant carcasses had been counted by Patrick Hamilton in Tsavo, and tourists had reported seeing a bullet-riddled elephant giving birth at the roadside. Another friend taking clients on safari in the North had heard about fifty shots one night and discovered four dead elephants the following morning; and in another incident two tourists were shot dead by bandits in Meru National Park.

For weeks the Press commented on the Leakey-Muhoho controversy as accusations hurtled back and forth across Nairobi between the Museum and the Wildlife Ministry. Eventually Leakey offered to resign from the Museum as its director, but the majority of the Press stayed on his side and, as the Somali incursions grew even bolder, an increasingly determined President Moi ordered all national parks' staff to shoot poachers on sight.

However, despite large military operations which had been going on all year, elephants were still being killed in alarming numbers, and the poachers continued unhindered. Then came the news that the five white rhinos in Meru National Park – the only ones in Kenya – had been shot at night by poachers while in their enclosure. It was one of their most provocative acts so far, and Perez Olindo was shocked to the core.

For President Moi, the shooting of Meru's prized white rhinos was the last straw. Perez Olindo was told to leave and Richard Leakey became the new director of National Parks. Esther, our Maasai cook, told me when I came home one day. She had heard the announcement on the afternoon news. Speechless with disbelief, I rang them at once and heard they had both been taken completely by surprise. Yes, it was true, Olindo told me. He had flown back from Amboseli where he had been investigating the latest Somali attacks on tourists, only to be informed by his tearful secretary that he was to pack up his office and quit. It was a painful blow for him, but in his charming way he managed to smile away his bitterness. He was too good a man to be lost for long to conservation and was instantly snapped up by the African Wildlife Foundation.

Leakey's arrival was a milestone in Kenya's wildlife politics, and came just in time for the elephants. It was a shrewd move on the part of the president; for it is doubtful if anyone else could have saved the Wildlife Department from near collapse. Leakey, in turn, pledged himself to save the country's elephants and rid the department of its rotten eggs, and we offered to help him in any way we could.

Olindo's department was bankrupt at the time of the Tsavo elephant count, and Leakey now picked up the crumbs. 'I don't even have a secretary,' he told us, 'and if I did I have no money for her salary. I've just gone through the files and answered seventy letters by hand.' I told him I was just about to leave for the USA to lobby for the closure of the ivory trade and raise funds, and would send him the most urgent items he needed within weeks.

While Iain was conferring with his colleagues in London, I was lecturing in twelve major US cities. 'Ivory kills,' I told the audience at the end of each lecture. 'In Kenya we have practically reached the end of the line. In the last fifteen years we have lost 85 per cent of our elephant population. The United States imports 25 per cent of the world ivory, and most of it is of illegal origin. Those bracelets, necklaces and pendants you buy in the department stores are carved in Hong Kong, and most of the tusks used by the Hong Kong carvers come from poached elephants. The USA buys 97 per cent of its carved ivory products from Hong Kong! What we are talking about is hundreds of thousands of elephants and hundreds of tonnes of ivory. Elephants and people continue to be shot each day to provide this market with ivory.'

Support was instantaneous. Shocked by what they had heard, people gave generously. Their credit cards, they promised, would be returned to department stores selling ivory, and their Senators would be urged to close the trade. Our picture of Boadicea charging and Joyce Poole's poached faceless elephant appeared in massive advertisement campaigns and in the Press – asking people not to buy ivory. In my small way, I hoped I had made a dent in the international trade and helped to raise funds for Richard in his battle to clean up the department.

By the time I returned to Kenya from the USA, the concensus for a world ivory ban was rapidly taking shape. In May 1989, Lord Caithness, the British minister whom both Iain and I had met and urged to close the trade, had prompted Margaret Thatcher to halt all ivory exports and imports in the UK. This was good news. Britain, after all, bore a heavy responsibility for the years of slaughter in Africa. Since 1979 the tusks from at least four hundred thousand elephants had passed through the British colony of Hong Kong.

France followed Britain's lead, as did the USA and the whole of the European community. By mid-June, even Japan had decided to stop imports of worked ivory; and two weeks later, Steinway, the maker of the most prestigious pianos, had announced that no new pianos would have keys made out of ivory.

The history of the piano has had a profound effect on the fortunes of the African elephant. As pianos became increasingly popular from the mid-1800s in the United States, so workers in ivory factories became ever-more specialized and the uses for ivory expanded from combs and cutlery handles to more refined objects. They learnt that a billiard ball would roll straight only if it came from the dead centre of the tusk, and that female tusks were the best. By now the piano was fast becoming an essential piece of furniture, bringing music into every Victorian home.

The men who owned the ivory companies were regular church-goers who supported abolition of the slave-trade and preached high moral responsibilities. And yet with this flourishing business, when women used fine ivory brushes and combs on their long hair, and music sounded through their drawing rooms, they closed their eyes and ears to the agony of Africa. At the same time they supported the Arab traders who used slaves to carry their tusks to the East African ports. Most of the tusks were enormous. They weighed between thirty and fifty kilos each side and belonged to the great bulls that wandered the African continent at that time. Many more elephants must have died from wounds in these shooting sprees, and it was known that often only one out of ten slaves survived the long journey from the interior. With each luxurious stroke of the brush, every gentle touch of the keys, the most unspeakable suffering was caused to elephants and people alike.

By the turn of the century the United States was the largest manufacturer of pianos in the world, producing 350,000 in 1910. It took about seven hundred tonnes of tusks to provide the ivory for those pianos – the equivalent of thirteen thousand dead elephants in that year alone – but nobody seemed worried at the time.

Now, late in the century, at the eleventh hour, the world was coming to its senses. On 18 July 1989, a giant pyramid of ivory was constructed in the Nairobi National Park, guarded by armed men dressed in the green uniforms of the wildlife service. More than two thousand tusks had been piled up, worth at least $3 million at that time, and all of them were to be burnt. Nothing like it had ever been seen in Africa, but President Moi wanted to send a message around the world, to the traders in Hong Kong and the poachers in the bush, that Kenya was determined to put an end to ivory trafficking.

All the world's press were there to record the event and people gathered around the pyre as if to witness an execution. But the killing had already taken place and the corpses of the elephants left by the poachers now littered the parks, and the *mafuta mingi*, the fat ones, as they are known in our part of Africa, had made their profits and departed. Kenya had lost 130,000 elephants in this way – but the burning was a sign that the killing had to stop. From now on it was the poachers who would leave their bodies in the bush if they tangled with Richard Leakey's new anti-poaching force.

After President Moi had appealed to the world to stop buying ivory, the fire was lit and red flames engulfed the pinnacled tusks that reached out for the last time into the sky. Columns of smoke carried the smell of burnt ivory over the green plains in a wide grey band as if a ghostly procession of poached elephants had lain down to die. All night the fire glowed, and still the curved shapes held together like a bony carcass that refused to be destroyed. But by morning only a bed of ashes remained.

It was Richard Leakey's inspired but sad finale to put an end to thousands of years of elephant killing and ivory collecting. Leakey called on all Kenyans to stop the killing and put down their guns. Many of the traders were now being exposed by the media for bleeding the continent of one of its prime resources, leaving Africa ever poorer.

As the century turned into its last decade, so did the use for ivory. It was the beginning of the end of the battle for the elephants – and it happened in Kenya. For the first time in fifteen years something had been achieved, but for how long? So long as there was a market for ivory anywhere in the world the elephants would never be safe.

CHAPTER THIRTY-FOUR

IAIN: *The Year of the Elephant*

1989, Kenya, Switzerland

WHO were these men who caused so much chaos to Kenya's elephants and seemed so invincible? The Somalis in the bush were tough and aggressive. In the middle of the 1989 Tsavo elephant count, Joe Kioko, who often came under fire, flew an anti-poaching patrol with the sharp-eyed Laitoro, a young Rendille warden. They spotted men hiding beneath an acacia canopy at a waterhole and summoned the army helicopter gunship from Voi to spray the target. At the first shots the Somalis scattered into the bush. Tracer bullets ignited the grass and kicked up a cloud of smoke and dust, obscuring the view as the gunship continued to strafe the area. For a while the poachers shot back, then fell silent.

Looking down on the inferno, Joe Kioko in his Cessna 180 could not believe anyone could be left alive. Patrick Hamilton joined the action in his Super Cub and the two planes circled above as police and rangers closed in on the waterhole. But the Somalis were still in possession. Patrick spotted a man lying in wait, but was too late. The police were out of radio contact, advancing confidently across the open. What happened next was inevitable. A young constable stepped into the rifle sights of a concealed poacher who shot him dead at point-blank range. Many more shots were exchanged. As darkness fell the poachers were still in possession of the waterhole and the police withdrew. When they returned at dawn the Somalis had melted away.

Two days later I helicoptered in to the waterhole with Laitoro and Patrick and a film crew. There lay three dead elephants on a rock, killed some months before and camouflaged from the air with leafy branches. We found two poachers' bodies, one gnawed to a skeleton by hyenas, and I had to admire their courage in surviving the strafing, fighting the police, and at the end of the day remaining in control of the waterhole to carry off their wounded and retrieve their possessions.

It was this legend of Somali invincibility that Richard Leakey had to crack before he could regain the upper hand. The Somali poachers were not only tough. They had little to lose as many were quite destitute, having come across the border from their own country where a vicious civil war was raging. Some were army deserters, some were rebels, others probably still in the Somali army taking leave for a little private enterprise. Many had little idea of where they were going and could not even speak Swahili, the lingua franca of Eastern Africa.

The bottom line was that a ready market for poached ivory existed back in Mogadishu, sanctioned by the leadership, with easy access to the Middle East, whence it would go to the Far East to be carved or exported to Western and Japanese end markets.

Marcus Russell, a young safari guide with a camp in the east of the park, kept me informed of what was going on there at the height of the poaching. He was friendly to the ranger patrols and often helped them with small supplies of food and equipment. In return they gave him their confidence. Marcus told me of one case where a party of Somalis had been trapped in a small ravine surrounded by superior Kenya ground forces. Under intense mortar fire they quickly realized their number was up, but rather than surrender they prayed to Allah, sang a psalm and went on fighting until all were dead.

The story of how the rangers eventually re-established their ascendency was a truly crucial part of the battle for the elephants. Much can be credited to Richard Leakey's new leadership and the political support and the trust which he enjoyed. It was vital that the new Kenya Wildlife Service should have its own armed men. There was no substitute for skilled rangers on the spot all the year round, and Richard took the best men he could find to lead them, whether they were inside the department or outside.

Hardly had Richard taken over when news went round the world that George Adamson, the grand old lion man of Africa, had been shot dead with two of his assistants by Somali bandits near his camp in Kora. It was a dark hour for Kenya; but within days, Leakey's men had captured one of the ring-leaders.

Information gathering was another crucial element, knowing who the enemy were, how they moved and when they were coming. Informants brought intelligence from far outside the park. A new enthusiasm gripped the department. Risk there was and many rangers paid the supreme price. But despite numerous teething problems the department was well set on the road to recovery.

Behind the lines the EEC played a vital role in providing emergency supplies. I found myself in charge of a $550,000 programme to channel EEC money for the elephants through WWF and to gather elephant statistics and pay for surveys before the CITES meeting. My old friend Hugh Lamprey was in charge of the WWF office in Nairobi, and together we moved into high gear to help save elephants in Kenya and Tanzania.

Planes, radios, compo rations, fuel, spares and camp equipment began to flow towards the front-line parks. We helped persuade Western governments into joining the elephant cause along with well-known groups like Friends of Conservation and the African Wildlife Foundation, and a plethora of new groups that sprang up overnight in response to the crisis: Elefriends, Elefund, International Tusk Force, Côte d'Or Elephant Foundation and many others.

Throughout 1989 these pent-up forces were unleashed on the ivory trade. As the *New African* magazine put it: 'Ban the trade and a fortune in ivory reverts to being a pile of elephant teeth. Keep the trade open, and on present showing we are unlikely to have any elephants left to grow teeth.'

CITES' over-optimistic statements about the efficacy of the quota system came back to haunt them. Chris Huxley's brain-child crumbled. No wrong-doing was ever attributed to him, but what might have been the perfect plan for regulating the trade in ivory, devised as the template for all trade in wild species, turned out to be a house built on sand and never could have worked in Africa.

The CITES Secretariat came under harsh attack and accusations of corruption flew around. Some of these came from highly suspect sources, such as Mr Poon. No evidence was ever produced to support such allegations. Eugene Lapointe, the French-Canadian bureaucrat in charge of CITES for the past eight years, was not implicated, and later reported that bribes had indeed been offered, and that some of the traders had accused the Secretariat of taking money. 'When the opposition makes this sort of accusation,' said Lapointe contemptuously, 'it proves the system is beginning to bite.'

But the rumours persisted. For the first time, CITES found itself on the defensive, and Lapointe lashed out at the new conservation groups that had sprung into existence to defend the elephant. 'They have sprouted like mushrooms,' he said. 'Mushrooms are usually good but some of them are poisonous.'

With every week the distrust between CITES and the non-governmental conservation groups grew. In May, Pierre Pfeffer, a long-time French activist against the trade, joined in the fray. 'The problem is that CITES obtained their funding from the ivory traders, who contribute a portion of their revenue to the management of CITES,' he said. 'The more ivory trafficked the more revenue.' Pfeffer was outraged at CITES' support for yet more sales of Burundi ivory in which the veteran ivory trader Jacques Lewkowicz of France Croco, who had infuriated the Zaire minister in 1979, was one of the main bidders.

Pfeffer had touched on a raw nerve. The CITES Secretariat was supposed to be impartial; but under Lapointe it had come out clearly on the side of the traders, leading conservationists to suggest this could have something to do with the way it was funded.

Although CITES is financed primarily by the parties to the convention and is administered by the United Nations Environmental Programme, its rules allow the Secretariat to raise additional money from outside sources; and in 1988, as CITES had come under intense scrutiny over the failure of its elephant policy, it had emerged that Lapointe's organization had been accepting money from the ivory traders. Ever since the CITES ivory unit had been set up in 1985, its budget had been heavily subsidized by 'no-strings' contributions from the ivory trade to the tune of at least $200,000. Among the contributors were several of the major ivory traders suspected of shady dealings.

There was nothing illegal in these transactions but their revelation left CITES' credibility badly damaged. The repercussions were felt even inside CITES itself, where Joe Yovino, who had been head of the ivory unit, resigned in frustration. 'When I saw my salary was coming from K.T. Wang that just did it,' he told *Time* magazine.

At last the ivory issue was centre stage. As the full horror of the killing of Africa's elephants and the looting of its parks emerged, and the real nature of the traders and their cosy relationship with CITES was exposed, world opinion swung solidly in favour of banning the trade at the earliest opportunity.

That chance would come in October 1989, when CITES was due to debate the whole ivory-trade issue in Lausanne, Switzerland. Everybody knew this would be the most decisive moment in the entire history of the fight to save the elephant, and as the conference loomed closer both sides drew up their battlelines.

On the one side was Eugene Lapointe and his CITES Secretariat, who firmly believed that the best way to save elephants was to maintain the demand for ivory, putting a price on tusks so that producer countries would have an incentive to protect their herds.

Behind Lapointe were the Zimbabweans under Rowan Martin, together with South Africa and the other southern states, and the ivory traders of Hong Kong and Japan – a curious alliance bound together only by their common interest in propping up a discredited trading system which had made many people rich but failed utterly to protect the elephant.

On the other side were a formidable array of conservation groups from all over the world, backed by Tanzania, Kenya, Chad and Somalia, the USA and all of the European Community Nations who wanted an end to the ivory trade once and for all.

As support for an ivory ban grew, the defenders of the trade fought back with increasing desperation. Not long before the CITES convention was due to open, the Zimbabwe Wildlife Department spelled out its unyielding opposition in East Africa's *Swara* magazine.

Zimbabwe had a conservation philosophy which had proved to be supremely successful, they said. An ivory ban would, at the stroke of a pen, take away the value of elephants which had increased over the years. The success of their policies of culling and trading had resulted in more elephants than ever before. Zimbabwean farmers were legal owners of the wildlife on their land, which made them value wild animals, including elephants, and look after them for profit. The proposed ban smacked of the idea that wildlife belonged to Westerners. 'We do not like the way the West is dictating terms to us when they understand so little about the issues involved,' the polemic continued. 'Instead of spending money on publicity about the ivory issue it would be better for them to give us that money to control poaching.

'Do not take your lead from the countries in Africa that have failed to conserve their animals – the Kenyas and Tanzanias – where elephants are indiscriminately and illegally killed. Do not listen to the panicked voices of conservationists who have failed. Listen to us, copy our success, spread it through Africa; don't destroy it.'

If the ivory trade was banned the price would go up and it would be driven into the hands of the black market, said the Zimbabweans. 'The choices you will be making at CITES in October will destroy or conserve the elephants – forever. Do your bit to save the elephants. Make it worth our while to keep them. Keep legitimate trade legal. Encourage it.'

This was stirring stuff, but it did nothing to demolish the arguments for the prosecution of the ivory trade. These reiterated the huge increase in the trade which had expanded five-fold, from around two hundred tonnes a year in 1950 to nearly a thousand tonnes a year in the 1980s.

As for predictions that a ban would drive the trade underground, they were absurd, since it was reckoned that at least 90 per cent of all ivory currently on the market had been obtained illegally anyway. Despite the imposition of the CITES plan to control the ivory trade, it had fallen into the hands of unscrupulous men who had evaded every restriction thrown in their way.

Above all, the Zimbabweans seemed happy to write off the rest of the continent north of the Zambezi, where five out of every six African elephants still lived. Culling and trading might work in Zimbabwe, but it was not a policy that could be exported to central Africa or to countries such as Kenya and Tanzania, where men were still dying in the never-ending war against the poachers. Viewed in these terms, such pro-trade attitudes seemed short-sighted and selfish. As one cynical observer put it, 'Zimbabwe is determined to fight for its right to trade ivory down to the last Tanzanian elephant.'

For my part, I had believed for many years that the facts would speak for themselves. Sometimes, as in Uganda and CAR, I had been proved right and surveys had led to action. But all too often nothing had happened, even when alarming revelations had emerged. This happened with the Selous survey of 1986, when neither the Tanzanian government nor the combined forces of WWF, IUCN and the Frankfurt Zoological Society had been able to get a realistic project together. In Kenya, too, facts had failed to save the elephants; but now in all these places things were happening; and at the root of it all was the stark truth that at least five hundred thousand elephants, and perhaps as many as seven hundred thousand had been lost in the decade, almost entirely due to the ivory trade, and it had taken a shock of this size to galvanize the world into action.

And then suddenly it was October and the CITES' delegates were descending on Lausanne with the eyes of the world's press focused on them. In the great ivory debate to follow the outcome would decide the fate of Africa's remaining six hundred thousand elephants.

The Tanzanians, led by Costa Mlay, their popular new director of wildlife, had been the first to call for an outright ban on all international trade in ivory. Kenya, the USA and EEC had immediately added their support, and a showdown with Eugene Lapointe's pro-trade faction was now inevitable.

The conference hall in Lausanne was packed. Of the 103 countries which had agreed the CITES treaty, ninety-one sent delegations and each state was entitled to one vote. Many other interested bodies were also there as observers. These were mostly non-governmental organizations such as WWF, who could speak but not vote; and the whole show was run by Lapointe and his secretariat of full-time CITES employees.

The delegates had come from all over the world to discuss problems affecting a host of endangered plants and creatures, from rare parrots and turtles to snowdrops and cyclads; but no other conference had ever been charged with such high emotion or so dominated by a single issue. That issue, as everyone knew, was the African elephant. At Lausanne there was a sense of history in the making. Everything we had fought for over the past two decades was about to be decided in the debate. If we lost now, so would the elephants, for this was their last chance.

At the opening ceremony Prince Bernhard of the Netherlands left no one in any doubt as to where his sympathies lay, and reminded delegates that the aim of the convention was to save endangered species. 'If there is any doubt about a decision concerning the fate of wildlife,' he pleaded, 'let the benefit of the doubt always be in favour of the wildlife.' Then the gloves were off and the conference was under way.

Eventually, after CITES' officials and conservation groups had been slugging it out for the first few rounds, a compromise was offered. The idea, supported by TRAFFIC, WWF and others, was that a two-year moratorium would be followed by limited trading by those southern African countries with sound elephant management records. It failed because of the intransigence of the Zimbabweans and their allies, who demanded that all southern African nations should be treated as a single bloc. This was clearly unacceptable since it would have placed countries like Zimbabwe and Botswana, with healthy elephant populations, in the same league as Zambia, where poaching was still serious, Mozambique, which was in the middle of a civil war, and Angola, which did not even belong to CITES.

By now the first week of the conference had almost passed with neither side gaining enough support to win the necessary two-thirds majority. Then came another attempt at a compromise. This was the so-called Somali amendment, which proposed full protection for the African elephant, but with special criteria to allow some controlled trade if appropriate in the future. There followed a clumsy attempt to block it by the Swiss chairman, Peter Dollinger, who said it was so similar to a previous amendment that he would not consider it. But after strong protests from the Somali delegation at the end of the session it was agreed that their proposal would be properly considered after the weekend break.

By Monday afternoon when the conference had reassembled to deal with the elephant issue, the tension in the hall was unbearable. Just before the final voting began I was asked to give a brief report on the current status of the African elephant. It gave me a last chance to put the whole case in perspective. I gave credit to the southerners; but the crucial figure was the overall loss of over half a million elephants in ten years compared to fifty thousand gained in Zimbabwe and Botswana.

Then came the moment we had all been waiting for. A last-ditch attempt to impose voting by secret ballot was overwhelmingly rejected and the countdown began. First came the contentious proposal to exempt all the southern African states from any ivory-trade ban. Had it succeeded it would have put paid to any real hope of saving the elephants; but, as each delegation called out its decision, it soon became evident that we had cleared the first hurdle and the amendment was lost by seventy votes to twenty, with one abstention.

Then came the call for an outright ban; and that, too, failed to win a two-thirds majority, with fifty-three votes in favour, thirty-six against, and two abstentions.

That left all our hopes pinned to the Somali amendment, which would make ivory trading illegal throughout the world, at least for the next two years, denying traders the chance to launder illegal stocks through countries that might have been exempted had other alternative amendments succeeded.

The vote seemed to take forever. As if in a dream I saw the hands go up. China voted against. So inevitably did Burundi, South Africa and Zimbabwe; but they were not enough. Somewhere someone started clapping, then suddenly everybody was on their feet applauding. It was as if an innocent man who was condemned to death had been reprieved.

The amendment was carried by seventy-six votes to eleven, with four abstentions. To the side I could see Allan Thornton and his EIA sleuths dancing a victory jig, while Eugene Lapointe sat shaking his head in disbelief on the stage. The Zimbabweans handed in their reservation on the spot, and were to be followed later by Botswana, Malawi, Zambia and South Africa. Oria and I could hardly believe it. Passions had raged throughout the conference but in the end it was the numbers game, backed up by reason and inescapable facts that had won the day.

After the sound and fury of the CITES meeting there was time to celebrate the victory. Conservation organizations were happy with their individual roles as each wanted to tell the world about it. As for me, I felt only a profound sense of relief that a cease-fire had at last been won for the elephants. But the price was a deep rift with some of our southern colleagues.

Before leaving Europe I wrote to Charles de Haes, director of WWF International, to tell him how happy I was with the

CITES outcome. It had taken WWF a lot of heart-searching to go for the ban, but I was relieved once more to feel in tune with their policy. I had experienced the full force of establishment disapproval. For years I had known what it means to be frozen out of decision-making at the centre. The words of an IUCN officer still rang in my ears. 'If you don't belong to an organization, what credentials could you possibly have to attend this elephant meeting?' Luckily the EEC had come to my rescue and given me the necessary credentials!

In the next two years WWF were able to report that they had invested over $2.5 million in elephant conservation in Africa all over the place. The elephant had indeed become a conservation flagship.

Eugene Lapointe was removed from office, but remained unrepentant to the end, asserting that the ban was a serious mistake, engineered by charities with vested interests in the crisis; and CITES never did release the names of the ivory traders, although most of these leaked to the private sector. Ali Suleiman, one of the chief ivory traders from Burundi was reported murdered in Brussels. Murders were also committed in South Africa as the ivory Mafia began to fall out among themselves.

As for the opposition, at one extreme nothing will change their thinking. Huxley, the ex-CITES' official, wrongly accuses the conservation lobby and CITES parties of fraudulently exaggerating the threat to elephants and of using figures they knew to be untrue so that they could raise more money on the elephant's back. Elephant population declines, he asserted in an article in the *Independent*, were guessed at, then exaggerated in order to engineer an 'elephant crisis', and the strategy of the NGO was to mislead the public about the true status of the African elephant by avoiding scientific debate and appealing only to the emotions. I could only conclude he had not read the Ivory Trade Review Group report.

Even now, Ian Parker still maintains that according to 'biological theory' humans and elephants are competitors and cannot coexist on the same range, the implication being that elephants must disappear as man expands, and the ivory trade cannot be held to blame. He spends much time now in Botswana, a country friendly to ideas of elephant culling, where he can fulminate against those who brought about the ivory ban.

But these are the politics of defeat and despair. What of symbiosis, and the fact that elephants can benefit economies simply by people coming to look at them in national parks? In Kenya live elephants are now worth far more than dead ones. In a good year they can earn Kenya $25 million or more in tourist revenue.

Now that the shadow of the poacher has receded for the time being, other spectres still remain to haunt Africa: drought, famine, AIDS, chronic overpopulation, soil erosion, wrecked ecosystems, maladministration, corruption, a debt of $270 billion, arms budgets which have risen ten times as fast as incomes, and civil wars without end. Reported in the Western press, this litany of suffering portrays a continent in a stage of terminal collapse, imploding in a hopeless vortex of despair.

However, this is another case of over-simplification. Although human tragedies are widely reported the success stories are all too often ignored. And there is space enough for the continent to swallow Europe, America and India and still find room for elephants.

Kenya can now hold up its head with pride. The results show in the elephant statistics, the one true independent measure, which over the years have told such a gloomy tale.

New counts in the Aberdares, Laikipia, Mt Kenya, Meru and Tsavo show a dearth of fresh carcasses. Amboseli and Masai Mara remain free of poaching. Most important is the change in Tsavo, where the once invincible poachers have for the timebeing been defeated. In 1988 about one thousand elephants were poached, but in 1990 it fell to a mere fifteen. In the 1991 count only one 'recent' elephant carcass was spotted – a calf killed by a lion. The elephants of Tsavo have had a bumper crop of baby elephants, and are now ranging back into the former no-go areas north of the Galana River. The park has been swept clean from end to end. Stephen Gichangi, an old-time warden, who remained true through all the bad times, is now in charge and revels in the success.

There is a good and wholesome feeling about the Kenya Wildlife Service today. Corrupt officials have retired or have been transferred. The sullen faces and eye-avoiding mannerisms of former days have gone. Friendships with wardens and rangers are now easy to make and we all feel we are on the same side.

Many of the things we struggled for over the years have been fulfilled in Kenya, and it makes us feel that all those long, hard years of struggle and heartbreak were worth it. We have a dynamic, talented and forward-looking Wildlife Service, not an alien graft from colonial days, but a genuine African institution full of keen youngsters from the university, offering hope for the future of wildlife and the environment in Kenya.

For the poachers the motivation for killing elephants has gone, too. Formerly an elephant with ivory was like a paper bag stuffed with money left lying in the bush. Now it is dangerous to trespass in the national parks. The rangers may know you are coming before you enter. Your tracks are likely to be picked up and the men who follow may shoot you on sight and ask questions later. Above all, the ivory you seek is not worth what it was, and even then you may not be able to sell it.

Tanzania also offers gleams of hope. The government's 'Operation Uhai' succeeded in making massive ivory hauls and many arrests. Elephant poaching has dropped almost to zero and wide-ranging aerial surveys made in 1991 found no fresh elephant carcasses. New projects have been started in Ruaha and in the Selous. For Oria and me, the reprieve the Manyara elephants are now enjoying is perhaps the most significant.

After years of chaos Uganda, too, is climbing out of its trough. The country is settling down politically, civilian life is reviving. The elephants of Murchison still drink in the Nile, and the EEC project is doing its best to help protect them.

Good news has also come in from some of the other places we visited. The elephants of Gabon still stroll on the beaches and the desert elephants of Namibia are now protected. Those in Kruger appear more secure than ever. The new South African Endangered Species Protection Unit has penetrated some of the ivory and rhino-horn networks, and as the country emerges from its political isolation one can only hope that international traffickers who have found an easy working refuge there will be isolated and exposed.

Elsewhere the news is mixed. In Mali only the Gourma desert elephants are unmolested; the rest have disappeared. Many populations have been devastated in Central and West Africa since our 1979 journey there and elephant poaching continues in some places and is diminished in others. We have little hope for Sudan.

All over Africa, ivory is still there in stockpiles, hidden in dusty go-downs, buried by the sackful in the bush, locked away in private vaults, waiting to get out. According to one of Leakey's agents there were 184 tonnes of ivory in Mogadishu, but no buyers. Instead of going through the roof as critics of the ban had warned, the price of ivory to a poacher fell through the floor, from around $30 to less than $3 a kilo.

News from the Far East has been good. There, Tom Milliken's powers of persuasion have been evident, and Taiwan, once feared as a potential ivory loop-hole country, has twice burnt its ivory. In 1991, except for Japan, the trade was reported as totally collapsed throughout the Far East by Esmond Bradley-Martin who toured the twelve countries.

But in much of Africa the same grisly crew of crooks, poachers, corrupt officials and 'ivory consultants' is still waiting to exploit a relaxation or abolition of the ban. All that Oria and I know is that if the ivory trade is allowed to flourish the elephants will suffer. After all that has happened, no matter what the cost, the trade must now be kept closed. Perhaps this will happen. At least some of the biggest traders of the past have switched to other activities – Dorado back to his diamonds, Madame van Erpe into drugs and jail, Poon emigrating out of Hong Kong to start a new life in Canada.

It was certainly a long struggle and the victory of 1989 is by no means secure. However, the elephants and the wilderness they represent are surely worth a lifetime's effort. Now we have entered a more hopeful era in which the elephant has engaged a new world-wide sympathy. All over Africa, young people are involved, looking at the elephant and its chances of survival. Never again will the fate of the elephant be debated by only a handful of recalcitrant scientists. Today, the species is under international public scrutiny, and Oria and I can only hope that it will do better in our shrinking world than it has over the last twenty years.

EPILOGUE

ORIA: *The Survivors*

1990, Manyara

L EAVING Naivasha, roadside children in ragged clothes stood
out like beacons as we sped by, holding up rabbits and
red plums for sale. Everything was tinged with gold. It
was December 1990 and we were heading south again, down into
Tanzania, drawn back to Manyara where our lives among the
elephants had begun so long ago. Forgotten was all thought of
people, conferences, papers and computers as the wind streamed
across our faces, blowing away the cares of twenty years. The scent
of dry grass was in the wind, and the grass ran rippling across the
plains as far as the eye could see, to the foot of the great mountain,
Kilimanjaro, blue with distance in the heat.

We were happy in Manyara, and would be again, though
much had changed. The elephants were far fewer, but scientific
work in the park continued, and a new researcher, Melly
Reuling, was trying to identify the individual elephants which
had survived the holocaust now that the poaching had stopped.
We had heard that she had found Virgo, the matriarch with
whom we had always enjoyed the greatest trust, and were
going back in the hope of renewing our acquaintance with
our old friend.

We arrived at nightfall, just as the first fire-flies were beginning to shine under the trees. Forest streams fed by clear springs gushed across our path, disappearing into dense clumps of dwarf palms where two elephants were browsing. I was always envious of Iain being able to identify them as casually as one recognizes neighbours walking in the street. But now, for the first time, he did not know who they were.

Standing where I stood before, but now with greying hair and grown children, I look out upon a place I knew so well and listen to the sounds of morning. Francolins call as the sun arrives, burnishing the coppery leaves of the terminalia trees. Water slides down a bare rock, trickling past a gaunt baobab to lose itself in the pink sand of the dried-up river bed. Baboons scramble down to eat, foraging for the astringent fruit of the tamarind. It is the dry season and everything is waiting for rain.

Following a familiar path I reach a house where no one lives, that once was home to us. Two decades have passed, but here many things remain the same. With his body slightly shrunken, clothed in the same green park uniform, Mhoja has come to our camp especially to be with us. His face is sadder and older; but like a seasoned warrior he keeps his anguished heart closed. He would say, 'lamenting is woman's talk.'

'*Karibu*,' he murmurs with a gentle smile as I approach with my two grown daughters. 'Welcome.' Smoke rises from the old tin hut as the kettle boils and tea is made. Saba has returned to the place of her birth, a young woman turned twenty, with Dudu her sister, eighteen months younger.

We had taken this extraordinary world so much for granted then. At that time we never realized how unique our life was. Nor could we have imagined that most of the elephants whose world we shared would be dead by the time our children grew up. Rumours would come our way every few years, that Virgo had been sighted, drifting like a ghost among the trees. We had kept our fingers crossed, praying that she would evade the poachers, unlike so many of Manyara's other great matriarchs – named after Greek Goddesses or heroic British Queens – who had instead become skulls and bones and ivory trinkets. Now out of them all, only three survive. The elephant we knew as Tuskless was there with her daughters. Broken Leg, approaching thirty and barren, with her uneven tusks and crippled leg, had also been spared. Some hunters fear that God may take vengeance on he who kills a cripple. And Virgo had recently been sighted again by Melly Reuling. We could not believe that she had managed to avoid death for so long. Was she now the oldest matriarch?

Between 1966 and 1970, ninety babies were born in the park. In Boadicea's kinship group alone, eighteen babies had been born during that period and Bottle Brush was one of them. Now Bottle Brush, miraculously, at twenty-one is alive and has just had a baby, her first. Under normal conditions she would have started reproducing in her mid-teens and by now already have had a second one. But from 1971 onwards, Bottle Brush had witnessed the destruction of her entire family. Isabelle, Leonora, Giselle and Slender Tusks were the first to go, followed by Boadicea and Jezebel. Within four years all the leaders of the family had been wiped out. That still left the other matriarchs – Curie, Right Hook, Diana, Calypso, Laila, Bahati and Hera – to look after the small families until they, too, became 'missing, presumed killed'.

And the brothers and other big males, where were they? None seemed to be around. Only a gaggle of orphans which huddled close to Virgo. Melly claimed something strange was going on – there were no babies. Bottle Brush's small baby was the only one she had sighted in Manyara. None of us knew if it was due to constant harassment by poachers or a lack of suitable breeding males, but probably it was both.

We decided to divide into two cars, and set out to look for the missing elephants. Both Saba and Dudu had been working on their own elephant projects during their year off from school and university. Now, long brown legs dangling through the Land-Rover's open roof hatches, they scanned the dense thickets and tangles of creepers, joining Melly, Iain and Mhoja in their search. We found them shortly before midday, a mass of elephants hiding from the sun beneath the extending branches of an umbrella tree.

It was one of those loose family units made up of teenage female orphans that hung around with Virgo, said Melly. Being the oldest elephant in the park now, Virgo seemed to be associated with several groups of orphans, moving with one or another. We wondered who they could be. They were all about the same age and size – survivors from the 1970 clan of babies. One had a short left tusk and no breasts. She was known as Maridadi (beautiful in Kiswahili). She had become extremely tame and would often walk right up to

Melly in the car and stand there. Now she was resting, standing side by side with Bottle Brush, with whom she had formed a close bond, while the small baby slept beneath them.

The bush was so thick that visibility was minimal as we edged our way after them when they began to move on. Then, without a sound, Virgo suddenly appeared. Like a ghost from the depth of the green underworld, her huge grey head loomed out above us, less than three metres from our car.

It was the long-awaited meeting we had talked about for years. I looked up at her wise-seeming visage, now so deeply lined, as if setting eyes on a dear and long-lost friend, which indeed she was. 'How wonderful to see you,' I felt like saying. 'It's been such a long time.' Cautiously she extended the tip of her trunk, sniffing the air, and I longed to reach out to her, as we did in the old days, thinking, You're still alive after all these years. How did you manage it? But instead we kept acutely still and scarcely dared to breathe.

'Hello Virgo,' Iain called with a quiet voice, as he had always done, sliding from the door in one long move to stand and face her. For a brief moment we thought some kind of recognition had transpired. Iain took one step forward and called her name again but she threatened slightly with a nod of her head. Then they both stood their ground, just watching. She was about forty-five now – born at the end of the Second World War – and I wondered what kind of a life she'd had. Stored inside that wrinkled head of hers was the recent story of Manyara. But we could only guess and calculate, through carcass counts and years of monitoring, what had really happened to these elephants. We longed to make friends with her again but we knew the risks were too great. Both her children, which we had named after ours, had fallen to the poacher's bullets. As if we had been sharing our thoughts Iain returned to the car and drove slowly away. 'She may well have recognized something,' he said, 'but let her mistrust man.'

Returning along the lake's edge, we bumped into Bottle Brush again. With her companions she had moved around a big wallow in the black cotton soil and was now pushing and splashing in the mud. Suddenly one of the younger females dashed out of the wallow followed by another, running as fast as she could. It was Maridadi. Peering through my binoculars, I suddenly focused on a small blob in the mud amid the columns of legs and trunks. Pua, the matriarch, was trying to push it with her foot and another to lift it with her tusks. With a shock I realized the baby had fallen in and could not get out.

For a while there was so much noise and confusion that I could hardly follow what was going on. The elephants surrounded the baby, their temporal glands flowing down the sides of their faces. Each one in turn tried to push it with a trunk or a leg and then the mother returned and attempted to lift it with her tusks, but to no avail. Virgo with her one tusk was unable to lift the baby even when she tried to heave it out with her foot. Then one by one – as if following an unseen signal – they trooped away.

The baby looked exhausted. Every inch of its body was covered with a thick coat of mud as it stood all alone, bellowing for help.

Suddenly an appalling thought came to us. '*Simba*,' said Mhoja giving voice to our fears. 'Lions will come and it will have no chance.' There was only one thing to do if the only newborn baby in Manyara was not to be left to the mercy of the predators. We set off to look for help, driving flat out towards the ranger post at Endabash. There, Mhoja soon gathered his troops and with ropes and spades they followed us back to the wallow.

We arrived to find that Bottle Brush and Maridadi had returned and were standing over the baby. With the sun dropping rapidly behind the hills we had to act fast. It was quite easy to chase the two elephants away, and then in a flash, Melly, Iain and Mhoja and the rangers leapt into the wallow.

Instantly the mud wrapped itself around their legs, pulling them down. The stench was unbearable. On reaching the baby they heaved and pulled with all their strength until suddenly, out it came.

As soon as it was free everyone ran for their cars in case the mother returned. But instead of rushing for cover, the little elephant followed the cars as fast as its muddy legs could go, immediately bonding to us, since the mother was nowhere around. Then, when it realized it could not keep up, it stopped and stood in lonely desolation, screaming and growling its distress call for the mother.

But not a sound erupted from the surrounding forest into which the elephants had gone. It was as if the earth had swallowed them up. Even the birds had fallen silent. At last Maridadi returned alone, but for some inexplicable elephantine reason she failed to take the baby with her and hurried away again. And so, bracing ourselves for the likelihood of having an orphan on our hands, we made baby-sitting plans for the night and returned to where the tiny elephant stood calling. Instantly it latched on to Melly's car while shadows lengthened and night fell. She had to keep the engine of her Land-Rover running, simulating elephant rumbles to calm down the baby, and when it overheated and needed to be switched off, the baby ran into the bush.

Another hour passed with the sound of gentle footsteps as the baby walked round and round, stopping now and then to lean against the warmth of the tyres, blasting out a loud 'suckle protest' call in the hope of finding milk, while we wondered how we would get through the night, keeping the hyenas and lions away. When the moon rose and the lake turned to silver beneath the dark encircling hills, Melly and Iain took the baby home to Ndala.

We had no proper milk and dared not give it anything but water, which it drank eagerly. Its odour and restlessness and hungry bellowings filled the house. It was, we soon discovered, a female. She must have been no more than a few weeks old, covered in soft hair with pink, round ears and a miniature trunk. We named her Muddy-Melly.

Sleeping with the baby was assigned to Iain. After preparing a wall of mattresses for her, he lay down on the table and offered his thumb for her to suck, while trying to snatch some sleep himself in between long heart-wrenching calls of hunger and distress that echoed up the Ndala Valley. In the small hours, lions roared around the camp; but at least she was safe for now.

Waking early, rumpled and dishevelled after a sleepless night, we slipped away in convoy, with Muddy-Melly in our midst weakened by a twelve-hour fast, to look for her family. While one car searched for fresh prints in the dust, the other waited by the lake clearing with this baby from another world. Together Melly and Saba followed the little elephant as it trundled along the shore near the mud wallow. But of Bottle Brush and Maridadi and the rest, there was no sign.

The responsibility for Muddy-Melly's survival weighed heavily on our shoulders. Her short life was running out hour by hour. Without milk she would not be able to live much longer; yet still she stood, her little head bobbing with curled-up trunk, refusing to sleep. After much consultation I returned to camp to make her a weak mixture of skimmed powdered milk. The milk might cause her stomach to scour but we would have to take that risk.

Racing down the winding track I suddenly came upon a wall of elephants crossing the road, and slid to a halt in a cloud of dust. 'Who the hell are these?' I yelled aloud.

One elephant had been feeding as I approached, tearing down branches with its coiled trunk. Now, at the sound of my voice, it stood frozen in the act of eating, its trunk still raised among the leaves, the gaping mouth exposing a bright pink tongue and the stub of a left tusk.

I tried to recognize them through my binoculars. Then I stared again at the elephant with its left tusk exposed and realized who it was. It was Maridadi. She and her companions were a good deal further north than we had expected, but that was typical of elephants. Without wasting another second, I hurried to find the baby.

By now Muddy-Melly had finally collapsed with exhaustion and was sleeping under a makeshift shelter next to the car. She lay like a foetus, eyes closed, with deep breaths surging from her trunk like the ebb and flow of the sea. 'I've found the family; I'm sure it's Maridadi,' I shouted to the girls. Neither of them believed me, and after some interrogation they reluctantly packed the car with cushions, and lifted Muddy-Melly into the back. While Melly drove, Saba clasped the calf firmly to her chest. We let them go ahead.

Not far from where they had been sighted stood Muddy-Melly's family. Somehow Muddy-Melly knew they were there and started bawling. With no time to waste Melly stopped the car behind a bush and threw open the back door. 'I leapt out,' Melly told me later, 'and pulled Muddy-Melly out like a sack so the mother could see her. All the time she was protesting loudly.'

For a moment the little elephant stood totally confused. Saba jumped into the driving seat and was already moving away as Melly flung herself through the open door. The baby, realizing she was being abandoned by her foster mother, turned and ran after them as fast as she could with a long resounding cry. 'Go for it, Saba,' yelled Melly. 'Faster, faster,' she cried, leaving Muddy-Melly to her fate.

Out of the trees in a cloud of dust stormed the oncoming grey solid wall of alarmed females on the war path. As the car vanished from sight Muddy-Melly let out one last heart-rending cry. Then the anxious matriarchs were upon her like the bows of plunging ships, ears spread like shields, stretching out their trunks to grab their long-lost baby and pull her gently into a stockade of legs.

Saba and Melly stopped and watched through tear-filled eyes for any sign of the baby, but Bottle Brush, Maridadi and Pua had formed a barricade around her, calming her with mellow rumbles of reassurance before escorting her back into the safety of the trees. There they spent the next few days in the Bagayo woodlands with Virgo, not moving more than a few hundred metres while Muddy-Melly remained under a bridge of elephant tummies regaining her strength.

During the months that followed, great care was taken not to repeat the drama at the mud wallow, and Muddy-Melly was sighted regularly by Melly and Mhoja, growing stronger and fatter all the time. The last time she was sighted was far out on the lake shore, with Bottle Brush, Pua, Virgo and Maridadi in close attendance, silhouetted against a pink frieze of flamingoes. It was clear that she had completely recovered from her ordeal, but she was still desperately vulnerable and would need all the protection the matriarchs could provide.

She represented a new elephant generation, the first baby to be born at Manyara since the ivory ban. With her went all our hopes and fears for the future. She was a symbol of everything we had struggled for, and we wondered what kind of life lay in store for her. Would she survive to enjoy ripe old age like Virgo or would she be gunned down and made into something functional to sell? A stool from her foot, gloves from her ears, a chess set from her tusks and a paper weight from the tip of her trunk?

Nothing more we could say or do would help her now. She was small yet, but she would grow; and as she marched out into her bright world, hurrying to keep up with the rest of her family, we wished her well.

Photographic Credits

All photographs were taken by Iain and Oria Douglas-Hamilton except the following:

Front end paper: Blythe Loutit
Rear end paper: Frans Lanting

First Section
p.1: Lee Lyon, National Geographic Society
p.4 (above & below): William Campbell
p.6 (bottom left): Jean Gorse
p.7: Jeanette Hanby/David Bygott
p.16 (left): Iain and Oria Douglas-Hamilton, National Geographic Society
p.17: Rick Weyerhaeuser, National Geographic Society
p.22 (above): Jean de Brunhoff, Hachette
p.23 (above): Jean de Brunhoff, Hachette
      (below): Lee Lyon, Survival Anglia Ltd.

Second Section
p.1 below: Bruno Lamarche
p.2 (top left): Forestièr, *Paris Match*
p.3 (top right): Pierre Vernet
      (above left): Lee Lyon, Survival Anglia Ltd.
      (above right): Forestièr, *Paris Match*
      (middle): Azoulay, *Paris Match*
p.5 (below): William Campbell
p.7: J. P. Girard

p.8 (above): Forestier, *Paris Match*
p.9: Deutsch, *Paris Match*
p.10 (above): *Paris Match*
    (below): Jean Luc Temporal
p.11 (below): Jean Luc Temporal
p.16: Michael Fay

Third Section
p.8: Bill Winter
p.9: W. R. Garrett
p.12 (below): Iain and Oria Douglas-Hamilton, National Geographic Society

Fourth Section
p.4 (left): Louise Gubb
    (middle right): Joyce Poole
    (below left): Daphne Sheldrick
p.5 (top): Louise Gubb
    (middle, Ian Parker): *Mail on Sunday*
p.6 (above): Joyce Poole
    (below left and right): William Campbell
p.9: Louise Gubb
p.12: Iain and Oria Douglas-Hamilton, National Geographic Society

The regional maps were projected by Fran Michelmore in collaboration with UNEP.

Whilst every effort has been made to credit photographers, the publishers regret any omissions or error.

Bibliography

These references are chosen for relevance or as a guide to further reading on elephants.

African Elephant and Rhino Specialist Group (AERSG), Minutes of meetings held from 1976-91

Barnes, R.F.W., 'The Status of Elephants in the Forests of Central Africa'. Results of a Reconnaissance Survey by the Wildlife Conservation International team, Vol 2: Ivory Trade Review Group Technical Reports, 1989

Barnes, R.F.W. and Douglas-Hamilton, I., 'The numbers and distribution patterns of large mammals in the Ruaha-Rungwa area of southern Tanzania'. J. Appl. Ecol. 19-411-425, 1982

Bosman, P. and Hall–Martin, A., *Elephants of Africa*, C. Struik, Cape Town, 1986

Burrill, A., Douglas-Hamilton, I. and Mackinnon, J., 'Protected Areas as Refuges for Elephants', (in *Review of the Protected Areas System in the Afrotropical Realm*), IUCN, 1986

Burrill, A. and Douglas-Hamilton, I., 'African Elephant Database Project: Final Report – Phase One – GRID Case Study Series No. 2', Global Environment Monitoring System, UNEP/WWF/ELSA, 1987

Bryden, H. A., 'The Decline and Fall of the South African Elephant', *Fortnightly Review, 79: 100–108*, 1903

Caughley, G., Dublin H. and Parker, I.S.C., 'Projected Decline of the African Elephant', Biological Conservation 54:157–64

Conniff, R., 'When the Music in our Parlours Brought Death to Darkest Africa', *Audubon* magazine, July 76–93, 1987

Cumming, D.H.M. and Jackson, P., 'The Status and Conservation of Africa's Elephants and Rhinos', Proceedings of 1984 AERSG Hwange meeting, IUCN, 1984

Cutler, 'The killing of elephants in Zaire', US State Department telegram, 1978

DiSilvestro, R. L., *The African Elephant: Twilight in Eden*, John Wiley & Sons, New York, 1991

Douglas-Hamilton, I., Statements to US Congressional Hearings in relation to proposed legislation on the African Elephant before the Merchant Marine and Fisheries Committee. US Congressional Records, 1977, 1979, 1988

'African Elephant Ivory Trade Study', Report to US Fish and Wildlife Service, (Typescript), 1979

'Elephants Hit by the Arms Race: Recent Factors affecting Elephant Populations', *Pachyderm (2):11–13*, 1983

'Elephant Population Trends and their Causes', *Oryx Vol 21 (1):11–23*, 1987

'The Great East African Elephant Disaster', *Swara 11(2):250–254*, 1988

'African Elephant Population Study', *GRID: African Elephant Database Project – Phase II*. The Commission of the European Communities/WWF/GEMS/UNEP, 1988

'Overview of Status and Trends of the African Elephant', Ivory Trade Review Group Technical Reports, Vol. 2, Typescript, 1989

Douglas-Hamilton, I. and O., *Among the Elephants*, William Collins and Sons, 1975

Douglas-Hamilton, I. and Burrill, A., 'Using Elephant Carcass Ratios to Determine Population Trends', African Wildlife: Research and Management: 98–105, 1991

Douglas-Hamilton, I., Hirji, K., Mbano, B., Olivier, R.C.D., Tarimo, E., and De Butts, H., 'Aerial Census of Wildlife in the Selous Game Reserve', WWF Project 3173 report, Ministry of Natural Resources and Tourism, Dar es Salaam, Typescript, Tanzania, 1986

Douglas-Hamilton, I., Froment, J. M., Doungoubé, G. and Root, J., 'Récensement aerien de la faune dans la zone nord de la Republique Centrafricaine', FAO: CAF/78/006 Document de travail 5, 1985

Douglas-Hamilton, I. and Hillman, A.K.K., 'Elephant carcasses and skeletons as indicators of population trends', International Livestock Centre for Africa Monographs, 4:113–129, 1981

Douglas-Hamilton, O., 'Africa's Elephants, Can They Survive?', *National Geographic*, 158(5):570–603, 1980

The Elephant Family Book, Picture Book Studio, 1990

Dublin, H. T. and Douglas-Hamilton, I., 'Status and Trends of Elephants in the Serengeti–Mara Ecosystem', Afr. J. Ecol. Vol 25:19–23, 1987

Du Toit, R. F., Cumming, D. H. M. and Stuart, S. N., 'African Elephants and Rhinos: Status Survey and Conservation Action Plan', Proceedings of 1987 AERSG Nyeri meeting, IUCN, 1989

Eltringham, S. K., *Elephants*, Blandford Press, 1982

Gary, R., *The Roots of Heaven*, Michael Joseph, 1958

Haigh, J. C., Parker, I. S. C., Parkinson, D. A., and Archer, A. L., 'An Elephant Extermination', Environmental Conservation. 6(4):305–310, 1979

Hall–Martin, A., 'Elephant Survivors', *Oryx 15 (4):355–362*, 1980

'Conservation and management of elephants in the Kruger National Park, South Africa', Proceedings of 1981 AERSG Hwange meeting, IUCN, 1981

Hanks, J., *A Struggle for Survival: The Elephant Problem*, C. Struik, 1979

Ivory Trade Review Group (ITRG), 'The Ivory Trade and the Future of the African Elephant', (Vol. 1: Executive Summary; Vol 2: Reports on Elephant Status and the Ivory Trade), Ivory Trade Review Group Technical Reports, Typescript, 1989

Kayanja, F. and Douglas-Hamilton, I., 'Case History of Uganda's National Parks: Impact of the Unexpected', *Swara 6(3):8–14*, 1983

Laws, R. M., 'The Tsavo Research Project', J. Reprod, Fert. Suppl. 6:495–531, 1969

Laws, R. M., Parker, I. S. C., and Johnstone, R. C. B., *Elephants and Habitats in North Bunyoro, Uganda*, Clarendon Press, 1970

Luxmore, R., Caldwell, J., and Hithersay, L., 'The Volume of Raw Ivory entering trade from African producing countries from 1979 to 1988', Vol 2: Ivory Trade Review Group Technical Reports, Typescript, 1989

Martin, E. B., 'The Craft, the Trade, the Elephants', *Oryx 15 (4):363–366*, 1980
'The World Ivory Trade', *Swara 6(4):28–32*, 1983
'The Japanese Ivory Industry', WWF Japan 1985, 1985
'After the Ivory Bans', Wildlife Conservation: Vol. 93 (6):28–31, 1990

Martin, E. B., Caldwell, J. R., and Barzdo, J. G., 'African Elephants, CITES and the Ivory Trade', CITES, 1986

Meredith, M., 'The Ivory Trade in Congo; and Illegal Flows of Ivory in Southern Africa', Vol 2: Ivory Trade Review Group Technical Reports, Typescript, 1989

Meulenaer, Tom De, and Meredith, M., 'The Ivory Trade in Zaire', Vol. 2: Ivory Trade Review Group Technical Reports, Typescript, 1989

Michelmore, F., Beardsley, K., Barnes, R. F. W., and Douglas-Hamilton, I., 'Elephant Population Estimates for the Central African Forests', Vol. 2: Ivory Trade Review Group Technical Reports, Typescript, 1989

Milliken, T. and Melville, D., 'The Hong Kong Ivory Trade', Vol 2: Ivory Trade Review Group Technical Reports, Typescript, 1989

Moss, C. J., *Elephant Memories*, William Morrow, 1988

Mulder, M. D., and Caro. T., 'Slaughter of the Elephants', *New Scientist*, July: 32–34, 1980

O'Connell, M. A. and Sutton, M., 'The Effects of Trade Moratoria on International Commerce in African Elephant Ivory', A Preliminary Report, World Wildlife Fund and The Conservation Foundation, 1990

Offerman, P., 'La Capture et la Domestication des Elephants dans La Province Orientale', Bull Agricole du Congo Belge, 21:384–387, 1930
'Les Elephants du Congo Belge', Corps des Lieut. Hon. De Chasse du Congo Belge Bull, 3(9):85–95, 1951

Olindo, P. M., Douglas-Hamilton, I., and Hamilton, P. H., '1988 Tsavo Elephant Count', *Swara 11 (3):23–24*, 1988

Omar, H. S., 'Save the Elephants from Extinction in Somalia', Somalia Range Bulletin, 12: 67–70, 1981

Parker, I.S.C., 'The Ivory Trade Report to I. Douglas-Hamilton on behalf of the US Fish and Wildlife Service', 6 vols, Typescript, 1979
Ivory Crisis, Chatto and Windus, 1983

Parry, D., 'Slaughterhouse of the Giants', Quagga, 7: 32–33, 1983
Payne, K., 'Elephant talk,' *National Geographic*, 176 (2):264–277, 1989
Pfeffer, P., *Amnistie Pour les Eléphants*, 1989
Pilgram, T. and Western, D., 'Elephant Hunting Patterns', *Pachyderm (3):12–13*, 1983
    'Managing elephant populations for ivory production', *Pachyderm, 4:9–11*, 1984
Poole, J. H., 'The Effects of Poaching on the Age Structure and Social and Reproductive Patterns of Selected East African Elephant Populations', Vol 2: Ivory Trade Review Group Technical Reports, Typescript, 1989
Poole, J. H. and Moss, C. J., 'Musth in the African Elephant', Loxodonta africana, Nature, 292: 830–831, 1981
Poole, J. H., Payne, K., Langbauer, W. R., Jr., and Moss, C. J., 'The social contexts of some very low frequency calls of African elephants', Behavioral Ecology and Sociobiology 22:385–392, 1988
Redmond, I., *The Elephant Book*, Walker Books, 1990
Ricciuti, E. R., 'The Ivory Wars', Animal Kingdom 83(1), 1980
Robinette, L. and Blankenship, L., 'Sense not Sentiment on Culling the Game', Africana Vol. 6 No. 10:12–15, 1978
Sheldrick, Daphne, *The Tsavo Story*, Collins & Harvill Press, 1973
Sheldrick, D.L.W., 'Report on Poaching in the Tsavo National Park', Typescript, 1976
Temporal, J. L., 'La Chasse Oubliée', Gerfaut Club, 1989
Thomsen, J. B., 'Conserving the African Elephant', CITES fails, US acts, TRAFFIC (USA) 9(1) 1–3, 1989
Thornton, A. and Currey, D., *To Save an Elephant*, Doubleday, 1991
Tinker, J., 'Who's Killing Kenya's Jumbos?', *New Scientist*: 452–455, 1975
TRAFFIC, Many detailed reports on the Ivory Trade, Traffic Bulletins, 1979–91
Verschuren, J., *Mourir Pour Les Eléphants*, Editions L. Cuypers, Bruxelles, 1975
Western, D., 'Africa's Elephants and Rhinos: Flagships in Crisis', *Tree 2(11)*, 1987
    'The Ecological Role of Elephants in Africa', *Pachyderm (12):42–45*, 1989

Index

NOTE: The initials NP stand for National Parks

Abdi (poacher), 313–14
Aberdare National Park, 35, 51, 110,
   343
Aboubakar, Lambara, 158
Adupa, Mishak, 182, 191–2, 226,
   228
Aerial counting, *passim*; 28, 40,
   107, 147, 175–7; CAR, 277–8,
   286; Kenya, 28–9, 103, 109;
   Murchison Falls NP 94–5,
   182; Queen Elizabeth NP,
   181–2; Selous, 76, 78, 79, 81, 83–4
Africana, 244
African Elephant Action Plan, 176–8
African Elephant and Rhino
   Specialist Group, (AERSG), 250,
   264, 293–5; first meeting, 250–51;
   Nyeri meeting, 1987, 302–4
African Elephant Bill, 124, 317
African Elephant Specialist Group,
   62, 97, 119–20, 176, 179, 243;
   first full meeting, 184–6; Hwange
   meeting, 215–17, 243; disbanded,
   249–50; *see also* African Elephant
   and Rhino Specialist Group
African Wildlife Foundation, 57,
   198, 241, 267–8, 317, 329, 335

Aga Khan, Prince Sadruddin, 316
Akagera NP, 57–60, 62
Amboseli NP, 108, 109, 250, 303–4,
   316, 329, 343
Amin, Idi, 90–91, 95, 96, 180, 209
Among the Elephants, 45–6, 55
Anderson, George, 198
Anglia Television, 21–2, 44, 59
Angola, 30–31, 252, 321
Animal Kingdom, 179–80
Anti-poaching measures, *passim*;
   194–5, 196, 197, 266–7; Kidepo,
   205, 208–9; Sheldrick, 36–7
Ardrey, Robert, 124
Arms race and elephants, 263
Asia Week, 301
Assaba Mountains, 138–9, 143
Assala, 165–6
Awadalla el Awad, Mohamed, 265
Balinga, Victor Sunday, 157–8
Bamingui-Bangoran NP, 277, 278–9,
   280, 281–2
Baraka, Zaidi, 299
Barnes, Richard, 303, 324; and
   Karen, 254
Barre, Mohamed Siad, 327
BBC Wildlife Magazine, 266

Beard, Peter, 39
Beilenson, Anthony, 125, 317
Belgium, 48–50
Bell, Richard, 250
Bendabule, Agostino, 95, 203–4,
    207, 209, 223, 228; killed in plane
    crash, 225, 233, 237
Bernhard of the Netherlands,
    Prince, 316, 340
Birigenda (ranger), 197
Blashford Snell, Colonel John, 205
Block, Jack, 40
Bokassa, Jean Bedel, 133, 144,
    159, 170, 273–4, 279;
    and La Couronne, 171;
    overthrow, 185, 274
Bongo, President of Gabon, 160,
    161
Botha, P.W., 321
Botswana, 341, 342
Bradley Martin, Esmond, 250–51,
    265, 266, 345
Breytenbach, Colonel, 322
Bryceson, Derek, 44–5, 98–9, 100,
    102–3
Bukuku, Citoyen Mwangaya, 135
Bulgaria, 211
Burengo, Mhoja, 18, 19, 27–8,
    100–1, 337–8, 350; and death of
    Boadicea, 54–5; drought (1976),
    99
Burrill, Anne, 302–3, 304
Burundi, 57, 299–300, 319,
    321, 323, 336; and Lausanne
    CITES meeting, 341; trader
    from Burundi murdered, 342
Caille, René, 145–6
Caithness, Lord, 330
Cameroon, 151, 152, 154, 154–9; at
    Hwange meeting, 216
CAR (Central African Republic),
    118, 158–9, 170–71, 176,
    339; Clive Spinage and, 170,
    185; elephant numbers in,
    264, 271, 273–82, 285–6, 293,
    295; ivory trading, 129, 152,
    171, 323, 325; methods of
    killing, 30; poaching, 253–4, 274
Carey, Ambrose, 320–21

Carr, Chuck, 295
Carr, Norman, 174
Carving, 151–2, 153–4, 158–9
Caughley, Graeme, 84, 319–20
Certificates of origin *see* ivory
    documents
Chad, 264, 293, 295, 337
Chaitou, Hassan, 142
Charities created for elephants, 335
China, 211, 341
Chong Pong, 322
CITES (Convention on
    International Trade in
    Endangered Species), 29–30, 134,
    137, 275, 306, 342; Appendix
    One list, 305; Buenos Aires
    conference, 296; financing of,
    297; and ivory bans, 170, 177,
    337, 339; ivory sales, 297–9,
    300; and ivory trade, 267, 268–9,
    316; Lausanne, 339–42; Nairobi
    committee meeting, 319; quota
    system, 294–9, 300, 325, 335–7;
    sponsor trade study, 319; treaty,
    135, 137; and Zimbabweans, 320
Clarke, Ken, 112
Cobb, Steve, 320, 324
Coetsee, Clem, 218–19, 221
Collecte, La, 277, 287, 291
Congo, 47–8, 176; ivory trade
    from, 171, 325; and Poons, 323
Conway, Bill, 56, 98, 124
Cook Report, 323
Coolidge, Hal and Muffy, 211–12
Counting, technical difficulties,
    177–8; *see also* surveys
Couronne, La, 129, 170, 176,
    287; History in CAR, 274, 285
Cropping, 70; Uganda, 93;
    Zimbabwe, 296, 338; *see also*
    culling
Crop raiding, 50, 60, 80, 144
Croze, Harvey, 62, 119, 302
Culling, 42, 62, 116–19, 175, 342;
    and economics, 121–2, 123, 296,
    338; at Hwange, 217–21; and
    ivory trade, 216; Kruger NP, 69,
    70–71; suggested at Manyara,
    98, 100, 102–3, 104; in Rhodesia

Culling *continued*
  and Zimbabwe, 120–23, 215–16,
  338; in Rwanda, 57–60; at Selous,
  80; suggested at Tsavo, 37–9, 74;
  Uganda, 89–90, 93
Cumming, David, 185, 250, 294,
  303, 305
Currey, Dave, 305
Dacko, David, 273, 274
Daily Nation, 106
DANIDA, 75–6
Davitz, Michael, 127
de Brunhoff, Jean and Cecile, 48
de Haes, Charles, 173–4, 269, 341–2
Denmark, 75–6
de Schryver, Adrien, 60–61, 134
Deforestation, 162; *see also* trees
De Wet Potgieter (journalist), 322
Diop, Birame, 153
Dollinger, Peter, 340
Dorado brothers, Julian and Pablo,
  171, 285, 286–7, 345
Douglas-Hamilton, Diarmaid, 64,
  65, 71, 72, 74; and lobbying on
  Uganda, 241; *Soldier of Fortune*
  supplies, 232–3
Douglas-Hamilton, Dudu, 21,
  46, 184, 204–5, 229, 258; visits
  George Adamson, 328; return to
  Manyara, 347–8
Douglas-Hamilton, Iain, *passim*;
  accused of gunrunning,
  177, 211–12; childhood,
  64–5; held at gunpoint, 222;
  honorary chief park warden,
  196–9; loses chairmanship of
  elephant group, 251; made
  anti-poaching specialist, 223;
  meets President Kolingba, 291
Douglas-Hamilton, Oria, 128,
  205–6, 212–14; and Beauty
  without Cruelty, 251–2; meets
  Iain, 16–18; observes cull in
  Hwange, 217–21
Douglas-Hamilton, Saba, 18,
  21, 47, 184, 229, 258–61, 347–53
Doungoubé, Gustave,
  277–8
Dowling, Kevin, 323–4

Drought, 35, 38–9, 73, 98, 101–3,
  148–50
Dublin, Holly, 251, 269–70, 318
Dupuy, André, 138, 243
East African Wildlife Society, 310,
  312, 328
East African Wildlife Symposium,
  Third, 89
Edroma, Eric, 89, 92, 180–82, 185,
  187
EEC, 198–9, 280, 312, 337, 342;
  and ban on ivory trade, 268–9,
  339; delegation visits Kidepo,
  226, 228–32; emergency
  supplies in Kenya, 335; Masai
  Mara game reserve study,
  318; project in Uganda, 344;
  providing funds, 205, 223,
  228; *see also* Europe; John; Rod
Elephant and Ecosystems Campaign,
  174
Elephant Conservation Act, 318
Elephant Extermination, An, 59
Elephants, *passim*; in adverse
  conditions, 73, 149; on beach,
  165; behaviour, 19–20, 26–7,
  70–71, 100, 165–6, 250, 303–4;
  in desert, 134, 147, 149, 344;
  individuals: Gabon, 50–51;
  Kruger, 70; Manyara, 18,
  20–22, 26–9, 54–5, 96, 100, 330,
  346–53; Tsavo, *289*, *Loxodonta
  africana pharoensis*, 138–9, 161;
  in mountains, 138–9; physical
  characteristics, 69–70, 73,
  219–20; reaction to poaching,
  108; in Red Data Book, 119–21
Eltringhan, Keith, 93
Environmental Investigation
  Agency, 305, 320, 341
Eskanazi, Bepo, 134
Ets Manyi, 169
European Ivory Traders
  Association, 177
FAO, 271, 293
First World Wilderness Congress,
  124
Forest elephant, 165–6, 324
France, 134, 211, 212, 330

Frankfurt Zoological Society, 99, 225, 339
Froment, Ingrid, 277, 281
Froment, Jean-Marc, 275–8; Bokassa's palace, 281; in 1984, 283–5, 287, 290, 292, 293
Gabon, 49, 152, 160–67, 171, 303, 344
Galana game ranch, 112, 312
Galana River, 35, 343
Gallman, Kuki, 253–4; 256–7; 262
Gallman, Paolo, 256
Gangala na Bodio, 48–52
Garamba NP, 52–3, 276
Garrett, Bill, 212, 233, 235, 236
Gary, Romain, *Roots of Heaven*, 23, 87, 131, 189, 237, 247
Ghana, 216
Gichangi, Stephen, 343
Gourma, the, 146–7
Grayson, Patrick, 321
Greenpeace, 305
Grzimek, Bernhard, 90–91, 99
Guizard, Pierre, 162, 167
Guizard, René, 163–6
Gwynne, Michael, 302
Hall-Martin, Anthony, 185, 243
Hamilton, Patrick 'Chui', 309–10, 311, 313, 328, 333–4
Hanks, John, 319
Hausa traders, 154, 157, 158
Holland, 211
Holt, Patrick, 180, 182, 191, 193–4, 196, 204
Hong Kong, 125, 299, 318, 320, 330, 337; importance in world market, 300–302; imports of ivory, 40, 96, 129, 265; Ivory Trade study, 172; Parker in, 133, 169, 170
Human population and elephants, 124, 140, 143–4, 249, 267; competitors, 342; effect of human conflict, 252; in Gourma, 149–50
Hurt, Robin, 264, 275, 276
Huxley, Chris, 266, 268–9, 335, 342; AERSG meeting, Zimbabwe, 295–6;

Huxley *continued*
and ivory sales, 297 8, 299
Hwange, 215–17, 243, 244, 264; and CAR, 275; meeting of African Elephant Special Group, 215–17, 243; National Park, 120–23, 325
Independent, 342
Institute for Nature Conservation, Zaire, 135, 169
Ionides, C.J.P., 'Old Iodine', 80–81
IUCN (International Union for the Conservation of Nature), 29, 211, 223, 312, 342; African Elephant Action Plan, 176–7, 179; attacked by Parker, 267; general assembly in USSR, 169–70; at Hwange meeting, 216; and ivory ban, 269, 305; Ivory Trade study, 126–7, 173–4, 177; and ivory trade, 185, 186, 306; and surveys, 339; Survival Science Commission, 62, 179; and TRAFFIC, 297; *see also* African Elephant Specialist Group
Ivory Coast, 151
Ivory documents, 129, 135, 154, 157–8, 168–9, 171, 172, 176, 252, 265, 294, 299
Ivory laundering, 296–307
Ivory stores, 84, 101, 114, 127, 157, 290
Ivory trade, *passim*; 29–30, 120, 137, 150, 185; in Abidjan, 151–2; and AERSG, 250–51; amnesty, 337; control of, 119, 249, 267, 304, 337–8; and elephants, 39, 40, 293; First World Wilderness Conference, 124–5; history of, 76, 135–7, 155, 172, 284; in Ivory Coast, 153–4; in Kenya, 40, 42–3, 105; politics of, 178, 252, 266; price rises, 40, 41–2, 127, 137, 263, 276; self-regulation, 126, 129, 174; in Senegal, 137; study of, 107, 110–12, 133; in Sudan, 264–6; in Uganda, 93–4, 96; in Zaire, 53, 134; *see also* ivory documents; Parker, Ian; poaching; quota systems

Ivory Trade study, 126–7, 172–3, 173–4, 177
Ivory Trade Review Group, 319–20, 324, 325, 342
Jackman, Brian, 264
Jackson, Peter, 264
Japan, 172, 325, 330, 337
Jarman, Peter, 41, 42–3, 107, 115
Jenkins, Peter, 37, 106, 108
Johannesburg *Sunday Times*, 322
John (EEC bodyguard), 196, 201–2, 206, 235; in Kampala, 222–3; in Kidepo, 207, 208, 211
Johnson, Marion, 154
Johnson, Stanley, 268
Joseph (cook), 163–6
Jumbe, Aboud, 100, 102
Kafue NP, 174
Kaokoveld, 72–4, 243
Kayanja, Professor Fred, 244
Kee Chong ivory factory, 301
Kennedy, Senator Edward, 241
Kenya, 41, 105–15, 176, 244, 326–32, 343–4; and CITES Lausanne meeting, 337, 339; at Hwange meeting, 216; and ivory trading, 105, 113–15, 126, 129, 252, 297; poaching in, 36, 74, 110–13, 129, 176; Wildlife department, 106, 111, 310–11, 312; Wildlife Service, 343–4; *see also* Aberdare, Amboseli, Masai Mara Park, Tsavo
Kenyatta, Mzee Jomo, 76, 105, 126, 128
Kidepo Park, 37, 187, 202–9, 211, 222, 227–42, 243; and Sudanese raiders, 204, 205, 207–8, 225, 232, 233–4, 230–42
Kioko, Joe, 176, 309, 333
Knysna, 64–5, 71–2
Kolingba, President of CAR, 287, 289–90, 291
Kora NP, 327, 328, 335
KROLL Associates, 319–20
Kruger NP, 65, 67–71, 97, 322–3, 344; and ivory, 252; poaching in, 243
Kyeyune, Peter, 195, 205

Labongo, Alfred, 94, 182–3; anti-poaching force, 233; Kidepo, 206, 241, 242; seizes weapons, 205; Uganda 1980, 191, 194, 197, 201, 203
Laboureur, Jean, 280, 282, 285
Lai family, 323
Laikipia, 253, 256, 343
Laitoro, 333
Lamarche, Bruno, 134, 145, 146, 148–9, 185
Lamprey, Hugh, 335
Langenwalter, Bob, 213–15
Laplume, Commandant, 49–50, 51
Lapointe, Eugene, 299, 336, 337, 342; at Lausanne, 339–41
Lausanne, meeting of CITES at, 337, 339–42
Laws, Dr Richard, 37–8, 89, 92, 97, 119
Leakey, Richard, 107, 312, 328–9, 330, 331; and Somali poachers, 334–5
Lerner, Karen, 125
Lessendjina, Madame, 169, 171
Lewkowicz, Jacques, 179, 301, 336
Logwe, Sergeant Peter, 234–5, 237–9
London Zoological Society, 324
Loxodonta africana pharoensis, 138–9, 161
Luangwa Valley NP, 84, 174–5, 319, 322
Luka (tracker), 255–6
Lulimbi, 94–5
Lwezaula, Fred, 184
Lyon, Lee, 21, 60–61, 95; death, 56–7, 61; photographs Boadicea, 21–2
McIlvaine, Bob, 57
McMeekin, Diana, 302
Madogo, Bwana, 80
Makita (tracker), 163–6
Malan, Magnus, 321
Malawi, 341
Mali, 145–50, 344
Malpas, Rob, 93, 180, 181, 184, 191, 193
Mane, Moussa, 138

Manovo-Gounda-Saint Floris
Park, 277, 279, 280, 281, 284–6
Mansion, Colonel Jean-Claud, 277,
279–80, 287–91
Manyara, 15–16, 17, 18–22, 25–31,
33, 96, 118, 344, 347–53; counting
carcasses in, 109–10; death
of Boadicea, 54–5; decline in
population, 306; drought, 98–104;
Survival Anglia film, 21–2,
44; visit of Aboud Jumbe, 100
Maramagambo Forest, 91–2
Markham, Beryl, 66
Martin, Rowan, 270, 294–5, 316;
CITES Lausanne meeting, 337;
Zimbabwe AERSG meeting, 294
Masai Mara Game Reserve, 41,
108, 118, 269–70, 275, 343; EEC
study, 317–18
Mauritania, 133, 134, 138–44
Mayer, Harold, 259
Meredith, Martin, 324
Meru NP, 37, 108–9, 110, 118;
new counts, 343; tourists shot
dead, 328; white rhinos shot, 329
Milliken, Tom, 323, 325, 345
Minga, Henry, 184, 264
Miombo Research Station, 77
Miramuibi (engineer warden), 225–6
Mission des Elephants, la, 49–50
Mkomazi NP, 312
Mlay, Costa, 339
Mobutu, Sese Seko, 133, 169, 324
Mogadishu, 334
Moi, Daniel arap, 129, 310, 329, 331
Monitor, 125, 300
Moss, Cynthia, 250, 303, 315,
316, 317; *Elephant memories*, 304
Mounter, Julian, 113–14
Moussa, Abdou, 158
Moxson (gunbearer), 218–19, 221
Mozambique, 69, 252
Mugabe, Robert, 215, 216
Muhoho, George, 327–8
Mull, J.A., 213–14, 259
Munro, David, 127, 179
Murchison Falls NP, 192–5, 199,
202, 222, 224, 276, 344; counts,
41, 94, 95, 182–4, 243; and

Murchison Falls NP *continued*
culling, 37, 118; poaching, 37,
192–5, 228; Richard Laws in, 89
Mutinda, Jonathan, 42
Mweka College of Wildlife
Management, 110, 116, 224, 311
Muzorewa, Bishop Abel, 120, 121,
215
Nairobi Seminar, 41
Nairobi NP, 45, 331
Naivasha, *passim*; 18, 46, 51, 84,
227–8, 256–7; African Elephant
Office, 62
Namib, the, 72
Namibia, 243, 344
National Geographic Society, 212,
233, 236, 241, 305
Nature Watch, 26, 28
Ndosireho, Sefa, 203–4, 208, 209;
EEC delegation visit, 228; killed
in plane crash, 225, 233, 237
Nepal, 51, 224
New African, 327, 335
New Scientist, 106, 315
New York Times, 74
New York Zoological Society, 40,
56, 98, 124, 179–80, 241; Wildlife
Conservation International
Division, 295
Nicholson, Brian, 81
Nimeri, Gaafar, Muhammed, 241
Niokolo Koba NP, 137–8, 243
Northern Rhodesia, 174
Nwara, Simon, 155–6
Nyerere, Julius, 74, 76, 81
Obote, Milton, 90, 206, 222, 245
Observer (London), 300
Odendaal Commission, 73
Ogutu, Matthew, 106
Okello, Francis, 196–7
Okong, Klau, 192, 194, 196
Ol Ari Nyiro, 253–4, 255–7
Ol Donyo Lengai, 18
Olindo, Dr Perez, 310, 311, 313,
316–17, 325, 329
Omon, Sergeant, 194, 195
Onaah, Lt.-Col., D.S.O., 92, 96
Onfine, Kakiese, 169, 170
Operation Uhai, 344

Pachyderm, 263
Paraa Lodge, 95, 95, 202
Paris Match, 321–2
Parker, Ian, 37, 179, 317, 319–20, 342; AERSG, 250–51; African Elephant Special Group, 185, 216; attacks WWF and IUCN, 243–4; and Burundi stockpile, 299–300; and CITES ivory sales, 298; in Hong Kong, 133, 169, 170; *Ivory Crisis*, 59–60, 266–8; at Manyara, 39–40; Nairobi seminar, 41–2; and Rwanda, 57–60; studies of ivory trade, 107, 125–7, 129, 172–3, 177; *Sunday Times* article, 266; telegram to African Wildlife Foundation, 267–8; and Uganda, 90, 92, 94, 96
Parkinson, Tony, 57–60
Pascal (Gabon), 163–6
Payne, Katherine, 304, 315, 316
Pearce, Professor David, 324
Pettifer, Julian, 30–31
Pfeffer, Pierre, 315, 336
Pianos, 330–31
Pienaar, Tol, 69, 70
Pilgram, Tom, 268
Piramoi, Sergeant, 231, 238
Plage, Dieter, 21, 59, 61
Poaching, *passim*; 117–18, 138, 193–4, 195; CAR, 280; Kidepo, 204, 207, 234–6; in Luangwa, 175; Nairobi seminar, 42–3; in Rhodesia, 122; Selous, 81; Tsavo, 36, 55, 105–7, 110–13, 313–14, 333–5; Uganda, 92, 183, 191–2
Poole, Joyce, 302–3, 315, 316, 317, 325, 330
Poon family, 301, 320, 323, 336, 345
Poppleton, Captain Frank, 223–4, 234, 241, 244
Price, Sandy, 267–8
Puccioni, Vanni, 319
Pygmies, 156–7, *161*, 276
Queen Elizabeth NP, 89, 91, 180, 243; numbers of elephants, 94–5, 118, 181
Quotas, ivory, 294–9, 296, 317, 318, 336; *see also* ivory trade

Rabemtullah, 299
Rankin, Singer, 302
Red elephants, 35, *288*
Reilly, Bill, 317
Reuling, Melly, 346, 348, 351–3
Rhino: black, 103, 109, 124, 215, 249, 253, 255; white, 329
Rhodesia, 118, 120–23, 215–16; *see also* Zimbabwe
Robinette, Les, 116, 118–19
Rod (EEC bodyguard), 206
Rodgers, Alan, 75–9, 125
Rohrsted, Tué, 228, 318, 319
Rollais, Gilbert, 171
Root, Alan, 102
Root, Joan, 275, 277, 281
Ross, Iain, 37
Royal Chitwan NP, 51
Ruaha NP, 103, 118, 344
Russell, Marcus, 334
Rwanda, 56–62
Sahel, 146–50, 264
Savimbi, Jonas, 321
Scherlis, John, 100–101
Schindler, Paul, 302
Scott, Sir Peter, 62, 106, 175, 186; and culling, 116–18, 175; *The Elephant Dilemma*, 116, 117–18
Selous, Frederick Courteney, 77, 79, 80
Selous Game Reserve, 75–6, 77–84, 97, *97*, 103, 108, 118, 175, 339; number of elephants down, 317, 325; number of tusks per elephant, 125; new projects, 344
Senegal, 135–8, 139, 172, 243
Serengeti, 37, 62, 270, 275; counting in, 103, 108, 109, 118, 318–19; *see also* Masai Mara NP
Serengeti Research Institute, 103
Senghor, Leopold, 137–8
Sheldrick, Daphne, 315
Sheldrick, David, 36–9, 106, 128, 266, 309; Tsavo, 33–5, 43, 102, 110–12
Shirre company, 298
Singapore, 300
Société Nouvelle France Croco, 134, 169, 171, 180, 301, 336

Soldier of Fortune, 232–3
Somalia, 118, 327, 337; fall in
  elephant population of, 243, 264;
  ivory sale, 297–9; at Lausanne
  CITES meeting, 340; Somali
  bandits in Kenya, 313, 333–5
Sotrequa, 169
South Africa, 73, 118, 251, 321,
  322; at Hwange meeting, 217;
  at CITES Lausanne meeting,
  337, 341; exports of ivory, 322–3
South African Endangered Species
  Protection Unit, 344
Southern Africa, 62, 64–74, 117; *see
  also* individual countries
Spinage, Clive, 170, 253, 278,
  282, 283; at first full meeting of
  African Elephant Group, 185, 274
Ssale, Paul, 223, 224–5, 226
Stanley (aircraft attendant), 311
Stevens, Christine, 305, 315, 317
Sudan, 171, 232, 264–6, 325;
  dead elephants, 30, 243, 293,
  295; *see also* Sudanese raiders
Sudanese raiders, 204, 205, 207–8;
  Kidepo, 224, 225, 230–42
Suleiman, Ali, 342
Sunday Standard of Nairobi, 297
Sunday Telegraph, 236
Sunday Times (Johannesburg), 322
Sunday Times (London), 264, 266
Surveys of Elephants, *passim*; 56,
  110, 115, 150, 253, 317, 339;
  CAR, 283–6; East Africa, 40–41;
  Kenya, 41, 106–10, 112, 114–15,
  128, 310; Southern Africa, 62,
  68; Tanzania, 75, 81, 98–103,
  109–10; Uganda, 37, 89–90,
  108; *see also* individual countries
Survival Anglia, 21–2, 44
Survival Service Commission, 62
Swara magazine, 337
Taiwan, 300, 345
Tanzania, 65, 75, 81, 103, 299,
  338, 343; Director of National
  Parks, 31; at Hwange meeting,
  216; ivory store, 84; and ivory
  trade, 252, 337; preservation
  policies in, 74, 83; *see also*

Tanzania *continued*
  Manyara, Mweka, Ndala, Ruaha,
  Selous, Tarangire NPs
Tarangire NP, 103, 118
Tatika, Tatala, 276
Ter Haar, Johann, 198, 228, 229–30
Thatcher, Margaret, 330
Thornton, Allan, 305, 320, 341
Time magazine, 337
TRAFFIC, 296–7, 306, 323–5, 340
Train, Russell, 252
Trees, destruction of, 25, 116, 123;
  Ivory Coast, 152–3; Luangwa,
  175; Manyara, 25, 98–9, 102;
  Murchison Falls NP, 95; Tsavo,
  37, 38
Trevor, Simon, 39, 112, 311
Tsavo, 33, 43, 57, 110–13, 118,
  119, 127–8, *288, 289*; and
  culling, 37–8, 102; deteriorating
  situation, 200, 308–13, 317;
  elephant numbers, 84–5, 108,
  110, 118, 311–12; poachers
  in, 106, 110, 112–13, 176,
  326–9; radio-collared elephant
  shot near, 41; tourists held
  up in, 326; Wata bowmen, 266
Turkana, Lake, 47
Turner, Myles, 38
Tusks, *passim*; 40, 69–70, 137,
  152, 155; amount leaving
  Africa, 124–5; analysis of
  weights, 127, 268, 289–90;
  burnt, 331–2; Cameroon,
  158–9; confiscated, 41, 134, 289;
  Rhodesia, 122; value of, 316–17
Twins, elephant, 100–102, 104
Uganda, 37, 88–95, 108,
  180–87, 199–211, 339, 344;
  aid programme, 242–3;
  anti-poaching efforts, 233,
  234–41; export of ivory through,
  171; *see also* Murchison NP,
  Queen Elizabeth NP, Kidepo
Uganda Institute of Ecology, 88
UNITA, 30–31, 321, 322
United Arab Emirates, 300,
  320
United Kingdom, 300, 323, 324, 330

United Nations, 278; UN
  Development Programme, 199,
  205, 275–6; UN Development
  Project Team, 223; UN
  Environmental Programme
  (UNEP), 302, 336; UNEP Global
  Environmental Monitoring
  System, 302, 304, 306, 312
USA, 56, 97, 129, 329, 337;
  attempts to legislate for
  elephants, 125, 172; Cameroon
  embassy, 155; campaign to ban
  import of ivory, 125–6, 177;
  Fish and Wildlife Service, 126,
  127; imports to, 330; Peace
  Corps, 139–40, 142; and pianos,
  330–31; and Sudanese army; 232
USSR, 211
van Erpe, Madame, 171, 345
van Note, Craig, 300, 321
Van Wyk, Dr Piet, 67–8
Vaneco, 169, 179
Vassoko-Bolo Reserve, 278, 279
Vernet, Pierre, 147–8
Vesey-Fitzgerald, Desmond, 70
Virunga NP, 59
Voi, 35, 311, 333
Wakamba people, 110, 309
Wang, K.T., 300, 301, 336–7
Watson, Murray, 264, 265, 298
Western, David 'Jonah', chairman of
  AERSG, 249–51, 263; and ivory
  trade, 306, 317, 319, 320, 324; to
  Japan, 325; telegram to African
  Wildlife Foundation, 266–8;
  Zimbabwe meeting (AERSG),
  294, 295
Weyerhauser, Rick, 180, 184, 191,
  193
Wells, Melissa, 199
West Germany, 211
Whyte, Jenny Bell, 56
Wijngaarden, Willem, 128
Wildlife Awareness Week, 128, 225

Wildlife Services, 57
Wong, George, 126
Wonga Wongué Reserve, 160
Woodley, Bill, 35–6, 106, 110, 176,
  309
World Bank, 105, 176, 307
World Conservation Strategy, 252,
  294
World Wilderness Congress, 124
WWF (World Wildlife Fund – later
  renamed World Wide Fund for
  Nature), 106, 117, 126, 177, 212,
  241, 264; allocation of funds,
  98, 185, 223, 275, 293, 320;
  attacked by Parker, 244, 267; and
  ban on ivory trade, 269, 303–4,
  316–17; at Hwange meeting, 216;
  and ivory trade, 29, 173, 186,
  306, 342; at Lausanne CITES
  meeting, 342; and Rhodesia, 216;
  and surveys, 271, 312, 339; and
  TRAFFIC, 297; US branch, 198,
  234, 252, 315, 316–17
Youssif, Saumare, 143
Yovino, Joe, 299, 337
Yusta, 101
Zaire, 85, 97, 129, 133–5, 153, 167;
  army shooting elephants, 134;
  counts of elephants, 94, 293;
  elephant school, 48–52; exports
  to Ivory Coast, 152; Institute
  for Nature Conservation, 169;
  ivory trade, 168–70, 171, 176,
  252, 274, 295, 323–4; military
  and ivory, 169; and Poons, 323;
  see also Garamba NP, Lulimbi
Zambia, 174, 216, 252, 322, 341; *see
  also* Luangwa Valley NP
Zimbabwe, 120–23, 215–16;
  AERSG meeting, 294; at CITES
  Lausanne meeting, 341; use of
  elephants, 294, 296, 316, 337–8;
  Wildlife Department, 270, 294
Zorga, Jean-Marie, 154–5